Public Service Performance

Perspectives on Measurement and Management

Edited by

George A. Boyne, Kenneth J. Meier, Laurence J. O'Toole Jr. and Richard M. Walker

CAMBRIDGE UNIVERSITY PRESS
Cambridge, New York, Melbourne, Madrid, Cape Town, Singapore,
São Paulo, Delhi, Dubai, Tokyo, Mexico City

Cambridge University Press
The Edinburgh Building, Cambridge CB2 8RU, UK

Published in the United States of America by Cambridge University Press, New York

www.cambridge.org
Information on this title: www.cambridge.org/9780521172936

© Cambridge University Press 2006

First published 2006
First paperback edition 2010

A catalogue record for this publication is available from the British Library

ISBN 978-0-521-85991-2 Hardback
ISBN 978-0-521-17293-6 Paperback

Contents

Figures

Tables

Notes on contributors

Rachael Addicott is a Lecturer in Health and Public Sector Management at the School of Management, Royal Holloway University of London. Rachael is a member of the Centre for Public Services Organizations and her research interests include organizational change in public service organizations and network governance – particularly in health care.

Rhys Andrews is currently a research associate in the Centre for Local and Regional Government Research, Cardiff University. He has over five years experience of researching public services in Wales and England, undertaking a variety of projects studying policy implementation, project delivery and performance in a range of public and voluntary sector bodies. His research interests are now focused on strategic management, organizational environments and public service performance. He is currently working on an Economic and Social Research Council study analysing strategy, structure and service improvement in Welsh local government. He has published articles in the *Journal of Public Administration Research and Theory, Public Administration* and other journals.

George A. Boyne MA, MLitt, PhD is Professor of Public Sector Management at Cardiff Business School. His publications include five books and almost 100 articles in academic journals. He has obtained, as principal or co-applicant, research funding of over £5 million from bodies including the Economic and Social Research Council, the Leverhulme Trust, the Joseph Rowntree Foundation and UK central government departments. From 2003 to 2005 he was an ESRC/EPSRC Advanced Institute of Management Research Fellow. He is an Associate Editor of the *British Journal of Management* and the *Journal of Public Administration Research and Theory*. He has acted as an adviser to UK bodies such as the Audit Commission, the National Audit Office and the Local Government Association, and is a member of the United Nations Expert Group on Public Sector Effectiveness.

Gene A. Brewer is Associate Professor of Public Administration and Policy at the University of Georgia School of Public and International Affairs. He is an internationally recognized public management scholar who publishes in some of the top-ranked journals in the field. His current research interests include public sector reform, governmental performance, and bureaucratic accountability in democratic political systems. He is an editorial board member of the *Public Administration Review*, and an overseas advisor for the UK's Advanced Institute for Management Research, Cardiff University, in Wales.

Youseok Choi is a doctoral student in social welfare at the University of Wisconsin-Madison. His studies focus on evaluating performance of welfare service delivery systems and welfare reform. His research interests include comparative social policy and management of social service organizations.

Young Han Chun is an assistant professor of public administration at Yonsei University, Seoul, Korea. He holds a BA and an MPA from Seoul National University and a DPA from the University of Georgia. His dissertation, *Goal ambiguity in public organizations*, has won three national dissertation awards including the Leonard D. White Award. His research focuses on organizational innovation, strategic planning and performance management in the public sector, and goal attributes in public organizations. He has published articles in such journals as *Journal of Public Administration Research and Theory, Korean Public Administration Review*, and *Korean Journal of Public Administration*.

Ewan Ferlie is Professor of Public Services Management and Head of School at the School of Management, Royal Holloway University of London. He is also Director of the Centre for Public Services Organizations there. He has published widely on organizational change processes in the public services, especially health care, and is co-author of *The New Public Management in Action* (Oxford University Press, 1996) as well as numerous articles.

Melissa Forbes is a joint doctoral student in public policy and sociology at the Ford School of Public Policy at the University of Michigan-Ann Arbor. Her research interests centre around institutional and organizational change, especially the effect that institutional change has on corporate environmental behaviour and environmental policy.

Carolyn J. Heinrich is an Associate Professor at the LaFollette School of Public Affairs and Associate Director of the Institute for Research on Poverty at the University of Wisconsin-Madison. Her research focuses on social welfare policy, public management, and social programme evaluation. Heinrich is co-author of several books on the empirical study of governance and public management, including *Improving Governance: A New Logic for Empirical Research* and *Governance and Performance: New Perspectives*. Recent articles have appeared in the *Review of Economics and Statistics, Journal of Policy Analysis and Management*,

Journal of Labor Research, Journal of Drug Issues, Journal of Human Resources, Public Administration Review, and *American Journal of Evaluation*. She is a founding board member of the national Public Management Research Association, an elected member of the Policy Council of the Association for Public Policy Analysis and Management, and the editor of the *Journal of Public Administration Research and Theory*.

Carolyn J. Hill is an Assistant Professor of Public Policy at Georgetown University in Washington, DC. She received her Master's degree in public policy from the La Follette Institute at the University of Wisconsin-Madison, and her PhD from the Harris Graduate School of Public Policy Studies at the University of Chicago. Carolyn's research focuses on the design, management, and performance of publicly-supported programmes, particularly those that serve poor families. She is co-author, with Laurence E. Lynn, Jr. and Carolyn J. Heinrich, of *Improving Governance: A New Logic for Empirical Research*.

Graeme A. Hodge is Professor of Law at Monash University in Australia. An adviser to Australasian governments, he has contributed to journals in public administration and management, social and economic policy, regulation and law. His research interests cover privatization, contracting, public-private partnerships, accountability and regulation.

Kimberley R. Isett, PhD, MPA is an Assistant Professor of Health Policy and Management at Columbia University's Mailman School of Public Health. After completing her doctoral work, she spent eighteen months as an NIMH post-doctoral research fellow at the Cecil G. Sheps Center for Health Services Research at the University of North Carolina at Chapel Hill, under the mentorship of Joseph P. Morrissey. Her work focuses on interorganizational collaboration, public management, and the delivery of services to vulnerable populations. Her work has been recognized by the Academy of Management's Health Care Management and Public and Nonprofit Divisions, as well as receiving the designation of the best published article in the American Review of Public Administration in 2004.

Patrick Kenis is Professor at the Faculty of Social and Behavioural Sciences at Tilburg University, the Netherlands where he is also Head of the Department of Policy and Organization Studies. He also lectures at TIAS (the Business School of Tilburg University) of which he is a member of the Academic Board. Previously he has worked at the Free University, Amsterdam, the University of Konstanz, Germany, the European Centre for Social Welfare Policy and Research, Vienna and the European University Institute, Florence. He received his PhD in Social and Political Sciences from the European University Institute in

Florence, Italy. He has published articles in such journals as the *Academy Management Review, Methodology – European Journal of Research Methods for the Behavioral and Social Sciences, IEEE Transaction on Visualisation and Computer Graphics, Journal of Theoretical Politics, International Journal of Sociology and Social Policy* and *European Journal of Political Research, Economic and Industrial Democracy* as well as several books and numerous chapters. His research interest focuses on the organizational and network responses in different areas.

Yi Lu is a PhD candidate in the Department of Public Administration and Policy, School of Public and International Affairs at the University of Georgia. Prior to coming to the University of Georgia, she completed the MPA programme at the University of Missouri-Columbia and was a research assistant at the Community Policy Analysis Center. Her research focuses primarily on networked-setting management and financial management.

Laurence E. Lynn, Jr. is the George H. W. Bush Chair and Professor of Public Affairs at the Bush School of Government and Public Service at Texas A&M University. His most recent book, co-authored with Anthony M. Bertelli, is *Madison's managers: Public administration and the constitution*, published by Johns Hopkins University Press. He is the 2005 recipient of the Public Management Research Association's H. George Frederickson award for career contributions to public management scholarship.

Kenneth J. Meier is the Charles H. Gregory Chair in Liberal Arts and Professor of Political Science at Texas A&M University and Professor of Public Management at the Cardiff School of Business, Cardiff University. His eclectic research interests include public management, the relationship between bureaucracy and democracy, minority politics, and quantitative methods.

H. Brinton Milward is the McClelland Professor of Public Management at the University of Arizona. Milward is jointly appointed in the Departments of Management and Policy, Political Science and Sociology and he is a Faculty Associate at the Udall Center for Studies in Public Policy. His research interests revolve around the intersection of public policy and management. He has focused much of his recent work on understanding how to efficiently and effectively manage networks of non-profit organizations that jointly produce public services like mental health. His most recent work is comparing private firms and non-profit agencies that deliver the same services under government contracts. He and Keith Provan have received an IBM Grant to write '*The public manager's guide to network management*'. His recent article 'Dark networks as problems' has been widely cited for its application of network analysis to terrorist networks, human trafficking, drug smuggling, and other illegal activities.

M. Jae Moon is a faculty member at the Department of Public Administration of Korea University. Before joining Korea University, he was at the Bush School of Texas A&M University (2002–2004) and the Graduate School of Public Affairs at the University of Colorado at Denver (1998–2002). His research interests include public management, information technology/environmental policy, and comparative public administration. His research has recently appeared in major public administration and policy journals. He was Book Review Editor for *Public Administration Review* (2002–2005).

Donald P. Moynihan is Assistant Professor of Public Affairs at the Robert M. La Follette School of Public Affairs at the University of Wisconsin-Madison. His research and teaching interests include performance management, homeland security, citizen participation and public budgeting. He is the author of *Rethinking performance management*, forthcoming from Georgetown University Press. He has published in volumes and journals that include *Public Administration Review, J-PART, Administration & Society, Public Performance and Management Review, Governance, Journal of Policy History,* and *Review of Public Personnel Administration.* His article 'Why reforms don't always have to work to succeed: A tale of two managed competition initiatives' won the 2002 award for best journal article from the Public and Nonprofit Division of the Academy of Management. Another article, 'Capacity, management and performance: Exploring the links', was selected as the best article published by the *American Review of Public Administration* during 2003. Moynihan earned his master of public affairs and PhD in public administration from the Maxwell School of Citizenship and Public Affairs at Syracuse University.

Mary O'Mahony is a Professor of International Industrial Economics at the University of Birmingham Business School and a Senior Research Fellow at the National Institute of Economic and Social Research (NIESR) where she has worked since 1987. She is also an AIM Public Service Fellow. She has led projects on a wide range of topics, including deriving internationally consistent measures of fixed capital stocks, measuring productivity levels and growth rates in manufacturing and market services, and the impact of human capital and information technology on international relative productivity levels. Her current research interests include measuring productivity in public services such as education and health and she has recently participated in a study measuring output and productivity in the UK National Health Service. She currently serves on advisory boards for the ONS on measuring output in the education sector and for the Department of Health on productivity measurement in adult social services.

Laurence J. O'Toole, Jr is Margaret Hughes and Robert T. Golembiewski Professor of Public Administration and head of the Department of Public Administration and Policy in the School of Public and International Affairs at the University of Georgia (USA). He is also appointed Professor of Comparative Sustainability Policy Studies at Twente University, the Netherlands. He has published extensively on public management, performance, and governance networks. Currently he serves as co-editor for public management of the *Journal of Policy Analysis and Management*.

Sanjay K. Pandey is an assistant professor in the Department of Public Administration at the University of Kansas. His last academic position was with Rutgers University, Campus at Camden where he directed Phase II of the National Administrative Studies Project (NAsP-II). His research and teaching interests are in public management and health policy.

Keith G. Provan, PhD, is Eller Professor, School of Public Administration and Policy, University of Arizona, Tucson, Arizona, USA. His primary interests are organization theory, health and human services delivery systems, and interorganizational networks in the public, non-profit, and business sectors. He has published extensively in all these areas. Professor Provan's current and recent work has focused on the evolution, governance, and effectiveness of networks in child and youth health, mental health, chronic disease prevention, and tobacco control. His PhD is from the State University of New York, Buffalo.

Hal G. Rainey is Alumni Foundation Distinguished Professor in the Department of Public Administration and Policy of the School of Public and International Affairs at the University of Georgia. His research concentrates on organizations and management in government, with emphasis on performance, change, leadership, privatization, and comparisons of governmental management to management in the business and nonprofit sectors. The third edition of his book, *Understanding and managing public organizations*, was published in 2003. He was recently elected as a Fellow of the National Academy of Public Administration.

Anne C. Rouse is Associate Professor of IT and Business Strategy at the Deakin Business School, Deakin University, Australia. She has been researching outsourcing since 1997, and her doctoral thesis on outsourcing risks and benefits won the 2003 ACPHIS prize for 'best Australasian PhD' in information systems.

Peter C. Smith is Professor of Economics and director of the Centre for Health Economics at the University of York. His research interests include the finance and performance of public services, topics on which he has published widely. He has advised numerous national and international agencies, including the World Bank, OECD and the World Health Organization.

Philip Stevens is a Research Fellow at the National Institute of Economic and Social Research. Since arriving at the institute in 2000, his work has included: work on the effect of tuition fees on universities; investigations of different methods of cost efficiency analysis for local government; an investigation of the role of efficiency in explaining international income differences; secondary analysis of the Employers Skills Survey; a feasibility study of the analysis of public sector productivity; and an examination of issues surrounding the recruitment and retention of staff in the HE sector. He is currently working on developing new approaches to measuring and understanding NHS outputs and productivity; an analysis of low-wage work in Europe; and an examination of the star ratings system in NHS acute trusts.

Richard M. Walker is Professor of Public Management at the School of City and Regional Planning at Cardiff University and Centre of Urban Planning and Environmental Management at the University of Hong Kong. His research interests are in the performance consequences of management with particular reference to strategy, management reform, innovation and red tape. Research articles on these and other topics have appeared in *Journal of Policy Analysis and Management, Policy and Politics, Journal of Public Administration Research and Theory, Public Administration*, and *Public Administration Review*.

Eric W. Welch is an Associate Professor in the graduate programme in public administration at the University of Illinois at Chicago. He earned his PhD in public administration at Syracuse University and has since participated in research projects at the Center for Economic Studies, the International Institute for Applied Systems Analysis, the Great Cities Institute, and the Japan National Institute for Environmental Studies. His current research interests concern issues in electronic governance, environmental policy and comparative administration. Professor Welch has recently published articles in such journals as *Political Communication, British Journal of Political Science, Governance, Administration and Society*, and *Journal of Public Administration Research and Theory*.

Wilson Wong is an associate professor of the Department of Government and Public Administration, the Chinese University of Hong Kong. He received a Bachelor of Social Science from the Chinese University of Hong Kong, an MPA and a PhD in public administration from the Maxwell School, Syracuse University. Professor Wong's core research areas include public management and organization theory, e-government and globalization, and public budgeting and finance. His journal articles and book chapters have been published by *Administration and Society, Brookings Northeast Asia Survey, Environmental Management, Governance, Public Administration Review, Journal of Public Administration Research and Theory*, Hong Kong University Press, and M. E. Sharpe. Prior to his Chinese University position, he had been a research associate at the Center for Policy Research (CPR) at Syracuse University. In 2002–2003, Professor Wong served as a visiting fellow in the Center of Northeast Asian Policy Studies (CNAPS), Brookings Institution.

1 Introduction

George A. Boyne, Kenneth J. Meier, Laurence J. O'Toole Jr and Richard M. Walker

Introduction

The performance of public organizations around the globe is constantly under scrutiny by a variety of stakeholders including politicians, citizens, service users and government inspectors. In the UK, the Labour administration has placed public service improvement at the centre of its domestic agenda and recent events such as the major terrorist attacks of 9/11 in the US, the response of public agencies to Hurricane Katrina and the SARS outbreak in the Far East clearly demonstrate the pressure on public organizations to perform well. Knowledge of routes to higher levels of performance in public organizations is, therefore, of critical importance.

However, there is only limited evidence on the determinants of performance in public organizations (Boyne 2003; O'Toole and Meier 1999). A range of important questions persist about the performance of public bodies. This edited volume seeks to contribute new knowledge on the issues of performance measurement and management in public organizations by focusing upon three questions:

- What approaches should be adopted to measure the performance of public agencies?
- What aspects of management influence the performance of public agencies?
- As the world globalizes, what are the key international issues in performance measurement and management?

In focusing upon these fundamental questions, the contributors to this book debate methodological and technical issues in the measurement of performance in public organizations and provide empirical analyses of the determinants of performance. The book also provides some important groundbreaking work by considering the international dimensions of these issues. Prior to considering these issues in more detail, and discussing the chapter contributions, we describe the meeting from which the papers presented here emerged.

The determinants of performance in public organizations seminar

In May 2004 the editors of this book organized a major international seminar on the 'Determinants of Performance in Public Organizations' at Cardiff University. The purposes of the seminar were to bring together scholars working at the leading edge of research on the performance of public organizations, give greater prominence to this area of academic inquiry, and delineate an agenda for further research. The conference participants are collectively mapping the research frontier on the determinants of organizational performance – especially on the role of management in public service improvement. The publication of this book completes the process of publishing all the papers presented at the seminar. Seven of the papers can be found in a symposium edition of the *Journal of Public Management Research and Theory* edited by Boyne and Walker (2005) and published in October 2005.[1]

The seminar was sponsored by the Advanced Institute for Management Research (www.aimresearch.org) and the Public Management Research Association (www.pmranet.org). The Advanced Institute for Management Research (AIM) is a £17 million flagship initiative that was launched in 2003 by the UK's Economic and Social Research Council (ESRC) and the Engineering and Physical Sciences Research Council (EPSRC). The AIM seeks to build capacity for effective management research that addresses academic, business, public service and policy audiences. The AIM has four objectives, to:

- conduct research that will identify actions to enhance the UK's international competitiveness;
- raise the scientific quality and international standing of UK research on management;
- expand the size and capacity of the active base for UK research on management;
- develop the engagement of that capacity with world-class research outside the UK and with practitioners as co-producers of knowledge about management and other users of research within the UK.

The public services formed one theme within the AIM rubric. A dozen AIM research fellows were appointed to work on the public services. These fellows, as a group, have undertaken systematic reviews of existing work and new theoretical and empirical research. They have also laid out research agendas in their areas of work and identified capacity building requirements in the UK social science community. This book is edited by two of those Fellows (Boyne and Walker) and two AIM International Visiting Fellows (Meier and O'Toole). George

---

1 The papers published in the symposium edition of the *Journal of Public Management research and Theory* were written by Andrews, Boyne, Meier, O'Toole and Walker; Brewer; Chun and Rainey; Forbes and Lynn; Hill; Martin and Smith; and Pitts.

A. Boyne's work focused on public service failure and turnaround and Richard M. Walker examined the relationship between innovation and organizational performance. As International Visiting Fellows, Kenneth J. Meier and Laurence J. O'Toole brought their expertise on public management and performance and research methodologies to a UK audience.

The AIM seminar at Cardiff University was co-sponsored by the Public Management Research Association (PMRA) which is a non-profit academic membership association that has grown out of the bi-annual series of Public Management Research Conferences based in the US. PMRA seeks to further research on public organizations and their management and serve as a voice for the public management research community. The event marked PMRA's first foray overseas as it seeks to internationalize its networks and membership, and to nurture theory building and systematic testing of theory consistent with the canons of social science, using the full range of quantitative and qualitative methodologies in public management.

Fifteen papers were delivered over the two-day event that was held from 6 to 8 May 2004 in the Glamorgan Building at Cardiff University. The papers, listed alphabetically, were:

Rhys Andrews (Cardiff University), George A. Boyne (Cardiff University), Kenneth J. Meier (Texas A&M University and Cardiff University), Laurence J. O'Toole Jr. (University of Georgia) and Richard M. Walker (University of Hong Kong and Cardiff University). *Diversity and organizational performance: An empirical analysis*

Gene A. Brewer (University of Georgia). *In the eye of the storm: Frontline supervisors and federal agency performance*

Yousek Choi and Carolyn J. Heinrich (University of Wisconsin-Madison). *Privatization and performance-based contracting in public welfare programs: The challenge of promoting accountable administration*

Young Han Chun (Yonsei University) and Hal G. Rainey (University of Georgia). *Consequences of goal ambiguity in public organizations*

Rachael Addicott and Ewan Ferlie (University of London – Royal Holloway). *Determinants of performance in cancer networks – A process evaluation*

Melissa Forbes and Laurence E. Lynn Jr. (Texas A&M University). *Studying governance: Are the United States and the rest of the world in step?*

Katharina Hauck, Nigel Rice, Peter C. Smith and Andrew Street (University of York). *Explaining variations in health authority performance: A multivariate hierarchical modelling approach*

Carolyn J. Heinrich (University of Wisconsin-Madison) and Carolyn J. Hill (Georgetown University). *How does governance influence substance abuse treatment strategies? State policies and naltrexone adoption*

Gregory Hill (Texas A&M University). *Long-term effects of managerial succession: An application of the Boyne/Dahya model*

Graeme A Hodge (Monash University) and Anne Rouse (University of Melbourne). *Outsourcing government information technology services: An Australian case study*

Patrick Kenis (Tilburg University*). Control as a determinant of performance in public organizations*

Mary O'Mahony (National Institute of Economic and Social Research). *Outcome based measures in international comparisons of public service provision*

Sanjay K. Pandey (Rutgers University), David H. Coursey (Florida State University), and Donald P. Moynihan (Texas A&M University). *Management capacity and organizational performance: Can organizational culture trump bureaucratic red tape?*

David W. Pitts (University of Georgia). *Diversity, representation and performance: Evidence about race and ethnicity in public organizations*

Keith G. Provan (University of Arizona), Kimberley Roussin Isett (Texas A&M University) and H. Brinton Milward (University of Arizona). *Cooperation and compromise: A network response to conflicting institutional pressures in community mental health*

The seminar was also attended by other academics and practitioners, including H. George Frederickson (University of Kansas) and M. Jae Moon (who also contributes to this volume with his co-authors) and Derek Egan (Office of the Deputy Prime Minister, England). The formal and informal discussions at the seminar provided an important opportunity for this mix of established and more junior academics to develop new directions in public management research. Much of that thinking is reflected in the chapters in this book, and further avenues yet to be explored are identified in the concluding chapter.

Measuring and assessing performance in public agencies

This book deals with qualitative and quantitative approaches to the measurement of public service performance. Longstanding interest has been expressed in the measurement of performance in public agencies (see Ostrom 1973; Park 1984; Kelly and Swindell 2002) and the most appropriate way to analyse such data (Heinrich and Lynn 2001; Martin and Smith 2005; Gill and Meier 2000).

Empirical studies of the performance of public organizations have been limited. This may reflect traditional concerns amongst public administration scholars with organizational processes rather than outputs and outcomes. In addition, many studies of 'policy outputs' have taken costs or resource utilization as the dependent variable (Boyne 1996; see also Smith, Chapter 5). Though questions about expenditure are important for public management scholars, the focus of practitioners (and, more recently, researchers) has shifted along the public service production line from financial inputs to service delivery and performance.

This change of emphasis has opened up important new agendas for public management scholars. The performance of public organizations is contested and multidimensional; for example, Boyne's (2002) review of dimensions of performance included measures of output quantity, output quality, efficiency, effectiveness, accountability, equity, probity, democracy and impact. Although many such classifications exist, little clarity has been offered on the most appropriate ways to measure organizational performance, or how to analyse performance data. These questions are of immediate academic and practical concern. As governments around the world rate the performance of their public agencies, be it cities in China, federal agencies in the US, local governments and health services in the UK or the Putting Service First Scheme in Australia, the types of data used and the way that data is manipulated become important issues. The practical consequences of these regimes are not inconsiderable. In the UK, for example the regimes that rate hospitals or local authorities have major consequences for future resources flows and the autonomy of these agencies. Work by Andrews *et al.* (2005) in England has shown how such regimes do not take account of the context within which organizations operate and thereby penalize those working in difficult conditions.

These performance management regimes often rely upon scorecards as the means to communicate oversight agencies' assessments to citizens. Although such summaries of performance (often in league tables) may be readily interpreted by the layperson, the construction of scorecards is complex involving different types of assessment of performance, and uses a mixture of qualitative and quantitative techniques (see Weimer and Gormley, 1999 and Andrews *et al.*, 2006 for a discussion). The use of performance data from different sources has been an issue of longstanding debate in public management (see Park 1984). The central question posed here is: what is the best source of performance data? Two types of data are typically presented, perceptual or 'subjective' data and archival or 'objective' data. In public management the majority of the debate has been conceptual, with little empirical evidence presented on the relative validity and reliability of these types of performance data (though see for example, Kelly and Swindell 2002).

Important questions about the hotly-debated merits of subjective and objective evaluations of performance are tackled in Chapters 2 and 3. In Chapter 2, entitled 'Subjective and Objective Measures of Organizational Performance: An Empirical Exploration', Rhys Andrews, George A. Boyne and Richard M. Walker assess the relative merits of different methods of measuring performance. The questions they pose include: What types of measures should be used? Are the different types of measure valid? Who is best placed to make assessments – stakeholders in the organization or those outside it? The authors analyse a new dataset from Welsh local government which includes measures of internal and external perceptions of performance. Their analysis reaffirms that organizational performance in the public sector is complex and multidimensional. Its complexity relates to the number of dimensions of performance and the number of stakeholders. The performance of public organizations cannot be reduced to a single dimension, and is inescapably contestable.

Chapter 3 by Gene Brewer entitled 'All Measures of Performance are Subjective: More Evidence from US Federal Agencies' develops this theme. Using data from the 2000 Merit Principles Survey, US Merit Systems Protection Board, the chapter examines the role of frontline supervisors in the twenty-two largest Federal agencies, and explores their contributions to organizational performance and effectiveness (see Brewer 2005 for a full discussion of these results). Attention in this chapter is focused on the validity, reliability, and sensitivity of perceptual measures of organizational performance, as reported by civil servants. To explore issues of common-source bias, Brewer splits the sample: one part of the organization assesses management, the other performance. The results suggest that common-source bias is perhaps more limited than is sometimes claimed.

Performance measures are derived from a variety of sources including inspections, user and citizen satisfaction surveys and archival data. The performance assessments of oversight agencies are often qualitative in form, based on observations and interviews. Little consideration has been given to the use of qualitative data in the literature on performance in public agencies. Chapter 4 by Rachael Addicott and Ewan Ferlie, entitled 'A Qualitative Evaluation of Public Sector Organizations: Assessing Organizational Performance in Healthcare' demonstrates how qualitative data can be used in studies of organizational performance. Qualitative methods are argued to capture the experiences of users, contribute towards positive social and organizational change though action research and offer insights into why things work. Their approach is to track organizational processes through longitudinal and comparative case studies. This methodology is applied to a complex managed cancer network in the UK's National Health Service. Methods utilized include a Delphi panel, interviews, documentary analysis and observation. The example shows how these techniques can be used to construct assessments of organizational performance.

In Chapter 5, entitled 'Quantitative Approaches towards Assessing Organizational Performance', Peter Smith provides a comprehensive critique of the application of quantitative techniques to the study of the performance of public organizations. He reviews techniques for the analysis of one performance indicator and studies that use multiple performance measures in a single model. While providing a comprehensive overview of the application of these techniques, Smith is keen to point out that for most public organizations service delivery or programme evaluation is reliant on multiple measures of performance. The case is made for the use of seemingly unrelated regressions in future studies of the determinants of performance in public organizations for two reasons.

First, the technique does not suffer from some of the technical problems associated with Stochastic Frontier Analysis or Data Envelopment Analysis. Second, it moves beyond the typical piecemeal modeling of individual performance indicators and does not place excessive demands on data or modelling methodology. Smith concludes by noting the need to use other research methods alongside quantitative techniques.

The performance consequences of management

Empirical studies of the impact of management on the performance of public organizations are scarce (Boyne 2003, 2004). Prior wisdom suggests that the actions of public servants are constrained by the rule of law and the external environment within which they operate. Over recent years a small number of researchers (many of whom make contributions to this book) have demonstrated that a range of management variables influence the performance of public organizations, including innovation, leadership, managerial quality, and strategy. In this section of the book a number of major public management trends are explored. The question of the nature of goals in public organizations has long been debated (Rainey 2003). A central theme of this debate is about the clarity of goals in public organizations, and the consequences that arise from opaque goals. Linked to this are questions about control mechanisms within and without public agencies. A key argument in the public management literature is that vague goals are compounded by poor control arrangements, both internal and external. In recent decades there has been a growth of network forms of governance and a spread of contracts with external suppliers of public services. Networks are likely to enhance problems of goal ambiguity and control while contracting, theoretically, should reduce these problems. The chapters in this section of the book explore the performance consequences of these management arrangements.

Chapter 6 addresses an issue of central importance to the management of public organizations: goal ambiguity. Young Han Chun and Hal G. Rainey build on the important work (2005a; 2005b) that has been exploring the determinants and performance impacts of goal ambiguity, taking the case of thirty-two US federal agencies and using their published strategic plans and performance reports as statements of their goals. In this chapter they move on to examine the 'Consequences of Goal Ambiguity in Public Organizations'. They study the relationship between three aspects of goal ambiguity (directive, evaluative and priority) and measures of red tape, decentralization, reward expectancy, and job satisfaction. The findings support the value of clear goals and objectives for public organizations. In particular Chun and Rainey argue that clear goals can reduce procedural regulations, support more decentralization, and increase levels of reward expectancy and job satisfaction. Nonetheless, tensions between the need for managerial clarity and political opaqueness are recognized as a key issue in public management.

In Chapter 7, Patrick Kenis discusses 'Performance Control and Public Organizations'. The chapter reviews the concept of performance control, which is a cybernetic process of setting objectives, measuring performance, and feeding back information. Two extreme examples of performance control are examined: management performance control and agency control. In relation to each part of the cybernetic process, Kenis offers propositions on the likely relationship between performance management control and agency control. The review concludes that there is no one best form of performance control and that prescriptions in this area are likely to be difficult to identify.

Red tape, one of the concerns of Chun and Rainey, is salient to public organizations around the world. Frequently, public organizations are criticized for procedural regulations that adversely affect their performance, and governments increasingly seek to reduce levels of red tape. New public management and reinvention sought to enhance organizational flexibility, but little academic work has examined the performance consequences of red tape. In Chapter 8, Sanjay K. Pandey and Donald P. Moynihan examine 'Bureaucratic Red Tape and Organizational Performance: Testing the Moderating Role of Culture and Political Support'. The authors use data collected from managers in US state health and human service agencies as part of the National Administrative Studies Project. Pandy and Moynihan conclude that red tape does have a negative impact on organizational performance. However, their results show that if levels of developmental culture and political support are high then an increase in red tape is associated with improved performance, suggesting that organizations adapt in different ways to similar constraints. Thus red tape per se is not bad; rather, its impact depends on other characteristics of public organizations.

In Chapter 9, Kenneth J. Meier, Laurence J. O'Toole Jr. and Yi Lu focus on networks and organizational performance. In their chapter entitled 'All That Glitters Is Not Gold: Disaggregating Networks and the Impact on Performance', they note that much theoretical discussion has been presented about the ways that many public programmes are implemented in complex interorganizational networks of public, private and non-profit sector units, and how managers create, sustain, and nourish such networks. In recent years a growing body of empirical research has analysed the impact of network arrangements on public programme performance. Meier, O'Toole and Li contend that largely omitted in the discussion of networks to date has been attention to the possibility that network contact and network interaction might not be beneficial to the performance of the organization at the network's center. This chapter addresses both the positive and negative forces that network nodes bring to bear on the policy performance of a core organization. The analysis focuses on 500 US school districts over a three-year period. Although earlier research has demonstrated that managerial networking has a consistent positive impact on organizational performance, this study disaggregates the network into its component parts to demonstrate that the interaction with some nodes reduces performance. Meier, O'Toole and Lu provide further evidence to validate the management matters argument, however they also suggest that what matters is perhaps more complex that hitherto demonstrated.

Keith G. Provan, Hendry Brinton Milward and Kimberley Roussin Isett examine the evolution and performance of a network of community-based, non-profit, health and human service agencies providing publicly funded services to adults with serious mental illness in Chapter 10. In 'Network Evolution and Performance Under Public Contracting', data from Tucson/Pima County in Arizona is examined from two points in time; first, shortly after the introduction of a new system of funding by the state, based on financial risk under managed care; and then, four years later, after the system had matured. Despite concerns that the new system would increase competition and force agencies to emphasize cost control at the expense of services, their findings indicate that performance did not suffer and that collaboration among key provider agencies increased substantially. The authors draw conclusions concerning the impact of risk-based public contracting on network performance and evolution.

Chapter 11, 'The Design and Management of Performance-based Contracts for Public Welfare Services' sees Youseok Choi and Carolyn J. Heinrich explore the pioneering Wisconsin Work (W-2) programme of public welfare reform. This changed the administrative structure for public welfare services delivery from county government administration to one that allows for private sector management of programmes and performance-based contracting. The authors ask some fundamental questions about contract design and administration. They provide a detailed longitudinal case study of the Wisconsin Works programme. This chapter demonstrates the complexities that public agencies are likely to face in service contracting, one of which is the incomplete nature of contracting arrangements. The primary difficulties experienced were renegotiation and problems of contract administration and management. Choi and Heinrich argue that if public sector contracting is dominated by economic assumptions of completeness and efficiency then the results are likely to be inadequate.

The complexities and uncertainties of contracting are the theme of Chapter 12 where Graeme A. Hodge and Anne C. Rouse examine 'Outsourcing Government Information Technology Services: An Australian Case Study'. They examine the policy promises made when outsourcing IT services, and review the range of global evidence to date on the effectiveness of this technique. The chapter provides a detailed analysis of the outsourcing experience of several major federal government operations in Australia. The authors contrast the empirical experience of a US$1billion contracting deal with the promises made. Their central finding is that the modest 15 per cent saving promised initially was largely not delivered. The reasons for this are analysed and contrasted against the common assumptions made in determining successful outsourcing performance. Finally, the chapter draws together a series of general lessons on the outsourcing of IT at a time when governments are increasingly intent on adopting private means for providing public sector services and infrastructure. The main lesson is that IT outsourcing is more complex and risky than has hitherto been acknowledged.

Global questions in measurement, management and performance

This book takes some of the detailed questions examined earlier and locates them on the international stage. Chapters 13 and 14 by O'Mahony and Stevens and Welch, Moon and Wong consider issues of measurement, while Forbes, Hill and Lynn examine the international evidence on management and the governance in Chapter 15.

Chapter 13: 'International Comparisons of Output and Productivity in Public Service Provision: A Review' by Mary O'Mahony and Philip Stevens considers the feasibility of international comparisons of public service provision at the aggregate sector level, taking the examples of health and education. The authors make a persuasive case for measuring public service output and productivity in ways that mirror the methods used in the market sector. The body of the chapter deals with how output and productivity measurement can be achieved across international borders, with an application to the education sector. The core of their argument is that private and public services are comparable because they both seek to meet consumer demand, and public preferences should, therefore, dictate how services are evaluated. As we noted in the earlier discussion, such studies are now possible because of data availability, which in turn means that, as O'Mahony and Stevens conclude, it will become increasingly possible to extend the types of models presented in this chapter to examine more complex public management relationships in other contexts.

Melissa Forbes, Carolyn J. Hill and Laurence E. Lynn Jr. turn the readers' attention to the international research literature on management and government performance. In Chapter 14, 'Public Management and Government Performance: An International Review' Forbes, Hill and Lynn apply the 'logic of governance' (Lynn *et al.* 2001) analytical framework to a database of nearly 1,000 articles from over fifty countries. The chapter offers a synthesis of the prior studies by Forbes and Lynn (2005) and Hill and Lynn (2005) on '*how researchers understand* what works and how it works'. On methodology, the authors note clear variations between US and non-US research, with the latter more likely to favor 'linear' managerialist hypotheses. They speculate that this may reflect the federal, diffuse and polycentric nature of the US system, in contrast to unitary or statist regimes. The most substantive finding of their study is that hierarchy continues as the backbone of governance, raising questions about the extent of the recent emphasis upon networked or horizontal governance in the public management literature and in the rhetoric of public and political debates on the nature of public service delivery.

The issue of cross-national performance measurement is at the centre of the contribution by Eric W. Welch, M. Jae Moon and Wilson Wong. Their chapter, 'What Drives Global E-government? An Exploratory Assessment of Existing E-government Performance Measures', begins with a discussion of the multiple institutional interests in tracking the use of e-government and the multitude of measures that have followed from this. Many of these measures are already adopted widely in studies that inform policy makers on the drivers of e-government performance, without any systematic evaluation of their validity. The authors take a step back to examine the fundamental question of the validity of those measures and how this may have affected the research findings on what factors actually drive global e-government. Welch, Moon and Wong find different approaches to constructing e-government measures, low correlations among e-government measures, and low to moderate consistency in the relationships between major independent variables and e-government measures. They conclude that much work needs to be done in this field: more precise definitions and better theory development are prerequisites to meaningful e-government measures – a global challenge for academics and practitioners working in this field.

Public management and organizational performance: From non-issue to big issue

The performance of public organizations, and the role of management in helping or hindering the quest for better results, has been prominent on the agenda of policy makers for a quarter of a century. The advent of new public management posed significant new questions to which academics had, initially, few answers. Although they entered the fray a little late, public management researchers are rapidly developing theories and evidence that illuminate the impact of management on public service improvement. This book confirms that significant progress has been made in conceptualizing both management and performance, and in testing the relationship between them.

Nevertheless, further developments in a number of aspects of this research agenda are required. In the concluding chapter of the book, the editors identify major questions concerning theory, methods, measures and data sets that confront the research community. Answers to these questions will provide valuable information to policy makers on the management reforms that make a difference to public services. In addition, research that deals successfully with these questions will reinforce the shift in public service performance from a neglected issue to the defining theme of the field of public management.

REFERENCES

Andrews, R., Boyne, G. A., Law, J. and Walker, R. M. (2005) 'External constraints on local service standards: The case of comprehensive performance assessment in English local government', *Public Administration*, **83**: 639–656.

Andrews, R., Boyne G. A. and Walker, R. M. (2006). 'Strategy content and organizational performance: An empirical evaluation', *Public Administration Review* **66**. 52–63.

Boyne, G. A. (1996) *Constraints, choices and public policies.* London: JAI Press.

Boyne, G. A. (2002) 'Concepts and indicators of local authority performance: An evaluation of the statutory framework in England and Wales', *Public Money and Management*, **22** (2): 17–24.

Boyne, G. A. (2003) 'Sources of public service improvement: A critical review and research agenda', *Journal of Public Administration Research and Theory*, **13**: 767–794.

Boyne, G. A. (2004) 'Explaining public service performance: Does management matter?', *Public Policy and Administration*, **19** (4): 110–117.

Boyne, G. A. and Walker, R. M. (2005) 'Determinants of performance in public organizations' Symposium edition, *Journal of Public Administration Research and Theory*, **15**: 483–639.

Brewer, G. A. (2005) 'In the eye of the storm: Frontline supervisors and federal agency performance', *Journal of Public Administration Research and Theory*, **15**: 505–527.

Chun, Y. H. and Rainey, H. G. (2005a) 'Goal ambiguity in US federal agencies', *Journal of Public Administration Research and Theory*, **15**: 1–30.

Chun, Y. H. and Rainey, H. G. (2005b) 'Goal ambiguity and organizational performance in US federal agencies', *Journal of Public Administration Research and Theory*, **15**: 529–557.

Forbes M. and Lynn, L. E. Jr. (2005) 'How does public management affect government performance? Findings from international research', *Journal of Public Administration Research and Theory*, **15**: 559–584.

Gill, J. and Meier, K. J. (2000) Public administration research and practice: A methodological manifesto', *Journal of Public Administration Research and Theory*, **10**: 157–200.

Heinrich, C. J. and Lynn, L. E. Jr. (2001) 'Means and ends: A comparative study of empirical methods for investigating governance and performance', *Journal of Public Administration Research and Theory*, **11**: 109–138.

Hill, C. J. and Lynn, L. E. Jr. (2005) 'Is hierarchical governance in decline? Evidence from empirical research', *Journal of Public Administration Research and Theory*, **15**: 173–195.

Kelly, J. M. and Swindell, D. (2002) 'A multiple-indicator approach to municipal service evaluation: Correlating performance measurement and citizen satisfaction across jurisdictions', *Public Administration Review*, **62**: 610–620.

Lynn, L. E. Jr., Hienrich, C. J. and Hill, C. J. (2001) *Improving governance: A new logic for empirical research.* Washington DC: Georgetown University Press.

Martin, S. and Smith, P. C. (2005) 'Multiple public service performance indicators: Toward an integrated statistical approach', *Journal of Public Administration Research and Theory*, **15**: 599–613.

Ostrom, E. (1973) 'The need for multiple indicators of measuring the output of public agencies', *Policy Studies Journal*, **2**: 85–91.

O'Toole, L. J. Jr. and Meier, K. J. (1999) 'Modeling the impact of public management: The implications of structural context', *Journal of Public Administration Research and Theory*, **9**: 505–526.

Park, R. B. (1984) 'Linking objective and subjective measures of performance', *Public Administration Review*, **44**: 118–127.

Rainey, H. G. (2003) *Understanding and managing public organizations*. 3rd edn. San Francisco: Jossey-Bass.

Weimer, W. T. and Gormley, D. L. (1999). *Organizational Report Cards*. Cambridge, MA: Harvard University Press.

2 Subjective and objective measures of organizational performance: an empirical exploration

Rhys Andrews, George A. Boyne and Richard M. Walker

Introduction

Governments around the globe now seek to judge the performance of their public services. This has given rise to the introduction of a range of complex and sophisticated regimes to provide information to politicians, managers and the public on organizational success or failures. Examples include an index of measures of performance of Chinese cities (China Daily 2004), the Comprehensive Performance Assessment in English local government (Audit Commission 2002), the Government Performance Results Act 1992 in the US, the Service Improvement Initiative in Canada, the Putting Service First scheme in Australia, Strategic Results Area Networks in New Zealand, Management by Results in Sweden, and Regulation of Performance Management and Policy Evaluation in the Netherlands (Pollitt and Bouckaert 2004). Researchers have increasingly turned their attention to public service performance (e.g., see the Symposium edition of *Journal of Public Administration Research and Theory* 2005 (Boyne and Walker 2005), on the determinants of performance in public organizations). Despite such progress, a persistent problem for public management researchers and practitioners has been the conceptualisation and measurement of performance.

Previous research has shown that organizational performance is multifaceted (Boyne 2003; Carter *et al.* 1992; Quinn and Rohrbaugh 1983; Venkatraman and Ramanujuam 1986). This is because public organizations are required to address a range of goals, some of which may be in conflict. Consequently, public organizations are obliged to focus attention on multiple dimensions of performance. Boyne's (2002) review of these dimensions isolated five conceptual categories – outputs, efficiency, effectiveness, responsiveness and democratic outcomes. Outputs include the quantity and quality of services; efficiency is concerned with the cost per unit of outputs; effectiveness refers to the achievement of formal objectives; responsiveness includes measures of satisfaction, as judged by direct service users, wider citizens and staff; democratic outcomes are concerned with accountability, probity and participation. These categories are found in a variety of academic studies, and in the performance measures used by governments and public organizations.[1]

If some clarity has been brought to the criteria of performance, uncertainty still exists over the best way to measure and operationalize these criteria. For example, governments use aggregated or broad and individual or narrow measures of performance to judge the progress of public agencies. Aggregate measures draw together performance data from a number of sources to produce an overall score for an organization or service. The results of aggregate measures are often presented in a scorecard (Weimer and Gormley 1999). Individual measures typically focus on one dimension of performance in one service area and are reported as specific performance indicators. However, using aggregate measures may mask the contributions of particular management practices, while using individual ones could result in what educationalists call 'teaching to the test'. A growing literature exists on the perverse outcomes of performance management regimes (Ashworth *et al.* 2002; Power 1997).

In this chapter we assess the relative merits of different methods for measuring performance. Should performance measures be objective or subjective?[2] If subjective, should they be based on the perceptions of stakeholders who are internal or external to the organization? What is the relationship between objective and subjective measures, and between internal and external perceptions of performance? Academics have debated for over three decades the merits of subjective and objective measures of performance (Ostrom 1973; Park 1984; Carter *et al.* 1992; Kelly and Swindell 2002). While studies of the measurement of the performance of firms have explored this issue, little work has been undertaken on public organizations. Performance is generally accepted to be a less complex concept in the private sector because most stakeholders agree that strong financial results are essential to business success. By contrast, no single dimension of performance is as paramount in the public sector, and different stakeholders may have widely different interpretations of success and failure.

Our aim is to compare subjective and objective measures of public service performance. The comparability of these measures has major implications for attempts to understand and measure the performance of public organizations. To this end we initially define objective and subjective measures of performance and discuss issues of measurement validity. We then move on to present an empirical analysis of the relationship between subjective and objective

---

1 The dimensions of organizational performance typically used in public sector studies are usually drawn from the '3Es' model of economy, efficiency and effectiveness or the IOO model of inputs-outputs-outcomes. For a more detailed discussion see Boyne (2002).

2 The terms objective and subjective measures are widely used in both the social science measurement and the management literatures. While their use might be provocative, they are used in this chapter as shorthand to distinguish between different ways of measuring performance. As becomes clear in our discussion there are problems associated with the use of both types of measure. All measures are ultimately 'perceptual' rather than 'factual'.

measures of performance across a range of services and dimensions of performance and through time. Our conclusions reflect on the relative merits of subjective and objective performance measures.

The definition and measurement of objective and subjective performance

Both objective and subjective measures of performance have been used in studies of the determinants of performance in public organizations (Brewer 2004; Gould-Williams 2004; Pandey and Moynihan, Chapter 8 of this volume; Andrews *et al.* 2006; Meier and O'Toole 2003). However, public sector studies have rarely used objective and subjective measures in combination (though see Walker and Boyne in press; Kelly and Swindell 2002) and much of the literature has treated these measures as equivalent (Wall *et al.* 2004). This section of the chapter defines objective and subjective measures and deals with a number of technical issues of measurement which suggest that the objective and subjective measures are equally susceptible to problems of validity.

Defining objective and subjective measures of performance

Objective measures have been viewed as the gold standard in public management research. They are typically regarded as the optimum indicators of public sector performance because they are believed to reflect the 'real' world accurately and 'minimize discretion' (Meier and Brudney 2002: 19). An objective indicator should, therefore, be impartial, independent, and detached from the unit of analysis. To reduce discretion and be objective, a measure of performance must involve first the precise assessment of a dimension of performance[3] and second involve an external process to verify its accuracy. Many measures meet these criteria. For example school exam results are a good example of objective measures – they reflect an element of the effectiveness of schools, and students' achievements are validated through the marking of their work by external examiners. Furthermore, this information is publicly available and open to scrutiny by the community. Such data have been used by Meier and O'Toole in their programme of research on management and performance in Texan School Districts. In England and Wales, external performance measures have been available for local governments since 1992 (Boyne 2002). However, the Audit Commission Performance Indicators did not always measure performance (e.g., many early indicators simply measure spending), and while they were published by the Commission only some of them were checked for accuracy. They were, therefore,

---

3 This may include aggregate measures of overall organizational effectiveness or a particular dimension of performance.

of dubious value and unreliable; indeed, anecdotal evidence suggests that data were often 'made up' by local service managers. This position has now changed. The new Best Value Performance Indicators (BVPIs) more closely reflect core dimensions of public service performance, and are audited by external agencies.

A subjective measure may be biased or prejudiced in some way and is not distant to the unit of analysis. Subjective measures, like objective ones must refer to a dimension of performance that is relevant to the organization, that is, subjective judgements may be made either by members of an organization, such that judgements of performance are internal, typically obtained from surveys of managers – or they may be based on external stakeholders, such as consumers or inspectors employed by regulatory agencies. While these measures are external, they typically have not been subjected to independent scrutiny.

Some judgements of performance include aspects of subjective and objective measures; for example the Executive Branch Management Scorecard used by the US government (Government Executive 2004) and the inspection system used in many British public services (Boyne *et al.* 2002). In the latter case, government inspectors make judgements on public organizations based upon a mixture of objective performance data, subjective internal measures of performance from agency staff, subjective external perceptual measures from uses and their own impressions during a site visit.

The validity of objective and subjective measures of performance

A number of validity issues exist in relation to all types of measures of performance. The process of operationalizing the performance of public agencies raises a number of interesting questions about the use of objective measures, the most difficult of which relates to the extensive number of dimensions of performance in the public sector. Boyne (2002) identified eighteen dimensions of performance and concluded that only six of these were captured in recent BVPIs. Areas omitted included issues of fundamental importance to the delivery of public services such as responsiveness and equity. If objective measures are not able to deal with the complexity of performance in public organizations, serious attention must be paid to the use of subjective measures. Indeed the use of subjective measures is often defended in the literature because objective measures are simply not available, or do not tap all of the appropriate dimensions of performance.

Subjective measures are seen to be limited because they suffer from a number of flaws, of which common-method bias is believed to be the most serious (Wall *et al.* 2004). Common-method bias is caused by informants' general predilection towards giving similar responses to separate survey questions (i.e. using only the higher or lower points on a response scale). This causes problems when survey respondents make judgements on both management and performance, and these variables are then used in a statistical model. Furthermore, reliance upon recall together with uncertainty about informants' knowledge of actual performance may also undermine the accuracy of subjective measures (Golden 1992).

Validity is not, however, a problem only for subjective measures. Serious questions have also been posed about the accuracy of objective measures, following major accounting scandals in private firms such as Exxon or WorldCom and evidence of 'cheating' on indicators in the public sector (Bohte and Meier 2000). Furthermore, the objective measures often used in management research are financial, and can be questioned because organizations may make decisions about capital and revenue expenditure subject to anticipated profit – in short, financial measures may also be socially constructed. This problem is also witnessed in relation to external subjective measures of performance in the public sector because scorecards are collated by officials of regulatory agencies through field visits.

One solution to these problems is to use a combination of subjective and objective performance measures to compensate for the deficiencies of using either in isolation. However, when studies adopt both types of measure, their limitations are not always systematically addressed and they are sometimes seen as interchangeable. It could be argued that the latter approach is not problematic because a range of evidence on private organizations demonstrates that there are positive and statistically significant correlations between objective and subjective measures of overall performance, some in the region of $r = .8$ (Bommer *et al.* 1995; Delaney and Huselid 1996; Dess and Robinson 1984; Dollinger and Golden 1992; Powell 1992; Robinson and Pearce 1988). Such findings, however, are only achieved when measures of the same dimensions of performance are used (Guest *et al.* 2003; Voss and Voss 2000). Moreover, consensus on the most important criterion of performance is likely to be greater in the private rather than the public sector. No single dimension of performance is as important for public organizations as financial results are for private organizations.

Although the distinction between objective and subjective measures is clear in principle, some cross-contamination is bound to occur in practice. For example, the content of performance indicators reflects perceptions of the dimensions of services that are important to external stakeholders; and internal perceptions of performance are influenced by scores on performance indicators. The evidence as it exists suggests that the best course of action for public management researchers and practitioners is to use both objective and subjective measures to capture diverse interpretations of organizational performance and to address the limitations of each type of measure.

It is important to recognize that judgements of performance by different stakeholders are likely to be identical only when:

- the same criteria of performance are used;
- the weights attached to the criteria are the same;
- the same indicators are used to operationalize these criteria;
- the information is regarded as equally credible by different groups;
- expectations of the level of achievement against the indicators are the same.

If any one of these conditions is not met, the relationship between subjective and objective measures of performance, and between different subjective measures, will become weaker. Eventually, as all the conditions are relaxed, these relationships may fall close to zero.

An empirical comparison of objective and subjective measures of performance

In this section we compare and contrast objective and subjective performance measures through an analysis of services in Welsh local authorities. The services we examine cover all main local government functions in the UK: education, social services, housing, waste management, highways maintenance, planning, public protection, leisure and culture, and benefits and revenues. Subjective and objective measures of the following dimensions of performance are available for these services: effectiveness, output quality, output quantity and equity. We compare objective performance data and internal and external subjective perceptions of performance in 2002 and 2003. The data sources, measures and methods of data manipulation necessary to permit comparison are now discussed for each type of performance measure. Full data on the performance indicators used in our analysis and the services that are included are shown in Table 2.1.

Objective performance

Objective performance for all major services in Welsh local authorities is measured every year through the production and publication of performance indicators set by their most powerful stakeholder: the National Assembly for Wales, which provides over 80 per cent of local government funding. The National Assembly for Wales Performance Indicators (NAWPIs) are based on common definitions and data which are obtained by councils for the same time period with uniform collection procedures (National Assembly for Wales 2001). All local authorities in England and Wales are expected to collect and collate these data in accordance with the Chartered Institute of Public Finance and Accountancy 'Best Value Accounting – Code of Practice'. The figures are then independently checked for accuracy, and the Audit Commission assesses whether 'the management systems in place are adequate for producing accurate information' (National Assembly for Wales 2001, 14).

Table 2.1 Objective performance measures 2002–2003

	Effectiveness	Quality	Quantity	Equity
Education	% Unqualified school-leavers (inverted) Average General Certificate in Secondary Education (GCSE) score % 5+ GCSEs A*-C % 1+ GCSEs A*-G % KS2 Maths level 4 % KS2 English level 4 % KS2 Science level 4 % KS3 Maths level 5 % KS3 English level 5 % KS3 Science level 5 % GCSE C+ in English/Welsh, Maths/Science	% Reception–Year 2 classes with 30+ pupils (inverted) % Year 3–6 classes with 30+ pupils (inverted) % Special Educational Needs statements in 18 weeks	% Excluded pupils attending 10 hours tuition a week (inverted) % Excluded pupils attending 10–25 hours tuition a week % Excluded pupils attending 25+ hours tuition a week	Primary school exclusions (inverted) Secondary school exclusions (inverted)
Social services	% Care leavers 1+ GCSE A*-G	% Looked after children with 3+ placements during the year (inverted) % Adult clients receiving a needs statement % Child protection cases reviewed	Older people helped to live at home Adults 65+ assessment rate Adult nights respite care	
Housing	% Rent collection[1] % Rent arrears (inverted) % Write-offs (inverted)	% Homelessness applications decided in 33 days Average social housing re-let times (inverted) % Repairs in time Time non-urgent repairs (inverted)		Commission for Racial Equality Housing code of practice
Waste		Missed household waste collections (inverted)[2] % Population served by kerbside recycling		

Highways	Pedestrians killed or seriously injured (inverted) Cyclists killed or seriously injured (inverted) Motorcyclists killed or seriously injured (inverted) Car users killed or seriously injured (inverted) Others killed or seriously injured (inverted) Pedestrians slight injury (inverted) Cyclists slight injury (inverted) Motorcyclists slight injury (inverted) Car users slight injury (inverted) Others slight injury (inverted)	% Faulty street lamps (inverted) Days traffic controls in place for road works (inverted) % Repairs carried out for damaged roads and pavements	% Pedestrian crossings with disabled facilities
Planning		% Planning applications processed in 8 weeks % Standard searches carried out in 10 days	
Public protection	Burglaries (inverted) Vehicle crimes (inverted)	% Food inspections carried out for high risk food premises % Food inspections carried out for other premises	
Leisure and Culture		% Equipped playgrounds meeting national standards	Swims Playgrounds
Benefits and revenues	% Renewal claims on time % Cases processed correctly	Average time for processing new claims (inverted) Average time for processing notifications of changed circumstances (inverted)	

1. This performance indicator was not collected in 2003. Thus the effectiveness measure for that year is made up of only two housing PIs.
2. For this indicator the large maximum scores (874 in 2002, 507 in 2003) meant that we subtracted all the given missed bins scores from 1,000 to create the inverted indicator.

The dimensions of performance covered by each NAWPI are shown in Table 2.1.

Examples include:

- *Output quality* – the number of days that traffic controls were in place on major roads, the percentage of planning applications processed in eight weeks and the average time taken for processing new welfare benefit claims.
- *Output quantity* – the percentage of excluded school pupils attending more than 25 hours tuition a week, the proportion of elderly people helped to live at home and the number of playgrounds maintained by an authority.
- *Effectiveness* – the average General Certificate in Secondary Education (GCSE) score, the percentage of rent arrears and the percentage of welfare benefit claims processed correctly.
- *Equity* – the percentage of primary and secondary school exclusions, the authority's score on the Commission for Racial Equality's Housing Code of Practice and the percentage of pedestrian crossings with facilities for disabled people.

For our analysis we used seventy-two of the one-hundred service delivery NAWPIs available for 2002 and 2003. Although these cover a number of different dimensions of performance, our analysis focuses only on those dimensions for which there were indicators in at least two service areas. Analysing dimensions of performance using data from only one service area would have excessively restricted the sample size, because the maximum number of cases for which we have subjective data in a single service area is fourteen. We are also forced to omit some dimensions of performance from our analysis, such as staff satisfaction and efficiency, because objective indicators on these dimensions are not set by the National Assembly for Wales. To make the indicators suitable for comparative analysis across different service areas, we divided each of them by the mean score for Welsh authorities, inverting some (e.g., the percentage of unqualified school-leavers) so scores above the mean always indicated higher performance.[4] This also allowed different indicators to be added together to create composite measures of objective performance.

We created aggregated measures of output quality, output quantity, effectiveness and equity for each service by first adding groups of relevant indicators together. A single measure of each performance dimension was then constructed for all services by standardizing the total score for each service area. This was done by dividing each aggregated group of service area indicators by the mean score for that aggregated measure. So, for instance, to create the standardized output quantity measure we first added together the scores for three indicators of quantity of education delivered (percentage of excluded pupils attending ten hours tuition a week (inverted), percentage of excluded pupils attending ten to twenty-five hours of tuition a week, and percentage of excluded pupils attending

4 We inverted indicators by subtracting the given scores from 100.

more than twenty-five hours a week) and divided the aggregate score in each local authority service by the mean score. We then repeated this method for output quantity indicators in social services and leisure and culture, thereby deriving a single measure of output quantity across the three service areas.

The standardized groups of indicators were treated as individual scores on effectiveness, quality, quantity and equity for each local authority service in Wales. Individual scores were then used as measures of objective performance suitable for comparison with subjective perceptions of service performance. Our aggregation method also meant that each indicator was weighted equally, ensuring that our analysis was not unduly influenced by particular indicators. Factor analysis was not used to create proxies for each performance dimension because the number of cases per service area is too small to create reliable factors (for a concise explanation of this problem, see Kline 1994).

Internal subjective performance

Internal subjective performance measures for our analysis were derived from an electronic survey of managers in Welsh local authorities. The survey explored informants' perceptions of organization, management and performance.[5] Four single-item measures capturing four dimensions of organizational performance were used for our analysis: effectiveness; output quality; output quantity; and equity. We also asked survey respondents about efficiency, value for money, consumer satisfaction, staff satisfaction, and social, economic and environmental well-being, but NAWPIs do not cover these and cannot be included in our comparison of subjective and objective measures. Survey respondents were asked to assess how well their service was currently performing in comparison with other services in Wales on each performance dimension. Informants placed the performance of their service on a seven-point Likert scale ranging from 1 (disagree that the service is performing well) to 7 (agree that the service is performing well). Multiple informant data were collected from corporate and service level staff in each organization. Two echelons were used to overcome the sample bias problem faced in surveying a higher proportion of informants from one organizational level. Corporate officers and service managers were selected because attitudes have been found to differ between these positions (Aiken and Hage 1968; Payne and Mansfield 1973; Walker and Enticott 2004). In each authority, questionnaires were sent to up to two corporate informants, and up to ten managers in each of the nine service areas covered by objective performance measures. Our analysis in this chapter is conducted only on service managers, because the objective performance indicators and external subjective measures of performance are available at the service level.

5 A copy of the full questionnaire is available on request from the authors.

The number of service informants and respondents differed for each authority because the extent of contact information provided varied across services. The number of informants also changed year on year as a result of personnel changes. A maximum of eighty-nine questionnaires per authority were sent to service managers, and the maximum number of responses from service managers received was thirty-eight.

The survey data were collected in the autumn of 2002 and the autumn of 2003 from Welsh local authorities (for an account of electronic data collection procedures see Enticott 2003). The sample consisted of twenty-two authorities and 830 informants in 2002, and twenty-two authorities and 860 informants in 2003. Seventy-seven per cent of authorities replied (17) and a 29 per cent response rate was achieved from individual informants (237) in 2002. In 2003, 73 per cent of authorities replied (16) and a 25 per cent response rate was achieved from individual informants (216). Our comparison of the equivalence of objective and subjective measures of performance is conducted on ninety-five of the 198 services in Welsh councils in 2002 and on eighty-four of those services in 2003. Most of the services we analysed responded to both years of the survey, but a small number responded only in either 2002 or 2003. The remaining services in this sub-set did not respond to the survey.

To generate service level data suitable for our analysis informants' responses for each service area were aggregated. The average score of these was then taken as representative of performance in that service area. So, for instance, if in one authority there were two informants from the education department, one from school improvement and another from special education needs, then the average of their responses was taken to be representative of the education department as a whole. These scores formed a measure of internal subjective service performance that we compared with objective measures of performance. The small number of respondents in some departments in some councils immediately raises the possibility that their perceptions of service performance may be unreliable, thereby further weakening any observed relationship between objective and subjective measures.

External subjective performance

External subjective performance measures for our analysis were derived from inspection reports for local services in 2002 and 2003. Inspectors are agents of central government, but they are also accountable to their direct employer (usually the Audit Commission) and bring a range of professional values to their task. No explicit statement is available that reveals the dimensions of performance that are included in their assessments or the relative weights that inspection teams attach to them. Their judgements are based on analysis of an authority's organizational context, performance data, 'reality checks' and a range of 'direct inspection methods' (Audit Commission 2000: 15). Judgements on service performance range from 0 stars (poor) to 3 stars (excellent), and were converted into categorical data (1–4) for the purposes of our analysis. The inspection reports also categorize services on their capacity to improve; however, these judgements refer to organizational characteristics rather than service performance, and so are not included in our analysis. Even for service performance alone, however, it is clear that inspectors are drawing not only on NAWPIs, but also on other sources of information and, possibly, different criteria of performance.

To compare inspection judgements and objective performance we created an overall mean objective performance score for each inspected service. This was done by first adding together the performance indicators in each service area used in our analysis. We then standardized the aggregated performance indicator scores for each service area by dividing them by the mean score for those areas. These standardized scores were finally treated as comparable measures of objective performance for inspected local authority services, by dividing them by the mean score for inspected services.

To compare inspection judgements and internal subjective performance we created an overall mean subjective performance score for each inspected service. This was done by aggregating the effectiveness, quality, quantity and equity scores of inspected services and dividing the aggregated results by the mean aggregated score. This standardized score was then treated as an internal subjective performance measure for inspected services.

The programme of external inspection covered only around 20 per cent of services in each year. To generate a larger sample size for our comparison of inspection judgements and performance we averaged the performance scores for 2002 and 2003. These scores were then standardized by dividing them by the mean objective and subjective performance scores for all services inspected between 2002 and 2003.

Results

The results for our comparison of objective and subjective performance are presented in Tables 2.2 to 2.13. The tables show our findings on the relationship between objective and internal subjective performance, objective and external subjective performance, and internal and external subjective performance.

Objective measures and internal subjective measures

We used Kendall's tau-b non-parametric test of association to analyse bivariate correlations between measures of internal subjective and objective performance because this method is the most suitable for the small size of our sample (Kendall, 1970). Tables 2.2 to 2.5 show the correlations by performance dimension for the

Table 2.2 Effectiveness correlations 2002–2003

	1	2	3
1 Objective effectiveness 02			
2 Objective effectiveness 03	.418**		
3 Subjective effectiveness 02	.172+	−.074	
4 Subjective effectiveness 03	.209*	.128	.228**

N = 46
\+ = significant at the 0.10 level (1-tailed)
* = significant at the 0.05 level (1-tailed)
** = significant at the 0.01 level (1-tailed)

Table 2.3 Output quality correlations 2002–2003

	1	2	3
1 Objective quality 02			
2 Objective quality 03	.444**		
3 Subjective quality 02	.060	.009	
4 Subjective quality 03	.007	.135+	.319**

N = 65
\+ = significant at the 0.10 level (1-tailed)
* = significant at the 0.05 level (1-tailed)
** = significant at the 0.01 level (1-tailed)

Table 2.4 Output quantity correlations 2002–2003

	1	2	3
1 Objective quantity 02			
2 Objective quantity 03	.390**		
3 Subjective quantity 02	−.154	−.033	
4 Subjective quantity 03	.260*	.176	.139

N = 27
\+ = significant at the 0.1 level (1-tailed)
* = significant at the 0.05 level (1-tailed)

Table 2.5 Equity correlations 2002–2003

	1	2	3
1 Objective equity 02			
2 Objective equity 03	.741**		
3 Subjective equity 02	.041	.216	
4 Subjective equity 03	.111	.125	.107

N = 17
** = significant at the 0.01 level (1-tailed)

two years analysed. Tables 2.6 to 2.9 show the correlations between performance dimensions within each year for objective and subjective measures. The number of cases for each set of correlations varies due to the different response rates for each year of the electronic survey of Welsh councils, changes in the size of the NAWPI data set caused by missing or unreliable data (e.g., some returns for the proportion of special school pupils excluded in 2002 were identified as potentially incorrect by auditors), and the smaller number of indicators available for certain performance dimensions in some service areas. Each set of correlations comprises those services where objective and subjective performance scores could be derived for 2002 and 2003. The units of observation for all our analyses are services.

Table 2.2 indicates that the objective measure of effectiveness is positively correlated across the two years. The correlation of .418, however, suggests that objective performance on this dimension exhibits a moderate degree of stability. Likewise, our subjective measure of effectiveness is positively correlated for the two years analysed, but the size of the correlation (.288) implies only a low degree of stability. Our measures of objective and subjective effectiveness are positively, though weakly, correlated in 2002, but uncorrelated in 2003. This finding implies that the two aspects of effectiveness are not equivalent, and that our measures may be tapping different components and criteria of effectiveness which are unrelated to each other. For example, our measure of subjective effectiveness may reflect service managers' perceptions of overall effectiveness, while our measure of objective effectiveness gauges achievement on a small number of headline performance indicators. Finally, there is a small positive correlation between objective effectiveness in 2002 and subjective effectiveness in 2003. The evidence of a relationship between these two measures may be attributable to a performance 'feedback loop', wherein subjective perceptions of effectiveness have been influenced by prior objective performance results (March and Sutton 1997).

Table 2.3 shows that our objective measure of output quality is positively correlated across the two years studied, as is our subjective measure. The moderate correlations (.444 and .319) suggest that our separate measures of output quality exhibit a degree of stability through time. Objective and subjective quality are positively and weakly correlated only in 2003, with no relationship apparent in 2002. The modest longitudinal relationships for objective and subjective measures taken separately are therefore not repeated across those measures. Table 2.4 indicates that our objective measure of output quantity is positively correlated for the two years analysed, with the correlation (.390) implying a moderate degree of stability. However, our subjective measure exhibits no stability over time. This may be a consequence of the lower reliability associated with the small dataset, that is used for our analysis of this dimension of performance. In addition, some turnover in the survey respondents within each service year

Table 2.6 Objective performance correlations 2002

	1	2	3
1 Objective effectiveness			
2 Objective output quality	.036		
3 Objective output quantity	.059	−.070	
4 Objective equity	−.201+	−.499**	.409*

+ = significant at the 0.10 level (1-tailed)
* = significant at the 0.05 level (1-tailed)
** = significant at the 0.01 level (1-tailed)

Table 2.7 Objective performance correlations 2003

	1	2	3
1 Objective effectiveness			
2 Objective output quality	.088		
3 Objective output quantity	−.034	−.057	
4 Objective equity	−.094	.181+	.056

+ = significant at the 0.10 level (1-tailed)
* = significant at the 0.05 level (1-tailed)
** = significant at the 0.01 level (1-tailed)

Table 2.8 Subjective performance correlations 2002

	1	2	3
1 Subjective effectiveness			
2 Subjective output quality	.753**		
3 Subjective output quantity	.692**	.841**	
4 Subjective equity	.283**	.167+	.213**

+ = significant at the 0.10 level (1-tailed)
* = significant at the 0.05 level (1-tailed)
** = significant at the 0.01 level (1-tailed)

Table 2.9 Subjective performance correlations 2003

	1	2	3
1 Subjective effectiveness			
2 Subjective output quality	.673**		
3 Subjective output quantity	.668**	.771**	
4 Subjective equity	.392**	.326**	.237*

+ = significant at the 0.10 level (1-tailed)
* = significant at the 0.05 level (1-tailed)
** = significant at the 0.01 level (1-tailed)

on year may make our internal subjective performance measures less stable than those for objective performance. There is no support for a relationship between our objective and subjective measures of service quantity in the same years. Nevertheless, there is again some evidence of a 'feedback loop' between perceptions of performance in 2003 and objective performance in 2002.

Table 2.5 shows that the only positive correlation for performance on equity is for the objective measure across each of the two years considered. The strength of this correlation (.741) suggests that objective performance on equity is approaching inertia. The other correlations indicate that there is virtually no equivalence between perceptions of equity through time. It could be the case that the subjective measures are simply not related to existing objective measures of equity, which omit major issues such as distribution of services by ethnicity, gender, social class, age and geographical area. This clearly illustrates the difficulty of comparing objective scores on a few narrow criteria of equity with subjective scores that take a much broader view of this dimension of performance. To explore the apparently weak relationship between different measures of performance further, we correlated the objective and subjective measures of performance for each year.

Table 2.6 shows that only objective equity is correlated with other dimensions of objective performance in 2002. There is a moderately strong negative correlation between output quality and equity (−.499), which suggests that organizations are faced with a trade-off between equity and quality. By contrast, the moderate correlation (.409) between equity and output quantity implies that improvements in one may be accompanied by improvement in the other. The weak negative correlation between effectiveness and equity again suggests the presence of trade-offs between different dimensions of performance. Table 2.7 shows that in 2003 there is only a weak positive correlation between objective quality and equity. This suggests both that the relationship between different objective measures is unstable through time and that, overall, they are tapping different dimensions of performance. These findings reveal an unusual amount of instability in objective performance, which is often found to display high levels of auto-correlation through time. This may be attributable to the use of aggregated rather than separate indicators or to particular issues associated with performance in Welsh local government.

Table 2.8 shows that there are strong positive correlations between most of the different dimensions of subjective performance in 2002. Subjective effectiveness, quality and quantity are all positively correlated at about .7 or more. However, equity is weakly correlated with the other performance dimensions. The high correlations for effectiveness, quality and quantity imply that the survey respondents have convergent views on these performance dimensions. The evidence may also indicate the presence of common source bias within the data set. It is not obvious, however, why common source bias would be present in the measures of service outputs and effectiveness, but not in the measures of equity. Table 2.9 shows that the pattern of relationships for subjective performance dimensions remains stable through time, with the correlations for equity and the other dimensions becoming slightly stronger.

External subjective measures and internal subjective and objective measures

We used descriptive statistics to analyse the relationship between external subjective, internal subjective and objective performance because this method is the most suitable for the small number of inspected services. Table 2.10 shows the range of values and their standard deviations for each of these aspects of performance in 2002, 2003 and for both years aggregated. Tables 2.11–2.13 show the mean subjective and objective performance scores for those authorities judged by inspectors as 1 (poor), 2 (fair), 1 and 2 (poor or fair), and 3 (good) for the same time periods. More Welsh services provided objective performance data for audit and inspection than responded to our survey. As a result, the n for the objective performance mean is higher than for the subjective performance mean.

The tables indicate that, in general, as inspectors rate services more highly, the mean subjective and objective performance scores for these services also rise. This suggests that inspectors' judgements are positively, if loosely, related to the substantive and perceived achievements of local service providers. However, there are two exceptions to the pattern. The mean subjective performance score for good services in 2003 is lower than that for fair services, which contrasts with the higher mean objective performance score for services receiving the better inspection judgement in the same year. This finding is repeated for the aggregated figures shown in Table 2.13. These results may be caused by the lower data reliability associated with the small number of subjective performance scores in 2003, or could reflect more serious divergence between internal and external perceptions of performance.

Conclusion

Organizational performance in the public sector is complex and multidimensional. It is, therefore, important to assess the relative failure or success of different organizations on a range of criteria and measures. Different stakeholders are likely to have the same view of performance only when a highly restrictive set of conditions (concerning criteria, weights, indicators, data reliability and expectations) is met. Prior literature tends to contain the assumption that objective measures are better than subjective measures of performance. However, no truly 'objective' measures of public service performance exist, any more than there are objective measures of art and music. Public service beauty is in the eye of the stakeholder. The supposedly objective measures that are

Table 2.10 Descriptive statistics for subjective and objective performance in inspected services

	Minimum	Maximum	S.D.
Subjective performance 02	.84	1.23	.12
Subjective performance 03	.83	1.19	.13
Subjective performance 02–03	.83	1.23	.12
Objective performance 02	.68	1.38	.12
Objective performance 03	.46	1.27	.18
Objective performance 02–03	.45	1.37	.16

Table 2.11 Inspection results and mean subjective and objective performance 2002

BV Performance score	Subjective performance mean	Objective performance mean
1 (poor)	0.88 (n = 1)	0.92 (n = 3)
2 (fair)	1.01 (n = 11)	1.02 (n = 17)
2 and 1	1.00 (n = 12)	1.01 (n = 20)
3 (good)	1.01 (n = 4)	1.03 (n = 12)

Table 2.12 Inspection results and mean subjective and objective performance 2003

BV Performance score	Subjective performance mean	Objective performance mean
1 (poor)		0.83 (n = 1)
2 (fair)	1.01 (n = 6)	1.00 (n = 13)
2 and 1		0.99 (n = 14)
3 (good)	0.99 (n = 5)	1.01 (n = 9)

Table 2.13 Inspection results and mean subjective and objective performance 2002–2003

BV Performance score	Subjective performance mean	Objective performance mean
1 (poor)	0.88 (n = 1)	0.89 (n = 4)
2 (fair)	1.01 (n = 15)	1.00 (n = 25)
2 and 1	1.00 (n = 16)	0.98 (n = 29)
3 (good)	1.00 (n = 9)	1.02 (n = 21)

available are usually imposed on service providers by their governmental superiors, so reflect a particular set of politically and historically contingent judgements on what is important and desirable. Furthermore, such objective indicators are also swayed by data availability and ease of measurement, so inevitably present a partial (in every sense) picture of performance.

Just as objective measures are biased by political and technical constraints, so subjective perceptions of performance are likely to be influenced by the objective indicators that service providers are required to collect and report. Thus some positive correlation should be expected between objective and subjective measures of performance, but this is unlikely to be high unless both types of measure focus on exactly the same components of services and dimensions of performance. Our analysis of different sets of performance information in Welsh local government has shown that these conditions for the comparability of different views of performance are rarely met. The objective indicators that we analysed covered sub-components of performance criteria such as effectiveness and equity; and although the subjective indicators of these concepts were broader, their exact content was difficult to discern. The performance criteria and weights that entered the performance judgements of service managers and external inspectors are largely unknown.

The major lesson from our analysis is that objective and subjective measures of performance provide different pieces of the performance jigsaw. They are rarely measures of precisely the same elements of performance, so it is unsurprising that they are not closely correlated. It cannot be concluded that subjective perceptions of performance are 'wrong' simply because they are weakly related to objective measures. Except when either subjective or objective measures are distorted by low reliability or deliberate error, neither is an inherently superior estimate of organizational performance in the public sector.

REFERENCES

Aiken, M. and Hage, J. (1968) 'Organizational interdependence and intra-organizational structure', *American Sociological Review*, **33**: 912–930.

Andrews, R., Boyne, G. A. and Walker, R. M. (2006) 'Strategy content and organizational performance: an empirical analysis', *Public Administration Review*, **66**: 52–63.

Ashworth, R., Boyne, G. A. and Walker, R. M. (2002) 'Regulatory problems in the public sector: theories and cases', *Policy and Politics*, **30**: 195–211.

Audit Commission (2000) *Best value inspection in Wales*. London: HMSO.

Audit Commission (2002) *Comprehensive performance assessment*. London: Audit Commission.

Bohte, J. and Meier, K. J. (2000) 'Goal displacement: assessing the motivation for organizational cheating', *Public Administration Review*, **60**: 173–182.

Bommer, W. H., Johnson, J. L., Rich, G. A., Podsakoff, P. M. and MacKenzie, S. B. (1995) 'On the interchangeability of objective and subjective measures of employee performance: a meta-analysis', *Personnel Psychology*, **48**: 587–605.

Boyne, G. A. (2002) 'Concepts and indicators of local authority performance: An evaluation of the statutory framework in England and Wales', *Public Money and Management*, **22**(4): 17–24.

Boyne, G. A. (2003) 'What is public service improvement?', *Public Administration*, **81**: 221–228.

Boyne, G. A., Day, P. and Walker, R. M. (2002) 'The evaluation of public service inspection: a theoretical framework', *Urban Studies*, **39**: 1197–1212.

Boyne, G. A. and Walker, R. M. (eds.) (2005) *Journal of Public Administration Research and Theory*, **15**: 483–639.

Brewer, G. A. (2004) 'In the eye of the storm: frontline supervisors and federal agency performance'. Paper presented at the Determinants of Performance in Public Agencies Conference, Cardiff University, May.

Carter, N., Klein, R. and Day, P. (1992) *How organisations measure success: The use of performance indicators in government*. London: Routledge.

China Daily (2004) '33 indexes evaluate government performance.' Accessed on 28 September 2004. www.english.people.com/cn/2004/08.02/eng 20040802_151609.html.

Delaney, J. T. and Huselid, M. A. (1996) 'The impact of human resource management practices on perceptions of organizational performance', *Academy of Management Journal*, **39**: 949–969.

Dess, G. G. and Robinson, R. B. (1984) 'Measuring organizational performance in the absence of objective measures: the case of the privately-held firm and conglomerate business unit', *Strategic Management Journal*, **5**: 265–273.

Dollinger, M. J. and Golden, P. A. (1992) 'Interorganizational and collective strategies in small firms: environmental effects and performance', *Journal of Management*, **18**: 695–715.

Enticott, G. (2003) 'Researching local government using electronic surveys', *Local Government Studies*, **29**(3): 52–67.

Golden, B. R. (1992) 'Is the past the past – or is it? The use of retrospective accounts as indicators of past strategies', *Academy of Management Journal*, **35**: 848–860.

Gould-Williams, J. (2004) 'The effects of "high commitment" HRM practices on employee attitude: the views of public sector workers', *Public Administration*, **82**: 63–81.

Government Executive (2004) Daily Briefing 29 January 2004. Retrieved 19 May 2004 from www.govexec.com.

Guest, D. E., Michie, J., Conway, N. and Sheehan, M. (2003) 'Human resource management and corporate performance in the UK', *British Journal of Industrial Relations*, **41**: 291–314.

Kelly, J. M. and Swindell, D. (2002) 'A multiple-indicator approach to municipal service evaluation: correlating performance measurement and citizen satisfaction across jurisdictions', *Public Administration Review*, **62**: 610–620.

Kendall, M. G. (1970) *Rank correlation methods*. 4th edn. London: Griffin.

Kline, P. (1994). *An easy guide to factor analysis*. London: Routledge.

March, J. G. and Sutton, R. L. (1997) 'Organizational performance as a dependent variable', *Organization Science*, **8**: 698–706.

Meier, K. J. and Brudney, J. L. (2002) *Applied statistics for public administration*. Orlando: Harcourt College.

Meier, K. J. and O'Toole, L. J. (2002) 'Public management and organizational performance: the impact of managerial quality', *Journal of Policy Analysis and Management*, **21**: 629–643.

Meier, K. J. and O'Toole, L. J. (2003) 'Public management and educational performance: the impact of managerial networking', *Public Administration Review*, **63**: 689–699.

National Assembly for Wales (2001) Circular 8/2001, Local Government Act: guidance on Best Value Performance Indicators 2001. Cardiff: National Assembly.

National Assembly for Wales (2003) *National Assembly for Wales Performance Indicators 2001–2002*. Available from: www.lgdu.gov.uk.

National Assembly for Wales (2004) *National Assembly for Wales Performance Indicators 2002–2003*. Available from: www.lgdu.gov.uk.

Ostrom, M. (1973). 'The need for multiple indicators of measuring the output of public agencies', *Policy Studies Journal*, **2**: 85–91.

Pandy, S., Coursey, D. H. and Moynihan, D. P. (2004) 'Management capacity and organizational performance: can organizational culture trump bureaucratic red tape?' Paper presented at the Determinants of Performance in Public Agencies Conference, Cardiff University, May.

Parks, R. B. (1984) 'Linking objective and subjective measures of performance', *Public Administration Review*, **44**: 118–127.

Payne, R. and Mansfield, R. (1973) 'Relationships of perception of organizational climate to organizational structure, context and hierarchical position', *Administrative Science Quarterly*, **18**: 515–526.

Pollitt, C. and Bouckaert, G. (2004) *Public management reform: A comparative analysis*, Oxford: Oxford University Press.

Powell, T. C. (1992) 'Organizational alignment as competitive advantage', *Strategic Management Journal*, **13**: 119–134.

Power, M. (1997) *The audit society*. Oxford: Oxford University Press.

Quinn, R. E. and Rohrbaugh, J. (1983) 'A spatial model of effectiveness criteria: towards a competing values approach to organizational analysis', *Management Science*, **29**: 363–377.

Robinson, R. B. and Pearce II, J. A. (1988) 'Planned patterns of strategic behavior and their relationship to business-unit performance', *Strategic Management Journal*, **9**: 43–60.

Venkatraman, N. and Ramanujam, V. (1986) 'Measurement of business performance in strategy research: a comparison of approaches', *Academy of Management Review*, **11**: 801–814.

Voss, G. B. and Voss, Z. G. (2000) 'Strategic orientation and firm performance in an artistic environment', *Journal of Marketing*, **64**: 67–83.

Walker, R. M. and Boyne, G. A. (2006) 'Public management reform and organizational performance: an empirical assessment of the UK Labour government's public service improvement strategy', *Journal of Policy Analysis and Management*, **25**: 371–394.

Walker, R. M. and Enticott, G. (2004) 'Using multiple informants in public administration: revisiting the managerial values and actions debate', *Journal of Public Administration Research and Theory*, **14**: 417–434.

Wall, T. B., Michie, J., Patterson, M., Wood, S. J., Sheehan, M., Clegg, C. W. and West, M. (2004) 'On the validity of subjective measures of company performance', *Personnel Psychology*, **57**: 95–118.

Weimer, D. L. and Gormley, W. T. (1999) *Organizational report cards*. Cambridge, MA: Harvard University Press.

3 All measures of performance are subjective: more evidence on US federal agencies

Gene A. Brewer

Introduction

This chapter has twin aims. First, I address the important matter of measuring organizational performance and argue that it is a socially-constructed concept; thus, all measures of performance are subjective. I then propose a framework to evaluate such measures. This framework consists of three criteria: validity, reliability, and sensitivity. A perceptual measure of organizational performance is introduced, and this measure is shown to satisfy these criteria as well or better than most measures. However, perceptual measures are vulnerable to common source and related bias. Two ways to assess the viability of this threat are suggested and demonstrated.

Second, this perceptual measure of organizational performance is utilized in an empirical analysis. I test a hybrid model that predicts organizational performance in the twenty-two largest federal agencies using data from the 2000 Merit Principles Survey, US Merit Systems Protection Board. This model features supervisory management and several related constructs as prominent variables. The findings show that management matters a great deal. Frontline supervisors play an important role in organizational performance, and supervisory management is an important determinant of high performance in federal agencies. High performing agencies also tend to have skillful upper-level managers, strong cultures that value employees and emphasize the importance and meaningfulness of the agency's work, and policies that empower those employees. These agencies also tend to have a strong performance orientation, and they strive for workforce diversity. The concluding section reflects on the difficulty of measuring organizational performance in the public sector; offers some practical advice for policy-makers and public managers; and makes some suggestions for future research.

Measuring organizational performance

This study begins with a methodological question of some importance. How can organizational performance be measured adequately in the public sector, with government's expansive range of programme activity, vague and often conflicting goals, and a highly charged political environment that includes multiple principals vying for control over the policy agenda, public administrators exercising considerable discretion in policy implementation, and citizens joining the fray? Part of the answer lies in the fact that organizational performance is a socially-constructed concept and all measures of performance are subjective. This is especially true in the public sector where competing views of reality exist and many important disputes are settled by elections or mutual accommodation rather than by more objective or rational means. In the public sector (and elsewhere), organizational performance is an elusive concept that – like beauty – lies in the eye of the beholder. This is why perceptual measures are appropriate.

Measures of organizational performance should satisfy three crucial criteria: validity, reliability, and sensitivity. But can a perceptual and somewhat subjective measure of organizational performance such as the one utilized in this study satisfy these criteria? In the discussion that follows, I introduce the measure – present evidence – which suggests it satisfies these criteria, and conclude that it is probably superior to most measures of organizational performance utilized in the research literature and in public policy-making. Then, I discuss the threat of common source and related bias and demonstrate two ways to assess it.

This study taps survey data drawn from a large sample of federal government employees to develop a perceptual measure of organizational performance. The construct is measured with eight survey items that tap its different dimensions. These dimensions come from two sources. First, Boyne (2003) identified the following 'headline dimensions' of service performance: quantity of outputs, quality of outputs, efficiency, equity, outcomes, value for money, and consumer satisfaction. Second, Brewer and Selden (2000: 688–689, Figure 3.1) formulated a 2×3 typology of organizational performance consisting of internal and external dimensions that focus on the core administrative values of efficiency, effectiveness, and fairness (for similar approaches, see Quinn and Rohrbaugh 1983; Selden and Sowa 2004; Walker and Boyne in press; Kim 2005; Brewer 2005). The resulting index includes most dimensions of the construct, and it produces an alpha reliability coefficient of .83.[1]

This is a perceptual measure of organizational performance, but there are many precedents for it (for a list of studies, see Brewer 2005: 511). Most of these studies use employee perceptions of organizational performance and many of them focus on public agencies, as does the present study (also see Brewer 2005;

---

1 All of the indexes used in this study were created by adding the measurement items that composed them. In a few instances, measurement scales were equalized before adding.

Brewer and Lee 2005; Kim 2005). Several studies have shown that perceptual measures of organizational performance correlate positively with moderate to strong associations with more objective measures (for a list of studies, see Brewer 2005: 511). Walker and Boyne cite a range of evidence that demonstrates '... there are positive and statistically significant correlations between objective and subjective measures of overall performance, some in the region of $r = .8$' (in press). The authors add that performance is a multi-dimensional construct, and the strongest correlations are found between measures that tap similar dimensions (also see Wall *et al.* 2004).

The perceptual measure of organizational performance utilized in this study is robust. Respondents come from all hierarchical levels and functional areas of the agencies studied, thus incorporating most perspectives. They are asked to assess different aspects of performance in both their work units and the larger organization, which provides a panoramic view of federal agency performance. The measures utilized in this study are unobtrusive – they come from a secondary data set that was collected for other purposes. Respondents could not have anticipated that this study would be mounted, or that it would use the eight survey items listed in the appendix to measure organizational performance. Furthermore, the respondents were guaranteed absolute anonymity when completing the survey. In all likelihood, their responses were relatively unbiased. Collectively, these informants and their assessments are thought to provide a valid and reliable indicator of federal agency performance. The combined index thus provides a sensitive, encompassing measure. It is evaluated on the criteria of validity, reliability, and sensitivity.

In measurement theory, there are two types of validity: the extent to which a researcher accurately identifies all theoretical dimensions of a construct, and the extent to which the construct's operational definition accurately taps these theoretical dimensions. As already mentioned, one crucial point is that organizational performance is a socially-constructed concept; thus, *all measures of performance are subjective*. The perceptual measure of organizational performance used in this study comes from federal employees, but it would be equally subjective if drawn from citizens, clients, stakeholders, audit agencies, members of Congress, the White House staff, or 'expert researchers'. In fact, one might argue that employees know their organizations better than anyone else.

Reliability is another important criterion. Reliability is evidence that a measure distinguishes accurately between subjects and over time. There are three dimensions of reliability: a measure's equivalence – different raters or instruments should produce consistent measures; its stability – it should yield the same results over time, unless what is being measured changes; and its internal consistency – in multiple-item scales, all items constituting the measure are related to the same concept or phenomenon. Reliability can be assessed both qualitatively and quantitatively (Meier and Brudney, 1993: 102–103). Some of both are provided in earlier discussions. Here, some additional quantitative evidence is presented. Inter-rater reliability is computed by dividing the sample and correlating measures of organizational performance in the two halves. They correlate at .86 (p <.001), suggesting that the measure is highly reliable and consistent. In addition, the variable has a range of 12–80 and a standard deviation of 10.72 – certainly within bounds. The alpha reliability coefficient for the multiple-item scale is .83 – well above the customary threshold of .70.

In addition to being valid and reliable, a measure must also be sensitive. Sensitivity is a function of the measure's precision or calibration. In this research, considerable effort was devoted to developing a sensitive measure. The survey administrators asked respondents a battery of questions related to organizational performance, and respondents scored their answers on Likert-type scales. The researcher then matched the survey questions with the theoretical dimensions of organizational performance and utilized the respondents' answers to measure this construct. The resulting measure seems more sensitive than most.

One potential threat is common source and related bias, which can occur when a single set of survey respondents are relied upon to provide measures of both the independent and dependent variables in a study (Podsakoff and Organ 1986; Wall *et al.* 2004; Walker and Boyne 2006).[2] To assess the viability of this threat, Harman's (1967) one-factor test was employed following the approach outlined by Podsakoff *et al.* (1984). According to this method, if a substantial amount of bias is present, all variables will load on a single factor or a general factor will emerge that accounts for most of the variance. In the present study, neither condition exists. This finding thus partially allays concerns about such bias. Later, I return to the nagging threat of common source and related bias and provide further evidence that it is not problematic.

In summary, the measure of organizational performance developed and utilized in this study seems more valid, reliable, and sensitive than most measures utilized in the research literature and in public policy-making. For example, consider how well organizational performance has been measured in the following cases:

- The Bush administration included a 'management scorecard' in its fiscal year 2005 budget and assigned federal agencies a green, yellow, or red light based on how well they were implementing the President's management agenda.
- The Government Performance Project, a joint effort by Syracuse University and the Pew Charitable Trusts, recently released its latest 'report card' on the states. Each state was graded in four areas – information, infrastructure, money, and people – and assigned an overall grade ranging from A– to C–.
- Coggburn and Schneider (2003) recently published a study on the effects of management quality on state government performance, which they define as state

2 'Common source and related bias' refers to several different threats that are described in the literature; i.e., common source, common method, common response, and single-source bias.

policy priorities and commitments. Their measure is the difference between the percentages of state government spending on welfare versus highways.
  The International City/County Management Association's Center for Performance Measurement has developed a wide variety of performance measures on specific services and encouraged member governments to compare and adopt 'best practices'.

Based on the foregoing discussion, all of these measures seem to be lacking in validity, reliability, and/or sensitivity. Another thing they tend to overlook is the need to develop an omnibus measure of organizational performance that can be used to improve service delivery and promote good government across the full spectrum.

The emerging human capital crisis

We now turn to the substantive part of this study. For some time, there have been ominous signs of an emerging human capital crisis in the federal government. This 'quiet crisis' has received increasing attention from federal management agencies and on Capitol Hill. President Bush recently acknowledged the gravity of the crisis by placing 'Strategic Management of Human Capital' at the top of his management agenda (US Office of Management and Budget 2001).
  There is a growing awareness that a major part of the human capital crisis is in frontline supervisory management. Several recent studies have acknowledged the chronic nature of this supervisory management problem, and how it has exacerbated the larger human capital crisis in the federal government (Light 2002; National Academy of Public Administration 2003; National Commission on the Public Service 2003; US Merit Systems Protection Board 2001, 2003; US Office of Personnel Management 2001). These studies seem to agree that supervisory management is the crucial link between human capital and high performance in the public sector.
  Public management scholars have spent considerable time and effort trying to answer the question, 'does management matter in public organizations?' Yet, they have not examined the role of frontline supervisors carefully enough. There are many reasons to believe that frontline supervisors – who are near the heat of action – play an important role in high-performing organizations.

Dilemmas of the frontline supervisor

The National Academy of Public Administration defines front-line supervisors as: '. . . individuals responsible for the work of non-supervisory employees' (2003: 2). According to this definition, there are about 125,000 front-line supervisors in the federal government (National Academy of Public Administration 2003: 2). Yet, there are many more employees with supervisory responsibilities, and some evidence to suggest that these upper-level supervisors experience the same or greater difficulty with core supervisory tasks such as performance management (US Merit Systems Protection Board 1998, 1999, 2003). Thus, this study expands the definition of first-line supervisors to include this larger group of employees with supervisory responsibilities. They are referred to collectively as 'frontline supervisors'.

From 1991 to 2001, 1.5 supervisory jobs were lost for every non-supervisory job, and the supervisory span of control increased from 7:1 to 8:1 in the federal government (National Academy of Public Administration 2002: 7–12). Federal leaders are a rapidly aging and highly experienced segment of the federal workforce, and they are among the first to go when agencies trim their employment rolls (National Academy of Public Administration 2002; US Office of Personnel Management 2001). Thus, downsizing and attrition has contributed to what Paul Light (1995) describes as 'the thickening of government'. It has also resulted in skill imbalances that may undermine the ability of federal agencies to carry out their missions (US Department of Labor 1992; US Merit Systems Protection Board 2001).

The US Merit Systems Protection Board (2001, 2003) surveyed federal workers and found that many employees believe their supervisors have relatively good technical skills, but lower management skills. This is understandable since federal agencies tend to hire at the entry level which places greater emphasis on the applicant's technical skills (National Academy of Public Administration 1997; Partnership for Public Service 2002). Many employees also report that their supervisors do not deal effectively with low-performing employees, echoing numerous studies and reports on the subject. Supervisors generally do a good job in the technical aspects of their work, but they do less well with the human resource management aspects (US Merit Systems Protection Board 1998: 1).

Frontline supervisors may be the federal government's most important leadership asset in sheer numbers and direct impact (National Academy of Public Administration 2003, 2004). Experts agree that agencies could improve the selection, development, and management of their supervisors (National Academy of Public Administration 2003, 2004; US Merit Systems Protection Board 1992, 1998, 1999; US Office of Personnel Management 2001). The National Academy of Public Administration recommends that agencies should balance technical competencies with managerial and leadership competencies, which should reflect 'agency-specific mission challenges, values, and leadership environment' (National Academy of Public Administration 2003: 38). The bottom line is that supervisory responsibility is a central role – not a collateral duty.

Frontline supervisors must do more with less and 'communicate their organization's vision, lead change, build high-performing work teams, and coach and mentor employees – all while coping with enormous challenges and change' (National Academy of Public Administration 2003: 13). The price of poor supervision includes lowered job performance, difficulty in retaining good employees, and an increased number of problems that require third-party intervention (Hale 2003; National Academy of Public Administration 2003, 2004). Thus, there are strong reasons to believe that supervisory management is the catalyst that produces high performance.

Data and methods

This study will utilize data from the US Merit Systems Protection Board's Merit Principles Survey 2000. The survey sample included 17,250 full-time permanent civilian employees working in the largest federal executive branch agencies. (The US Postal Service and intelligence agencies were excluded.) The sample was selected randomly from the federal workforce of over 1.5 million employees, but it was stratified by agency to permit cross-agency comparisons (for details, see Brewer 2005: 510, Table 1). The response rate was 43 per cent – similar to other government-wide surveys conducted contemporaneously (e.g., see National Partnership for Reinventing Government and US Office of Personnel Management 2000). Respondents provided information about their jobs and related issues (for details, see Brewer 2005: 509; US Merit Systems Protection Board 2003).

The theoretical framework for this study is Boyne's (2003) model of government performance and service improvement, as supplemented by several other sources (e.g., Rainey and Steinbauer 1999; Lynn *et al.* 2000; Brewer and Selden 2000; Boyne and Walker 2002; Meier and O'Toole 2002). Specifically, Boyne identified five clusters of variables that empirical studies have investigated. These clusters include: resources; organization; markets; regulation; and management. A sixth cluster was added: individual factors. For a list of the constructs in each cluster and their measurement items, see the appendix. Several of the more important constructs are discussed here.

The perceptual measure of *organizational performance* introduced earlier in this study will be used as the dependent variable in this analysis. The independent variables are described next. Management variables include *frontline supervisory status, supervisory proficiency, performance management, satisfaction with higher management, support for workforce diversity*, and two measures of organizational culture: *meaningful/engaging work* and *efficacy*. The variables *frontline supervisory status* and *supervisory proficiency* are of particular interest in this study. The first variable serves two purposes: it helps to assess the raw importance of frontline supervisors in the federal service, and it serves as a control variable. The second variable, *supervisory proficiency*, estimates frontline supervisors' competence in that role. This variable is measured with eight survey items that probe different elements of the construct. These elements include task proficiency, management skills, social welfare skills, communication skills, etc. Since these skills are often described as separate traits in the literature, this study had hoped to keep them separate. However, the consistency of the responses shows that these traits come bundled.[3] This suggests that poor supervisors tend to perform poorly on most aspects of their job, while good supervisors tend to be well-rounded individuals.

Resource variables include *sufficient resources, sufficient number of employees*, and *sufficient training*. Organization variables include *recent downsizing* and *size of work unit*. Markets variables include *recommend government employment* and *private sector competition*. Two regulation variables are included: *familiarity with the Government Performance and Results Act* and *cutting personnel system red tape*. Finally, Brewer and Selden (2000: 689) identified two types of factors that affect organizational performance in federal agencies: agency-level factors and individual-level factors. The authors found that these factors work in concert. Boyne's five categories seem to measure the former set of variables, so an additional set is included for the latter. *Individual performance* is included in the model because it probably contributes to federal agency performance. The variables *pay satisfaction* and *job satisfaction* are also included in the model. Empirical research suggests that job satisfaction is not strongly linked to individual performance. However, it may be related to the overall sustained success of the organization (for rationales, see Brewer and Lee 2005; Kim 2005; US Merit Systems Protection Board 2001; Rucci *et al.* 1998).[4]

Several other variables were tried but dropped from the final equation because they were weak, insignificant, or problematic. These include: demographic variables; agency dummy variables; policy or mission-type variables; and interaction variables.

Findings and discussion

Table 3.1 ranks federal agencies by performance. Their overall mean on the combined performance index is 71.78.[5] Agency means range from 67.75 to 76.99 on the 100-point scale, suggesting that federal agencies are performing relatively well on the whole.

Overall, federal agencies did particularly well on the performance element of effectiveness – measured by the linkage between work activities and agency mission, but they did not do so well on the performance element of fairness – measured by how well they dole out recognition and rewards based on merit. The relatively large standard deviation on this item (2.61 on a 10-point scale)

3 When factor analysed, these items load on a single factor with an Eigenvalue of 5.58462 which explains 70 per cent of their total variance. When combined, they produce an alpha reliability coefficient of .81.
4 Federal employee job satisfaction seems to be declining over time. The US Merit Systems Protection Board (2001) finds that employees who are satisfied with their supervisor differ markedly from those who are dissatisfied. This latter group is about twice as likely to say they intend to look for another job, and they generally report more negative and pessimistic responses to the survey questions.
5 The combined performance index was converted to a 100-point scale to facilitate comparison and interpretation.

Table 3.1 Federal agencies ranked by performance: means and standard deviations

Agency	Mean	Standard Deviation
1. Commerce	76.99	10.73
2. National Aeronautics and Space Administration	75.50	11.88
3. Defense: Air Force	74.36	14.09
4. Defense: Army	73.72	13.13
5. State	73.48	11.32
6. Defense: Other	73.17	13.25
7. Housing and urban development	72.61	13.32
8. Health and human services	72.36	12.49
9. Veterans administration	72.32	12.51
10. General services administration	72.01	14.64
11. Labor	71.88	13.14
12. Defense: Navy	71.39	14.06
13. Transportation (except Federal Aviation Administration)	71.35	13.62
14. Justice	70.62	13.96
15. Education	70.60	13.44
16. Interior	70.20	12.49
17. Environmental protection agency	70.09	13.62
18. Social security administration	69.93	13.51
19. Energy	69.13	13.59
20. Treasury	69.02	12.86
21. Agriculture	68.65	14.68
22. Federal Aviation Administration	67.75	12.45
OVERALL	71.78	13.37

Note: The organizational performance indexes are converted to a 100-point scale to facilitate comparison and interpretation. The indexes are composed of the items shown in the appendix.

suggests that it might be a useful lever for improving agency performance. Efforts to improve employee perceptions of fairness and equity could significantly improve their perceptions of the agency's performance.

The highest performing agencies are the Commerce Department, National Aeronautics and Space Administration, and the Air Force. The lowest performing agencies are the Departments of Treasury and Agriculture, and the Federal Aviation Administration. This latter finding is particularly disturbing because of the 11 September 2001 terrorist attacks that occurred soon after these data were collected (see National Commission on Terrorist Attacks Upon the United States, 2004, for details on agency performance problems and management failures).

This study and other extant data suggest that fairness and equity issues may be a root cause of poor agency performance (e.g., see Kurland and Egan 1999; Brewer 2003; US Merit Systems Protection Board 2003). Agencies spend considerable time promoting instrumental goals rather than substantive ones, and top agency management is neither trusted nor considered very competent by many agency employees. Difficult or impossible missions may also contribute to poor agency performance.

In earlier stages of this research project, the attitudes of supervisors and non-supervisors were compared and supervisors were found to be more positive and optimistic about work-related issues, their agency's performance, and their own supervisor's competence and effectiveness (Brewer 2005). The reasons for these differences are not altogether clear, but federal agencies probably benefit from having a core of positive, optimistic employees in their supervisory ranks. These findings also spotlight two key questions that were raised earlier: Does management matter overall? Do frontline supervisors have an appreciable effect on federal agency performance? These questions are addressed next.

In the next stage of the analysis, management variables and other related items are tested in a multivariate model constructed from the literature on organizational performance. All respondents (frontline supervisors and other employees) are included in the analysis.[6] Table 3.2 reports the results of an ordinary least squares multiple regression analysis predicting federal agency performance. The equation explains 63 percent of the variation in performance across the twenty-two largest federal agencies. The results are highly significant, providing confidence at the .001 level.[7]

Among the individual factors affecting federal agency performance, management-related variables exert the strongest influence. Examination of the standardized coefficients reveals that the two measures of organizational culture – *meaningful/engaging work* and *efficacy* – have large effects, while the following items are also important predictors: *frontline supervisory status, supervisory proficiency, performance management, satisfaction with higher management, and support for diversity.* All of these items achieve statistical significance at either the .01 or .001 level. Thus, the central research questions in this study are answered affirmatively. Management *does* matter, and frontline supervisors *are* important determinants of federal agency performance – both via their raw presence in the workforce and their skilled management contributions.

Among the individual factors, one variable emerges as important. *Individual performance* is a strong and significant predictor of federal agency performance. Among the resource variables, only *sufficient number of employees* has a positive effect on federal agency performance. Staffing levels apparently make a difference. This finding also confirms the notion that excessive downsizing and workforce reductions will undercut federal agency performance.

Both of the market variables are significant predictors of federal agency performance. These variables include *recommend government employment and*

---

6 List-wise deletion of missing data caused some attrition in cases. However, efforts to salvage cases via pair-wise deletion or replacing missing values with the mean did not substantially improve the model's fit or significantly change the power and significance of the predictor variables.

7 A correlation matrix showed no evidence of problematic multicollinearity among independent variables. In addition, no condition number (C-index) was larger than 6.5, and no variance inflation indexes were larger than 2.7.

Table 3.2 Predicting organizational performance

Variables	Unstandardized coefficient	Standard error	Standardized coefficient
Resources:			
Sufficient resources	20.66	16.79	.02
Sufficient number of employees	49.65***	13.73	.05
Sufficient training	8.70	16.74	.01
Organization:			
Recent downsizing	−3.21	12.20	−.00
Size of work unit	−.48	.32	−.02
Markets:			
Recommend Government employment	53.10***	16.24	.05
Private sector competition	40.26**	13.74	.04
Regulation:			
Familiarity with GPRA	−11.43	12.89	−.01
Cutting personnel system red tape	73.55***	8.56	.13
Management:			
Frontline supervisory status	102.17**	37.11	.04
Supervisory proficiency	9.25***	2.90	.06
Performance management	51.45***	6.38	.14
Satisfaction with higher management	156.76***	15.96	.15
Support for workforce diversity	60.83***	12.53	.06
Culture – meaningful/ engaging work	68.31***	5.06	.23
culture – efficacy	43.30***	4.54	.20
Individual factors:			
Individual performance	110.16***	8.32	.18
Pay satisfaction	−7.11	14.17	−.01
Job satisfaction	−36.08	22.45	−.03

$R^2 = .63$ 　　　　　　　　Adjusted $R^2 = .63$
F Value $= 234.48$*** 　　Sample size $= 2{,}662$
$*p = .05; **p = .01; ***p = .001.$

private sector competition. The former item is a reverse-content question. Respondents who strongly recommended government employment were considered to be tacitly giving the private sector a weaker recommendation. The latter item queried respondents directly about their views on outsourcing their work to the private sector. Together, these items suggest that agencies in a competitive market environment may perform better if they have a loyal and strongly committed workforce.

The first regulation variable is disappointing. However, this variable may not provide a good test.[8] The second regulation variable – *cutting personnel system*

---

8 One reviewer questioned whether regulation is a major factor affecting federal agencies, noting that Boyne's (2003) work was derived from a UK context where regulation is a major theme in theory and practice. The answer is a guarded yes. In the US, efforts to reduce red tape and institute other types of regulatory reform do seem to affect federal agencies (Wilson 1989; Gore 1993; Brewer 2003).

red tape – has a large and statistically significant effect. Efforts to reduce red tape are regulatory innovations that may be related to organizational performance (Wilson 1989; Gore 1993; Bozeman 2000; Rainey 2003).[9] In this case, reducing personnel system constraints and working around burdensome red tape to enforce performance standards and deal effectively with poor performers seems to improve federal agency performance.

None of the organization variables produce strong results or achieve statistical significance. Policy-makers and public managers often focus on reorganizing government agencies to improve their performance. This was the case when President Bush and Congress recently created the Department of Homeland Security – a move that consolidated twenty-two agencies and 180,000 employees into a single cabinet-level department designed to combat terrorism more effectively. Yet, the findings reported in this study suggest that such reorganizations may have little overall effect on performance.

Overall, this study provides a good test of Boyne's (2003) framework as supplemented by other sources, and it confirms that management matters a great deal in federal agency performance. In particular, frontline supervisors – who work in the eye of the storm – seem to play an important role. Both their presence and proficiency has a direct effect on organizational performance, and it probably has a myriad of indirect effects as well. In all likelihood, frontline supervisors are key figures in building and sustaining an organizational culture that promotes high performance, and they indirectly influence many other factors that impact federal agency performance.

In addition, the results confirm that high performing agencies tend to have skillful upper-level managers, strong cultures that value employees and emphasize the importance and meaningfulness of the agency's work, and policies that empower those employees. These agencies also tend to have a strong performance orientation, and they strive for workforce diversity.

Further assessing the threat of common source and related bias

Lastly, we return to the potential threat posed by common source and related bias. This type of bias is perhaps the most serious and difficult-to-overcome threat facing survey-based research. Here, further analysis is conducted to assess the viability of this threat in the present study. The analysis is conducted as follows. Survey respondents are randomly assigned to two groups so that different groups can be utilized to measure the independent and dependent

---

9 Bozeman (2000, 12) defines red tape as: 'Rules, regulations, and procedures that remain in force and entail a compliance burden but do not serve the legitimate purposes the rules were intended to serve' There are two types of red tape: internal and external. Internal red tape imposes a burden on members of the organization, while external red tape imposes a burden on citizens or clients who interact with the organization.

variables, respectively. This severs the link that transmits common source and related bias. Then, individual-level means are replaced with agency-level means for the dependent variable *organizational performance*. To preserve more cases for analysis, individual-level means are retained for the independent variables, thus fixing the unit of analysis at the individual level (N = 2,908) rather than the agency level (N = 22). Finally, the hybrid model of federal agency performance developed earlier and tested in Table 3.2 is re-estimated for the following models:

Model 1: *Linkage intact* – responses from the full sample of respondents are used to estimate both the independent and dependent variables, thus keeping the linkage intact that transmits common source and related bias.

Model 2: *Linkage severed* – the sample is split and responses from different sub-samples are used to estimate the independent and dependent variables, thus severing the linkage that transmits common source and related bias.

The results are shown in Table 3.3. The amount of variance explained by the two models is relatively low at .07 per cent. However, this low level of explanatory power is expected since the dependent variable is now being measured at the agency level rather than the individual level, as was done in Table 3.3.[10] Both models are statistically significant at the .001 level, and their general pattern of findings is fairly consistent. These models, thus, provide a fair proving ground for the test that follows.

If common source and related bias is present, the first model should outperform the second – the first model allows such bias to be transmitted while the second model does not. Yet the results show that the models are very similar in the total amount of variance explained, the explanatory power of the individual variables, and the levels of statistical significance achieved. This similarity provides additional evidence that common source and related bias is not problematic in the present study.

Conclusion

This study has developed and tested a perceptual measure of organizational performance that seems to meet three crucial criteria: validity, reliability, and

---

10 One reviewer pointed out that the weaker explanatory power of these models might actually be evidence of common source and related bias. However, I contend that the original and re-estimated models (Tables 3.2 and 3.3) should not be compared. The original model uses individually-reported scores for the dependent variable while the re-estimated models use agency-level means. We should thus expect the original model to have greater explanatory power because individual responses to the survey questions are internally consistent and reflect those individuals' unique perspectives. This is desirable, and it does not necessarily mean that such responses are biased.

Table 3.3 Assessing the threat of common source and related bias

Variables	Model 1: Linkage intact unstandardized coefficient	Model 2: Linkage severed unstandardized coefficient
Resources:		
Sufficient resources	1.79	2.67
Sufficient number of employees	13.44***	13.65***
Sufficient training	−13.32**	−15.32**
Organization:		
Recent downsizing	−14.86***	−13.94***
Size of work unit	.05	.10
Markets:		
Recommend Government employment	−12.51*	−12.66**
Private sector competition	16.50***	15.39***
Regulation:		
Familiarity with GPRA	−20.14***	−18.63***
Cutting personnel system red tape	.01	−.16
Management:		
Frontline supervisory status	20.49	16.94
Supervisory proficiency	−1.25	−1.42
Performance management	17.80***	17.60***
Satisfaction with higher management	−1.02	3.44
Support for workforce diversity	11.39**	10.30**
Culture – meaningful/engaging work	−9.92***	−9.66***
Culture – efficacy	2.88*	3.50*
Individual factors:		
Individual performance	7.43**	5.78*
Pay satisfaction	−8.45*	−7.26
Job satisfaction	2.35	.28
$R^2 =$	.08	.07
Adjusted $R^2 =$	.07	.07
F Value =	13.07***	12.18***
Sample Size =	2,908	2,908
$*p = .05; **p = .01; ***p = .001.$		

sensitivity. However, this measure is also vulnerable to the threat of common source and related bias. Efforts to assess the viability of this threat suggest that it is not problematic in the present study, but these results are not conclusive. Survey researchers actually want respondents to have an internally consistent set of attitudes. This internal consistency is good because much of science is about discovering orderly patterns and observable distinctions. However, it comes dangerously close to being common source and related bias when the same group of respondents is used to measure the independent and dependent variables in a study. Thus, common source and related bias is very hard for survey researchers to identify and filter out.

The management implications of this study are straightforward. Management matters in federal agencies, but only when it is competent and skillfully applied. Public managers must motivate and empower employees, create sustainable organizational cultures, emphasize performance at the individual, work unit, and organizational levels, and promote workforce diversity. Furthermore, this study shows that frontline supervisors are an important part of the management team. These employees play a crucial role in improving federal agency performance, and more emphasis should be placed on their recruitment, selection, and retention, and on their training and development. Again, their competence and skill are key elements in improving federal agency performance.

Efforts to eliminate frontline supervisors to save money, streamline operations, and empower street-level employees may have a perverse effect: these supervisors are among the most positive and optimistic members of the federal service, and they are important conduits for transmitting public service ethics and values to the next generation of public servants. Outsourcing public jobs to improve governmental performance also seems paradoxical: the very elements that need to be strengthened to improve federal agency performance are those that seem to be most lacking in the private sector. These elements include: high levels of public service motivation, organizational cultures that link to the public interest; robust conceptions of organizational performance that include fairness and equity criteria; and commitment to achieving a representative workforce that mirrors the social and demographic origins of society.

Future research can build on this study in several ways. First, researchers should try to improve the perceptual measure of organizational performance used here, and continue to assess how well it corresponds with more objective measures of the construct. Ideally, future research should include both subjective and objective measures. Another avenue of research that sorely needs developing is further study of the complex interrelationships and gnarly interactive effects between management and other factors that affect organizational performance. Finally, future research should take an international bent and focus more on comparisons between nations and the performance of their different levels of government.

Acknowledgement

This chapter evolves from a paper presented at 'The Determinants of Performance in Public Organizations: Advancing Knowledge in Public Management Conference' in Cardiff, Wales, 6–8 May 2004, and appearing in *Journal of Public Administration Research and Theory* **13**, 1 (October 2005): 5–26. The author is grateful to Paul van Rijn of the US Merit Systems Protection Board for providing the data analysed in this study, and the editors who made helpful comments.

REFERENCES

Boyne, G. A. (2003) 'Sources of public service improvement: A critical review and research agenda', *Journal of Public Administration Research and Theory*, **13**: 367–394.

Boyne, G. A. and Walker, R. M. (2002) 'Total quality management and performance: An evaluation of the evidence and lessons for research on public organizations', *Public Performance and Management Review*, **26**: 111–131.

Bozeman, B. (2000) *Bureaucracy and red tape*. Upper Saddle River, NJ: Prentice Hall.

Brewer, G. A. (2003) 'When core values and missions collide: Gut-wrenching change in the US Department of Agriculture'. Paper presented at the Seventh Public Management Research Conference, Georgetown University, 9–11 October.

Brewer, G. A. (2005) 'In the eye of the storm: Frontline supervisors and federal agency performance', *Journal of Public Administration Research and Theory*, **15**: 505–527.

Brewer, G. A. and Lee, S. Y. (2005) 'Federal agencies in transition: Assessing the impact on federal employee job satisfaction and performance'. Paper presented at the Eighth Public Management Research Conference, University of Southern California – Los Angeles, 29 September–1 October.

Brewer, G. A. and Selden, S. C. (2000) 'Why elephants gallop: Assessing and predicting organizational performance in federal agencies', *Journal of Public Administration Research and Theory*, **10**: 685–711.

Coggburn, J. D. and Schneider, S. K. (2003) 'The quality of management and government performance: An empirical analysis of the American states', *Public Administration Review*, **63**: 206–213.

Gore, A. (1993) *Creating a government that works better and costs less: The report of the National Performance Review*. Washington, DC: US Government Printing Office.

Hale, J. (2003) *Performance-based management: What every manager should do to get results*. San Francisco: Jossey-Bass.

Harman, H. H. (1967) *Modern factor analysis*. Chicago: The University of Chicago Press.

Kim, S. (2005) 'Individual-level factors and organizational performance in government organizations', *Journal of Public Administration Research and Theory*, **15**: 245–261.

Kurland, N. B. and Egan, T. D. (1999) 'Public v private perceptions of formalization, outcomes, and justice', *Journal of Public Administration Research and Theory*, **9**: 437–458.

Light, P. C. (1995) *Thickening government: Federal hierarchy and the diffusion of accountability*. Washington, DC: The Brookings Institution.

Light, P. C. (2002) *The troubled state of the federal public service*. Washington, DC: The Brookings Institution.

Lynn, L. E. Jr., Heinrich, C. J. and Hill, C. J. (2000) *Governance and performance: New perspectives*. Washington, DC: Georgetown University Press.

Meier, K. J. and Brudney, J. L. (1993) *Applied statistics for public administration*, 3rd edn. Belmont, CA: Wadsworth Publishing Co.

Meier, K. J. and O'Toole L. J. Jr. (2002) 'Public management and organizational performance: The effect of managerial quality', *Journal of Policy Analysis and Management*, **21**: 629–643.

Meier, K. J. and O'Toole L. J. Jr. (2004) 'Unsung impossible jobs: The politics of public management'. Paper presented at the Annual Meeting of the American Political Science Association, Chicago, IL.

National Academy of Public Administration (1997) *Managing succession and developing leadership: Growing the next generation of public service leaders.* Washington, DC: National Academy of Public Administration.

National Academy of Public Administration (2002) *The 21st century federal manager: A study of changing roles and competencies: Preliminary research findings,* Report 1 of the 21st Century Federal Manager Series, Washington, DC: National Academy of Public Administration.

National Academy of Public Administration (2003) *First-line supervisors in the federal service: Their selection, development, and management,* Report 2 of the 21st Century Federal Manager Series, Washington, DC: National Academy of Public Administration.

National Academy of Public Administration (2004) *Final report and recommendations: The 21st Century Federal Manager Series.* Washington, DC: National Academy of Public Administration.

National Commission on Terrorist Attacks Upon the United States (2004) *The 9/11 Commission report: Final report of the National Commission on Terrorist Attacks Upon the United States.* New York: Norton.

National Commission on the Public Service (2003) *Urgent business for America: Revitalizing the federal government for the 21st Century.* Washington, DC: National Commission on the Public Service.

National Partnership for Reinventing Government and the US Office of Personnel Management (2000) *Government-wide employee survey.* Washington, DC: National Partnership for Reinventing Government and the US Office of Personnel Management.

Partnership for Public Service (2002) *Mid-career hiring in the federal government: A strategy for change.* A Report by The Partnership for Public Service, Washington DC: The Partnership for Public Service.

Podsakoff, P. M. and Organ, D. W. (1986) 'Self-reports in organizational research: Problems and prospects', *Journal of Management,* **12**: 531–544.

Podsakoff, P. M., Todor, W. D., Grover, R. A. and Huber, V. L. (1984) 'Situational moderators and leader reward and punishment behaviors: Fact or fiction?', *Organizational Behavior and Human Performance,* **34**: 21–63.

Quinn, R. E. and Rohrbaugh, J. (1983) 'A spatial model of effectiveness criteria: Towards a competing values approach to organizational analysis.' *Management Science,* **29**: 363–377.

Rainey, H. G. (2003) *Understanding and managing public organizations.* 3rd edn. San Francisco: Jossey-Bass.

Rainey, H. G. and Steinbauer, P. (1999) 'Galloping elephants: Developing elements of a theory of effective government organizations', *Journal of Public Administration Research and Theory,* **9**: 1–32.

Rucci, A. J., Kirn, S. P. and Quinn, R. T. (1998) 'The employee-customer profit chain at Sears', *Harvard Business Review,* **76** (1): 83–97.

Selden, S. C. and Sowa, J. E. (2004) 'Testing a multi-dimensional model of organizational performance: Prospects and problems', *Journal of Public Administration Research and Theory,* **14**: 395–416.

US Department of Labor (1992) *Government as a high performance employer: A SCANS report for America 2000. Report of The Secretary's Commission on Achieving Necessary Skills.* Available at: www.ttrc.doleta.gov/SCANS/Govhpe.htm

US General Accounting Office (2000). *Human capital: Managing human capital in the 21st century, GAO/T-GGD-00-77.* Washington, DC: U.S. General Accounting Office.

US Merit Systems Protection Board (1992) *Federal first-line supervisors: How good are they?* Washington, DC: US Merit Systems Protection Board.

US Merit Systems Protection Board (1998) *Federal supervisors and strategic human resources management.* Washington, DC: US Merit Systems Protection Board.

US Merit Systems Protection Board (1999) *Federal supervisors and poor performers*. Washington, DC: US Merit Systems Protection Board.

US Merit Systems Protection Board (2001) *Merit principles survey 2000*. Washington, DC: US Merit Systems Protection Board.

US Merit Systems Protection Board (2003) *The federal workforce for the 21st century: Results of the merit principles survey 2000*. Washington, DC: US Merit Systems Protection Board.

US Office of Management and Budget (2001) *The President's management agenda FY 2002*. Available at: www.whitehouse.gov/omb/budget/fy2002/mgmt.pdf

US Office of Personnel Management (2001) *Supervisors in the federal government: A wake-up call*. Washington, DC: US Office of Personnel Management.

Walker, R. M. and Boyne, G. A. (2006) 'Public management reform and organizational performance: An empirical assessment of the UK Labour Government's public service improvement strategy', *Journal of Policy Analysis and Management*, 25: 371–394.

Wall, T. B, Michie, J., Patterson, M., Wood, S. J., Sheehan, M., Clegg, C. W. and West, M. (2004) 'On the validity of subjective measures of company performance', *Personnel Psychology*, 57: 95–118.

Wilson, J. Q. (1989) *Bureaucracy: What government agencies do and why they do it*. New York: Basic Books.

APPENDIX: Measurement items, means, and standard deviations

Dependent variable

Organizational Performance (mean = 57.53, s.d. = 10.72, range 12–80, Alpha = .83).

- In the past 2 years, the productivity of my work unit has improved.
- How would you rate the overall productivity of [your work unit]?
- How would you rate the overall productivity of [your organization]?
- Overall, how would you rate the quality of work performed by your work unit as a whole?
- Overall, how would you rate the quality of work performed by the larger organization that includes your work unit?
- To what extent do you feel that [the work performed by your work unit] contributes to the accomplishment of your agency's mission?
- To what extent do you feel that [the work performed by your organization] contributes to the accomplishment of your agency's mission?
- Recognition and rewards are based on merit in my work unit.

Independent variables

Resources:

Sufficient resources – I have the resources to do my job well (range 1–5)

Sufficient number of employees – My work unit has a sufficient number of employees to do its job (range 1–5)

Sufficient training – I receive the training I need to perform my job (range 1–5)

Organization:

    Recent downsizing – My work unit has been downsized in the last five years (range 1–5)

    Size of work unit – What is the total number of employees in your immediate work unit, including the supervisor and team leader(s)?

Markets:

    Recommend Government employment – I would recommend the government as a place to work (reversed) (range 1–5)

    Private sector competition – A private sector company could perform the work of my work unit just as effectively as my work unit (range 1–5)

Regulation:

    Familiarity with GPRA – I am familiar with the Government Performance and Results Act (GRPA) (range 1–5)

    Cutting personnel system red tape (mean = 4.98, s.d. = 2.28, range 2–10, Alpha = .92)

      In my work unit, corrective actions are taken when employees do not meet performance standards.

      In my work unit, steps are taken to deal with a poor performer who cannot or will not improve.

Management:

    Frontline supervisory status – Are you a supervisor? (range 0–1)

    Supervisory proficiency (mean = 24.61, s.d. = 8.40, range 8–40, Alpha = .81)

      My supervisor has good management skills.

      My supervisor has good technical skills.

      My supervisor looks out for the personal welfare of members of my work unit.

      My supervisor keeps me informed about how well I am doing.

      My supervisor deals effectively with poor performers.

      My supervisor deals effectively with misconduct on the job.

      My immediate supervisor encourages my career development.

      Overall, I am satisfied with my supervisor.

    Performance management (mean = 11.43, s.d. = 3.59, range 4–20, Alpha = .81)

      My performance standards are clearly linked to my organization's goals and objectives.

      The performance appraisal system motivates me to do a better job.

      The standards used to evaluate my performance are fair.

      The performance appraisal rating system has helped increase communications about my job between my supervisor and me.

    Satisfaction with higher management – Overall, I am satisfied with managers above my immediate supervisor (range 1–5).

Support for workforce diversity – Workforce diversity should be taken into account when choosing among the best qualified candidates (range 1–5).

Culture – Meaningful/engaging work (mean = 22.85, s.d. = 4.57, range 5–30, Alpha = .68).

- I am often bored with my job (reversed).
- The work I do is meaningful to me.
- I know what is expected of me on the job.
- My present job makes good use of my skills and abilities.
- To what extent do you feel that [the work you personally perform] contributes to the accomplishment of your agency's mission?

Culture – efficacy (mean = 22.46, s.d. = 6.18, range 7–35, Alpha = .86)

- Information is shared freely in my work unit.
- At the place I work, my opinions seem to count.
- A spirit of cooperation and teamwork exists in my work unit.
- In the past two years, I have been given more flexibility in how I accomplish my work.
- I am treated with respect in my work unit.
- Employees participate in developing long-range plans in my work unit.
- I am satisfied with the recognition I receive for my work.

Individual factors:

Individual performance (mean = 16.99, s.d. = 2.24, range 3–20, Alpha = .69)

- How would you rate [your] overall productivity?
- Overall, how would you rate the quality of work [you] perform?

Pay satisfaction – Overall, I am satisfied with my current pay (range 1–5).

Job satisfaction – Overall, I am satisfied with my job (range 1–5).

4 A qualitative evaluation of public sector organizations: assessing organizational performance in healthcare

Rachael Addicott and Ewan Ferlie

Introduction: The growth of qualitative evaluation

There has been growing interest in using evidence-based policy as a more rational basis for decision making in public policy in various countries in the 1990s (Dopson *et al.* 2005). This trend has been an influence on the post-1997 New Labour government in the United Kingdom (UK) where its so-called 'modernization' of government (Cm4310 1999) seeks to improve the use of research and evidence to ascertain 'what works'. Policy making is here a continuous learning process with iterations with an improving research base to build the 'experimenting society' (Oakley 2000), first promised in the wake of pioneering evaluations into the Great Society programmes in the US in the late 1960s, then forgotten and rediscovered in the 1990s.

These ideas have been prominent in the evidence-based medicine movement in healthcare. Healthcare has a strongly developed research tradition, both in traditional biomedical science (where the Cochrane Collaboration[1] undertakes overviews or 'meta analyses' of available randomized controlled trials (RCTs)) and more recently in multidisciplinary and social science informed forms of health services research. An area of rising interest has been the evaluation of service delivery and organization in healthcare (Fulop *et al.* 2001), where non-traditional methods of qualitative and action research are apparent. There is increasing demand for evaluation from governmental funders, including (perhaps counterintuitively) qualitative as well as quantitative research.

Ferlie and McNulty (1997) present a more positive picture of demand for qualitative research within the UK government than the American case painted by Rist (2000: 1015) who concluded 'there is no broad based and sustained tradition

---

1 The Cochrane Collaboration is an international organization that produces and disseminates systematic reviews of healthcare interventions and encourages the search for evidence in the form of clinical trials and other studies of interventions.

within contemporary social science of focusing qualitative work specifically on policy issues, especially given the real time constraints that the policy process necessitates'. By contrast, there is more to the UK evaluation wave than production of quantitative data for RCTs or quasi-experiments, valuable though these studies are, with an additional concern for rigorous qualitative work to inform policy. This may take the form of qualitative studies alone or large-scale, multi-method studies, which bring together a number of disciplines. For example, a multidisciplinary evaluation of a major healthcare innovation in the UK National Health Service (NHS) will often bring together clinical academics (studying clinical outcomes), health economists (studying cost effectiveness), and organizational sociologists (studying organizational process) in a large research team.

This demand springs from a number of sources. First, there is a desire to capture the experience of the user of public services as an integral part of policy 'outcomes' in the broadest sense. Qualitative methods, such as focus groups, play an important role in this field. Secondly, funders often want to use research to contribute to positive social and organizational change, as well as to provide academic research findings. This creates a growing space for action research (Meyer 2001). Thirdly, policy makers often wish to know not only 'what works' but also 'how it works', in the sense of identifying the organizational and managerial processes (and 'change mechanisms' in the words of Pawson and Tilley (1997)), associated with 'good' policy outcomes. Organizational process research (Ferlie and McNulty 1997) contributes to this policy need through analysis of the management of change and strategic decision making within public services organizations.

Organizational performance in NHS cancer networks: A worked example

We recently undertook a qualitative evaluation of organizational performance in the five NHS-managed clinical networks (MCN) for cancer across London (Ferlie and Addicott 2004), funded by the Research and Development arm of NHS London. In this section, we analyse this study as an example of qualitative evaluation, discussing the methods used and some wider questions thrown up by the study.

To begin, UK public sector organizations, such as the NHS, have been increasingly encouraged by New Labour reforms (Cm4310 1999; Newman 2001) to explore novel methods of coordinating services across pre-existing vertical or functional boundaries to become more 'joined-up'. In the 1990s, networks were emerging as a new, innovative organizational form in the public sector and cancer networks were established in the NHS, replacing previous internal market based arrangements (Calman and Hine 1995), to ensure a more seamless patient journey across different healthcare providers and the better diffusion of knowledge and good practice out from traditional centres of excellence. These networks covered large populations and clusters of healthcare providers – five were established in London, covering a population of about 1.5 million each. NHS London was interested in exploring the functioning and performance of these five new organizations and commissioned us as external evaluators to undertake a qualitative study.

Using the principles of organizational process research, we examined the 'performance' of the five London MCNs for cancer. This chapter details the process undertaken for assessing the success of these networks and explores issues involved in deriving success criteria. The chapter also describes our key organizational conclusions and reflects more broadly on the practice of organizational process research as an approach to qualitative evaluation.

Qualitative research and evaluation paradigms

First we discuss epistemological issues in a field where methodological 'paradigm wars' (Oakley 2000) have been evident. Traditionally, the quantitative paradigm has been dominant in social and scientific research and evaluation, however techniques derived from the qualitative paradigm have emerged over the last twenty or so years as an increasingly influential basis for exploring social phenomena (Flick 2002). Qualitative methodologies commonly suffer from criticism by positivists for being non-generalizable, subjective and invalid (Kvale 1996; Foddy 1993), and still recently qualitative evaluation has been regarded as 'more in the realm of the potential rather than the actual' (Rist 2000: 1015) by one sceptic. More recent accounts (Fulop *et al.* 2001) move beyond these paradigm debates to consider circumstances in which adherents of different paradigms can work together fruitfully, perhaps in large multidisciplinary teams.

The positivist paradigm of evaluation tends to use RCTs or quasi-experiments as preferred research techniques, sometimes explicitly positioned as such in a 'hierarchy of evidence' model. Contrary to qualitative research, the quantitative paradigm typically creates a research design that allows for explicit generalization of findings, with an emphasis on measurement and causality (Oakley 2000).

As in the wider research methods literature, qualitative evaluation has emerged as a significant alternative to traditional quantitative methods. Various qualitative evaluative approaches can be distinguished. One approach includes action research where there is often a value-laden commitment to participation and positive social and organizational change (Meyer 2001). Some action researchers (Eden and Huxham 1996) draw attention to the explicit need to develop substantive theory by undertaking a linked set of action research projects. Guba and Lincoln's (1989) model of 'fourth generation evaluation' is naturalistic and participative in character, and could be considered to have a natural affinity to qualitative data (although stressing that quantitative data will also often be useful). Greene (2000) suggests that qualitative evaluators may rather engage in 'storytelling', with an emphasis on understanding and authenticity.

Clearly qualitative approaches to evaluation are more appropriate to answering certain questions. Rist (2000) proposes that qualitative methods are especially influential for issues of problem definition, understanding prior initiatives and assessing community and organizational receptivity as well as the impact of different intervention strategies. Qualitative evaluation can explore how a programme is understood by various stakeholders, including users. The qualitative paradigm is of particular relevance to the study of personal experiences and narratives (Flick 2002) with an analysis and interpretation of 'how people create and maintain their social worlds' (Neuman 1991: 62). Qualitative evaluation (as opposed to basic qualitative research) does not simply produce interesting academic knowledge, but should seek to answer policy and practice questions. It is a branch of evaluation, and not pure curiosity driven research.

Criticisms of qualitative research and evaluation often focus on problems of low external validity, so that results tend to be localized with little meaningful, generalizable message about policy. However, Pawson and Tilley (1997) argue that their model of 'realistic evaluation' (which consists of qualitative and also quantitative methods) is also theory driven evaluation. Critiquing the methods used in RCTs and quasi-experiments, they produce a theory of why policy interventions do or do not work and hence build theoretical external validity. Typically, this theory will be substantive or middle range rather than grand theory.

Organizational process approaches similarly develop middle range theory (rather than grand theory) across a comparative set of qualitative cases, mixing empirical and theoretical aspects of external validity (Ferlie 2001). There is little use of quantitative data in 'pure' organizational research. There is a concern (Ferlie and McNulty 1997; McNulty and Ferlie 2002) for locating change 'outcomes' (often of an intermediate rather than final nature) across comparative cases and hence building explanations across a substantial qualitative dataset.

For qualitative evaluation to be considered 'rigorous', there needs to be an assured procedure. 'Evaluations conducted qualitatively can make little contribution to social policies and programs if they are not perceived as credible – defensible, enlightening, and useful' (Greene 2000: 987). Using multiple data sources, or 'triangulation', is a method for strengthening the empirical grounding of qualitative research and providing assurance of rigor, as is the move from single to comparative case designs, with thought about the basis on which cases are selected (Yin 1994).

We now move on to consider a concrete example of organizational process methods as a form of qualitative evaluation: the study of the creation, evolution and impact of MCNs in NHS London.

Organizational performance in UK cancer services: A worked example of qualitative evaluation

MCNs for cancer were intended to streamline patient care and foster the flow of knowledge between professions and healthcare organizations. It is an important management innovation within healthcare, yet we have little independent evaluation of its impact. MCNs in the NHS have been defined as 'linked groups of health professionals and organizations from primary, secondary and tertiary care working in a coordinated manner, unconstrained by existing professional and (organizational) boundaries to ensure equitable provision of high quality effective services' (Edwards 2002: 63).

Each MCN is 'coordinated' by a network management team (NMT) facilitating communication between the professional groups and organizations that comprise the network – family doctors, community health nurses, hospital based clinicians (medical and nursing), managers, palliative care representatives, and cancer commissioners. Each NMT comprises four core staff – a manager, lead clinician, lead nurse, and a service improvement coordinator. MCNs established various tumour groups (TG) including representatives from professional groups, responsible for establishing protocols, guidelines and so-called care pathways (see Figure 4.1).

MCNs were proposed as a more effective way of coordinating cancer services for patients who require care across a range of organizations than internal market based models. Cancer was the first clinical network model established and is a prototype for other areas. However, the NHS also can adopt such fashionable managerial changes without providing an evaluation of their worth (Ferlie and Pettigrew 1996: S94).

The overall aim of this evaluation was to provide an analytic commentary on the creation, development and *impact* of the MCN model on London-based cancer services. We were interested in exploring impact and performance and how these may vary by locality, in keeping with the tenets of organizational process research (Ferlie and McNulty 1997; McNulty and Ferlie 2002). We were more interested in intermediate process-based indicators than final clinical outcomes, again in keeping with our more managerialist stance.

Few studies have evaluated the effectiveness of networks within healthcare. Those that have typically examine the number of services offered, reductions in hospitalization rates, effects on clinical outcomes and the maintenance of standards (Kates and Humphrey 1993). Bogason (2004) suggests that it is difficult to use traditional evaluation methods for studying networks, because evaluators are unsure what they will encounter. The organizational form – in particular an innovative form such as MCNs – is not known, the lines of responsibility are unclear and there are traditionally no defined tasks of implementation. Networks lack clear goals and outcome criteria on which to base an evaluation,

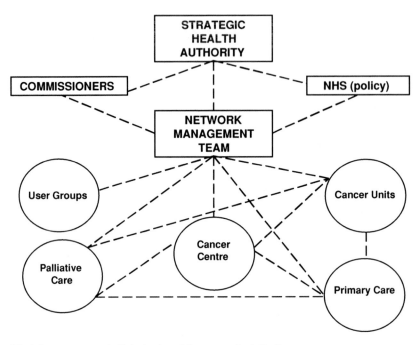

Figure 4.1   What does a managed clinical network for cancer look like?

and there is no baseline data against which to measure improvement. Kates and Humphrey argue that aspects of networks can be difficult to quantify, such as interorganizational relationships.

Qualitative evaluation can explore these important but complex issues. The first stage in our study considered which indicators of performance should be used within the evaluation and how they should be derived. A consensus development method was utilized to establish indicators of performance. Consensus methods have been utilized to develop agreement in areas of uncertainty, or where there is a lack of, or contradictory, evidence on a certain topic. The three commonly used methods for establishing or developing consensus are consensus development panels, nominal group processes and the Delphi technique (Bowling 1999; Jones and Hunter 2000).

Consensus development panels entail facilitating a group of experts to discuss a specified topic to improve understanding or develop consensus. This method can be expensive and time consuming to organize, and requires a high level of coordination. Alternatively, the nominal group process operates similarly but also asks the nominated experts to decide on their individual views and rank their ideas before attending the initial meeting. The results are summarized and presented to the members of the group at a subsequent meeting and the group then discuss the rankings and their individual differences, re-ranking ideas based on the discussion. Like the consensus development panel, a facilitator is required.

This approach suffers from the same limitations as the above approach and the need for multiple meetings ensures that the method may be time consuming (Bowling 1999).

In the end, we used a Delphi technique (Bowling 1999) to derive success criteria, that is what did different respondents perceive as key success factors of a MCN for cancer and could they converge on a consensus? The Delphi technique offsets the cost, time and organizational limitations of the previous two methods, and is discussed in the following section.

Developing measures of performance – the Delphi technique

The Delphi technique is a group consensus-building process, used to establish agreement in areas of uncertainty, or where there is a lack of, or contradictory, evidence. The technique is conducted via mail, fax or e-mail, so information is exchanged remotely (Dunham 1998).

Traditional group decision making is frequently dominated by one individual, or individuals with vested interests, and the Delphi technique is structured to avoid this shortcoming. There are variations in the use of the Delphi technique. In the first instance, members of an expert group are typically asked to answer several open-ended questions about their ideas or experiences on a topic. When the responses are returned they are compiled into a second questionnaire under summarized topic headings or statements and sent back to the group for the experts to comment on the strengths and weaknesses of each of the ideas and identify any new concepts. Members of the group may be asked to rank the ideas from most promising to least promising. The results of this step are then summarized by the researcher, and if any disagreement remains among the group, sent back for a further cycle of feedback and re-ranking. The aspects of disagreement are explored and the reasons for the differences can be ascertained and analysed. The exercise is deemed to be complete when dominant, highly evaluated ideas have emerged via consensus. The literature shows the Delphi process typically consists of four rounds, however more recent evidence demonstrates that two to three rounds are preferred (Bowling 1999; Dunham 1998; Linstone and Turoff 1975).

We now discuss how the technique was utilized in developing success criteria for the evaluation of London MCNs. Twenty-eight stakeholders involved in cancer delivery, strategic planning, advocacy and commissioning were approached to participate. These stakeholders were deliberately recruited from a range of different groups involved in cancer services – clinicians, nurses, managers, primary care, users/volunteers and policy representatives – within the principles of pluralistic evaluation (which argues against a singular framework or perspective of evaluation). Deliberately exploring dimensions of structure, process and outcome (clinical and near-clinical but not final clinical), eight factors were

Table 4.1 Success indicators of a managed network for cancer

Source: Delphi study	Source: NHS cancer plan
Does the network have a clear management structure?	Have cancer units been designated?
Does the network have a clear strategy?	Have cancer centres been designated?
Are all patients considered by a multidisciplinary team?	Does the cancer network involve the following key players – health service commissioners (health authorities, primary care groups and trusts) and providers (primary and community care and hospitals), the voluntary sector, and local authorities?
Is the network operating on a patient focused basis?	Does the network closely involve the chief executives of provider NHS trusts and health authorities and PCTs?
Is there timely diagnosis and treatment for all patients?	Is the patient pathway smooth and seamless and are resources targeted where they are most needed to serve the cancer needs of their local population?
Is there evidence that patients are receiving high-quality treatment and care?	Have alliances developed to help reduce the risk of cancer, through action on smoking and diet?
Do patients report improved experiences, standards of care and quality of life since the development of the network?	Are there support and organizational development facilities available to regions and networks?
Has there been increased cancer prevention and earlier diagnosis since the introduction of the cancer network?	Have the Cancer Services Collaborative initiatives rolled out to all cancer networks?

consensually deemed by respondents to be important derived through two rounds of a Delphi process.

These eight bottom-up success indicators were then combined with eight top-down success criteria obtained from the *NHS Cancer Plan* (2000) – a recently published policy document, focused on improving prevention, acting on health inequalities, earlier detection, faster diagnosis and treatment, providing consistent high quality services, and improving quality of life through better care. The sixteen resulting success criteria – depicted in Table 4.1 – equally balanced bottom-up and top-down criteria.

Different conceptions of success

As the respondents were drawn from a range of stakeholder groups, we examined the distribution of responses from the 'raw', first round data. Not surprisingly, each prioritized issues important to their stakeholder group – for example, primary care representatives emphasized the importance of involving primary care, user representatives emphasized issues relating to users and carers. Policy makers and commissioners prioritized commissioning, leadership and structural reconfiguration, while clinicians emphasized multidisciplinary collaboration and research. This highlights a difference in what purchasers of healthcare consider to be important indicators of success, versus those providing direct patient care. In the second round, consensus emerged and the eight resulting indicators were identified.

Methodology for measuring performance

Following identification, we sought to 'test' these success criteria in the field to benchmark networks. The first step was to choose key dimensions for analysis (Pettigrew *et al.* 1992) and we ultimately examined three specific dimensions (or 'tracers') to benchmark the success criteria within the networks:

- centralization of specialist services;
- budget/resource allocation, and;
- education and training.

The first two tracers surfaced during initial investigations as major current concerns. Education and training provided a contrast of the possible knowledge management function. Our three tracers focused on a mix of structural, budgetary and knowledge issues and were used as a framework to 'test' the 16 success criteria. Clinical outcomes were deliberately omitted from the evaluation as it was considered too early in network development to make a judgement of clinical impact. On this basis, various 'themes for analysis' were developed, which formulated the basis for data collection and ultimately translated into specific interview questions.

Comparative case studies

We employed a qualitative approach to gain access to areas not readily penetrable by quantitative research, such as individual meanings and personal experiences. Pope and Mays (1996) propose that qualitative methods typically possess high internal validity, and better analyse how individuals and groups act and behave in natural settings. Comparative case studies provided an in-depth understanding of the relationships between the organizations and professional groups, and associated performance outcomes in the five London MCNs across the different networks (Pettigrew *et al.* 1992; Glaser and Strauss 1967). The evaluation incorporated a longitudinal component, with the five networks studied over two years.

To provide a more manageable design – given the large number of TGs – we focused on two types of cancer – gynaecological and urological – as well as the networks as a whole. Gynaecological and urological cancers were chosen for two reasons. Firstly, one is solely a female issue and one predominantly a male issue. Secondly, the structural centralization process for gynaecological cancer is more advanced than the urological restructure. Analysis of tumour types at different stages of development allowed for consideration of whether there is any learning between TGs and to track progression of networks through time.

The network data have been anonymized so each network is referred to as 'Network A', 'Network B' et cetera.

Triangulation

Using multiple data sources, or 'triangulation', is a method for generating theory and strengthening empirical grounding of research. Stake (2000) proposes that triangulation clarifies meaning and verifies repeatability of an observation or interpretation. Three data collection methods were utilized – semi-structured interviews, document analysis and observation at meetings.

Semi-structured interviews

Semi-structured interviews were conducted with 117 representatives from the organizations and key professional groups involved with the London MCNs – clinicians, managers, nurses, commissioners and policy makers. These representatives were from primary, secondary and tertiary care organizations, Primary Care Trusts, Strategic Health Authorities and the NMTs.

Semi-structured interviews were favoured over structured interviews, as these allowed more flexibility and room for interpretation. These interviews were conducted to understand the perspectives of these different groups, on their role within the networks and issues relating to the identified success criteria. All of the interviews were tape-recorded and transcribed.

Documentary analysis

Key organizational documents – meeting minutes and terms of reference, strategic planning documents, discussion papers and job descriptions – were analysed to provide a historical narrative of MCN development and a textual indication of communication between network organizations and groups. This documentation was also utilized to corroborate the information collected through other methods.

Pettigrew *et al.* (1992) propose that documentary analysis can sensitize the researcher to key questions and supplies a chronology of change. Notes made in margins are a useful source of extra information, however given the current reliance on electronic communication, written notes were not particularly prevalent. The research team was included in the e-mail distribution list for each network and was privy to e-mail exchanges between network members – contributing to the documentary data collection.

Observation at meetings

Thirty-three key network meetings were attended to gain further insight into how the groups relate in a professional environment, to obtain a more in-depth understanding of the operation of the networks and to provide further support for the data collected through the interviews and document analysis. Observational notes were taken regarding the content of interactions, observations of group dynamics, decision making, attendance and the time devoted to particular agenda items. Observation provides a more authentic image of group interactions, which could be different than behavior observed in one-on-one interviews (Pettigrew *et al.* 1992).

Data analysis

All collected data was coded using *QSR NV ivo* software – codes were developed to provide a basis for categorizing and analysing the data and the coding structure was then checked and validated by another researcher. The data was then scanned in a search for specific cases that illustrated and provided evidence for the themes (Neuman 1991; Reinharz 1992).

All of the data was integrated to provide in-depth, comparative case studies. We initially composed single network case studies – organized according to the same overall format – and then moved to comparative analyses. On the basis of this comparison, we now discuss how the MCNs performed in relation to some of the defined success criteria, and how those involved in the networks viewed 'performance'.

Comparing performance across cancer networks

This provides a more in-depth analysis of four particular success criteria, which we focus on here for reasons of space:

- Does the network have a clear management structure?
- Does the network have a clear strategy?
- Is the network operating on a patient-focused basis?
- Is there evidence that patients are receiving high-quality treatment and care?

These four indicators are chosen as relating closely to the initial recommendations of key policy documents (Calman and Hine 1995; National Health Service 2000; NHS Executive 2000). The first indicator relates to the structure of the networks, the second to their purpose and vision, the third to processes and the fourth to outcomes. The third and fourth indicators are part of the core, initial purpose of the cancer network model – to streamline patient care, ensuring that the patient becomes the 'hub' of the system and has access to high-quality treatment and care. The networks were evaluated on each of these indicators by focusing specifically on progress against the three previously discussed tracer issues – centralization of specialist services, budget and resource allocation and education and training activities. This section also provides data on network variation on these four success criteria.

Does the network have a clear management structure?

There was wide variation in the management structure of each of the networks. While some emphasized the importance of a flat structure, others deliberately developed a hierarchical configuration. These differences tended to reflect the level of clinical leadership within the NMT – MCNs with respected clinical leaders tended to follow a more hierarchical management structure, while those with greater teamwork or managerial leadership tended to have a flatter structure.

For instance, the large and knowledgeable infrastructure of the Network E NMT was valuable for influencing organizations and professions to participate in the network. Combined with the nationally eminent reputation of the NMT director, the size and visibility of the NMT appears to have contributed greatly to pulling together a range of organizations – sometimes grudgingly – to become part of the network.

Alternatively, Network A had an unusually flat NMT structure when compared to other London MCNs. Several stakeholders felt that there were times when a designated network leader may have been an advantage for overriding organizational resistance.

Does the network have a clear strategy?

Networks with flatter managerial structures tended to have less strategic clarity. Generally, the fundamental *purpose* of the network model was quite clearly understood – to provide coordinated and high-quality cancer treatment and care through collaboration and establishing common protocols and guidelines. However, the *strategy* of the network and its mission and values were often much less clearly comprehended. The lack of strategic clarity was pronounced among hospital management, where the flatter structure was unfamiliar to those accustomed to operating in a hierarchical environment.

Some networks experienced high turnover amongst NMT staff. Unsurprisingly, these networks suffered from a lack of strategic direction. Also, ground level staff within these networks reported poor or limited communication with NMT representatives.

To illustrate, stakeholders in Network B reported little contact with NMT representatives due to recent changeovers in NMT staff and the small number of personnel. The NMT operated in a hands-off manner, communicating with commissioners whilst service providers self-organized to implement the recommendations of the national plan. When asked about the NMT, service providers often referred to the cancer managers within their own organizations, with no awareness that the NMT existed.

Is the network operating on a patient-focused basis?

Two London networks have developed Partnership Groups as forums for including user representation in the planning and delivery of cancer services. These groups include user representatives and healthcare professionals and managers, who represent their organizations at a senior enough level to respond to issues raised by the users.

Because of the involvement of healthcare professionals in the Partnership Groups, user representatives are exposed to the organizational 'realities' of the NHS. The healthcare professionals communicate the structure and process of the health service – why there are delays in particular processes and why it takes considerable time to rectify these delays. The Partnership Groups provide a forum for incorporating user views, but are also used to communicate to users how cancer care and treatment is delivered through the networks.

The other three networks have limited user involvement and there is considerable debate regarding the appropriate way of engaging users. To illustrate, some clinicians in Network C reported that they would welcome user involvement in network activities, while others indicated that this undermined the special relationship between doctors and patients. Some clinicians felt that the role of the medical profession is to represent patients' interests and that 'users are often not able to judge whether what has been done to them is the right thing to do'.

Is there evidence that patients are receiving high-quality treatment and care?

Across the five networks, respondents felt that it was difficult to ascertain whether patients would have experienced any changes or improvements in their treatment and care since the development of the network model. Some felt that patient care had improved, however there was only limited research and no clear baseline for comparison. This may represent a weakness of the type of process research identified, and the study could have benefited from a 'clinical outcomes' strand, perhaps within a larger multidisciplinary team.

Some felt that the networks' focus on organizational restructuring and centralization could lose sight of individual patients and quality of care. Much of the discussion focused on 'political battling' between stakeholders to protect their practices and funding while at times the interests of patients were not the key priority – 'keeping hospitals happy' was taking precedence. The networks were overindulging in structural reconfigurations and meeting waiting time targets, whilst ignoring more processual or strategic issues.

Networks are judged on specific government targets, particularly on the maximum two-week wait between urgent GP referral and outpatient appointment (National Health Service 2000). Energy is concentrated on collecting and submitting data for this target, however, the networks lack an efficient system for collecting data relating to other quality indicators. Such data were largely absent. Again, this may identify a limitation of organizational process research.

Cancer network comparison and evaluation

The overall pattern is one of considerable variation between each MCN's performance on each of the indicators. On the basis of the data available and collected, the networks were ranked against each other on the sixteen identified criteria. There was no clear and consistent high performer. Networks C, D and E each performed well on particular indicators within the bottom-up and top-down groupings, ensuring that when these rankings were averaged, there were only small variations in the overall rankings for these networks. However, on the basis of the overall rankings, Networks A and B consistently performed most poorly. We reiterate that the differences between the overall, averaged rankings were minimal. Appendix A provides a table of the raw data, detailing the rankings for each of the individual indicators, and the overall rankings. This table also indicates the indicators for which we were unable to collect any data.

The implication is that it is difficult to clearly separate out high and low performers – inter-network variation in performance is more nuanced. Some networks were performing well on particular indicators (e.g., patient involvement) and poorly on others (e.g., strategy), while some networks were performing moderately on all indicators. The rankings should be interpreted with caution. The hope that a positive 'outlier' could be identified through evaluation, factors associated with such high performance explored and the learning spread out more widely across the system proved illusory.

We should add that in practice top-down success criteria proved more dominant within the healthcare system than the bottom-up criteria. Specifically, the recommendations in the *NHS Cancer Plan* (2000) that formed the basis for the latter eight of the identified success criteria were subsequently converted into specific standards for development in the *Manual of Cancer Services Standards* (NHS Executive 2000). MCNs are required to adhere to these, largely top-down, criteria and, in the main, they are doing so. There are limited resources for any initiatives, data collection or analysis that do not relate to centrally-driven standards and targets.

Alternatively, of the eight success criteria derived from the bottom-up Delphi study, only one has subsequently become a government performance target – *is there timely diagnosis and treatment for all patients*? Over the past three years, considerable resources have been allocated to adhering to the aforementioned 'two-week wait' target (National Health Service 2000) – through process redesign and subsequent data management.

Weighting the indicators from the *NHS Cancer Plan* (National Health Service 2000) in favour of those from the Delphi study was considered, particularly as these indicators have since become key deliverables of the MCNs. However, due to the nature of the pluralistic evaluation approach that we employed, we did not deem this to be an appropriate strategy. Pluralistic evaluation argues against a singular framework or perspective of evaluation, and as such the bottom-up indicators that were developed by the range of stakeholders through the Delphi methodology were considered equally valid as those top-down criteria derived from national policy.

Data were not routinely available to measure the other success criteria identified through the Delphi study, in particular in relation to direct patient experiences. Respondents felt that it was difficult to ascertain whether patients would have experienced any changes or improvements in their treatment and care since the development of the network model. Some felt that patient care had improved, however, there had been no research conducted and no clear baseline for comparison. This data gap weakens the ability of process research to answer key policy questions, unless complemented by additional primary quantitative research.

The data being collected and provided to the Department of Health is not necessarily what the responding service providers were interested in – there was some evidence that clinicians would prefer a broader perspective of what is happening to their patients, including survival, satisfaction and follow-up data. However, this is not the primary purpose of governmental data collection systems, focused on providing information about the extent to which local healthcare systems are meeting targets. The clinicians were more interested in data collection that is clinically relevant and were skeptical of waiting time targets, which are primarily focused on the quantity – not quality – of clinical service. Some felt that the strong focus on waiting time targets 'distorts the priorities' of the networks and the individual hospitals.

There was considerable discrepancy between what the Department of Health considered to be indicators of success, versus what clinicians delivering direct patient care regarded as important. Doctors in particular were concerned that the government targets distract from caring for patients, and instead create a system whereby speed and efficiency are more important than high quality patient care.

Conclusion

Some substantive reflections on the cancer networks study

The evaluation was able to undertake exploratory, but also policy-relevant research into the creation and impact of a new organizational form in healthcare, using qualitative and organizational process-based methods of longitudinal and comparative case studies. Moreover, the empirical design was of some considerable scope and scale, covering the whole of NHS London and so cannot be seen merely as a small-scale single case study with very low external validity (a common criticism of qualitative methods). We managed to operationalize the task of conducting an assessment of performance through deriving a basket of top-down and bottom-up performance indicators. We provided the funders with an analytic commentary on the creation, development, and to some extent impact and performance of the five MCNs at the end of the study, as commissioned to do.

However, there were some drawbacks and limitations to the study. A main conclusion of the study was that the assessment of performance was more complex and nuanced than originally anticipated. Initially we had expected to be able to locate high and low performers within the set of networks, explore organizational process reasons for this variation and identify key learning points to inform future organizational design. Ultimately, we concluded that the five MCNs studied displayed a highly mixed pattern of performance in relation to the identified success criteria and there was no clear 'top performer' which emerged across the indicators. This emphasizes the complexity of using qualitative evaluative techniques in clearly identifying and diffusing levels of high performance across public service organizations.

More broadly, the operationalization of the success criteria was problematic. Identifying success criteria through the Delphi technique was a straightforward and transparent process, however gathering qualitative data to 'measure' these success criteria was more challenging. The Delphi exercise and the *NHS Cancer Plan* (2000) produced many quantitatively phrased success criteria that were difficult to measure qualitatively in the field. The researchers were reliant upon documentary evidence and interview responses for 'answers' to these criteria, and in many cases the answers were not available.

Our methodology did not always produce clear answers and was also weak in linking measures of inputs and processes to final clinical outcomes. We were not able to access primary quantitative data to address all the success criteria identified. Where these quantitative data were not available, some of our questions could not be answered. For example, one indicator was whether there was evidence that all patients in the network were receiving 'high quality' treatment in care, presumably reflected in better long-term final clinical outcomes. We were not able to come to a final conclusion on this question due to lack of data. Interestingly, many of these questions were identified by network personnel as important indicators of success, however databases were still not being built up by the NHS to address them. We also found it difficult in practice to access user representatives to assess the extent to which they were effectively being involved in these networks.

Wider implications for qualitative evaluation

We have here presented a worked example of qualitative evaluation of organizational performance (so Rist (2000) may be too pessimistic when arguing that qualitative evaluations exist more in potential than in actuality) which was of considerable scope and scale – across the whole of London – rather than a small single case study from which it would be difficult to generalize. It was commissioned by policy funders to help them understand more about how a novel organizational form was developing and operating. It was well suited to undertaking exploratory research into a new managerial phenomenon – given the rapidity with which managerial models change in the public services, there may well be a continuing demand from policy makers for this sort of evaluation.

What learning would we take from this project if we were asked to do a similar study again? First, we would seek to form a multidisciplinary team with other researchers with complementary skills in quantitative evaluation, especially the measurement of clinical outcomes (such as public health physicians). We agree with Fulop *et al.* (2001) that multidisciplinary evaluations of complex interventions in health services can be powerful, and that researchers who adopt different methods, and even epistemologies, can nevertheless seek to work fruitfully together. Secondly, we would undertake greater effort early in the evaluation to locate appropriate user representatives and gather data from them. Both these developments would strengthen the robustness of the design. Nevertheless, qualitative evaluations of performance in the public services using large-scale organizational process methods (a comparative set of longitudinal cases; multiple stakeholder approach; explicit interest in performance assessment) represent an interesting and important addition to the evaluative armory.

Acknowledgement

The authors acknowledge the support of the then NHS London Research and Development Directorate. The views expressed are those of the authors and not necessarily of the funder.

REFERENCES

Bogason, P. (2004) 'Researching network governance' in *International Colloquium on Governance and Performance*. INLOGOV, Birmingham, pp. 1–20.

Bowling, A. (1999) *Research methods in health. Investigating health and health services*. Buckingham: Open University Press.

Calman, K. and Hine, D. (1995) *A policy framework for commissioning cancer services*. London: Department of Health.

Cm4310 (1999) *Modernising government*, Prime Minister and Minister for the Cabinet Office, London.

Dopson, S., Fitzgerald, L., Ferlie, E. and Locock, L. (eds.) (2005) *Knowledge into action? Evidence based health care in context*. Oxford: Oxford University Press.

Dunham, R. (1998) '*The Delphi technique*', University of Wisconsin – School of Business. Available at: www.instruction.bus.wisc.edu/obdemo/readings/delphi.htm

Eden, C. and Huxham, C. (1996) 'Action research for the study of organisations' in *The handbook of organisation studies*, Clegg, S., Hardy, C. and Nord, W. (eds.) Thousand Oaks, CA: Sage, pp. 526–542.

Edwards, N. (2002) 'Clinical networks', *British Medical Journal*, **324**: 63.

Ferlie, E. and Addicott, R. (2004) *The introduction, impact and performance of cancer networks: A process evaluation*, London: Tanaka Business School – Imperial College London.

Ferlie, E. and Pettigrew, A. (1996) 'Managing through networks: Some issues and implications for the NHS', *British Journal of Management*, **7**: S81–S99.

Ferlie, E. and McNulty, T. (1997) '"Going to market": Changing patterns in the organisation and character of process research', *Scandinavian Journal of Management*, **13**: 367–387.

Ferlie, E. (2001) 'Organisational studies', in Fulop, Allen, Clarke and Black (eds.) pp. 24–39.

Flick, U. (2002) *An introduction to qualitative research*, 2nd edn. London: Sage.

Foddy, W. (1993) *Constructing questions for interviews and questionnaires. Theory and practice in social research*. Hong Kong: Cambridge University Press.

Fulop, N., Allen, P., Clarke, A. and Black, N. (eds.) (2001) *Studying the organisation and delivery of health services', research methods*. London: Routledge.

Glaser, B. and Strauss, A. (1967) *The discovery of grounded theory: strategies for qualitative research*. New York: Aldine.

Greene, J. (2000) 'Qualitative program evaluation: Practice and promise' in *Handbook of qualitative research*, Denzin, N. and Lincoln, Y. (eds.) London: Sage, pp. 530–544.

Guba, E. and Lincoln, Y. (1989) *Fourth generation evaluation*. Newbury Park, CA: Sage.

Jones, J. and Hunter, D. (2000) 'Using the Delphi and nominal group technique in health services research' in *Qualitative research in health care*. Pope, C. and Mays, N., (eds.) BMJ: London, pp. 40–49.

Kates, N. and Humphrey, B. (1993) 'Psychiatric networks: They make sense, but do they work?' *Canadian Journal of Psychiatry*, **38**: 319–323.

Kvale, S. (1996) *InterViews. An introduction to qualitative research interviewing*. Thousand Oaks, CA: Sage Publications.

Linstone, H. and Turoff, M. (eds.) (1975) *The Delphi technique. Techniques and application*. USA: Addison-Wesley.

McNulty, T. and Ferlie, E. (2002) *Reengineering health care. The complexities of organizational transformation*. Oxford: Oxford University Press.

Meyer, J. (2001) 'Action research' in Fulop, Allen, Clarke and Black (eds.), *Studying the organisation and delivery of health service research methods*. London: Routledge, pp. 172–187.

National Health Service. (2000) *The NHS cancer plan*. London: Department of Health.

Neuman, W. (1991) *Social research methods. Qualitative and quantitative approaches*. Massachusetts: Allyn and Bacon.

Newman, J. (2001) *Modernising governance. New Labour, policy and society*. London: Sage.

NHS Executive (2000) *Manual of cancer services standards*. London: National Health Service.

Oakley, A. (2000) *Experiments in knowing. Gender and method in the social sciences*. Cambridge: Polity Press.

Pawson, R. and Tilley, N. (1997) *Realistic evaluation*. London: Sage.

Pettigrew, A., Ferlie, E. and McKee, L. (1992) *Shaping strategic change: making change in large organizations, the case of the National Health Service*. London: Sage.

Pope, C. and Mays, N. (1996) 'Qualitative methods in health and health services research' in *Qualitative research in health care*, Mays, N. and Pope, C. (eds.) London: BMJ Publishing Group, pp. 1–9.

Reinharz, S. (1992) *Feminist methods in social research*. New York: Oxford University Press.

Rist, R. (2000) 'Influencing the policy process with qualitative research' in *Handbook of qualitative research*, Denzin, N. and Lincoln, Y. (eds.) London: Sage, pp. 1001–1017.

Stake, R. (2000) 'Case studies', in *Handbook of qualitative research*. Denzin, N. and Lincoln, Y. (eds.) London: Sage, pp. 435–454.

Yin, R. (1994) *Case Study research. Design and methods*. 2nd edn. Newbury Park, CA: Sage.

Appendix A. How did the networks compare? (1 = lowest performing, 5 = highest performing)

	Network A	Network B	Network C	Network D	Network E
Source: Delphi study					
Does the network have a clear management structure?	1	2	3	5	4
Does the network have a clear strategy?	1	2	3	5	4
Are all patients considered by a multidisciplinary team?	2	3	4	1	5
Is the network operating on a patient-focused basis?	2	3	4	1	5
Is there timely diagnosis and treatment for all patients?	1	2	4	3	5
Is there evidence that patients are receiving high-quality treatment and care?	*	*	*	*	*
Do patients report improved experiences, standards of care and quality of life since the development of the network?	*	*	*	*	*
Has there been increased cancer prevention and earlier diagnosis since the introduction of the cancer network?	*	*	*	*	*
Total (average)	**7 (1.4)**	**12 (2.4)**	**18 (3.6)**	**15 (3)**	**23 (4.6)**
Source: NHS Cancer Plan					
Have cancer units been designated?	1	2	5	4	3
Have cancer centres been designated?	1	2	5	4	3
Does the cancer network involve the following key players – health service commissioners (health authorities, primary care groups and trusts) and providers (primary and community care and hospitals), the voluntary sector, and local authorities?	1	2	3	4	5
Does the network closely involve the chief executives of provider NHS trusts and health authorities and PCTs?	1	2	4	3	5
Is the patient pathway smooth and seamless and are resources targeted where they are most needed to serve the cancer needs of their local population?	3	1	2	5	4
Have alliances developed to help reduce the risk of cancer, through action on smoking and diet?	1	2	3	5	4
Are there support and organizational development facilities available to regions and networks?	1	2	4	5	3
Have the Cancer Services Collaborative initiatives rolled out to all cancer networks?	1	2	4	5	3
Total (average)	**10 (1.25)**	**15 (1.875)**	**30 (3.75)**	**35 (4.375)**	**30 (3.75)**

* Data not collected by network

Quantitative approaches towards assessing organizational performance

Peter C. Smith

Introduction

One of the major challenges confronting any commentary on public service performance is how to secure meaningful quantitative measures of performance. This difficulty should not be surprising. The impossibility of fully measuring the output of public services is one of the fundamental reasons why their provision cannot be left entirely to competitive markets, and why some sort of public sector regulation is required.

Nevertheless, over the last 25 years a growing capacity to measure aspects of public service performance has emerged, through what might be termed the 'performance indicator movement' (Bird *et al.* 2005). A confluence of forces has led to this revolution in the collection and use of public service performance data. On the supply side, the massive advances in information technology have greatly reduced the price of collecting and processing data. On the demand side there has emerged a growing popular and political scepticism of public service professionals and institutions, and calls for greater independent audit and accountability. Performance data appear to answer many of these concerns.

In the United Kingdom, the emergence of the performance indicator culture can be traced to 1981, when the national government mandated the collection of a suite of Local Government Comparative Statistics in England and Wales, and required local governments to publish in an annual report comparisons of their own performance with that of 'similar' institutions (Smith 1990; Carter *et al.* 1992). In 1983 the Audit Commission was set up with a remit to scrutinize the economy, efficiency and effectiveness of local governments in England and Wales, and one of the earliest tools it deployed was a 'profile' of each local government's performance compared with its closest comparators.

The earliest performance indicators in the UK were dominated by measures of costs and resource utilization, reflecting a heavy reliance on readily available administrative and accounting data. Since then, the scope of performance indicator systems has broadened considerably, and there have been concerted attempts to introduce more measures of the outcomes of public services. Whilst the design of most public service performance indicator systems continues to be circumscribed to some extent by the nature of routine administrative data, the scope of their coverage is steadily increasing, thereby offering a growing potential to secure more comprehensive and meaningful measures of public service performance (Atkinson 2005).

However, notwithstanding the growing opportunities for quantitative analysis, the analysis of public service performance is fraught with perils. Naïve scrutiny of performance indicators can give rise to seriously misleading inferences. Yet the growing body of techniques designed to offer more satisfactory analysis of performance data introduces its own dangers. The purpose of this chapter is therefore to offer a critical commentary on the quantitative analysis of public service performance data. It focuses on local rather than national services. This makes it possible to compare local institutions or jurisdictions seeking to offer similar services, such as schools, police and hospitals. I assume throughout that there exist some relevant (though not necessarily comprehensive) performance data that can serve as the basis for comparative quantitative analysis.

Univariate analysis

Once a performance indicator has been published, the temptation to rank local institutions according to attainment on the indicator is irresistible. Indeed, in England, unadjusted indicators of school success rates in public examination were deliberately placed in tabular form in the public domain with the objective of promoting parental choice of school (West and Pennell 2000). Likewise, early electronic packages of health service performance routinely ranked local services in the form of such 'league tables', with the prime intention of stimulating benchmarking amongst organizations (Smith and Street 2005).

Yet it is for most public services manifestly unreasonable and misleading to compare solely on the basis of an unadjusted performance indicator. Public service organizations usually have no choice as to where they operate, so, must often do so in starkly different environments. They cannot, in general, be expected always to secure similar outcomes. The questions therefore arise: how much local variation in performance is legitimately explained by uncontrollable circumstances? And can the performance measures be satisfactorily adjusted to account for different environmental circumstances so that they do offer valid comparisons of local institutions?

In principle, a central payer (such as a national government) could seek to compensate local organizations for differences in environment by implementing a suitable funding mechanism (Smith 2003). Such mechanisms usually seek to allow local organizations to deliver some 'standard' level of services, by directing increased funds to more disadvantaged localities or organizations. Once they have been implemented organizations should – in principle – be on a level playing field, and therefore able to deliver comparable performance. In practice, it is rare to find a funding mechanism that completely compensates for differences in environment. When comparing organizations it may nevertheless be important to bear in mind that some, albeit imperfect, attempt to adjust for environment has been made through variations in funding levels.

This section examines methods of analysing individual performance indicators to secure an understanding of comparative performance. In scrutinizing these methods it is important to keep in mind that examination of a single indicator of performance can often mislead, as it ignores variations in other dimensions of organizational performance. We return to the need for a more holistic view of performance in the next section. Here we examine four univariate analytic approaches: cluster analysis; risk adjustment; regression analysis; and multilevel analysis. The focus of all – in one way or another – is to adjust a single indicator for variations in the organizational environment.

Cluster analysis

Some of the earliest and most widely deployed approaches towards comparing performance involve the use of various forms of cluster analysis (Everitt *et al.* 2001). The requirement of such approaches is first to select various quantitative measures of a locality's social, economic and geographical circumstances relevant to the service in question. Based on these data, a measure of the similarity (or 'distance') between each locality and all others is then calculated. After selecting a cluster analysis algorithm, the localities can then be clustered into discrete groups exhibiting broadly similar characteristics according to the chosen measure of similarity. A simpler approach, that is often more satisfactory in the performance measurement domain, is simply to identify the 'nearest neighbours' of each locality according to the chosen similarity measure, and to use these as the basis for comparisons.

For example, the 'police monitors' used to compare the performance of police forces in England and Wales rely on the specification of the 'most similar forces' for each force's report card (Police Standards Unit 2004). Each police force is compared only with a subset of other forces that exhibit similar social and demographic characteristics.

For any observed organization, cluster analysis (or nearest-neighbour analysis) effectively divides the remaining organizations into just two categories – comparable, or not comparable. Quite arbitrary technical choices have to be made regarding the measure of similarity to be employed and the cut-off criterion for including organizations within a comparable cluster. The technique can lead to unfair comparisons if one organization's comparators are allowed to be 'less similar' to it than another's. Moreover, cluster analysis suffers from the problem that some organizations may lie to the edge of a cluster, and exhibit more similarity to some comparators outside its cluster than those within the cluster. It is for this reason that the nearest-neighbour analysis is to be preferred, because it seeks to place the organization under scrutiny at the centre of its comparison group.

The main virtue of clustering techniques is transparency. Although the method of choosing comparators is technically opaque (and vulnerable to arbitrary technical choices), once the analysis is complete it is a straightforward matter to compare every organization with the average of its comparator group. However, the techniques are a very crude method of adjusting for variations in environment. They assume organizations are fully comparable with the chosen comparators, but discard potentially useful information about those organizations not selected as comparators. Various methods of risk adjustment or standardization have therefore been developed to effect a more robust basis for comparison.

Risk adjustment

Some of the most important external influences on public service performance are the characteristics of service users or the more general population being served. For any particular service user, success in securing desired outcomes may often be highly dependent on user characteristics. For example, in health care, expected surgical outcomes might depend in part on patient age, in criminal justice the probability of securing a prosecution might depend on the nature of the crime, and in schooling the probability of securing an examination success might depend in part on the intellectual capabilities of the child.

For this reason, a variety of techniques have been developed that seek to adjust observed outcomes for the nature of the population 'at risk' (Iezzoni 1997). The essence of such methods is to construct a ratio of observed to expected outcomes amongst users. The analytic effort of risk adjustment therefore goes into estimating the expected outcome for the organization, given the population it serves. For example (using the examples mentioned above) this would require estimates of the expected number of deaths from a surgical procedure, the expected number of successful prosecutions, or the expected number of examination passes, given the characteristics of the service users. Observed outcomes can then be ranked relative to these expected values.

If just one user characteristic is taken into account as a risk factor, and it comprises a small number of discrete categories, the calculation required for risk adjustment can be very straightforward. Using the policing example, it might entail merely calculating the national average prosecution rate p_i for each crime type i. Then if the number of each crime type i in an area in a certain period is n_i, the expected number of prosecutions in that period is $n_1 p_1 + n_2 p_2 + n_3 p_3 + \ldots$ This estimate can be used as the denominator in the risk-adjusted measure of prosecution success. The numerator is the actual number of prosecutions, and the ratio gives the organization's performance after adjusting for the types of crime being investigated.

Although not differing in principle, risk adjustment methods become much more complex, and more demanding of data, as the number of characteristics for which adjustment is required increases. The methods have been developed to their highest level of refinement in health care, where an extensive risk adjustment research industry has evolved. It is nevertheless worth noting that – although advanced methods are now used in health care – they are the subject of considerable debate and controversy, and it is often difficult to secure a consensus as to the most appropriate risk adjustment methodology. For example, Iezzoni *et al*. (1996) examine fourteen alternative methods of adjusting hospital death rates from pneumonia for US hospitals. They find that, although there is some correlation between the results obtained, for some hospitals there were serious variations in the performance rankings obtained, depending on the risk adjustment method used.

An important virtue of most statistical methods is that they offer quantitative estimates of standard errors, which can be used to assess the confidence with which performance rankings are held (Goldstein and Spiegelhalter 1996). A Royal Statistical Society working party has strongly urged that all performance data should be accompanied by appropriate measures of uncertainty (Bird *et al*. 2005). However, it is important to note that conventional standard errors merely model the variation inherent in the data, and do not accommodate the possibility that the chosen model is itself incorrect.

Regression analysis

It is often the case that the characteristics on which risk adjustment methods are based are continuous rather than discrete variables (for example, the income level of benefit claimants). Under these circumstances, the 'expected' outcome can be estimated using statistical regression models. The dependent variable (outcomes) for each organization is modelled as a function of a series of putative environmental determinants of outcome and an unexplained 'error' term. This yields an algebraic model that offers an estimate of an organization's predicted outcome for a given set of environmental circumstances. The unexplained error term for any organization can then be used as an estimate of its divergence from the sample 'expected' outcome, and therefore of its relative performance (Feldstein 1967).

A number of technical difficulties arise in the deployment of regression methods. The analyst must check that the model is well specified, in the sense that it conforms to the statistical assumptions underlying regression analysis (Godfrey 1988). And it is also important that the explanatory variables used are genuinely external influences on performance, and are not merely correlates of good or bad performance. For example, it is observed that hospitals making high use of agency nurses tend to secure worse health outcomes, other things being equal. The key question from a performance modelling perspective is whether reliance on agency nurses is a genuinely external constraint on management, or whether it is within managerial control. Only in the former case should it be included in the regression model.

In summary, by including an external factor in a regression model, the analyst is allowing any poor performance associated with that factor to be 'excused' so there must be confidence that it is an unavoidable (exogenous) influence on performance. There is no secure analytic method of choosing variables for inclusion in the regression method used for such purposes. For example, use of a traditional statistical t-test might indicate a statistically significant influence of agency nursing on hospital performance. However, that alone cannot determine whether the nursing variable should be included in the performance model. Rather, an appeal must be made to other research evidence and professional judgement as to whether or not it is a legitimate exogenous influence on performance.

It is therefore important to note that it is not usually appropriate to use the standard approach towards statistical model building, in which variables are tested for inclusion in a regression model using a t-test or some analogous criterion (Greene 2000). A variable might pass such a test (a) because it is a genuinely exogenous influence on performance; or (b) it is correlated with inefficiency, either accidentally or because of deliberate managerial choices. In case (b), its inclusion in the regression model is inappropriate as it would effectively 'excuse' any element of inefficiency correlated with the variable.

An example of applying the regression approach might be the following model of police performance. Other things equal, the crime rate y_i in area i is known from research evidence to be highly dependent on the rate of unemployment x_i in an area, a factor beyond the control of police forces. It may therefore be reasonable to deploy a regression of performance y_i on unemployment x_i, and to use the residual from that model as an indicator of 'risk adjusted' performance. The intention is to adjust for the uncontrollable influence of unemployment on crime, and what remains is an indication of attainment after that adjustment has been made.

Figure 5.1 illustrates the principles. Amongst police forces, a very clear positive relationship is identified between unemployment and outcome, as measured by the crime rate. Without adjusting for unemployment, organization P_1 appears to have the best performance (lowest crime rate). However, the regression line shown in Figure 5.1 indicates the *predicted* crime rate, given a jurisdiction's unemployment rate. Adjustment for unemployment then uses the residual unexplained performance from this regression line as a basis for comparison. Under this criterion, P_1 is now deemed as securing performance poorer than that expected, given its unemployment environment, and it is now P_2 that is deemed the top performer, as it secures the largest (vertical) residual below the expected crime rate, as estimated by the regression line.

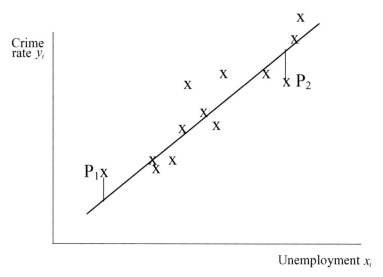

Figure 5.1   Univariate regression model

The use of regression models in this way is widespread (Propper and Wilson 2003). They beg many difficult questions. For example, this particular example presumes a linear relationship between explanatory variable and performance. Can that be justified? Economists usually assume that production functions are non-linear, implying a need to experiment with alternative functional forms. This is readily achieved using devices such as logarithmic transformations, but requires careful technical comparison of alternatives and a mechanism for choosing between competing models (Heckman *et al.* 1997).

In a similar vein, there may be external influences on police attainment other than unemployment (such as funding levels) that should be incorporated into the model. This too can be achieved easily using multiple regression methods, but requires technical judgements on the criteria for including additional variables.

Furthermore, the use of regression models presumes that a sample average relationship between unemployment and crime should be the basis for judging performance. That is, the regression line in Figure 5.1 is the average response in terms of crime rate to the local unemployment rate. Is this reasonable, or should some observations be omitted from the model, perhaps because they are anomalous in some way? For example, the data for one observation may have been contaminated by a strike of local court officials, and therefore does not represent typical practice.

These and other modelling considerations suggest a need for many technical choices in coming to a judgement on the most suitable statistical model to deploy as a basis for comparing performance. Many of these choices can have a profound impact on the analytic judgements that emerge. For example, local geography is often assumed to be an important determinant of ambulance service response times. In particular, more rural areas are presumed to suffer a disadvantage in securing short response times. Therefore, a critical determinant on the statistical estimate of performance of ambulance services may be whether or not a measure of rurality is included in the regression model, and – if it is – what particular measure of rurality is chosen. Therefore the analyst must at the very least make a clear statement about the technical choices that have been taken so that they are open to challenge and scrutiny.

Multilevel modelling

Most public services are organized hierarchically. For example individual teachers operate within schools, that in turn may be based in local government jurisdictions. A key policy question that therefore arises is: to what level of the hierarchy are variations in individual outcomes attributable? Statisticians have developed multilevel (or hierarchical) models to a high level of refinement in order to address such questions in domains such as schooling and other public services (Goldstein 1995; Rice and Jones 1997).

The essence of multilevel modelling is that all observations are located within a hierarchy of potential effects on performance, and that outcomes are to some extent attributable to the various levels of the hierarchy. The statistical models used to address the hierarchical structure are variations on the familiar regression theme. In its simplest form (just two levels) the underlying model merely adds an 'organization' effect to a model of individual attainment.

An example is the use of value-added models in education (Goldstein and Thomas 1996). Here the outcome variable is a pupil's eventual educational attainment secured while in the school. The environmental variable could be the calibre of the pupil on entry into the school, presumed to be beyond the school's control. A simple multilevel model can therefore be deployed, including prior attainment as an environmental variable and incorporating an organizational (school) effect. From a performance monitoring perspective, the interest is of course in each school's effect on attainment. The model secures an estimate of that effect, after adjusting for prior attainment. It therefore yields an estimate of the relative 'value-added' by the school.

Multilevel modelling shares many of the characteristics of regression modelling, but introduces additional technical choices, such as how to model the organizational (school) effect, and whether to allow the effect to vary across the range of environmental circumstances (pupil abilities). In the schooling context, multilevel models have been developed to a high level of refinement, but their use in other public service domains is less well developed (Heinrich and Lynn 2001).

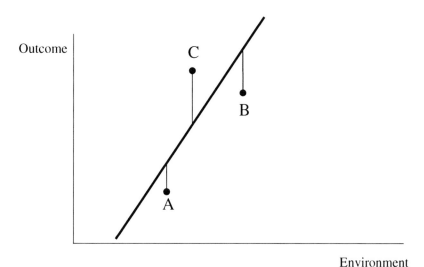

Figure 5.2   Performance ranking using only aggregate data

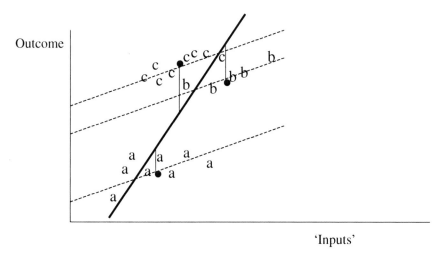

Figure 5.3   Changes in performance ranking based on hierarchical structure

The effect of using multilevel methods can be illustrated diagrammatically. Figure 5.2 shows the conventional aggregate regression model of average organization achievement on average environmental circumstances. In this illustration the regression line is shown by the solid diagonal. The residuals from this line suggest that the organizations' performance should be ranked in the order C, A, B.

In contrast, Figure 5.3 shows exactly the same data, but disaggregated to the individual level (service users are shown as lower case letters according to the organization that they used). The analysis suggests an average relationship between environment and outcome indicated by the parallel broken lines. However, organizations are clearly now ranked C, B, A, as C secures a higher average level than B, which in turn outperforms A, other things equal.

Multivariate analysis

The quantitative techniques considered so far examine a single measure of performance, seeking to adjust where necessary for uncontrollable influences on attainment. Such methods are undoubtedly valuable, and in some circumstances fit for purpose. However, almost all public services pursue multiple objectives, and focusing on a single indicator of performance will give only a partial picture of performance, and in many circumstances will be misleading. For example, suppose the performance of hospitals were judged solely on an efficiency measure, such as the average inpatient length of stay. Reliance on this single measure of performance clearly ignores other important aspects of hospital performance, such as the clinical quality of care. In particular, it cannot signal whether reduced length of stay is being secured at the expense of poorer health outcomes, arising from premature discharge of some patients.

Therefore, in parallel to the piecemeal analysis of individual performance measures, a great deal of research effort has also gone into developing overall measures of organizational performance, under the general banner of productivity analysis (Fried and Scmidt 1993; Coelli *et al.* 1998). The objective of productivity analysis is to secure a measure of the cost-effectiveness of an organization, confusingly referred to almost universally as a measure of efficiency. Whatever the terminology, the measure of organizational attainment is defined as a ratio of weighted outputs to weighted inputs. In a competitive market setting, a regulator could use market prices to weight outputs and inputs. However, a key difficulty in public services is to secure meaningful valuations, particularly of outputs, when there is no market to generate prices. The creation of composite performance measures relies crucially on securing estimates of the relative value placed by society on each output (Smith 2002). A central focus of productivity analysis is therefore on the weights to be attached to public service outputs. (Inputs generally are less problematic, and are often conflated into a single measure of total organizational costs.)

Two approaches have dominated the productivity literature: parametric econometric methods, pre-eminently various forms of stochastic frontier analysis (SFA), and the non-parametric methods known as data envelopment analysis (DEA). Although these methods approach the task in radically different fashions, they have the common intention of using the observed behaviour of all organizations to infer a production frontier, indicating the maximum feasible attainment.

They then offer estimates of the extent to which each individual organization falls short of the frontier. We first consider each of these approaches, and then turn to some possible alternative multivariate methods of assessing performance.

Parametric methods

The core of most parametric efficiency models is to develop either a cost function (under which costs are modelled as a function of a range of output measures) or a production function (under which a single measure of output is modelled as a function of a range of input measures). From a public service viewpoint, organizational costs are often readily observed, but it is usually much more difficult to develop a single composite measure of output. Therefore the interest is usually in the development of cost functions rather than production functions.

The simplest statistical approach to developing a cost function is to extend the univariate regression approach discussed in the previous section to its multivariate counterpart, in which costs are modelled as a function of a range of outputs and an unexplained error term, often using conventional ordinary least squares estimation methods. This yields an empirical model from which estimates of predicted expenditure can be inferred, given an organization's current levels of performance. The magnitude of the unexplained residual expenditure (the difference between actual and predicted expenditure) can be used as a basis for estimating the organization's overall efficiency.

The predicted expenditure from such models traces out a cost frontier, and in principle all organizations should lie on the frontier (if they are efficient) or beyond it (if their costs exceed the efficient level), implying that only positive residuals should be permitted. Yet, in contradiction to this assumption, the use of conventional multivariate statistical methods assumes a symmetric distribution of positive and negative unexplained variations from the estimated cost function.

This contradiction has led to the development of the parametric methods known collectively as stochastic frontier analysis (Kumbakhar and Lovell 2000). Their common feature is that they allow the unexplained error term in the model to be decomposed into two components: the conventional two-sided symmetric element, designed to model random noise, and a one-sided asymmetric element, designed to model inefficiency. Once unexplained variations in performance have been decomposed in this way, the analyst can infer the magnitude of the one-sided residual for each organization, which is attributed to inefficiency.

Thus SFA allows the analyst to model the cost function more realistically, by assuming that only positive deviations from the estimated frontier can be attributed to inefficiency. However, this greater realism comes at a considerable price. It requires strong assumptions to be made about the nature of the one-sided error term. It also requires that all one-sided error is attributed to inefficiency, and conversely attributes none of the symmetric error to inefficiency. These assumptions are highly contested, and have led some commentators to question the usefulness of SFA from a regulatory perspective (Smith and Street 2005).

Some of the difficulties brought about by applying SFA to a single cross-section of observations can be obviated by using panel data (i.e., a time series of observations is used for each organization, rather than a single measure) (Baltagi 1995). The important gain offered by panel data is the vastly increased ability to distinguish transient (random) variations in performance measures from persistent (systematic) variations that can form the basis for estimates of inefficiency. However, important technical assumptions must still be made, for example about how inefficiency is assumed to change over time, and there is a risk that any model is estimating historical rather than contemporary levels of inefficiency.

Non-parametric methods

Data envelopment analysis is based on similar economic principles to SFA, but uses very different estimation techniques, based on linear programming models (Thanassoulis 2001). It develops a production possibility frontier by identifying the organizations that 'envelope' all other organizations on the basis of a composite estimate of efficiency. For each organization, it seeks the linear combination of all other organizations that secures the same (or better) outputs at lowest use of inputs. Or conversely it can be used to search for the linear combination of all other organizations that use the same (or lower) inputs to secure the highest level of outputs. In DEA, the ratio of actual to optimal overall performance is referred to as inefficiency.

Compared to SFA, DEA has some attractive features. It requires no assumptions about the precise shape of the production frontier, or the distribution of the error term. It can handle multiple inputs and multiple outputs simultaneously, and it requires none of the stringent model testing that is required of parametric techniques. However, it also suffers from a number of drawbacks. Because the frontier is deterministic, it can be vulnerable to data errors. In practice, the DEA frontier is composed of a small number of highly performing organizations, and the performance of all other units is judged in relation to that frontier. Therefore, if the measurement of one key efficient organization on the frontier is incorrect, it can result in excessively negative judgements on many of the inefficient units. This high sensitivity to measurement of 'frontier' organizations is a symptom of a more general weakness of DEA, that – in contrast to parametric methods – there are no tests of whether a model fits the data well.

Moreover, from a regulatory perspective, DEA has the profound drawback that it permits flexibility in the weights attached to each output. Each organization can in principle be compared to the frontier according to an entirely different set of output weights. Thus, for example, an organization might be deemed DEA efficient only if a zero weight is placed on an important output. This appears to contradict the principle that organizations should be evaluated on a consistent basis, and has also exposed the technique to fierce criticism (Stone 2002). For this reason, many commentators advocate the use of DEA as a useful tool for exploring large and complex datasets, but not as a regulatory device for passing judgements or setting efficiency targets, because regulators would normally want to apply a consistent set of weights to all organizations, in line with regulatory priorities.

Seemingly unrelated regression methods

The dominant interest of many public service managers is in indicators of performance in specific service areas, rather than such aggregate measures of organizational performance. This suggests an interest in modelling individual indicators of performance, along the lines suggested in section 1. However, as discussed in this section, important relationships may exist between individual performance measures that are lost if this is pursued solely through the piecemeal development of univariate regression models of performance. Martin and Smith (2005) therefore demonstrate how a suite of performance indicators might be modelled simultaneously, using the methods of seemingly unrelated regressions (SUR).

To understand the potential importance of the need for simultaneous modelling, consider a very general production process with just two indicators of organizational performance, as illustrated in Figure 5.4. If all organizations were operating in identical environments, and using identical inputs, the frontier of feasible production could be illustrated by a single curve such as FF. Then all observations will lie on or inside this frontier. However, in general, public service organizations vary in both the environment they operate in and the resources they use. The position of the frontier will therefore differ between organizations. For example, the frontier F_2F_2 might indicate a revised frontier for a set of organizations operating with reduced levels of expenditure. The feasible mix of performance achieved by the organization at point A might be reduced to point A_2 if such a reduction were implemented.

Variations in the observed performance of two organizations might arise from five sources: environmental factors, resource levels, efficiency, substitution, and data quality. We consider these in turn.

1. The organizations might be operating in different environments, leading to variations in the feasible levels of performance. For example, schools might be operating in very different social and economic circumstances. Such influences on performance are often the most poorly understood and poorly measured aspect

Indicator 2

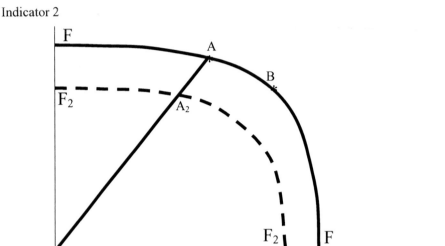

Figure 5.4   The production possibility frontier with two performance indicators

of the production process. As environmental circumstances improve, so we would expect to observe improvements in all performance measures (albeit to varying extents). Therefore, such variations will in general give rise to a positive correlation between performance measures.

2. The organizations might be devoting different levels of resource inputs to the services under scrutiny. Variations in resources act in a similar way to variations in environmental factors in altering the capacity of the organization to secure good performance. However they are often better understood and measured. Improvements in resources potentially increase the capacity for performance in all dimensions, and so should also give rise to a positive correlation between performance measures.

3. Conventional productivity models seek to focus attention on variations in overall efficiency, yet run into a difficulty because it is impossible to distinguish between organizational effects caused by unmeasured resources or environmental variations, and organizational effects caused by efficiency variations. Again, efficiency should be positively correlated with performance in all dimensions, therefore contributing to a positive correlation between performance measures.

4. If organizations are fully efficient, improved performance on one indicator can be secured only at the expense of a worse performance on others, as the organization moves round the efficient frontier. For example, in Figure 5.4, an efficient organization A can improve performance on indicator 1 only by reducing attainment on indicator 2 (moving, say, to point B). In contrast to (1) to (3) above, this substitution effect implies a negative correlation between performance measures.

5. Imperfections in data quality are inherent to all public services. These might affect relative measured performance in a variety of ways. For example, if the performance measures are of the form 'attainment per head of population', then an over-estimate of population would adversely affect performance in all domains, leading to a positive correlation between performance measures. If on the other hand the performance measures are expressed (say) in the form 'attainment in domain x per employee in domain x', then an imprecise allocation of employees between the different domains of performance might lead to a negative correlation between performance measures. Data imperfections could therefore contribute either positively or negatively to correlation measures.

There are therefore numerous reasons why performance on one indicator might be correlated positively or negatively with performance on another. So it may be important to move beyond the piecemeal modelling of individual performance indicators, and explicitly model covariance between indicators, without placing impossible demands on measurement instruments or modelling methodology. The essence of the SUR approach is to model such covariances by incorporating a latent variable, which can be thought of as an implicit unmeasured 'organizational' effect on performance across all indicators. It can be defined as any influence on overall organizational performance, whether or not it is within the direct control of the organization. Each of the five factors discussed above might contribute to the organizational effect, which therefore comprises a jumble of influences on measured performance.

Martin and Smith argue that such simultaneous modelling of performance measures is potentially important because:

- It economizes on the need for detailed modelling of individual performance measures. Rather than search for all the possible 'organizational' influences on performance, it infers a single latent organizational variable.
- It therefore economizes on the need to measure factors that affect performance across all performance measures, such as environmental variables. Instead, these are captured implicitly.
- By exploiting the important information implicit in the covariances between performance measures, it can reduce the very large confidence intervals frequently observed in single equation models, caused in part because of omitted or poorly measured explanatory variables.
- The more sensitive modelling of interactions may lead to different inferences about the level of an organization's performance on specific indicators. In principle, quite large changes in estimated residuals might arise as a result of the SUR modelling.

In short, compared with piecemeal modelling, the deployment of a SUR model of multiple performance indicators might secure marked reductions in standard errors, and accordingly more secure performance rankings of performance, without recourse to additional data or the highly questionable aggregation of performance indicators implicit in traditional productivity models discussed earlier. This is a promising area of research that has yet to be fully explored (Bailey and Hewson 2004; Hauck and Street in press).

Conclusion

None of the methods described here offers a panacea for the problem of analysing public service performance. Rather, they all offer useful alternative perspectives on the determinants of performance and on identifying the level of attainment of individual organizations. Moreover, quantitative approaches alone cannot answer all the questions about performance posed by politicians, regulators, managers, service users and the general public. However, used carefully in conjunction with other approaches, such as inspection, user surveys, and transparent governance, they offer great potential for enhancing our understanding of public services and promoting increased cost-effectiveness.

REFERENCES

Atkinson, T. (2005) *Measurement of government output and productivity for the national accounts*. Basingstoke: Palgrave Macmillan.

Bailey, T. and Hewson, P. (2004) 'Simultaneous modelling of multiple traffic safety performance indicators by using a multivariate generalized linear mixed model', *Journal of the Royal Statistical Society A*, **167**: 501–517.

Baltagi, B. (1995) *Econometric analysis of panel data*. New York: John Wiley.

Bird, S. M., Cox, D., Farewell, V. T., Goldstein, H., Holt, T. and Smith, P. (2005) 'Performance indicators: good, bad and ugly', *Journal of the Royal Statistical Society A*, **168**: 1–25.

Carter, N., Klein, R. and Day, P. (1992) *How organisations measure success: The use of performance indicators in government*. London: Routledge.

Coelli, T., Rao, D. S. P. and Battese, G. E. (1998) *An introduction to efficiency and productivity analysis*. Dordrecht: Kluwer.

Everitt, B., Landau, S. and Leese, M. (2001) *Cluster analysis*. London: Arnold.

Feldstein, M. S. (1967) *Economic analysis for health service efficiency: econometric studies of the British National Health Service*. Amsterdam: North-Holland.

Fried, L. K. and Scmidt, P. (1993) *The measurement of productive efficiency*. Oxford: Oxford University Press.

Godfrey, L. (1988) *Misspecification tests in econometrics*. Cambridge: Cambridge University Press.

Goldstein, H. (1995) *Multilevel statistical models*. London: Edward Arnold.

Goldstein, H. and Spiegelhalter, D. J. (1996) 'League tables and their limitations: Statistical issues in comparisons of institutional performance', *Journal of the Royal Statistical Society A*, **159**: 385–409.

Goldstein, H. and Thomas, S. (1996) 'Using examination results as indicators of school and college performance', *Journal of the Royal Statistical Society A*, **159**: 149–163.

Greene, W. H. (2000) *Econometric analysis*. Upper Saddle River, New Jersey: Prentice-Hall, Inc.

Hauck, K. and Street, A. In press. 'Performance assessment in the context of multiple objectives: a multivariate multilevel analysis', *Health Economics*.

Heckman, J., Heinrich, C. and Smith, J. (1997) 'Assessing the performance of performance standards in public bureaucracies', *American Economic Review*, **87**: 389–395.

Heinrich, C. J. and Lynn, L. E. Jr. (2001) 'Means and ends: a comparative study of empirical methods for investigating governance and performance', *Journal of Public Administration, Research and Theory*, **11**: 109–138.

Iezzoni, L., Shwartz, M., Ash, A., Hughes, J., Daley, J. and Mackiernan, Y. (1996) 'Severity measurement methods and judging hospital death rates for pneumonia', *Medical Care*, **34**(1): 11–28.

Iezzoni, L. (1997) *Risk adjustment for measuring healthcare outcomes*. 2nd edn. Chicago: Health Administration Press.

Kumbakhar, S. and Lovell, C. (2000) *Stochastic frontier analysis: an econometric approach*. Cambridge: Cambridge University Press.

Martin, S. and Smith, P. (2005) 'Multiple public service performance indicators: towards an integrated statistical approach', *Journal of Public Administration, Research and Theory*, **15**: 599–613.

Propper, C. and Wilson, D. (2003) 'The use and usefulness of performance measures in the public sector', *Oxford Review of Economic Policy*, **19**: 250–267.

Rice, N. and Jones, A. (1997) 'Multilevel models: applications to health data', *Health Economics*, **6**: 561–575.

Smith, P. (1990) 'The use of performance indicators in the public-sector', *Journal of the Royal Statistical Society A*, **153**: 53–72.

Smith, P. (2002) 'Developing composite indicators for assessing overall system efficiency', in P. Smith (ed.) *Measuring up: improving health systems performance in OECD countries*. Paris: OECD.

Smith, P. and Street, A. (2005) 'Measuring the efficiency of public services: the limits of analysis', *Journal of the Royal Statistical Society A*, **168**: 401–417.

Smith, P. C. (2003) 'Formula funding of public services: An economic analysis', *Oxford Review of Economic Policy*, **19**: 301–322.

Stone, M. (2002) 'How not to measure the efficiency of public services (and how one might)', *Journal of the Royal Statistical Society A*, **165**: 405–422.

Thanassoulis, E. (2001) *Introduction to the theory and application of data envelopment analysis*. Dordrecht: Kluwer Academic Publishers.

West, A. and Pennell, H. (2000) 'Publishing school examination results in England: incentives and consequences', *Educational Studies*, **26**: 423–436.

6   Consequences of goal ambiguity in public organizations

Young Han Chun and Hal G. Rainey

Introduction

Assertions that goal ambiguity in public organizations has a major influence on those organizations abound in the public management literature (for a review, see Rainey 1993). For instance, the Government Performance and Results Act (GPRA) of 1993 assumes that the reduction of goal ambiguity will improve organizational performance in US federal agencies. Strategic planning initiatives in many other nations have similar implications (Boyne and Walker 2004). New Public Management reforms and reforms in other nations have often sought to create more market- and business-like arrangements for government organizations, often involving efforts to clarify and specify goals and performance objectives (e.g., Barzelay 2001; Pollitt and Bouckaert 2000). However, one finds little empirical evidence of the impact of goal ambiguity on organizational performance and other important organizational characteristics such as structural dimensions, behaviours, and work attitudes. Severe conceptual and methodological challenges in investigating organizational goal ambiguity appear to account for this scarcity of evidence. Previous studies of goal ambiguity have usually relied on managers' responses to survey questions about whether their organizations have vague or clear goals (e.g., Rainey *et al.* 1995). Such surveys have found no differences between public and private managers in their ratings of the clarity of their organizations' goals. For public management experts, these results come as a surprise since they do not support the frequently repeated assertion that public organizations have less goal clarity than business firms. For researchers, this anomaly raises the question of whether relying on managers' survey responses provides an effective way to investigate goal ambiguity. Would one get different results using a different research strategy? The situation suggests the value of developing new conceptual and methodological approaches to analysing goal ambiguity.

This chapter examines the effects of goal ambiguity on structural dimensions and work attitudes in US federal agencies, relating new measures of goal ambiguity to measures of red tape, decentralization, reward expectancy, and job satisfaction. The chapter reports a third part of a larger study that develops a new strategy for research on goal ambiguity and tests theoretical arguments about the 'antecedents' and 'consequences' of the construct. The first part of the study suggested a multidimensional conception of goal ambiguity and developed new measures of the four dimensions described below (Chun and Rainey 2005a). The first article successfully validated the new measures by finding results to support hypotheses about the relations between those measures of goal ambiguity and variables often asserted in the literature to be antecedents of it, using a sample of 115 US federal agencies. These antecedents included the agency's financial publicness (the proportion of their funding which came from government allocations as opposed to sales or user charges), the need for political compromise over the agency's policies and actions, regulatory responsibility, complexity of the policy problems the agency confronts, and others.

Then, the second part of this research project reported evidence of relations between goal ambiguity and organizational performance (as perceived by organizational members) in US federal agencies (Chun and Rainey 2005b). Many management experts have claimed that goal ambiguity in organizations impedes organizational performance (e.g., Drucker 1980; Wilson 1989). Similarly, the tenets of management by goal clarification have played a key role in many managerial practices and policy initiatives, including Management by Objectives (MBO) in the 1970s and the Government Performance and Results Act (GPRA) in the 1990s. These initiatives actually involved a leap of faith because of the lack of evidence from systematic research. The second article tested this under-researched, yet critical presumption in the literature, drawing on a US government survey with a sample of more than 20,000 US federal employees working for thirty-two agencies. The results of the second article showed that most dimensions of goal ambiguity have significant negative relationships with such performance dimensions as: perceived managerial effectiveness; customer service orientation; productivity; and work quality. By finding results that are consistent with the literature, the second report provided further evidence to validate the new conceptual and methodological approach developed in this research project on goal ambiguity in public organizations.

This chapter takes another step by looking into the relations between goal ambiguity and consequences, focusing on such variables as: work satisfaction; reward expectancy; perceived red tape; and decentralization. Practitioners and policy makers have repeatedly made assertions about the impacts of goal ambiguity on organizational performance (e.g., Shalala 1998), while observations about effects on red tape, decentralization, work satisfaction, and reward expectancy have been discussed mostly among theorists on public bureaucracy (e.g., Dahl and Lindblom 1958; Downs 1967; Wilson 1989). Given that structural dimensions and work attitudes can act as important influences on organizational outcomes (Rainey 2003), examining the relations between goal ambiguity and these variables is important for both theoretical and practical reasons. To measure these consequence variables, the data source used for this study is the 2000 National Partnership for Reinventing Government (NPR) Survey conducted by the Office of Personnel Management (OPM). The survey sample is very large, involving 31,975 employees in forty-nine US federal agencies. We use a subset of this original sample that includes 25,814 employees in thirty-two agencies, the same sample used in the second article of this research project described earlier (Chun and Rainey 2005b).

Dimensions of goal ambiguity in organizations

For this study, *organizational goal ambiguity* refers to the extent to which an organizational goal or set of goals allows leeway for interpretation, when the organizational goal represents the desired future state of the organization. An organizational goal loses clear meaning and becomes ambiguous when it invites a number of different interpretations. This definition of organizational goal ambiguity (or clarity) is consistent with some previous conceptions of the construct (e.g., Locke *et al.* 1989). Goals can be ambiguous in various ways, and along different dimensions. We developed four dimensions of goal ambiguity, that refer to directing organizational activities, evaluating organizational performance, and making decisions about organizational priorities (Chun and Rainey 2005a).[1]

The measures for variables usually appear in the method section. Given the newness of the three concepts and measures of goal ambiguity, to aid the reader we describe the measures in this section as we introduce the concepts. As described below, the data for most of the dimensions of organizational goal ambiguity were collected from the agencies' strategic plans and performance reports. The Government Performance and Results Act (GPRA) of 1993 requires that virtually every federal agency describe the agency's goals and performance indicators in the strategic plans and annual performance plans and performance reports that must be submitted to Congress (US Office of Management and Budget 2001). This provides access to information about the formally stated goals of most federal agencies. (For more on the goal identification procedures, see Chun and Rainey 2005a.) The measures of the goal ambiguity dimensions we employ do not have a long history of use, so Chun and Rainey (2005a) provide extensive evidence of criterion validity, especially convergent validity. In general, convergent validity is established by demonstrating a high correlation between scores

1 The previous articles reported results for the variable 'mission comprehension ambiguity' which referred to the clarity of the organization's mission statement, measured by an index of the readability of the statement. This chapter does not discuss or report on that variable because it did not perform successfully in previous analyses, and to save space. We included this variable in the regression analyses reported later in this chapter, but it had very little effect on the results of those regressions and we deleted it from the tables we report to avoid confusion because we do not mention it in the text of the chapter.

from two different measures of the same construct (Schwab 1999). Ideally, the criterion and the measure being validated are collected by very different methods (O'Sullivan and Rassel 1995). Following this advice, we provide one or two alternative measures for each measure of the three dimensions of goal ambiguity. This evidence of convergent validity is described in detail in the previous reports of this research project (Chun and Rainey 2005a; 2005b).

Directive goal ambiguity

Directive goal ambiguity refers to the amount of interpretive leeway available in translating an organization's mission or general goals into directives and guidelines for specific actions to be taken to accomplish the mission (Scott 1992). Other scholars have treated this dimension – the room for interpretation in translating organizational missions into concrete activities and behaviours – as an important facet of goal ambiguity (Lowi 1979; Spicer and Terry 1996; Ginger 1998). For example, Lerner and Wanat's (1983) concept of 'fuzzy mandates' of public bureaucracy taps the same construct as directive goal ambiguity when they point out that fuzzy terms in legislation provide too little guidance for crisp implementation of the legislative mandates.

When the terms used in goal statements do not lend themselves to precise definition, goals lose clarity as directives for day-to-day decisions. To translate general and fuzzy formal mandates from legislation into specific guidelines, government agencies often have to refine statutory language by issuing administrative rules. We used the 'rules to laws ratio' (R/L ratio), that indicates the extent to which a federal agency needs to clarify vague Congressional intent or directions by adding specifications. This indicator is the ratio of the number of pages of administrative rules that the agency issues to the number of pages of legislation that the agency administers. This measure was drawn from Meier's work (1980) on agency power, where the R/L ratio was used as an indicator of autonomy in federal agencies because he posited that more ambiguity in statutes would allow more autonomy for agency officials. (For more on the R/L ratio, see Chun and Rainey, 2005a.)

Evaluative goal ambiguity

Evaluative goal ambiguity refers to the level of interpretive leeway that a statement of organizational goals allows in evaluating the progress toward the achievement of the mission. For performance evaluation, the organizational mission should be transformed into performance indicators and targets (Grizzle 1982). Organizations vary in the extent to which performance targets can be precisely described and in the extent to which valid and objective performance indicators are available (Smith 1999). Some organizations can express their performance targets in an objective and measurable manner that allows a minimum level of interpretive leeway. Other organizations have difficulty specifying objective, quantitative and outcome-focused performance indicators, and may use workload or process indicators rather than results or outcome indicators in performance evaluation (Merton 1957).

Evaluative goal ambiguity is measured by the percentage of subjective or workload-orientated performance indicators, as opposed to objective and results-orientated performance indicators, in each agency's performance plan. Franklin (1999) has used a similar measure in her study of strategic planning in Arizona state agencies. Data were collected from each agency's GPRA performance plan released in 1998–1999 or performance report released in 1999–2000. As with strategic plans, we collected the GPRA-required performance plans and reports either from the websites of the sample agencies or by contacting agency officials in planning units. In this study, 'subjective' performance indicators refer to measures based solely on individual perceptions about the level of organizational performance and frequently without a numerical target level. On the other hand, 'workload-oriented' performance indicators refer to input and output indicators as opposed to such 'results-oriented' ones as outcome and efficiency measures. It should be noted, however, that to distinguish 'results-oriented' indicators from 'workload-oriented' ones is not as simple as it sounds, since the difference between the two is not always clear. To deal with this problem, this study developed very specific criteria supplemented by examples in classifying the performance indicators reported in the GPRA plans and reports (see Chun and Rainey 2005a). In addition, inter-rater reliability was calculated for a subset of the sample of agencies. (For more on the reliability test, see Chun and Rainey 2005a.)

Priority goal ambiguity

Priority goal ambiguity refers to the level of interpretive leeway in deciding on priorities among multiple goals. To indicate priorities means to make decisions about which goals should take precedence over others at a given time, or to form a goal hierarchy in which the goals are vertically arranged through means-ends relationships (Richards 1986). The presence of multiple goals without any hierarchical arrangement and prioritization leaves much room for interpretation of such priorities and about which goals take precedence. This dimension is similar to several existing constructs in the goal ambiguity literature, such as goal focus (Weiss and Piderit 1999) and goal complexity (Lee et al. 1989).

For priority ambiguity, we used two indicators: (a) the number of long-term strategic goals, and (b) the number of annual performance targets. Previous research on goals in public organizations has used indicators such as these to measure the extent to which multiple organizational goals or goal-equivalents are simultaneously presented without any prioritization (Weiss and Piderit 1999; Franklin 1999). To combine the two indicators, the number of strategic goals and the number of annual performance targets, into a composite measure of priority goal ambiguity, it was necessary to standardize the indicators so that each was based on the same scale. The Z-scores of each of the indicators were used for this standardization and the average of the two Z-scores was calculated as the priority ambiguity score for each agency. (For more on the indicators, see Chun and Rainey 2005a.)

Conceptual framework and hypotheses

As described earlier, the present study focuses on four consequence variables: red tape; decentralization; reward expectancy; and job satisfaction.

Goal ambiguity and red tape

One of the most frequently-discussed consequences of organizational goal ambiguity is red tape or procedural regulations that are perceived to be excessive and detrimental by the members of the organization (see Bozeman 2000). Numerous authors have asserted that what we call directive goal ambiguity affects red tape in public organizations. These authors' observations vary, but generally converge on the assertions that government agencies often receive vague directives and mandates from legislative bodies or otherwise come to pursue diffusely-defined missions. Most government agencies do not have economic markets for their outputs and this deprives them of such performance measures as sales and profits; their executives operate under political pressures to control lower levels. The higher levels seek to control the lower levels through profusions of rules, directives, and requirements for hierarchical approvals; additional procedural constraints come from external sources such as oversight agencies; as a result, red tape proliferates (Dahl and Lindblom 1958; Downs 1967; Buchanan 1975; Warwick 1975; Lynn 1981; Rainey 1993). Rainey, Pandey, and Bozeman (1995) reported a positive relationship between managers' perceptions of goal ambiguity and their perceptions of higher levels of 'red tape'.

Priority goal ambiguity is also expected to have a positive association with red tape in public organizations. The presence of multiple goals in public organizations is often believed to lead to greater emphasis on procedural regulations (e.g., Buchanan 1975). Wilson (1989) suggested that the more external constituencies and the more goals and priorities in a government agency, the more likely the agency will develop standardized procedural constraints. Each procedural constraint, he argued, is aimed at minimizing the chance that an important goal or priority is not violated.

The survey data included responses to questions about whether the respondent's agency had eliminated or reduced several procedural constraints that reforms had targeted for elimination because of their excessively and inefficiently constraining effects. As described later, we used these to develop a measure of 'red tape reduction' which assumes that factors that increase red tape make it hard to reduce it. We tested the following hypotheses:

H1:   Federal employees in agencies with higher levels of directive goal ambiguity will perceive lower levels of red tape reduction.

H2:   Federal employees in agencies with higher levels of evaluative goal ambiguity will perceive lower levels of red tape reduction.

H3:   Federal employees in agencies with higher levels of priority goal ambiguity will perceive lower levels of red tape reduction.

Goal ambiguity and decentralization

Goal ambiguity in public organizations may be negatively related to organizational decentralization, or the degree to which power and authority are delegated to lower levels. Various authors contend that vague directives and mandates cause higher-level executives in government agencies to resist delegating their authority (e.g., Buchanan 1975; Warwick 1975; Lynn 1981). According to this interpretation, directive goal ambiguity should negatively relate to decentralization.

According to various authors, evaluative goal ambiguity should also relate negatively to decentralization. Meyer (1979), among others, argued that leaders in public agencies show reluctance to permit decentralization since there are few objective indicators that the leaders can use to hold lower levels accountable. Conversely, others observe that where public agency executives have access to clear, results-orientated performance measures, they show a greater tendency to delegate authority (e.g., Khademian 1995; Shalala 1998).

Priority goal ambiguity is also likely to be negatively associated with decentralization in public organizations. Downs (1967) suggested that the heterogeneity of goals in public bureaus leads to less delegation of discretion to subordinates. Wilson (1989) also observed that the more goals a public agency has, the more leaders seek to retain authority at the top, saying: 'It is easier to allow operators to exercise discretion when only one clear goal is to be attained. The greater the number and complexity of those goals, the riskier it is to give authority to operators' (133).

H4:   Federal employees in agencies with higher levels of directive goal ambiguity will perceive lower levels of decentralization.

H5:   Federal employees in agencies with higher levels of evaluative goal ambiguity will perceive lower levels of decentralization.

H6:   Federal employees in agencies with higher levels of priority goal ambiguity will perceive lower levels of decentralization.

Goal ambiguity and reward expectancy

Researchers who developed the Expectancy Theory of work motivation posited that human motivation for a behaviour is a function of an individual's perceived probability that the behaviour will lead to certain outcomes, and the individual's valuation of those outcomes (see Pinder 1998). A number of authors have argued that goal ambiguity in public organizations, especially in relation to performance evaluation, exerts a negative influence on reward expectancies. More ambiguous goals lead to more diffuse performance indicators. This makes it hard to design incentive systems that show employees how their efforts lead to performance that in turn leads to a reward. This also makes it hard for employees to see how their efforts link to group and organizational performance (Buchanan 1974; 1975; Perry and Porter 1982; Lan and Rainey 1992; Rainey 1993). Among the four dimensions of goal ambiguity, evaluative goal ambiguity should show the strongest relationship to reward expectancy.

H7:   Federal employees in agencies with higher levels of evaluative goal ambiguity will express lower levels of reward expectancy.

Goal ambiguity and job satisfaction

There has been little direct research which examines the relationship between organizational goal ambiguity and job satisfaction, but there are good reasons to hypothesize a relationship. Researchers have found that role ambiguity lowers job satisfaction, and organizational goal ambiguity should make it harder to avoid role ambiguity for individuals in the organization. Buchanan (1974, 1975) found in a survey that government managers expressed lower work satisfaction than managers in business firms. He interpreted this result as being due to the greater goal ambiguity in performance evaluation and the greater difficulty in prioritizing goals for the public organizations. This makes it more difficult, he argued, for public managers to sustain a feeling of efficacy that leads to job satisfaction.

H8:   Federal employees in agencies with higher levels of evaluative goal ambiguity will display lower levels of job satisfaction.
H9:   Federal employees in agencies with higher levels of priority goal ambiguity will display lower levels of job satisfaction.

Methodology

Data sources and sample

As described earlier, the data for the consequence measures were collected from the 2000 US Federal Employee Survey by the National Partnership for

Reinventing Government (NPR) and the US Office of Personnel Management (OPM). The survey was mailed in September 2000 to a random sample of 50,844 full-time employees in forty-nine federal agencies, and 31,975 surveys were returned for a response rate of 63 per cent. The sample was a representative cross-section of the target population of full-time federal civilian employees. A subset of this sample of the survey was used in the present study, that included 25,814 federal employees working for thirty-two federal agencies (a list of these agencies is available from the authors). Because of missing values, however, the number of respondents in each of the analyses below was somewhat lower than 25,814 and varied between analyses (for more information on the sample, see Chun and Rainey, 2005b).

Measures of the dependent variables

The questionnaire items in this analysis are described in **Appendix A**.

Reduction of red tape

As described in Appendix A, there were three questions in the survey that related to the perceptions of excessive procedural regulations: whether time cards had been eliminated; whether travel regulations had been simplified; and whether the hiring process had been streamlined. Procedural constraints on such areas as hiring, record keeping, and travel have often been the targets of complaints about red tape in public agencies. The questionnaire included these items to gather information about whether the agencies had actually implemented reforms to reduce constraints in these areas. These items were consistent with question-naire items used by previous research on red tape in public organizations (e.g., Rainey, Pandey and Bozeman 1995; Bozeman and Kingsley 1998; Pandey and Kingsley 2000). Factor and item analysis indicated high factor loadings for two of the questions and an acceptable Cronbach's alpha of .64, but led to the elimi-nation of the item about time cards. (For more on the results of the factor analysis, see Chun and Rainey 2005b.)

Decentralization

Based on measures used in previous research on centralization and hierarchical delegation in work organizations (e.g., Aiken and Hage 1968; Hage and Aiken 1969), two questionnaire items from the survey were identified as indicators of the extent to which power and authority were concentrated at higher levels. The two items assessed whether an individual's opinions seemed to count in the workplace and whether an individual has been given more flexibility in work.

Reward expectancy

The measure of reward expectancy was derived from answers to the questions 'Recognition and rewards are based on merit', and 'Creativity and innovation are rewarded'. These items tapped perceived possibilities of achieving rewards through performance and were in general consistent with questionnaire items used in previous research (e.g., Rainey *et al*. 1995). The two items were summed to create an index for reward expectancy.

Job satisfaction

The survey contained three questionnaire items pertaining to job satisfaction. As Appendix A indicates, these items concerned general job satisfaction, involvement in decisions, and recognition for doing a good job. Similar or identical questionnaire items have been used in many of the previous studies of job satisfaction (e.g., Bearden *et al*. 1993). Factor analysis and item analysis justified treating these items as a multi-item scale. (For more on the results of the factor analysis, see Chun and Rainey 2005b.)

Measures of the control variables

Individual-level controls

Since the measures of the consequence variables are based on individual perceptions, it is important to control for the respondents' personal attributes. Data on some basic demographic variables, however, including age, gender, and race, were not available in the data set because of the Freedom of Information Act provisions. Still, those on several important work-related individual characteristics, such as tenure, pay grade, job category, and managerial level, were available and we used them as control variables. (For more on individual-level control variables, see Chun and Rainey 2005b.)

Organizational-level controls

To control for organizational characteristics, we used seven variables, including organizational size, organizational age, institutional location, financial publicness, policy problem complexity, type of policy responsibility, and the need for political compromise among competing demands from constituencies. In the first report of this project (Chun and Rainey 2005a), we analysed the last five of these variables as 'antecedents' of goal ambiguity. The measure of *financial publicness* was the percentage of a federal agency's financial resources from government sources. The *need for political compromise* among competing demands from constituencies was measured by the number of clientele groups for a federal agency (Meier 1980; Rourke 1984). As the number of

Table 6.1 Descriptive statistics of consequence and independent variables

	N	Mean	Standard Deviation	Minimum	Maximum
Reduction of red tape	14,951	4.88	1.97	2.00	10.00
Decentralization	23,978	6.47	2.12	2.00	10.00
Expectancy	24,064	5.64	2.18	2.00	10.00
Job satisfaction	25,442	9.48	3.04	3.00	15.00
Directive ambiguity	25,814	4.45	3.94	0.97	16.27
Evaluative ambiguity	25,814	58.11	23.08	12.50	94.10
Priority ambiguity	25,814	−0.31	0.96	−1.14	3.96

Note: The number of respondents varied because of missing values.

clientele groups for a public organization increases, in general so do competing demands from the groups (Hargrove and Glidewell 1990). The *type of policy responsibility* (regulatory, non-regulatory, or hybrid) was identified based on two steps, using the *Congressional Quarterly's Federal Regulatory Directory* and the percentage of budget for personnel compensation. Professional staff ratio (PSR) was used as a proxy measure of *policy problem complexity*. The measure of *organizational size* was the natural logarithm of the number of full-time employees in 1997. The measure of *organizational age* was the number of years after the agency's establishment. *Institutional location* refers to whether a federal agency is inside the executive departments or outside. (These organizational-level controls are not described in the Appendix. For more on measuring them, see Chun and Rainey 2005a or contact the authors.)

While we will not discuss the regression results for these control variables below, the value of including them is evident in those results. For example, organizational size shows a very statistically significant relationship to each of the four dependent variables. Most organizational researchers would hypothesize these relations – e.g., that larger organizations have more trouble reducing red tape and decentralizing – but this makes it very important to take them into account in our analysis.

Results

Although the hypotheses were stated as bivariate relations, we tested them with ordinary least squares (OLS) regression analyses in order to control for the individual and organizational characteristics (for the results of tests to verify the assumptions regarding OLS regression analyses, see Chun and Rainey 2005b). The descriptive statistics for independent and consequence variables are presented in Table 6.1 and those for control variables are described in Chun and

Table 6.2 Results of regression analysis for reduction of red tape

Variables	Unstandardized coefficient	Standard error	Standardized coefficient
Individual-level factors			
Tenure	.06***	.01	.06
Pay grade	−.06**	.02	−.03
Professional	−.02	.05	−.00
Administrative	−.33***	.06	.06
Technical	−.08	.07	.01
Clerical	−.44***	.09	.04
Wage grade	−.12	.10	.01
Team leader	−.06	.05	−.00
Supervisor	−.20***	.05	−.03
Manager	−.20**	.06	−.02
Executive	−.14	.13	.00
Organizational-level factors			
Organizational size	−.12***	.02	−.06
Organizational age	−.001***	.00	−.05
Institutional location	−.17***	.05	.03
Problem complexity	−.003*	.00	.03
Competing demands	−.003**	.00	.04
Financial publicness	−.003***	.00	.05
Non-regulatory policy	−.31***	.06	.07
Hybrid policy	−.22**	.07	−.05
Goal ambiguity dimensions			
Directive ambiguity	−.007***	.00	−.06
Evaluative ambiguity	−.07***	.00	−.08
Priority ambiguity	−.02**	.02	−.04

R^2 = .048	Adjusted R^2 = .047
F Value = 32.30***	Sample size = 14665

* Significant at .05 level
** Significant at .01 level
*** Significant at .001 level

Rainey (2005b). (A correlation matrix for all the variables is available from the authors.)

Red tape

Table 6.2 shows the regression results for reduction of red tape. Hypothesis 1, that directive goal ambiguity would be negatively related to the perception of red tape reduction, was supported by the data (beta = −.06, p < .001). Employees working for agencies with higher levels of directive goal ambiguity perceive lower

Table 6.3 Results of regression analysis for decentralization

Variables	Unstandardized coefficient	Standard error	Standardized coefficient
Individual-level factors			
Tenure	−.003	.00	−.00
Pay grade	.25***	.01	.12
Professional	.11**	.04	.02
Administrative	.21***	.05	.03
Technical	.18**	.06	.02
Clerical	.56***	.07	.05
Wage grade	−.001	.00	.00
Team leader	.38***	.05	.05
Supervisor	.38***	.05	.05
Manager	.74***	.06	.07
Executive	.83***	.13	.04
Organizational-level factors			
Organizational size	−.12***	.02	−.04
Organizational age	−.0006	.00	−.01
Institutional location	.33***	.04	.05
Problem complexity	.01***	.00	.09
Competing demands	.001	.00	.02
Financial publicness	.0003	.00	.00
Non-regulatory policy	.24***	.05	.05
Hybrid policy	−.13*	.07	−.02
Goal ambiguity dimensions			
Directive ambiguity	−.01**	.00	−.03
Evaluative ambiguity	−.001	.00	−.01
Priority ambiguity	−.07**	.02	−.03

R^2 = .054	Adjusted R^2 = .053
F Value = 57.87***	Sample Size = 23427

* Significant at .05 level
** Significant at .01 level
*** Significant at .001 level

levels of red tape reduction. Evaluative goal ambiguity was also hypothesized to have a negative association with the reduction of red tape, as noted by Hypothesis 2. The data supported this hypothesis as well (beta = −.08, p < .001). The results also supported Hypothesis 3, that priority goal ambiguity would be negatively related to the perceived reduction of red tape (beta = −.04, p < .01).

Decentralization

Table 6.3 presents the regression results for decentralization. Hypothesis 4 predicted that directive goal ambiguity would have a negative impact on

Table 6.4 Results of regression analysis for expectancy

Variables	Unstandardized coefficient	Standard error	Standardized coefficient
Individual-level factors			
Tenure	.0001	.00	.00
Pay grade	.12***	.01	.05
Professional	.15***	.04	.03
Administrative	.08	.05	.01
Technical	−.002	.06	.00
Clerical	.34***	.08	.03
Wage grade	−.07	.08	−.00
Team leader	.18***	.05	.02
Supervisor	.55***	.05	.07
Manager	.85***	.06	.08
Executive	1.57***	.14	.07
Organizational-level factors			
Organizational size	−.08***	.02	−.03
Organizational age	.001***	.00	.04
Institutional location	.35***	.05	.05
Problem complexity	.01***	.00	.10
Competing demands	.002*	.00	.02
Financial publicness	.002**	.00	.03
Non-regulatory policy	.38***	.05	.08
Hybrid policy	−.09	.07	−.01
Goal ambiguity dimensions			
Directive ambiguity	.01	.00	.02
Evaluative ambiguity	−.006***	.00	−.07
Priority ambiguity	−.16***	.02	−.07
R^2 = .049		Adjusted R^2 = .048	
F Value = 52.79***		Sample Size = 23510	

* Significant at .05 level
** Significant at .01 level
*** Significant at .001 level

decentralization and the data supported the hypothesis (beta $= -.03$, p $< .01$)). Hypothesis 5, that evaluative goal ambiguity would also have a negative impact on decentralization was not supported (beta $= -.01$, p $> .05$). Hypothesis 6 predicted a negative relationship between priority goal ambiguity and decentralization and the results supported the hypothesis (beta $= -.03$, p $< .01$).

Reward expectancy

Table 6.4 shows that Hypothesis 7, which proposed that evaluative goal ambiguity would be negatively related to reward expectancy, was supported by the

Table 6.5 Results of regression analysis for job satisfaction

Variables	Unstandardized coefficient	Standard error	Standardized coefficient
Individual-level factors			
Tenure	.002	.01	.00
Pay grade	.22***	.02	.07
Professional	.17**	.06	.02
Administrative	.15*	.07	.01
Technical	.09	.09	.00
Clerical	.37***	.11	.02
Wage grade	.05	.10	.00
Team leader	.36***	.07	.03
Supervisor	.39***	.07	.03
Manager	1.06***	.09	.07
Executive	1.49***	.20	.04
Organizational-level factors			
Organizational size	−.16***	.02	−.04
Organizational age	.0009	.00	.01
Institutional location	.51***	.07	.05
Problem complexity	.01***	.00	.06
Competing demands	.005***	.00	.03
Financial publicness	.003**	.00	.03
Non-regulatory policy	.39***	.08	.06
Hybrid policy	−.04	.10	−.00
Goal ambiguity dimensions			
Directive ambiguity	.01	.01	.02
Evaluative ambiguity	−.006***	.00	−.04
Priority ambiguity	−.10**	.03	−.03

R^2 = .037	Adjusted R^2 = .036
F Value = 41.82***	Sample size = 24875

* Significant at .05 level
** Significant at .01 level
*** Significant at .001 level

data (beta $= -.07$, p $< .001$). Although we had stated no hypotheses about it, priority goal ambiguity showed a significant and negative relationship with reward expectancy (beta $= -.07$, p $< .001$).

Job satisfaction

In support of Hypotheses 8 and 9, Table 6.5 shows a significant negative relationship between evaluative goal ambiguity and job satisfaction (beta $= .04$, $p < .001$) and between priority goal ambiguity and job satisfaction (beta $= -.03$, $p < .01$).

Discussion and conclusions

The interpretation of the results should take into account the performance of the goal ambiguity measures in the previous reports of this research project (Chun and Rainey 2005a, 2005b). The validity of the new measures of goal ambiguity used in the present study was clearly demonstrated by the findings in the previous analysis of antecedents, together with the findings in the analysis of the impacts on perceived organizational performance. This provides evidence supporting the use of these measures to test hypotheses about consequence variables in addition to organizational performance. To be sure, one might say that the results of the present study are disappointing because all of the statistically significant findings have small effect sizes (small R-square statistics). Still, one can observe that it is encouraging to get results consistent with theoretical literature since the measures of the consequence variables came from a pre-existing survey that was designed for purposes other than this study. The present study shows statistically significant support for eight out of nine hypotheses drawn from theoretical discussions, even after controlling for an array of individual- and organizational-level variables.

In general, the results show that the measures of goal ambiguity have negative relations to measures of reduction of red tape, decentralization, reward expectancy and job satisfaction and that the different measures of organizational goal ambiguity had different patterns of relations with these variables. The significant and negative relationships of three goal ambiguity measures to red tape reduction add another finding, with more objective measures of goal ambiguity, to the small set of studies that have found similar results with more subjective measures of goal ambiguity (e.g., Lan and Rainey 1992; Rainey *et al.* 1995). The analysis also provides controls for many relevant variables. For example, Bozeman (2000) has emphasized the importance of controlling for managerial level in analysing red tape and other structural variables, and researchers have repeatedly found that managerial level relates to work satisfaction and similar variables. Our analysis provides a control for managerial level, as well as many other variables. These findings support the assertions of many authors, reviewed in the development of the hypotheses.

Contrary to our hypothesis, evaluative ambiguity showed no significant relationship to decentralization, failing to support the assertions that inability to state clear, results-oriented performance measures impedes decentralization in government agencies (e.g., Meyer 1979; Shalala 1998). The negative relationships for directive and priority goal ambiguity, however, do support assertions that vague mandates and multiple goals impede decentralization.

Evaluative and priority goal ambiguity showed significant negative relations to reward expectancy and work satisfaction. These results support observations about the greater difficulty that many public organizations may have due to difficulties in stating clear and results-orientated performance criteria (that would reduce evaluative goal ambiguity), and in setting clear priorities among goals (that would reduce priority goal ambiguity). As discussed in the literature review, authors have argued that these conditions make it harder to give clear performance goals to employees and to show them how their work influences the organization's performance, and this in turn lowers reward expectancy and work satisfaction (e.g., Buchanan 1974, 1975; Perry and Porter 1982; Rainey 1993). In addition, however, our analysis of variations among public organizations on these dimensions moves us in the direction of being able to analyse which ones have this problem, when, and to what degree. Directive goal ambiguity showed no significant relationship to reward expectancy and work satisfaction. The measure of directive goal ambiguity focuses on the volume of rules relative to the volume of the law. The result suggests that a vague mandate leading to more rules does not have a strong influence on employees' perception of work rewards and sense of satisfaction, and a weaker influence than the ability of people in the organization to state results-oriented and quantifiable performance indicators, and to prioritize goals.

Together with the findings in the previous report on the relation of goal ambiguity to organizational performance (Chan and Rainey 2005b), the results of the present study generally support the desirability of clear goals and objectives for government agencies. Our results support the conclusion suggested by many management experts, that goal clarification processes in government agencies can reduce excessively constraining procedural regulations, support more decentralization and hence autonomy in the workplace and increase levels of reward expectancy and job satisfaction. Yet the results in themselves cannot resolve such questions as whether some agencies simply have advantages over others in the feasibility of clarifying their goals, since assigned functions and political and institutional factors influence agency goals (Chun and Rainey 2005a). In addition, we need to keep in mind that various observers have pointed out that clarifying goals can provoke political controversy and have advised public administrators to move cautiously in expressing and divulging goals (Lindblom 1959); goal clarification can involve a managerially sound strategy but also a politically irrational approach. Further, to try to quantify something inherently unquantifiable can produce dysfunctional results and impede organizational effectiveness. To resolve these questions, we need more research with refined conceptual and methodological tools. Together with the previous articles of this research project (Chun and Rainey 2005a, 2005b), the present study shows where we stand now and provides valuable support for further development of better concepts and measures of the goal characteristics of government agencies.

REFERENCES

Aiken, M. and Hage, J. (1968) 'Organizational independence and intra-organizational structure', *American Sociological Review*, **33**: 912–930.

Barzelay, M. (2001) *The new public management: Improving research and policy dialogue.* Berkeley: University of California Press.

Bearden, W., Netemeyer, R. and Mobley, M. (1993) *Handbook of marketing scales.* Newbury Park, CA: Sage.

Boyne, G. A. and Walker, R. M. (2004) 'Strategy content and public service organizations', *Journal of Public Administration Research and Theory*, **14**: 231–252.

Bozeman, B. (2000) *Bureaucracy and red tape.* Upper Saddle River, NJ: Prentice-Hall.

Bozeman, B. and Kingsley, G. (1998) 'Risk culture in public and private organizations', *Public Administration Review*, **58**: 109–118.

Buchanan, B. (1974) 'Government managers, business executives, and organizational commitment', *Public Administration Review*, **35**: 339–347.

Buchanan, B. (1975) 'Red tape and the service ethic: some unexpected differences between public and private managers', *Administration and Society*, **6**: 423–438.

Chun, Y. H. and Rainey, H. (2005a) 'Goal ambiguity in US federal agencies', *Journal of Public Administration Research and Theory*, **15**: 1–30.

Chun, Y. H. and Rainey, H. (2005b) 'Goal ambiguity and organizational performance in US federal agencies', *Journal of Public Administration Research and Theory*, **15**: 529–557.

Dahl, R. and Lindblom, C. (1958) *Politics, economics, and welfare.* New York: Harper and Row.

Downs, A. (1967) *Inside bureaucracy.* Boston, MA: Little, Brown.

Drucker, P. (1980) 'The deadly sins in public administration', *Public Administration Review*, **40**: 103–106.

Franklin, A. (1999) 'Managing for results in Arizona: A fifth-year report card', *Public Productivity and Management Review*, **23**: 194–209.

Ginger, C. (1998) 'Interpreting roads in roadless areas: organizational culture, ambiguity, and change in agency responses to policy mandates', *Administration and Society*, **29**: 723–757.

Grizzle, G. (1982) 'Measuring state and local government performance: issues to resolve before implementing a performance measurement system', *State and Local Government Review*, **14**: 132–136.

Hage, J. and Aiken, M. (1969) 'Routine technology, social structure, and organizational goals', *Administrative Science Quarterly*, **14**: 366–376.

Hargrove, E. and Glidewell, J. (eds.) (1990) *Impossible jobs in public management.* Lawrence, KS: University of Kansas Press.

Khademian, A. (1995) 'Reinventing a government corporation: professional priorities and a clear bottom line', *Public Administration Review*, **55**: 17–29.

Lan, Z. and Rainey, H. (1992) 'Goals, rules, and effectiveness in public, private and hybrid organizations: More evidence on frequent assertions about differences', *Journal of Public Administration Research and Theory*, **2**: 5–28.

Lee, T., Locke, E. and Latham, G. (1989) 'Goal setting theory and job performance' in Pervin, L. (ed.) *Goal concepts in personality and social psychology.* Hillsdale, NJ: Erlbaum, pp. 291–326.

Lerner, A. and Wanat, J. (1983) 'Fuzziness and bureaucracy', *Public Administration Review*, **43**: 500–509.

Lindblom, C. E. (1959) 'The science of muddling through,' *Public Administration Review*, **19**: 79–88.

Locke, E., Chah, D., Harrison, S, and Lustgarten, N. (1989) 'Separating the effects of goal specificity from goal level', *Organizational Behavior and Human Decision Processes*, **43**: 270–288.

Lowi, T. (1979) *The end of liberalism*. New York: Norton.

Lynn, L. E. Jr., (1981) *Managing the public's business*. New York: Basic Books.

Meier, K. J. (1980) 'Measuring organizational power: resources and autonomy of government agencies', *Administration and Society*, **12**: 357–375.

Merton, R. (1957) *Social theory and social structure*. New York: Free Press.

Meyer, M. W. (1979) *Change in public bureaucracies*. Cambridge: Cambridge University Press.

O'Sullivan, E. and Rassel, G. (1995) *Research methods for public administrators*. White Plains, NY: Longman.

Pandey, S. and Kingsley, G. (2000) 'Examining red tape in public and private organizations: alternative explanations from a social psychological model', *Journal of Public Administration Research and Theory*, **10**: 779–799.

Perry, J. and Porter, L. (1982) 'Factors affecting the context for motivation in public organizations', *Academy of Management Review*, **7**: 89–98.

Pinder, C. (1998) *Work motivation in organizational behavior*. Upper Saddle River, NJ: Prentice Hall.

Pollitt, C. and Bouckaert, G. (2000) *Public management reform*. Oxford: Oxford University Press.

Rainey, H. (1993) 'Toward a theory of goal ambiguity in public organizations', in Perry, J. (ed.) *Research in public administration*. Vol. 2. Greenwich, CT: JAI Press, pp. 121–166.

Rainey, H. (2003) *Understanding and managing public organizations*. 3rd edn. San Francisco: Jossey-Bass.

Rainey, H., Pandey, S. and Bozeman, B. (1995) 'Research note: Public and private managers' perceptions of red tape', *Public Administration Review*, **55**: 567–574.

Richards, M. (1986) *Setting strategic goals and objectives*. 2nd edn. New York: West.

Rourke, F. (1984) *Bureaucracy, politics, and public policy*. Boston, MA: Little Brown.

Scott, W. (1992) *Organizations: Rational, natural, and open systems*. Englewood Cliffs, NJ: Prentice-Hall.

Shalala, D. (1998) 'Are large public organizations manageable?' *Public Administration Review*, **58**: 284–289.

Schwab, D. (1999) *Research methods for organizational studies*. Mahwah, NJ: Lawrence Erlbaum Associates.

Smith, D. (1999) *Make success measurable!* New York: John Wiley and Sons.

Spicer, M. and Terry, L. (1996) 'Administrative interpretation of statutes: A constitutional view on the "new world order" of public administration', *Public Administration Review*, **56**: 249–254.

US Office of Management and Budget (2001) *OMB Circular No. A-11*. Washington DC: US Office of Management and Budget.

Warwick, D. (1975) *A theory of public bureaucracy*. Cambridge, MA: Harvard University Press.

Weiss, J. and Piderit, S. (1999) 'The value of mission statements in public agencies', *Journal of Public Administration Research and Theory*, **9**: 193–223.

Wilson, J. (1989) *Bureaucracy*. New York: Basic Books.

Appendix A. Questionnaire items from the survey

Consequence variables (5-Point Likert-type items with 1 for 'strongly disagree' and 5 for 'strongly agree' or with 1 for 'not at all' and 5 for 'a very great extent').

Reduction of red tape (Cronbach's alpha = .65)

To what extent, has your organization implemented simplified travel regulations? (Not at all to a very great extent.)

To what extent has your organization streamlined the process for hiring employees?

Decentralization (Cronbach's alpha = .69)

In my organization, at the place I work, my opinions seem to count. (Strongly disagree to strongly agree.)

In the past two years, I have been given more flexibility in how I accomplish my work.

Expectancy (Cronbach's alpha = .73)

In my organization, recognition and rewards are based on merit. (Strongly disagree to strongly agree.)

In my organization, creativity and innovation are rewarded.

Job Satisfaction (Cronbach's alpha = .87)

Considering everything, how satisfied are you with your job? (Very dissatisfied to very satisfied.)

How satisfied are you with your involvement in decisions that affect your work?

How satisfied are you with the recognition you receive for doing a good job?

Individual level control variables

Tenure

How long have you been a Federal Government employee (excluding military service)?

1. Less than 1 year
2. 1 to 5 years
3. 6 to 10 years
4. 11 to 15 years
5. 16 to 20 years
6. 21 to 25 years
7. 26 to 30 years
8. 31+ years

Pay grade

What is your pay grade?

1. 01 to 05
2. 06 to 10
3. 11 to 12
4. 13 to 15
5. Above 15 (SL, ST, ALJ)
6. SES

Job category
What is your job category?

1. Professional
2. Administrative
3. Technician
4. Clerical
5. Other

Managerial level
What is your level of supervisory responsibility?

1. None, I am not a supervisor
2. Team leader
3. First line supervisor
4. Manager
5. Executive

7 Performance control and public organizations

Patrick Kenis

Introduction

This chapter is designed to contribute to the discussion on determining the performance of public organizations by investigating the relationship between performance control systems and performance. It cannot be assumed that performance control systems automatically lead to performance. Neither shall we assume that management control systems are the same as performance control. To do so would be a case of 'managementism' which has been described by Dubnick (2003: 9) as a phenomenon where 'management is seen as the premium mobile that shapes and drives the basic logic of the common research agenda for contemporary Public Administration'. Consequently, we will demonstrate that different forms of performance control do exist. Which form is the most likely to contribute to performance depends on a number of conditions.

In this chapter, we first give a definition of control systems; second, present different types of performance control systems; and third, formulate propositions about how different control approaches contribute to organizational performance. In the last part we discuss the limitations and the opportunities from these insights in providing a solid basis for improving the performance of public organizations.

The definition of performance control and types of performance control

Performance control is defined here as 'the process of monitoring performance, comparing it with some standards, and then providing rewards and adjustments' (see Ouchi 1977: 97). This definition should not be misinterpreted, as has often been done, by equating it with performance management, management control systems, management accounting systems, organizational control and management control (Ashworth *et al.* 2002). Control has often been interpreted as an administrative process 'designed to regulate the activities of organizational participants, and by implication, output' (Mills 1983: 445) via control mechanisms such as authority structures, rules, policies, standard operating procedures, budgets, reward and incentive systems (Abernethy and Stoelwinder 1995). All this suggests that performance control is studied mainly from the perspective of the manager or the controller, who use a set of practices or systems to elicit desired actions, or changes in agents' behaviour regarding certain outcomes.

In contrast, this chapter sticks to the generic definition of Ouchi, which conceptualizes performance control as a cybernetic process. A cybernetic process has generally been described as consisting of the following sequence of activities: setting the reference level (also sometimes called objective or standard), the measurement of performance via a comparison between the outcome and the pre-stated reference level; the feeding back of information about unwanted system variances and taking corrective action if necessary (see Green and Welsh 1988; Hofstede 1981). Only a process that fulfils these characteristics is considered to be performance control. It should be noted that the approach taken here is more and at the same time less than what has generally been discussed in the organizational literature. It is less because *only* those systems which can potentially be characterized by the complete cybernetic control process are included. It is more because it allows the inclusion of *any* type of performance control as long as it can potentially be characterized by the complete cybernetic control process. This is quite different from the bulk of the organizational literature where control in general and cybernetic control in particular have been described and analysed from a managerial perspective (see Rus 2005). In the organizational literature by definition the standards are set by the manager and by definition the manager is considered the controller. Both starting points are, however, by no means necessary according to the definition of cybernetic control. The fathers of cybernetic control (Wiener and Ashby) clearly did not define cybernetic control from a managerial perspective (see Wiener 1948; Ashby 1952; see also Follet 1937, 1951).

Distinguishing different forms of performance control is of paramount importance given the approach chosen here. It would be fatal to conclude that a public organization is not performing because a specific type of performance control cannot be observed. Consequently, we have to be as open as possible when identifying forms of performance control in public organizations.

On the basis of this definition we can investigate the different forms of performance control as present in organizational practice. For the sake of space and clarity, we distinguish between just two types of performance control: 'management performance control' and 'agent control'. These have been chosen as they are in many respects extreme forms – consequently, they provide a good basis for formulating propositions on the relationship between performance control and organizational performance.

Management performance control

This type of control is characterized by the highlighting of the presence of tools and instruments which are at the disposal of the controllers. A majority of the control, performance and accountability literature concentrates on this type of performance control. This attention fits a conventional functionalist contingency-based approach, which assumes that management control systems are adopted to assist managers (for a comprehensive review of the last twenty years of work in this field see Chenhall 2003). Few instruments and technologies have been developed to assist managers in their control task. The literature which fits this type concentrates on performance control management, with the emphasis on management. Consequently, there is a tendency here to confuse performance management with performance.

Different academic fields have contributed to this work. Organization studies was one of the first disciplines to discuss control tools for managers. This included the scientific management approaches, but equally organizational development approaches and contingency theory approaches. There is, apart from the more prescriptive and positivistic literature, also the literature that informs us about the limits of management control from the perspective of the controller (see e.g., Ackoff 1967, Ashworth *et al.* 2002, as well as Mintzberg's (1989) famous question: 'Why do managers not use the information as they apparently should?').

Institutional economics has also contributed substantially to the description and analysis of this type of performance control. Williamson's 'model of control loss' (Williamson 1971) and principal-agent theory (Alchian and Demetz 1972) fit this type. Principal-agent theory does take into account the agent (i.e. the controlled) but only in as far as the principal (the controller) needs instruments to control the agent's behaviour (see, in particular, Perrow 1986).

The field of accountancy is almost exclusively committed to the study of this type of performance control. Here, the dominant perspective is 'to affect the conduct of individuals in such a way that they act freely, yet in accordance with specified economic norms' (Miller 2001). And as Covaleski and Dirsmith observe: 'The prescriptive character of managerial accounting information espoused by this traditional school of thought is essentially internal and downward and also prescriptive in character' (1996: 6). The field of accountancy has developed, analysed and prescribed countless instruments to achieve this goal.

In the field of public administration this perspective is also rather prevalent. According to Dubnick, 'managerialism' dominates the field of public administration these days. Lately, however, it has taken a slightly different form called 'managementism' (Dubnick 2003). According to Dubnick (2003: 9) 'managementism' (represented by, e.g., Lynn 2001 and Lynn *et al.* 2000) makes no overt normative claims and is openly critical of easy answers, but nevertheless builds upon the foundational assumptions about the central role of management in both public and private sectors (see also Metcalfe 2001 and Salamon and Odus's 'The *Tools* of Government' 2002 [emphasis added]).

It should be clear that this system is historically very present in the literature and we can expect it to remain so in the future. I also expect researchers and others will keep searching for better and more effective tools for managers to control organizational performance.[1]

The prevalence of this type in the overall literature on performance control, however, is somewhat surprising, given the little (or at least very mixed) empirical evidence available on the relationship between the usage of tools and the actual performance of organizations (see Dubnick 2003, Boyne 2003a, Nicholson-Crotty and O'Toole 2004). A large part of this literature is prescriptive and advocates non-validated instruments and tools. The powerful rhetoric connected to this perspective seems to have gained the status of a 'rationalized myth' (see Meyer and Rowan 1977, Czarniawska-Joerges 1988, Modell 2004). It is yet to be seen to what extent this 'performance management' is actually 'in place' in public organizations and is thus likely to be related to performance.

Agent control

Czarniawska-Joerges (1988: 415) noted two tendencies in the organizational control literature: first, 'that organizational control, and even more so managerial control, is understood as a form of influence, steering or regulation exerted by managerial levels *vis-à-vis* non-managerial levels in organizations' and second, that the literature 'has concentrated on the means or methods of control' and concludes that 'such an approach can be explained, at least in part by the highly pragmatic and management-oriented character of most studies'. What she is pointing to here is that next to 'managerial control' (what we call 'management performance control') other forms of organizational control also exist. As we will see in more detail below, units within organizations often have significant control over standard setting and monitoring of their own performance. This is an empirical phenomenon we propose to label 'agent control'. This phenomenon has already been observed by many, but has never reached the level of consolidated attention. Zald (1978), for example, in his excellent article 'On the social control of industries', clearly emphasizes the importance of targets of control engaging in their own control practices. It is exactly this phenomenon which is defined here as agent control. Often agent control has been perceived (by the managerial literature) as goal-incongruent, deviant, anomalous, or pathological behavior (Dermer 1988). We believe this to be an empirical question.

---

1 Marshall Meyer (2002), for example, after having formulated a fundamental critique of the Balanced Scorecard, formulates a new performance instrument, the ABPA (Activity-based profitability analysis).

Combined with the cybernetic approach presented before, the question then becomes: which criteria do actors (whether they be individuals, groups or organizations) use to assess themselves, what type of information do they gather on how they are doing, and how do they use this information to eventually adjust to deviations; or, in a somewhat shortened version: 'how do actors know how they are doing, and what do they do with the information about how they are doing?' It should be clear by now that agent control is not limited to subordinates in an organization, but that it can be observed at every level of the organization (see e.g., Birnbaum 1990).

In order to be more specific about what exactly is meant here, it might be worthwhile to point first at some of the rare studies which have taken such a perspective and which are mainly from the field of public administration (for an excellent overview of studies from other fields see Rus 2005) and secondly, to indicate how agent control differs from other seemingly common phenomena as discussed in the literature.

Davies and Francis (1974), for example, found that the different types of personnel within hospitals agreed on the primary objective of the hospitals (i.e. the system) as being high-quality care, but they disagreed, based on their profession/occupation, as to the specific goals to be pursued. Furthermore, they found that the two most important criteria used by the NHS (i.e. the controlling agent) in performance evaluations of hospitals, such as bed occupancy and length of stay, were rated as being of the lowest importance by hospital staff members. Moreover, they also found a discrepancy in the goals to be pursued among organizational members, based on their professional/occupational adherence, which suggests that there are at least three sub-systems (nurses, junior doctors and consultants). Put in our words, it seems that agent control is a highly prevalent phenomenon in the organizations they studied (see also Chapter 4 of this volume by Addicott and Ferlie).

In another study Meyers *et al.* (2001) studied the governance and management of organizations delivering welfare at the local level in three US states. Their question was whether, and how, local welfare agencies have been able to operationalize goals consistent with the substantive policy goals of the state (i.e. the external controller of the agent). They found that the organizational goals in the local welfare organizations were substantially divergent from the top-down imposed-policy goals. More studies pointing towards the relevance and significance of agent control in public administration will be mentioned in the presentation of the propositions.

At this point it is also important to point out the difference between agent control and other seemingly related concepts such as self-control, self-evaluation, teamwork, self-managing teams, self-monitoring, self-regulation, self-leadership, professional control, social control and communities of practice. Although the study of these types of performance control can contribute to our understanding of agent control they are nevertheless different. There is no room to elaborate on this here, but Rus (2005) has shown that all these differ from agent control in one or more of the following ways: agent control focuses not on cognitive processes but on actual practices; it is not limited to exceptional situations; does not assume an integrated goal hierarchy; is not a management tool; can be exercised by any member of the organization; involves the controller and the controlled as the same; indicates that many norms can be relevant at the same time; and uses norms that do not need to be internalized. Of all these forms of control the 'communities of practice' type has been found to come closest to agent control.

After having introduced these two rather extreme forms of control we now turn to a presentation of propositions relating forms of performance control to organizational performance.

Propositions on the relationship between the type of performance control and organizational performance

The propositions presented are about how and when the two different control approaches distinguished here can be expected to have an impact on organizational performance. As a reminder, performance control has been defined here as the process of monitoring performance, comparing it with some standards and then providing rewards and adjustments. From this definition we can deduce that performance control has three dimensions: the reference used (also called objective or standard); the measurement of performance via a comparison between the outcome and the pre-stated reference level; and, the feedback of information about unwanted system variances and taking corrective action if necessary. How well a performance control type deals with these dimensions in a given situation is believed to determine its effectiveness.

In what follows we formulate a number of propositions relating the type of control performance to these three dimensions. The objective is mainly to demonstrate that there is no one best way of performance control, or in other words, it is not possible to develop general principles that are applicable to performance control at all times and places; any form of performance control is not equally effective, or in other words, performance control matters; and what the best form of performance control is depends on the nature of the context.

Propositions related to the criteria used

There are different possible situations in which clear criteria for assessing the effectiveness of an organization are not present, are rather unspecific or are not yet developed. We can think here of interorganizational networks, in which the need to collaborate is clear, but in which it is less clear what the criteria are for assessing whether the network is a success or not (see Korssen-van Raaij 2005). Or, as Boyne observed for the case of public organizations: (1) public organizations might not have clearly formulated formal goals, which means that goals could be ambiguous; (2) 'the formal goals that are explicit are likely to be broad mission statements rather than concrete objectives' (Boyne, 2003b: 215). Criteria can also be rather vague in terms of observing whether they have been achieved or not. Creativity, initiative, the creation of new knowledge, flexibility, etc., are all examples of such criteria (e.g., Bartlett and Ghoshal 1995). In addition, there is the fact that criteria are different depending on the current phase in which the organization finds itself. At early stages in their development outcome or impact criteria are not necessarily the best to assess whether the organization is performing well or not.

In all the situations described above it seems better to rely on the local, temporal and particularistic criteria of agents to assess the performance of the organization. Management control systems tend to focus on the short term and might bring in criteria which are inappropriate for a specific phase in which the organization finds itself or which do not do justice to the subtlety of some criteria (e.g., creativity or performance of schoolchildren) (see Bohte and Meier, 2000). It is much more likely that agents will take these specificities into account than any type of management performance system.

This can be stated formally as a research proposition:

P1: In organizations where clear objectives and goals are missing or are not yet developed, agent control is expected to contribute more to performance than management performance control.

Some organizations are characterized by the fact that they have staff who have precise ideas about the criteria they use in their work and on which the organization should be assessed. The most common example is the one in which professionals play an important role. Professionals do not usually relate to the organization's criteria for success, but more commonly to the criteria that are central to their profession and which they learned during their training. Riccucci *et al.* (2004) conducted a survey on the performance criteria discrepancy in public agencies between the organizational leaders and the actual street-level implementers. The authors surveyed 256 front-line workers, managers and policy makers in four US states and found that ' . . . front-line workers in local welfare systems consider goals related to eligibility determination to be more important to their agencies than goals related to either the employment or welfare deterrence/behavior modification goals of recent welfare reforms. Goal perceptions varied substantially, however, with agent setting, even after controlling for a variety of management and personal factors' (Riccucci *et al.* 2004: 445). Similarly, in a study of firefighters who lost their lives, Weick (1996) reports that they disobeyed the order to drop their tools (so they could run faster) because they had been heavily socialized by years of training to never drop their tools.

Maynard-Moody and Musheno (2000) found in a study of street-level workers that they simply apply the rules when the rules fit the individual situation of the client, but when the policy rules do not exactly fit the individual situation of the client, they tweak the rules as far as possible to help their clients.

The literature does not only report about these discrepancies, it also reports about the negative or dysfunctional consequences these discrepancies can have on performance. For example, Ashworth *et al.* (2002) demonstrated ritualistic compliance as a result of the discrepancy between externally imposed and agent goals, which easily can be seen to result in overall decreased performance of the organization. Other effects found as a result of this are: refusal to implement, poor performance by the agents, absenteeism, alienation, internal inactivity, etc. (Chatman 1991; Wilensky 1964). Not only on the individual level, but also on the organizational level such effects have been observed: for example, goal-displacement, cheating, collecting of useless data, etc. (Bohte and Meier 2000, Coplin *et al.* 2002).

The relationship between agents having distinct performance criteria and the effects on performance can be stated in the following proposition:

P2: In organizations where the staff has distinct criteria for assessing performance, the use of management performance control can be expected to lead to negative consequences and thus to a lower level of performance.

In many organizations a lot of criteria are used to assess performance. They might be as different as: efficiency, efficacy, quality, quantity, justice, good governance, learning, client directedness, innovativeness, etc. Some of these criteria are even in conflict – for example, efficiency and innovativeness. The question is, however, how this amalgam of criteria can lead to overall performance of the organization. There are two reasons to expect that a management control system is more effective in doing so than agent control.

The first is that research has discovered that in situations characterized by information equivocality and uncertainty, individuals engage in 'role making' (Grean 1967 in Mills 1983), that is they define what should be done and how it should be done, by defining boundaries of their own and thus decreasing the ambiguity of the situation. This is something Hill (2003) refers to when pointing to the inherent ambiguities contained in public service agencies, which result in role making, conflicting performance standards and the creation of new practices, in cases where there are no 'strong professional associations that establish norms of practice and procedure' (Hill 2003: 275). Although role making cannot be expected to have a negative effect on performance by definition (which would be the common position from a managerial perspective), it is clear that the phenomenon of role making will only increase the number of assessment criteria in the organization and will thus make achieving performance even more difficult.

Secondly, finding a balance between different types of criteria (which we believe to be contributing to the performance of the organization) is something that can better be achieved through an organization than through an individual. It is much easier, natural and more promising for an organization to be hypocritical than for a person (see Brunsson 1989). To contribute to performance the main task of the performance management control system in this case will be to integrate these different criteria.

Consistent with the above discussion, the following proposition can be stated, which relates the presence of competing criteria to the preferable form of performance control:

P3: In organizations where the staff is confronted with competing or even conflicting criteria of management, performance control can be expected to contribute more to performance than agent control.

Propositions related to measurement

Often activities in an organization cannot easily be measured. Something like learning or happiness cannot be tapped in the same way as, for example, the time spent with a client or getting to a meeting on time. Forms of performance management control are, however, very much dependent on objective and quantifiable information. Consequently, requiring objective and quantifiable information in such a situation might lead to the collection of information which is subsequently not used within the organization. However, it could be used by oversight institutions with the effect that they value and encourage or discourage organizations on doubtful grounds. Agents can be expected to take outcomes and effects less into consideration; they probably direct more attention to processes. In a study of how college presidents assess their performance Birnbaum (1990) found on the basis of thirty-two interviews with presidents that they had relied on both implicit and explicit information. Implicit information was gathered through their direct observations and tended to be subjective and non-comparable, since it had its origins in what they saw and heard. Birnbaum (1990) found that the majority of presidents assessed their effectiveness by basing it on implicit information gathered through personal observations. The majority were not satisfied with the official flow of information and actively sought to either exploit or construct new information channels. Some actively pursued information by either walking around or stopping by people's offices unannounced, which they called 'management by walking around'. This intuitive approach results according to Birnbaum (1990: 32) from 'training, immersion in details, and the ability to interpret ambiguous events from multiple perspectives . . . . It may be related to the ability to integrate rational, analytical, and deductive management styles on the one hand, with orientations that emphasize feelings, synthesis, and inductive techniques on the other . . .'.

It becomes clear that management performance systems can hardly compete with agent control when activities are difficult to measure objectively and when intuition plays a role.

Based on this logic, we offer the following proposition:

P4: When activities are not objectively measurable, agent control can be expected to contribute better to performance than performance management control.

Agent control can be seen as a form of self-evaluative judgement, which means that one needs to take into account certain constraints that might hamper this process, such as informational, cognitive and effective constraints (Campbell and Lee 1988). While these can have significant effects on the accuracy of the self-evaluative judgement, they are generally ignored in the organizational literature on self-regulation. They are mentioned in the more psychologically-orientated literature on self-appraisal. Regarding information constraints, Campbell and Lee (1988) state that when '. . . performing a job, an employee must consider what tasks are to be done, how they are to be performed, and what standards are to be used in judging the final outcome' (1988: 304). The argument is that if a person does not have any of this type of information, he or she will have difficulties in performing the job. Campbell and Lee (1988) also point to cognitive constraints in information processing of individuals due to the inherent limitations on human information processing capacity (Kahneman *et al.* 1982) and posit that individuals simplify the self-appraisal tasks by using specific schemas or heuristics, which in turn open the possibility of inaccurate self-appraisals. Moreover, self-appraisals can also be threatening to the individual in terms of self-esteem, thereby producing cognitive constraints (Campbell and Lee 1988). As Simon (1947) taught us so pertinently, organizations can exactly be seen as a solution to these types of constraints. Consequently, management performance control can be expected to lead to better performance in these cases. Stated as a formal proposition:

P5: In cases where informational constraints, cognitive constraints and affective constraints play an important role, performance management control can be expected to contribute more to performance than agent control.

Not only the accuracy and mode of measurement play an important role in contributing to performance but also the consequences of inaccurate measurements have to be taken into account. Inaccurate measurement of performance can potentially lead to wrong decisions on activities, investments, strategies and the like. What are the consequences of measurement errors on performance for different systems of performance control? Given the fact that performance management control is most often a tight system of objectives, measurements, targets, consequences and the like, it can be expected that a measurement error will reverberate unimpeded through the system and lead to wrong conclusions and decisions. Empirically speaking there is, of course, often much less danger since different studies have shown that '. . . most government agencies may collect data that is or could be used for performance measurement; however, they do not have a system in place in which those data are part of decision-making processes and have not made a serious commitment to do so, whether they profess it or not' (for similar conclusions Coplin *et al.* 2002: 700). This does not, however, mean that when they use it, it cannot contain performance errors leading to the consequences described above.

In contrast, an agent control system is principally rather loosely coupled compared to a management performance system. Measurement errors are much more tolerable in these systems. Birnbaum (1990) in his study on college presidents concludes that the expectations turn out to be quite stable, and the cognitive biases that maintain them should not be expected to shift as a result of discrete events. It may only be the case when negative feedback is consistent and received on a continuous rather than a discrete basis. It may not be important if presidents make moderate errors in self-assessments about their performance in specific cases, but it may be critical that they are able to detect and respond to changes in patterns that reflect the system state (Birnbaum 1990: 36).

Formulated as a proposition:

P6: Making moderate errors in measurement is less critical for performance in the case of agent control than in the case of performance management control.

Propositions related to feedback

Feedback refers technically speaking 'to the part of system or process output that returns to system or process input', which means that the system provides itself with information about its own governance (Vancouver and Day 2005: 164).

Feedback is considered important in any type of organization since it ensures that if the organization is not functioning according to the set criteria, something is done. An important difference is that between single-loop and double-loop learning. Argyris (1980: 291) defines double-loop learning as 'the detection and correction of errors [that] require changes in the underlying policies, assumptions, and goals. A thermostat is a single-loop learner because it detects when the room is too hot or too cold. A thermostat would be a double-loop learner if it questioned why it was set at 65 degrees or why it was measuring heat'. Single loop learning relates to the discrepancies and variations of set pre-standards. The logic of single loop learning cannot capture the fact that deviations might be considered 'good' because the plans were 'bad' (Luhmann 1973). Double-loop learning, on the other hand, describes a situation where a dynamic process between goals or criteria and measurements is foreseen. Since in management performance control systems there is a clear division of labour between the controller and the controlled, the chance that double-loop learning will occur is limited. Deviations are seen as deviations from the controller's standards; the fact that the controller considers deviations to result from bad plans or a poor design of the performance management control system is small (see e.g., Kenis 2003).

In agent control, the controller and the controlled are the same person and consequently the chance of discovering a relationship between the outcomes produced and the inputs and tools used is much higher. According to Jarzabkowski (2004: 536), who refers to the work of Orr (1990, 1996) on technicians, 'the micro-context provides an opportunity for adaptive practice. New knowledge about specific situations may arise from the social activities of dialogue and interaction' (Brown and Duguid 1991; Cook and Brown 1999), often about a problem or failure. For example, when the formal code of practice for mending a faulty photocopier is inadequate to the task, Orr's (1990, 1996) technicians engage in adaptive social interaction. They tell stories about the problem that generate new methods for its solution. New practice does not come from external sources, but from participating in the social process of problem-solving within that community.

Although managers are mostly associated with the use of management performance control systems, they themselves often use a mode of feedback that alternates between observations of performance and standards of performance. Preston's (1986) study of the design, implementation and the use of the computerized production information system observed that managers kept 'detailed personal records of routine or regular events which they personally defined as being important to themselves and to their work. Personal records included much of what managers found out through direct observation and interaction. The managers also made more formalized requests for figures, comments and memos from other people in the organization which in turn formed part of the manager's personal records' (Preston, 1986: 533). The outlined practices of collecting information as to their and their department's performance, via both direct observation and direct interaction and requests, were considered by the managers as contributing much more to the performance of their department than the data generated by the computerized production information system (that is, the official management performance control system).

All this points to fact that in these instances double-loop learning is deemed necessary, agent control contributes more to performance than management performance control. This can be stated formally as a research proposition:

P7: Agent control is expected to be a better form of performance control than management performance control for double-loop learning and thus performance.

Discussion and Conclusion

The aim of this chapter was to demonstrate that studying performance control is one way to contribute to our knowledge about the performance of public organizations. We have argued that different types of performance control can be distinguished. More specifically, two extreme forms have been presented in more detail: management performance control and agent control. Both forms differ in many respects and are prevalent in empirical reality, although agent control seems to have received much less attention in the academic literature.

The general conclusions of the chapter are first, that there is no best form of performance control, or in other words, it is not possible to develop a prescriptive performance control model which at all times and places contributes to performance. Secondly, not every form of performance control is equally effective in contributing to organizational performance, in other words, performance control matters; consequently, which form of performance control contributes best to organizational performance depends on a number of factors. These factors and the relationship between the type of performance control and organizational performance have been formulated in a number of testable propositions.

The main aim of the list of propositions is to demonstrate the relevance and significance of forms of performance control in the study of the performance of public organizations. We are aware that this is not a complete list of possible propositions. Many more could and should have been formulated, but given the limited space available and the limited state of the literature (especially with respect to agent control) this is not possible at present. It has become clear, however, that propositions which include characteristics of: the task, the controlled and controllers, the organization in which performance control takes place, the environment of the organization in which control takes place, and also the interdependencies between different types of control in an organization could all potentially have a direct, mediating or moderating effect on the relationship between forms of performance control and organizational performance.

Another omission from the chapter, also because of the limited state of the literature, is that we have not been able to limit our analysis to the case of public organizations alone. It has been necessary to include research carried out in the private and non-profit sector, although a large number of public sector studies have also been included. But what has already become very clear on the basis of the propositions is that both forms of control are potentially valuable for the performance of public sector organizations. On the basis of the propositions it cannot be concluded that either agent control or management performance control always contributes most to performance. Consequently, what has been said above about organizations in general also applies to public sector organizations, that is it is not possible to develop a prescriptive performance control model that is better for all times and places.

Another omission from the chapter is that we only discussed two types of performance control. Many more forms are, of course, present in organizations such as: self-regulation, professional control, self-management, social control, etc. Although we have argued that they differ from the two we have distinguished, we could not study them in great detail. The fact that forms of control in organizations relate to organizational performance, as has been proposed here, suggests that we should also start to study these forms in greater detail.

Finally we also have to introduce a caveat. We have demonstrated that there are good reasons to believe that the type of performance control used in an organizational setting is related to performance. In doing so, we have introduced a highly neglected phenomenon in the literature – agent control. This should not be interpreted as a superior form of control. Thus, while we do not posit that external controls are unrelated to performance, especially since agent control can also lead to control failures (a phenomenon which has received practically no attention in the related literature on self-regulation), we do believe that a focus on agent control practices could be especially relevant to the current trends in coordination. Thus, changes in organizational structures, such as the shift from hierarchical forms of control to more horizontal structures, as well as the increasing preponderance of network forms of organizing, have raised new questions as to appropriate forms of organizational controls. In these situations, we envision agent control practices as often demonstrating a high impact in terms of performance, since in these situations, traditional forms of control might become more and more problematic. In these cases, a complete closure of the cybernetic circle (including mutual processes between the different components) by prescriptive and pre-defined control systems will not only become more unlikely, but also cannot be expected to contribute to organizational performance. For public organizations, this might be the most important message of this chapter.

Acknowledgement

I would like to thank the participants of the Workshop on Determinants of Performance in Public Organizations (Cardiff University, 7–8 May 2004), Denise Korssen-van Raaij, Diana Rus and Larry O'Toole for their valuable comments on earlier drafts of this chapter. Needless to say, this chapter is the sole responsibility of the author.

REFERENCES

Abernethy, M. A. and Stoelwinder, J. U. (1995) 'The role of professional control in the management of complex organization', *Accounting, Organizations and Society*, **20**: 1–17.

Ackoff, R. L. (1967) 'Management misinformation systems', *Management Science*, **14**: 147–156.

Alchian, A. A. and Demetz, H. (1972) 'Production, information cost and economic organization', *American Economic Review*, **61**: 777–795.

Argyris, C. (1980) 'Some limitations of the case method: Experiences in a management development program', *Academy of Management Review*, **5**: 291–298.

Ashby, W. R. (1952) *Design for a brain*. New York, NY: Wiley and Sons.

Ashworth, R., Boyne, G. A. and Walker, R. M. (2002) 'Regulatory problems in the public sector: Theories and cases', *Policy & Politics*, **30**: 195–211.

Bartlett, C. A. and Ghoshal, S. (1995) 'Changing the role of top management: Beyond systems to people', *Harvard Business Review*, **7**(3): 132–142.

Birnbaum, R. (1990) '"How'm I doin?": How college presidents assess their effectiveness', *Leadership Quarterly*, **1**: 25–39.

Bohte, J. and Meier, K. J. (2000) 'Goal displacement: Assessing the motivation for organizational cheating', *Public Administration Review*, **60**: 173–182.

Boyne, G. A. (2003a) 'Sources of public service improvement: A critical review and research agenda', *Journal of Public Administration Research and Theory*, **13**: 367–394.

Boyne, G. A. (2003b) 'What is public service improvement?', *Public Administration*, **81**: 211–227.

Brown, J. S. and Duguid, P. (1991) 'Organizational learning and communities of practice: Towards a unified view of working, learning, and innovation', *Organization Science*, **2**: 40–57.

Brunsson, N. (1989) *The organization of hypocrisy*. Chichester: John Wiley and Sons.

Campbell, D. J. and Lee, C. (1988) 'Self-appraisal in performance evaluation: development versus evaluation', *Academy of Management Review*, **13**: 302–314.

Chatman, J. A. (1991) 'Matching people and organizations: selection and socialization in public accounting firms', *Administrative Science Quarterly*, **36**: 459–484.

Chenhall, R. H. (2003) 'Management control systems design within its organizational context: Findings from contingency-based research and directions for the future', *Accounting, Organizations and Society* **28**: 127–168.

Coplin, W. D., Merget, A. E. and Bourdeaux, C. (2002) 'The professional researcher as change agent in the government-performance movement', *Public Administration Review*, **62**: 699–711.

Cook, S. D. N. and Brown, J. S. (1999) 'Bridging epistemologies: The generative dance between organizational knowledge and organizational knowing', *Organization Science*, **10**: 381–400.

Covaleski, M. A. and Dirsmith, M. W. (1996) 'The budgetary process of power and politics', *Accounting, Organizations and Society*, **11**: 193–214.

Czarniawska-Joerges, B. (1988) 'Dynamics of organizational control: The case of Berol Kemi Ab', *Accounting, Organizations and Society*, **13**: 415–430.

Davies, C. and Francis, A. (1974) 'The many dimensions of performance measurement: There is more to performance than profits and growth', *Organizational Dynamics*, **3**: 51–65.

Dermer, J. D. (1988) 'Control and organizational order', *Accounting, Organizations and Society*, **13**: 25–36.

Dubnick, M. J. (2003) *Accountability and the promise of performance: In search of the mechanisms*. Paper prepared for delivery at the 2003 annual meeting of the American Political Science Association, 28–31 August, Philadelphia, PA and Conference of the European Group of Public Administration (EGPA), 3–6 September, Lisbon, Portugal.

Follett, M. P. (1937) 'The process of control' in L. Gulick and L. Urwick (eds.), *Papers on the science of administration*. New York, NY: Institute of Public Administration, pp. 161–169.

Follett, M. P. (1951) *Creative experience*. New York, NY: Peter Smith.

Grean, G. (1967) 'Role-making processes within complex organizations' in M. D. Dunnette (ed.), *Handbook of industrial and organizational psychology*. Chicago, IL: Rand McNally, pp. 1201–1245.

Green, S. G. and Welsh, M. A. (1988) 'Cybernetics and dependence: Reframing the control concept', *Academy of Management Review*, **12**: 287–301.

Hill, H. C. (2003) 'Understanding implementation: Street-level bureaucrats' resources for reform', *Journal of Public Administration Research and Theory*, **13**: 265–282.

Hofstede, G. (1981) 'Management control of public and not-for-profit activities', *Accounting, Organizations and Society*, **6**: 193–211.

Jarzabkowski, P. (2004) 'Strategy as practice: Recursiveness, adaptation, and practices-in-use', *Organization Studies*, **25**: 529–560.

Kahneman, D., Slovic, P. and Tversky, A. (1982) *Judgment under uncertainty: Heuristics and biases*. Cambridge: Cambridge University Press.

Kenis, P. (2003) 'Crisis in de gezondheidszorg: De wachtlijstproblematiek', *Bestuurskunde* **12**: 88–96.

Korssen-van Raaij, D. (2005) *Balancing on network norms: A partial presentation of a study on control in Dutch health care networks*. Paper presented at the EGOS Conference, Berlin.

Luhmann, N. (1973) *Zweckbegriff und systemrationalitat*. Frankfurt a.M: Suhrkamp.

Lynn, L. E. Jr. (2001) 'The myth of the bureaucratic paradigm: What traditional public administration really stood for', *Public Administration Review*, **61**: 144–160.

Lynn, L. E. Jr., Heinrich, C. J. and Hill, C. J. (2000) 'Studying governance and public management: Challenges and prospects', *Journal of Public Administration Research and Theory*, **10**: 233–261.

Maynard-Moody, S. and Musheno, M. (2000) 'State agent or citizen agent: Two narratives of discretion', *Journal of Public Administration Research and Theory*, **10**: 329–358.

Metcalfe, L. (2001) 'Reforming the European governance: old problems or new principles?', *International Review of Administrative Sciences*, **67**: 415–444.

Meyer, M. W. (2002) *Rethinking Performance Measurement*. Cambridge: Cambridge University Press.

Meyer, J. W. and Rowan, B. (1977) 'Institutionalized organizations: Formal structure as myth and ceremony', *American Journal of Sociology*, **83**: 340–363.

Meyers, M. K., Riccucci, N. M., and Lurie, I. (2001) 'Achieving goal congruence in complex environments: The case of welfare reform', *Journal of Public Administration Research and Theory*, **11**: 165–201.

Miller, P. (2001) 'Governing by numbers: Why calculative practices matter', *Social Research: An International Quarterly of Political and Social Science*, **68**: 379–396.

Mills, P. K. (1983) 'Self-management: Its control and relationship to other organizational properties', *Academy of Management Review*, **8**: 445–453.

Mintzberg, H. (1989) *Mintzberg on management: inside our strange world of organizations*. New York, NY: Free Press.

Modell, S. (2004) 'Performance measurement myths in the public sector: A Research note', *Financial Accountability and Management* **20**: 39–55.

Nicholson-Crotty, S. and O'Toole. L. J. Jr. (2004) 'Public management and organizational performance: The case of law enforcement agencies', *Journal of Public Administration Research and Theory*, **14**: 1–18.

Orr, J. E. (1990) 'Sharing knowledge, celebrating identity: War stories and community memory in a service culture' in D. S. Middleton and D. Edwards (eds.) *Collective remembering: Memory in society*, Beverley Hills, CA: Sage, pp. 169–189.

Orr, J. E. (1996) *Talking about machines: An ethnography of a modern job*. Ithaca, NY: Cornell University Press.

Ouchi, W. G. (1977) The relationship between organizational structure and organizational control. *Administrative Science Quarterly*, **22**: 95–113.

Perrow, C. (1986) *Complex organizations*. New York: McGraw-Hill.

Preston, A. (1986) 'Interactions and arrangements in the process of informing', *Accounting, Organizations and Society*, **11**: 521–540.

Ricucci, N. M., Meyers, M. K., Lurie, I. and Han, J. S. (2004) 'The implementation of welfare reform policy: The role of public managers in front-line practices', *Public Administration Review*, **64**: 438–448.

Rus, D. (2005) *Agent control in the organizational literature*. MA thesis manuscript: Tilburg University.

Salamon, L. M. and Odus V. E. (2002) *The tools of government: a guide to the new governance*. New York: Oxford University Press.

Simon, H. A. (1947) *Administrative behavior*. New York: Free Press.

Vancouver, J. B. and Day, D. V. (2005) 'Industrial and organisation research on self-regulation: from constructs to applications', *Applied Psychology: An International Review*, **54**: 155–185.

Weick, K. E. (1996) 'Drop your tools: An allegory for organizational studies', *Administrative Science Quarterly*, **41**: 301–313.

Wiener, N. (1948) *Cybernetics: Or control and communication in the animal and the machine*. Cambridge, MA: MIT Press.

Wilensky, H. L. (1964) 'The professionalization of everyone?', *American Journal of Sociology*, **70**: 137–159.

Williamson, O. (1971) *Corporate control and business behavior*. Englewood Cliffs, NJ: Prentice-Hall.

Zald, M. N. (1978) 'On the social control of industries', *Social Forces*, **57**: 79–101.

8 Bureaucratic red tape and organizational performance: Testing the moderating role of culture and political support

Sanjay K. Pandey and Donald Moynihan

Introduction

This chapter examines the relationship between red tape and performance, and proposes that organizational culture and political support can mitigate the negative effects of red tape. Bureaucratic red tape is a concept that both holds widespread popular appeal and is one of the few 'homegrown' theories in the field of public management. Despite this, academic work on red tape has not informed public management changes, or even the broader public management literature. Developments on conceptualizing and measuring red tape (e.g., Bozeman 1993; Pandey and Scott 2002) have had little direct influence on the thinking of reformers who seek to cut red tape (Gore 1993; Osborne and Gaebler 1992), or even the academic discussion of these reforms (e.g., Ingraham *et al.* 1997; Kettl and DiIulio 1995). While most scholars would probably accept the argument that red tape matters to performance, the recent emergence of an empirical literature on public sector performance also largely excludes explicit consideration of red tape (Ingraham *et al.* 2003; Lynn *et al.* 2001; O'Toole and Meier 1999).

Red tape, therefore, is an area of public management in which theoretical developments and practical concerns are pulling in different directions. For example, when Vice-President Gore discussed moving from red tape to results during the 1990s, he drew neither on groundbreaking theoretical work by Bozeman (1993) nor on Kaufman's (1977) seminal work. Such separation between theory and practice benefits neither enterprise. Our goal is to bridge this divide in the spirit of Kurt Lewin (1951: 169) who suggested that 'there is nothing so practical as a good theory'. A starting point for a practical theory is an assumption shared between practitioners and current theoretical approaches – red tape has a negative effect on performance. This chapter seeks to advance this basic theory by proposing and testing moderating mechanisms that mitigate the negative effect of red tape on performance. It develops and provides an empirical test for two alternative explanations – organizational culture and political support – that are expected to have such a moderating influence.

Theory and hypotheses

Developing the concept of red tape

Recognition of red tape as an organizational problem is relatively new. Early scholarly attempts conceptualized red tape at the individual level as in Merton's classic thesis about goal displacement or Gouldner's notion that red tape is intimately tied to an individual's perspective (Gouldner 1952; Merton 1940). The classic public administration perspective, rooted in interest group pluralism, has hewed close to Gouldner's perspective as expressed by Waldo (1946: 399): 'one man's red tape is another man's system' and echoed three decades later by Kaufman (1977: 4): 'one person's red tape may be another's treasured safeguard'.

It is only recently that there has been movement in the direction of rethinking of red tape as a system level variable, characterized by 'good people trapped in bad systems' (Gore 1993; Osborne and Gaebler 1992). This shift is best illustrated in Osborne and Gaebler's (1992: 110) words: 'The glue that holds public bureaucracies together, in other words, is like epoxy: it comes in two separate tubes. One holds rules, the other line items. Mix them together and you get cement'. This approach does not disparage public managers, but paints a rather empathetic picture recognizing the constraints under which they operate.

A key aim of recent reform movements, such as new public management (NPM) and reinvention, is on freeing public agencies from burdensome rules and providing the necessary flexibility to enhance performance (Hood 1991; Osborne and Gaebler 1992). These reforms focus on dysfunctional aspects of management systems, such as a concentration of organizational energy on process rather than results, and the constraints management systems impose on managerial authority in utilizing different resources. The solutions proposed by this literature target these dysfunctions, calling for reduced red tape and greater freedom in the areas of personnel, procurement, and financial systems (Thompson and Riccucci 1998).

Recent theoretical work on red tape shares many assumptions with reformers who see it as a barrier to public sector performance. Most prominently, Bozeman (1993, 2000) argues that while some rules are functional, others in the form of red tape exert a compliance burden and can therefore be expected to have a negative effect on performance. This assumption is reflected in Bozeman's (1993: 283) definition of red tape as 'rules, regulations, and procedures that remain in force and entail a compliance burden for the organization but have no efficacy for the rules' functional object'. Bozeman also draws a distinction between organizational red tape and stakeholder red tape. This chapter focuses on organizational red tape, which imposes a 'compliance burden for the organization but makes no contribution to achieving the rule's functional object' (Bozeman, 2000: 82). Although this definition provides a useful starting point, it has two key limitations – it is broad in scope and is not anchored to specific referents.

Pandey and colleagues offer a modification that helps overcome these limitations. Pandey and Kingsley (2000: 782) define red tape as 'impressions on the part of managers that formalization (in the form of burdensome rules and regulations) is detrimental to the organization'. This modification helps by avoiding 'the necessity of a detailed case study of every rule for determining organizational/social significance of the rule's functional object . . . and, rather than leaving determining organizational/social significance as an open matter, it provides a clear guideline. Simply put, red tape exists when managers view formalization as burdensome and detrimental to organizational purposes' (Pandey and Scott 2002: 565). Recent work (Pandey and Welch, 2005) has argued that our understanding of red tape will be advanced by focusing on specific management sub-systems, rather than relying on generic unanchored evaluations. For this reason, we employ measures of red tape in three key management domains – human resources, purchasing/procurement and information systems.

Based on a fundamental acceptance among both reformers and recent theoretical work that the burdens of system-level red tape have a negative effect on organizational performance, our first hypothesis is:

H1:   Red tape negatively affects organizational performance.

If burdensome rules and constraints cause lower performance, does eliminating rules and regulations improve performance? The basic logic of reformers is that improved performance through reorganized processes could not be achieved without giving managers the freedom necessary to make such changes (Moynihan and Pandey in press). However, organizations operating under similarly burdensome rules show significant variability in performance outcomes (Ban 1995). Bureaucratic red tape in different management systems does not completely determine performance – the effect of red tape on performance is moderated through other variables. We use the term moderation in its classic sense as described by Baron and Kenny (1986). Moderation occurs when a moderating variable either amplifies or mitigates the relationship between two variables of interest. Typically, an interaction term (a product of the independent and the moderating variable) in multiple regression is used to model the moderation effect.

We posit and test the effects of two moderator variables, namely organizational culture and political support for the organization. Before discussing these variables further, we briefly explain the underlying logic for the moderating role. To paraphrase a popular saying: red tape represents the triumph of means over ends. Reification of means in public organizations is facilitated by personnel, procurement and other systems, typically operating under statute or difficult to change administrative rules, with the locus of accountability at a higher level of governance than the focal organization. As a result, there is a tendency for sub-goals of different management systems to acquire unusual prominence. When sub-goals compete with rather than complement overarching organizational goals, the net result is a decline in organizational performance. The moderating factors we propose dampen the influence of 'sovereign' sub-goals and thereby improve performance. We discuss in greater detail the role played by the moderating factors below.

Organizational culture as a moderating factor

One perspective on organizational performance is that it is primarily one of control and coordination (Steiss 1982). The classical age of organization theory features the assumption that bureaucracies with streamlined command and control mechanisms successfully deal with control and coordination issues. There is support for this notion in historical work which shows that elaboration and entrenchment of the bureaucratic form led to better control and coordination mechanisms; which in turn had a positive impact on performance (Yates 1989). It is, however, a mistake to assume that it is merely the bureaucratic form of organization, with clear reporting lines, that holds the key to coordination and control issues.

Indeed, large hierarchies with many layers of reporting can distort both the downward and upward flow of information which in turn can negatively influence performance (Pandey and Garnett in press). While the size of the hierarchy is a salient consideration from a control/coordination perspective, an equal challenge is posed by the existence of management sub-systems that are not fully under organizational control. Ouchi (1980) was among the first scholars to point out that when bureaucratic control and coordination mechanisms fail, organizations rely on aspects of culture such as 'traditions' rather than 'rules' to facilitate control and coordination. Ouchi's (1980; 1981) argument that organizational culture is a key determinant of performance gained wide currency through the 1980s (Deal and Kennedy 1982; Peters and Waterman 1982, Schein 1992).

Systematic empirical examination of the impact of culture on performance of public organizations is rare. However, discussion of culture tends to emphasize its importance for performance (Boyne 2003; Brewer 2005; Rainey and Steinbauer 1999). Brewer (2005) finds that cultures characterized by efficacy and meaningful/engaging work are associated with higher performance. But by and large, the link between culture and performance is generally based on the premise that the culture is mission based (Rainey and Steinbauer 1999). As Boyne (2003: 371) notes: 'The core idea is that organizations that focus on results rather than procedures and have an external rather than internal orientation are likely to perform better.' The underlying logic for this relationship is that a mission-based culture will prompt managers to act with a greater entrepreneurial style rather than dwell on constraints. A mission-based culture, therefore, does not improve performance by eliminating red tape – it encourages managers to find ways to cope with and overcome it.

Carolyn Ban's (1995) research on federal agencies offers qualitative empirical support for this relationship. She finds that managers in the Environmental Protection Agency (EPA) were more adept at mitigating the negative effects of human resource constraints than managers in other agencies. Ban concludes that the EPA was able to stay within human resource constraints and yet succeed in achieving organizational goals due to a dynamic and entrepreneurial organizational culture. The EPA culture rewarded creative problem solving and risk taking in pursuit of the organizational mission.

Measuring culture presents some challenges that one does not encounter in qualitative studies. Ashkanasy *et al.* (2000) make a distinction between 'typing' and 'profiling' approaches in studies using questionnaire data. While the typing approach assigns a specific cultural type, profiling recognizes that an organization does not neatly fall into a single category. Therefore, it is best to view culture as a dimensional property with the unique culture of an organization comprised of a combination of different levels of the component dimensions. Consistent with this view, Zammuto and Krakower (1991), based on the work of Quinn and Rohrbaugh (1983), propose four dimensions of organizational culture – group culture, hierarchical culture, rational culture and developmental culture. In considering the role of culture in our theoretical model, we specifically focused on a culture dimension that can mitigate the negative effect of red tape. Especially suitable for this purpose is developmental culture, a cultural orientation that places high value on a focus on the organization (rather than people), flexibility, readiness, adaptability and growth (Zammuto and Krakower 1991). The developmental culture dimension is most similar to the mission-based culture that inspires managers to find ways to overcome inertial aspects of bureaucratic red tape. Therefore, we hypothesize:

H2: Organizations with developmental cultures will have higher organizational performance.

H3: Organizations with developmental cultures are better able to mitigate the negative effects of red tape on organizational performance.

Political support as a moderating factor

Much has been written about the value of political support for the operations of public organizations. Following the discrediting of the politics-administration dichotomy, a number of scholars have highlighted different ways in which political support influences organizational performance (Long 1949; Wilson 1989).

Thompson and Riccucci (1998) argue that a political system characterized by multiple principals and uncertain support can result in extremely cautious behaviour, avoidance of reasonable risk taking, lack of flexibility and a decline in innovation. In turn, one can expect these conditions to lead to decline in performance. Scholars have also made the point that agencies with an attractive mission are better positioned to develop and sustain political support (Rainey and Steinbauer 1999: 16). Our purpose, however, is not to explain what leads to high levels of political support, but to make an argument for the moderating effect of political support on the relationship between red tape and performance.

In making the argument for positive effect of political support, we focus on the role of elected officials. No group of political actors is more important to the operation of public agencies than elected officials. Through a variety of formal hierarchical as well as informal mechanisms, elected officials have the opportunity and ability to penetrate deeply into the inner workings of public organizations. Thompson (1967) has persuasively argued that relatively unhindered operations of the technical core of the organization are important for achieving high levels of performance. For public organizations, part of this technical core is made up of rules and procedures enshrined in different management sub-systems. This technical core is more open to external scrutiny and manipulation by a range of political principals. A practical example of this comes from the efforts of the Clinton administration to provide waivers from federal rules for any agencies or units that wished to avail of them. Thompson and Ingraham (1996) found that the ability to win these benefits often depended on whether the agency was dependent on a central agency (such as the Office of Management and Budget) and if so, their ability to overcome the objections that central agencies had to eliminating these waivers.

Organizations with low levels of political support are more vulnerable to external scrutiny and are, as a result, less free to coordinate the workings of different management sub-systems for maximizing organizational goals at the expense of sub-system goals. Vigorous external scrutiny means that organizations can ill afford to deviate from rules and procedures under which management sub-systems operate. Even if such deviations may, in principle, have been driven by performance considerations, opponents are likely to use these deviations to attack the agency. Organizations enjoying high levels of political support are not only able to maintain a viable technical core, but can also get the most out of it in terms of performance by coordinating the functions of different sub-systems optimally. Therefore we hypothesize:

H4: Organizations with high levels of political support from elected officials will have higher levels of organizational performance.

H5: Organizations with high levels of political support from elected officials are better able to mitigate the negative effects of red tape on organizational performance.

Data, measurement, model specification and findings

Sample selection and survey administration

The data for this study were collected in Phase II of the National Administrative Studies Project (NASP-II) which focused on state-level primary human service agencies. There was a lot of variation across states in the design and administration of these agencies (APHSA 2001). Twenty-four states had an umbrella agency, twenty had two large agencies and the rest had more than two agencies, bringing the total number of state primary human service agencies to eighty-five. Just two of the programmes administered by these agencies, Medicaid and State Children's Health Insurance Programme, serve over 50 m beneficiaries with total spending likely to exceed $300 billion in FY 2004 (Smith *et al.* 2004).

In addition to collecting information from secondary data sources, primary data was collected from a survey of senior managers in the agency (for more details see Pandey 2003; Moynihan and Pandey 2005). We explicitly instructed respondents to answer questions from the perspective of the agency at large. We received 274 responses for a response rate of approximately 53 per cent. These responses provided broad coverage with response(s) received from all but two of the agencies.

Measures

Because our unit of analysis is the organization, we aggregate responses by organization and use the mean score derived from all responses from a given organization. Lincoln and Zeitz (1980) have demonstrated that such measures, based on individual self-reports, are valid indicators of organizational properties. In order to enhance the validity of our measures we were very careful in choosing key informants – these key informants were senior managers performing roles that are likely to provide in-depth information on a wide range of salient issues facing the agency.

The number of respondents per agency ranged from 1 to 8, with a mean of 3.3 respondents per agency. It would have been ideal to have more respondents per agency, and perhaps it is limiting to assume that the views of a small number of respondents represent the agency. However, this is consistent with standard practice and indeed goes beyond it by relying on more than a single key informant to measure organizational properties. Tests for the consistency of intra-organizational responses also supported the assumption that respondents' answers mirrored those of others within the agency.[1]

1 To gain a rigorous estimate of the extent to which the aggregated responses represented organizational properties, rather than individual respondents' predispositions, we assessed intraclass correlation coefficients (ICC) across individual responses for each organization on the variables

Organizational performance measures

There is no clear consensus on the best approach for measuring organizational performance. Indeed, there were broad areas of disagreement in early efforts to define organizational effectiveness (Moynihan and Pandey 2005: 429). Thus, efforts to measure organizational performance need to begin with an explicit recognition of underlying choices and resultant trade-offs.

We measure organizational performance through questions about agency effectiveness in accomplishing its core mission and perceived service quality. Our approach is consistent with others measuring agency effectiveness based on manager's ratings (e.g., Brewer and Selden 2000; Mott 1972). Brewer (2005) notes additional precedents for using perceptual measures of performance in both public and private agencies. Such measures have been found to correlate with objective measures of performance, enjoying moderate to strong positive associations (Walker and Boyne 2006).

The ideal performance measurement situation is one in which there is widespread agreement about what the organization should be doing and that this goal can be accurately identified through a limited number of measures. However, these conditions rarely exist for public organizations. Despite subjective origins, perceptual measures have some benefits, although we do not suggest that they replace programme performance results, or stakeholder evaluations. First, the respondents are asked for their perspectives on the entire organization, rather than a specific programme. This avoids the necessity of equating programmatic measures of performance with organizational performance. Second, while external stakeholders can provide an alternative and valuable perspective on performance, it becomes more difficult to rely on these views where stakeholders are numerous and have conflicting viewpoints, a circumstance common to state-level primary human service agencies (Grogan and Patashnik 2003; Pandey 2002). The performance evaluations of one set of stakeholders might run contrary to others. Public managers are targeted by stakeholders to incorporate their goals, and are likely to have a more balanced perspective on the capabilities and difficulties involved in satisfying multiple stakeholder groups. In sum, while an employee-based perceptual measure will be broad and necessarily approximate, it relies on the views of those who know the agency best, and does not extrapolate organizational performance from highly specific programmatic measures or rely on one set of stakeholder perspectives to extrapolate organizational performance.

employed in the regression model (McGraw and Wong 1996). The measure indicates the proportion of variance between different respondents of the same organization, and the ICC estimates are based on mean squares obtained by applying analysis of variance models to these data (McGraw and Wong 1996). The ICC scores have an upper bound of 1, so higher positive scores close to 1 indicate a high degree of agreement between the different respondents. ICC statistics demonstrate high consistency in responses between members of the same organization in our sample: the lowest ICC is .661, and the next lowest is .833; the highest ICC is .989. The average ICC for organizations with multiple respondents is .944, and the standard deviation is .052.

Mission effectiveness was measured by asking the respondents to rate the following statement on a 0–10 scale, with 0 indicating not effective at all and 10 indicating extremely effective: *On an overall basis, please rate the effectiveness of your agency in accomplishing its core mission.* Service quality was measured by a summative index of four items (Gianakis and Wang 2000), each of which was rated on a 5-point Likert scale:

- Our agency can provide services the public needs.
- Our agency can satisfy public needs.
- Our agency can provide high quality of public service.
- Our agency can reduce criticism from citizens and clients.

Measuring independent variables

The first set of independent variables measure red tape in three key management sub-systems: human resources, procurement/purchasing and information systems. All these questionnaire items were rated on a five-point Likert scale. Human resources red tape was measured by a summative index of the following items (Rainey 1983; Pandey and Scott 2002):

- Even if a manager is a poor performer, formal rules make it hard to remove him or her from the organization.
- The rules governing promotion make it hard for a good manager to move up faster than a poor one.
- The formal pay structures and rules make it hard to reward a good manager with higher pay here.
- The personnel rules and procedures that govern my organization make it easier for superiors to reward subordinates for good performance (reversed).

A summative index of the following items was used to measure procurement red tape:

- The rules governing purchasing/procurement in my organization make it easy for managers to purchase goods and services (reversed).
- Due to standard procedures, procurement is based more on the vendor's ability to comply with rules than on the quality of goods and services.
- The rules governing procurement make it hard to expedite purchase of goods and services for a critical project.

Information systems red tape was measured by a sum of the following items:

- Rules and procedures on preparation of information system reports ensure that managers receive timely information (reversed).
- Procedural requirements for information system requests make it difficult for managers to obtain relevant information.

Table 8.1 Univariate statistics

Study variables	Items in scale	Cronbach's Alpha	Potential scale range	Midpoint	Mean	Standard deviation
Mission effectiveness	1		0–10	5	7.1	1.39
Service quality	4	0.72	4–20	12	16.5	2.28
Human resources red tape	4	0.69	4–20	12	15.2	2.59
Procurement/purchasing red tape	3	0.67	3–15	9	10.7	1.70
Information systems red tape	2	0.68	2–10	6	6.0	1.50
Developmental culture	3	0.72	3–15	9	8.8	2.14
Political support of elected officials	4	0.91	4–20	12	13.0	3.05

Developmental culture was measured with items adapted from Zammuto and Krakower (1991). Respondents were presented with brief descriptions of the organization's work environment and asked to express their agreement (on a five-point Likert scale) with the extent to which each description accurately portrayed their organization:

- My agency is a very dynamic and entrepreneurial place. People are willing to stick their necks out and take risks.
- The glue that holds my agency together is a commitment to innovation and development. There is an emphasis on being first.
- My agency emphasizes growth and acquiring new resources. Readiness to meet new challenges is important.

Political support from elected officials was measured using items developed by Gianakis and Wang (2000), with each items rated on a five-point Likert scale:

- Most elected officials in our state trust the agency.
- Most elected officials are very critical of the agency (reversed).
- Most elected officials believe the agency is competent.
- Most elected officials believe that the agency is effective.

Findings

We provide key details on each measure used in the study in Table 8.1. Interestingly, the mean scores on the two measures of organizational performance were somewhat higher than the midpoint of the scale. This does not, however, suggest that most organizations were superior performers. Rather, it may be indicative of a response style in which there was a tendency to use higher ratings. As indicated by the scores on human resources, procurement/purchasing and information systems red tape, it seems that red tape was a significant feature in these organizations. Scores on developmental culture, political support of elected officials are also displayed in the table.

Our primary modelling goal was to test for the moderating effects of organizational culture and political support from elected officials on red tape. Although we were not seeking to test for main effects of red tape on performance, we included the three red tape dimensions and a main effect of the moderating variable in the regression for purposes of comparison and complete specification. To test for three sets of moderating effects, we computed product terms by multiplying the moderating variable individually with three red tape dimensions – these product terms were computed after centreing the component variables.

For both measures of organizational performance, we estimated two regression equations, with the first testing the moderating effects of developmental culture and the second that of political support from elected officials. Given our concerns about statistical power and multicollinearity, only one set of interaction terms with one of the moderating variables was included in a regression equation (Jaccard *et al.* 1990). Regression diagnostics were performed to test for multicollinearity and influential data. For checking multicollinearity, we relied on variance inflation factors (VIFs). These values were well within tolerable limits, with the highest VIF standing at 3.12 (Belsely *et al.* 1980). We found few instances of influential data points in each regression and ascertained that the results were not overdetermined by these data points.

For each combination of performance measure and moderator variable, we estimated the following model:

Organizational Performance = *f*(Human resource red tape, Procurement red tape, Information systems red tape, Moderator variable, Product terms with moderator variable for the three red tape dimensions)

Table 8.2 presents the regression results for mission effectiveness as the dependent variable, with the first column presenting regression results for developmental culture as the moderator and the second column presenting the results for political support as the moderator. Both models were statistically significant, with adjusted R^2 of .665 and .607 respectively. The direction of the relationships between independent variables and mission effectiveness matched the hypotheses. Red tape dimensions were negatively related to effectiveness, although the procurement variable is not statistically significant. The main effects due to both moderator variables were statistically significant and in the expected direction indicating a positive relationship with performance.

Table 8.2 Multiple regression results for *mission effectiveness* as the dependent variable

Independent variables	Interactions with	
	Culture	Political support
Intercept	7.381****	9.447****
Human resources red tape	−0.0764* (−1.67)	−0.163*** (−3.67)
Procurement/purchasing red tape	−0.0763 (−1.19)	−0.069 (−1.07)
Information systems red tape	−0.130* (−1.75)	−0.174*** (−2.25)
Developmental culture	0.309**** (5.20)	
Political support		0.165**** (4.46)
Interaction of developmental culture with		
Human resources red tape	0.057** (2.49)	
Procurement/purchasing red tape	0.024 (1.03)	
Information systems red tape	0.029 (0.83)	
Interaction of political support with		
Human resources red tape		0.054**** (4.14)
Procurement/purchasing red tape		0.025 (1.21)
Information systems red tape		0.046* (1.96)
N	80	80
Adjusted R^2	0.665	0.607
F-value	23.71	18.68

Standardized betas displayed; **** $p < 0.0001$; *** $p < 0.01$; ** $p < 0.05$; * $p < 0.1$
T-scores displayed in parentheses.

We found partial support for moderation hypotheses as well (H3 and H5). The interaction term for human resources red tape and developmental culture was positive and statistically significant, indicating that high levels of developmental culture mitigated the negative effect of human resources red tape on mission effectiveness (H3). To facilitate understanding of moderation effect presented in Table 8.2, we provide a graphical depiction in Figure 8.1. The lines represent the relationship between human resource red tape and mission effectiveness at different levels of developmental culture. In plotting this interaction, we chose three levels of developmental culture (low = 3, medium = 8 and high = 13) and held the values of information systems and purchasing/procurement red tape at their mean. Figure 8.1 shows that at low developmental culture, mission effectiveness declined sharply as human resources red tape increased. At medium developmental culture, the slope of this decline was dramatically less steep and at high levels of developmental culture, there was a slight increase in mission effectiveness at high level of human resources red tape.

This pattern of relationships between red tape, the moderating variables and performance held across all the regression estimations. The interaction terms for

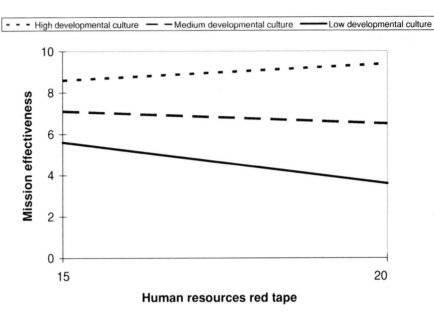

Figure 8.1   Moderating effect of developmental culture on mission effectiveness

both human resources red tape and information systems red tape, with political support as the moderator variable, were positive. This indicates that the negative effects of human resources and information systems red tape respectively on mission effectiveness were moderated by political support from elected officials. We provide graphic illustration of both these interactions at three different levels of political support (low $= 4$, medium $= 11$, high $= 18$) while holding other variables at their respective means. Both Figure 8.2 and Figure 8.3 showed a pattern similar to Figure 8.1. Under low levels of political support, mission effectiveness showed a steep decline as red tape increased. At a medium level of political support, this decline was less steep and under a high level of political support, there was a modest increase in mission effectiveness even as red tape increased.

The results of the regressions using service quality as the dependent variable are presented in Table 8.3. Both models, one with developmental culture and the other with political support as the moderator, were statistically significant with adjusted R^2 of 0.353 and 0.365 respectively. Regression coefficients for the three red tape dimensions were all negative in accordance with H1. However, only procurement red tape approached statistical significance in the first regression. In the second regression both procurement and human resources red tape were statistically significant. There was support for main effects for both moderator variables with respective coefficients being both positive and statistically significant (H2 and H4).

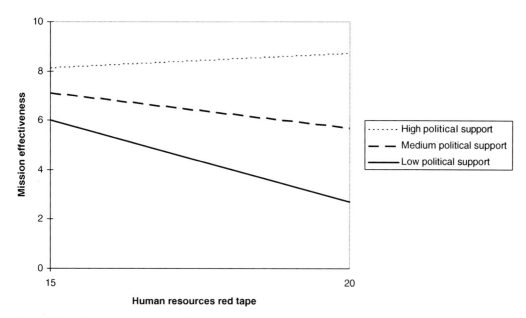

Figure 8.2   Moderating effect of political support on mission effectiveness: Human resource management red tape

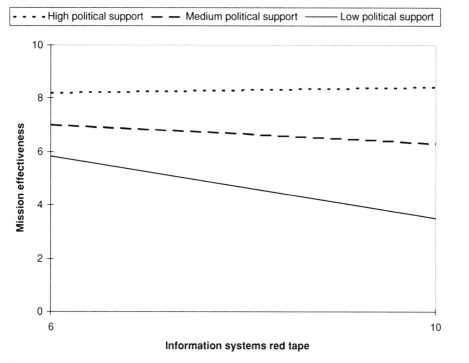

Figure 8.3   Moderating effect of political support on mission effectiveness: Information systems red tape

Table 8.3 Multiple regression results for *service quality* as the dependent variable

Independent variables	Interactions with	
	Culture	Political support
Intercept	17.914****	21.280****
Human resources red tape	−0.042 (−0.40)	−0.162* (−1.76)
Procurement/purchasing red tape	−0.239* (−1.79)	−0.249* (−1.97)
Information systems red tape	−0.188 (−1.13)	−0.222 (−1.39)
Developmental culture	0.351** (2.80)	
Political support		0.149** (2.01)
Interaction of developmental culture with		
Human resources red tape	−0.022 (−0.46)	
Procurement/purchasing red tape	0.116** (2.49)	
Information systems red tape	0.072(1.06)	
Interaction of political support with		
Human resources red tape		0.010 (0.39)
Procurement/purchasing red tape		0.133*** (3.41)
Information systems red tape		0.051 (1.15)
N	82	82
Adjusted R^2	0.354	0.365
F-value	7.41	7.73

Standardized betas displayed; **** $p < 0.0001$; *** $p < 0.01$; ** $p < 0.05$; * $p < 0.1$
T-scores displayed in parentheses.

Again, we found partial support for both moderator hypotheses (H3 and H5). The coefficients for the interaction term of procurement red tape, with developmental culture and political support, were both positive and statistically significant. Using parameters similar to earlier graphic depictions of the moderation effect, we provide a graphic illustration of moderation effect of developmental culture and political support respectively in Figures 8.4 and 8.5. The nature of relationships was similar to earlier patterns with both high level of developmental culture and political support separately providing mitigation of the negative effect of procurement red tape. At a high level of each of these moderator variables there was an increase in service quality in spite of increased procurement red tape.

Conclusion

Our goal in this chapter was to link disparate strands in the public management literature, specifically recent developments in red tape research with performance management. This is important because red tape figures prominently

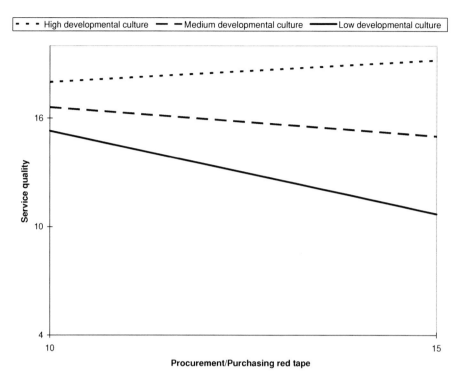

Figure 8.4   Moderating effect of developmental culture on service quality

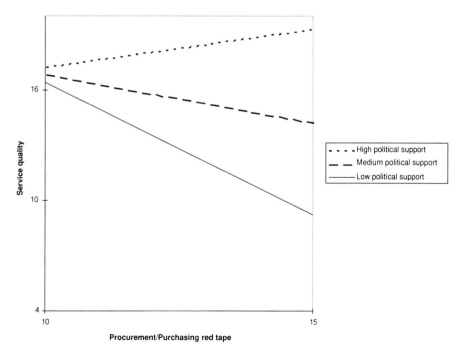

Figure 8.5   Moderating effect of political support on service quality

in real-world efforts to improve performance of public organizations. While there was some variation between models, all four regressions offered support for the three basic components of the theory we have proposed: that red tape negatively effects performance; that political support and culture matter to performance; and that political support and culture have moderating effects on the relationship between red tape and performance. The first two components of the theory are well-established claims, although they do not enjoy such clear empirical support. The third component is both theoretically novel and offers some nascent quantitative support to the limited case study evidence typified by Ban (1995).

Before discussing our findings, it is helpful to place the findings in the context of their limitations. Our results are based on a sample of managers working in state level human service agencies. Although we sample a range of senior managers from agencies that play a major role in delivering health and social services in the US, efforts to generalize beyond this set of agencies should proceed with caution. As noted earlier, the performance measures we use are based on assessments by senior managers only. While we make a case for the use of well-informed internal stakeholder assessments, replication using performance measures derived from other sources is necessary on both methodological and credibility grounds. Finally, although all the study measures show Cronbach alpha within acceptable range, further testing may be necessary for establishing construct validity. Such efforts could test divergent validity of constructs and they could also get into face validity considerations in measuring specific constructs. For example, one of the information systems red tape items seems to tap into construct space for both red tape and performance, and the service quality measures may get into both quality of services delivered by the agency and the agency's success in communicating about the quality of services it provides (Pandey and Garnett 2006).

Despite these and other potential limitations, our findings add value to the performance management literature by providing evidence for negative effect of different types of red tape on performance and also confirming insights on how these negative effects may be mitigated. The results are credible for a number of reasons. First, we lay out sound theoretical grounds for expecting that organizational culture and political support can mitigate the negative effects of red tape. Second, our data collection procedures followed the highest standards; we provided very clear and specific directions to the respondents and ended up obtaining responses from eighty-three out of eighty-five state-level human service agencies. Third, the absence of multicollinearity and significant influence from outliers provide indirect evidence that the results are not merely an artifact of overfitting data. Finally, other studies employing different samples and methodologies report similar findings (Ban 1995; Moon and Bretschneider 2002; Pandey and Bretschneider 1997).

How do our results, then, make a contribution to our Lewinian pursuit to develop and test theory that may be characterized as being quite practical? First, we find, not surprisingly, that red tape has a negative effect on performance. The practical and somewhat 'knee-jerk' response to the presumed relationship between red tape and performance has been to cut rules and red tape as a means for improving performance (Gore 1993; Osborne and Gaebler 1992). In some cases this has proved difficult, because some rules are deeply entrenched. For example, the Clinton administration was largely unable to adjust the core civil service statute that determined personnel rules (Thompson and Ingraham 1996). However, our findings about moderating effects of developmental culture and political support suggest that organizations can mitigate the negative effects of red tape through alternate modalities.

Indeed, we find that at high levels of the two moderating variables, increase in red tape is associated with improved performance. Although this finding is counter-intuitive and certainly warrants further investigation, it highlights the fact that red tape does not overdetermine organizational processes and outcomes. Organizations that vary in the proactive nature of their culture will behave differently when faced with the same set of constraints. Some will accept the constraints as given, and may even exaggerate their impact. Other organizations will seek to test the limits of these constraints, work around them, or interpret them in a way that allows a positive action bias. Organizations that enjoy higher political support will feel less constrained by rules and regulations because they do not operate in the shadow of a 'gotcha' approach to accountability where legislatures are actively policing organizational errors.

Moreover, others offer supporting evidence. Ban (1995) in her case study of four federal agencies shows that some agencies were better at overcoming personnel constraints and were more successful in recruiting qualified personnel. Bretschneider and colleagues (Moon and Bretschneider 2002; Pandey and Bretschneider 1997) using data from two separate questionnaire-based studies found that high levels of red tape prompted managers to be more innovative in using information technology. Moon and Bretschneider (2002: 288) offer the following explanation: 'As the transaction cost of red tape increases and reaches a certain point, the organization seeks an alternative solution to reduce the transaction cost'. We believe and indeed show that it is possible to go beyond the abstractions of transaction cost and offer explanations that explicitly account for the institutional context of public organizations.

What advice does this offer to public managers wary of the transaction costs imposed by red tape? Our findings here are similar to reports that a drug previously known to reduce the risks of heart disease is now found to lower risks for cancer as well. Public management scholarship has for years preached the benefits of a mission-based culture and strong political support for building successful public organizations. We are, in effect, prescribing the same recommendations, but for somewhat different reasons. Developmental culture and political support also help to reduce the negative effects of red tape on performance, thus offering a previously undiscovered benefit. Of course, it is relatively easy to tell public managers to change their organization's culture and increase its political support. It is quite another to actually do it. Indeed, these factors are difficult to change. Organizational cultures can be deeply entrenched, and political support depends to a large degree on agency mission and the composition of stakeholder support. However, public managers now may have one additional reason to make the effort.

Acknowledgement

We thank Ken Meier and Sheela Pandey for pointed and insightful comments. Data analysed in the chapter were collected under the auspices of the National Administrative Studies Project (NASP-II), a project supported in part by the Forum for Policy Research and Public Service at Rutgers University and under a grant from The Robert Wood Johnson Foundation to the Center for State Health Policy also at Rutgers University. Naturally, this support does not necessarily imply an endorsement of analyses and opinions in the paper.

REFERENCES

American Public Human Services Association (APHSA) (2001) *Public human services directory, 2001–2002*. Washington, DC: APHSA.

Ashkanasy, N. M., Broadfoot, L. E., and Falkus, S. (2000) 'Questionnaire measures of organizational culture' in Ashkanasy, N. M., Wilderon, C. P. M. and Peterson, M. F. (eds.) *Handbook of organizational culture and climate*. Thousand Oaks, CA: Sage 131–145.

Ban, C. (1995) *How do public managers manage?* San Francisco, CA: Jossey-Bass.

Baron, R. M. and Kenny, D. A. (1986) 'The mediator-moderator variable distinction in social psychological research: Conceptual, strategic, and statistical considerations', *Journal of Personality and Social Psychology*, **51**: 1173–1182.

Belsely, D., Kuh, E. and Welsch, R. (1980) *Regression diagnostics: Identifying influential data and sources of collinearity*. New York: John Wiley and Sons.

Boyne, G. (2003) 'Sources of public improvement: A critical review and research', *Journal of Public Administration Research and Theory*, **13**: 367–394.

Bozeman, B. (2000) *Bureaucracy and red tape*. Upper Saddle River, NJ: Prentice Hall.

Bozeman, B. (1993) 'A theory of government "red tape",' *Journal of Public Administration Research and Theory*, **3**: 273–303.

Brewer, G. A. (2005) 'In the eye of the storm: frontline supervisors and federal agency performance', *Journal of Public Administration Research and Theory*, **15**: 505–527.

Brewer, G. A. and Selden, S. C. (2000) Why elephants gallop: Assessing and predicting organizational performance in federal agencies. *Journal of Public Administration Research and Theory*, **10**: 685–712.

Deal, T. E. and Kennedy, A. A. (1982) *Corporate cultures*. Reading, MA: Addison-Wesley.

Gianakis, G. A. and Wang, X. (2000) 'Decentralization of the purchasing function in municipal government: A national survey', *Journal of Public Budgeting, Accounting and Financial Management*, **12**: 421–440.

Gouldner, A. (1952) 'Red tape as a social problem', in R. K. Merton, A. P. Gray, B. Yockey and H. C. Selvin (eds.) *Reader in bureaucracy*. pp. 410–418. Glencoe, IL: Free Press.

Gore, A. (1993) *From red tape to results: creating a government that works better and costs less: Report of the National Performance Review*. Washington, DC: USGPO.

Grogan, C. M. and Patashnik, E. (2003) 'Between welfare medicine and mainstream entitlement: Medicaid at the political crossroads', *Journal of Health Politics, Policy, and Law*, **28**: 822–858.

Hood, C. (1991) 'A public management for all seasons?', *Public Administration*, **60**: 3–19.

Ingraham, P. W., Joyce, P. G. and Donahue, A. D. (2003) *Government performance: Why management matters*. Baltimore, MD: Johns Hopkins University Press.

Ingraham, P. W., Thompson, J. R. and Sanders, R. (1997) *Transforming government: Lessons from the federal reinvention laboratories*. San Francisco, CA: Jossey Bass.

Jaccard, J., Turrisi, R. and Wan, C. (1990) *Interaction effects in multiple regression*. Newbury Park, CA: Sage.

Kaufman, H. (1977) *Red tape: Its origins, uses and abuses*. Washington D.C.: The Brookings Institution.

Kettl, D. F. and Dilulio, J. J. (1995) *Inside the reinvention machine: Appraising governmental reform*. Washington, DC: Brookings.

Lewin, K. (1951) *Field theory in social science: Selected theoretical papers*. New York, NY: Harper & Row.

Lincoln, J. R. and Zeitz, G. (1980) 'Organizational properties from aggregate data: Separating individual and structural effects', *American Sociological Review*, **45**: 391–408.

Long, N. E. (1949) 'Power and administration', *Public Administration Review*, **9**: 257–264.

Lynn, L. E., Heinrich, C. J. and Hill, C. J. (2001) *Improving governance: A new logic for empirical research*. Washington, DC: Georgetown University Press.

McGraw, K. O. and Wong, S. P. (1996) 'Forming inferences about some intraclass correlation coefficients', *Psychological Methods*, **1**: 30–46.

Merton, R. K. (1940) 'Bureaucratic structure and personality', *Social Forces*, **18**: 560–568.

Moon, M. J. and Bretschneider, S. (2002) 'Does the perception of red tape constrain II innovativeness in organizations? Unexplained results from simultaneous equation model and implications', *Journal of Public Administration Research and Theory*, **12**: 273–292.

Mott, P. E. (1972) *The characteristics of effective organizations*. New York: HarperCollins.

Moynihan, D. P and Pandey, S. K. In press. 'Creating desirable organizational characteristics: How organizations create a focus on results and managerial authority', *Public Management Review*.

Moynihan, D. P. and Pandey, S. K. (2005) 'Testing a model of public sector performance: How does management matter?', *Journal of Public Administration Research and Theory*, **15**: 421–439.

Osborne, D. and Gaebler, T. E. (1992) *Reinventing government: How the entrepreneurial spirit is transforming the public sector*. New York: Addison Wesley.

O'Toole, L. J. Jr. and Meier, K. J. (1999) Modeling the impact of public management: Implications of structural context. *Journal of Public Administration Research and Theory*, **9**: 505–526.

Ouchi, W. G. (1980) 'Markets, bureaucracies, and clans', *Administrative Science Quarterly*, **25**: 129–141

Ouchi, W. G. (1981) *Theory Z: How American business can meet the Japanese challenge*. New York: Avon Books.

Pandey, S. K. (2002) 'Assessing state efforts to meet baby boomers' long-term care needs: Case study in compensatory federalism', *Journal of Aging and Social Policy*, **14**: 161–179.

Pandey, S. K. (2003) National Administrative Studies Project (NASP-II): *A national survey of managers in state health and human services agencies*. Camden, NJ: Rutgers University.

Pandey, S. K. and Garnett, J. L. (2006) 'Exploring public sector communication performance: Testing a model and drawing implications', *Public Administration Review*, **66**: 37–51.

Pandey, S. K. and Welch, E. W. (2005) 'Beyond stereotypes: A multistage model of managerial perceptions of red tape', *Administration & Society*, **37**: 542–575.

Pandey, S. K. and Scott, P. G. (2002) 'Red tape: A review and assessment of concepts and measures', *Journal of Public Administration Research and Theory*, **12**: 553–580.

Pandey, S. K. and Kingsley, G. A. (2000) 'Examining red tape in public private organizations: Alternative explanations from a social psychological model', *Journal of Public Administration and Research and Theory*, **10**: 779–799.

Pandey, S. K. and Bretschneider, S. (1997) 'The impact of red tape's administrative delay on public organizations' interest in new information technologies', *Journal of Public Administration Research and Theory*, **7**: 113–120.

Peters, T. J. and Waterman, R. H. (1982) *In search of excellence: Lessons from America's best run companies*. New York: HarperCollins.

Quinn, R. E. and Rohrbaugh, J. (1983) 'A spatial model of effectiveness criteria: Towards a competing values approach to organizational analysis', *Management Science*, **29**: 363–377.

Rainey, H. G. (2003) *Understanding and managing public organizations*, 3rd edn. San Francisco, CA: Jossey Bass.

Rainey, H. G. (1983) 'Public agencies and private firms: Incentive structures, goals, and individual roles', *Administration and Society*, **15**: 207–242.

Rainey, H. G. and Steinbauer, P. (1999) 'Galloping elephants: Developing elements of a theory of effective government organizations', *Journal of Public Administration Research and Theory*, **9**: 1–32.

Schein, E. H. (1992) *Organizational culture and leadership*. 2nd edn. San Francisco, CA: Jossey-Bass.

Smith, V., Ramesh, R., Gifford, K., Ellis, E., Rudowitz, R. and O'Malley, M. (2004) *The continuing Medicaid budget challenge: State Medicaid spending growth and cost containment in fiscal years 2004 and 2005*. The Kaiser Commission on Medicaid and the Uninsured, October, Publication 7190.

Steiss, A. W. (1982) *Management control in government*. Lexington, MA: D. C. Heath and Company.

Thompson, F. J. and Riccucci, N. M. (1998) 'Reinventing government', *Annual Review of Political Science*, **1**: 231–257.

Thompson, J. (1967) *Organizations in action*. New York: McGraw-Hill.

Thompson, J. R. and Ingraham, P. W. (1996) 'The reinvention game', *Public Administration Review*, **56**: 291–298.

Waldo, D. (1946) 'Government by procedure' in F. M. Marx (ed.) *Elements of public administration*. Englewood Cliffs, NJ: Prentice Hall. pp. 381–399.

Walker, R. M. and Boyne, G. A. (2006) 'Public management reform and organizational performance: An empirical assessment of the UK Labour government's public service improvement strategy', *Journal of Policy Analysis and Management*, **25**: 371–394.

Wilson, J. Q. (1989) *Bureaucracy*. New York: Basic Books.

Yates, J. (1989) *Control through communication: The rise of system in American management*. Baltimore: Johns Hopkins University Press.

Zammuto, R. F. and Krakower, J. Y. (1991) 'Quantitative and qualitative studies of organizational culture', *Research in Organizational Change and Development*, **5**: 83–114.

9 All that glitters is not gold: Disaggregating networks and the impact on performance

Kenneth J. Meier, Laurence J. O'Toole, Jr. and Yi Lu

Introduction

Networks of actors rather than merely individual administrative agencies are significant in shaping the production and delivery of public policy. A burgeoning research literature proclaims as much, practical discussions on multiple continents treat the theme as important, and the academic research on networked arrays has become ever more convincing and detailed.

A dominant emphasis in this coverage has been on the value added by networked arrays over the 'lonely organizations' (Hjern and Porter 1982) that were highlighted in the traditional work of public administration and public management. Networks, the literature contends, enhance the avenues for dealing with wicked and complex problems that require partnerships and cooperation among public, private, and/or non-profit actors. They offer flexibility, adaptability, potential economies of scale, and greater possibilities for coproduction. They provide sensible fits for the demands of multilevel governance. Indeed, they would seem to be the institutional form of choice in an era of 'governance, not governments'. As recent movements such as the New Public Management sputter on, networks could become an imperative of the new century's public administration.

While these points may have considerable merit, particularly under carefully stipulated conditions, they overgeneralize and overreach. In this chapter, we argue that the glittering promise of networking may not be so golden after all. Some forms of networked interaction – with particular kinds of actors under particular conditions – might well produce little or nothing, while others are simultaneously advantageous for outcomes. In the auric world of networks, all that glitters is not gold.

To develop this point, we first characterize the dominant treatment of the network theme in public management. We indicate theoretical reasons why the usual interpretation might be invalid, or at least subject to important contingencies. We then disaggregate networking behaviour in a large sample of interdependent public management settings to test the notion that not all network nodes are equal, or equally functional for policy performance. We show how network influence interacts with the quantity of managerial networking activities. The chapter concludes with some implications for research and practice. In pursuing this analysis, we advance an earlier study by O'Toole and Meier (2004a) by examining findings from a recent time period and incorporating additional management influences aside from those related to the networking theme (see also O'Toole and Meier 2005).

Networks in a golden light

Networks are undeniably an important aspect of public management (Provan and Milward 1995; O'Toole 1997; Milward and Provan 2000; Cline 2000; McGuire 2002; Agranoff and McGuire 2003). European scholars have pressed the issue even more (Kickert, Klijn and Koppenjan 1997; Rhodes 1997; Bogason and Toonen 1998), emphasizing developments in the emerging European Union and international governance (Kohler-Koch and Eising 1999; Pierre and Peters 2000; Howse and Nicolaidis 2002). In the US, systematic research has documented the near-ubiquity of networked forms for the execution of public policy, certainly via national legislation and regulations (Hall and O'Toole 2000, 2004). Even beyond the explicit work on networks, the significant research devoted to the subject of 'governance' – with particular attention to the webs of state and non-state actors woven into intricate patterns of interdependence – testifies to the salience of the subject in contemporary analyses (Held 1996; Heinrich and Lynn 2000; Kettl 2000; Pierre and Peters 2000; Lynn, Heinrich and Hill 2001).

Perhaps not surprisingly, given that the emergence of networks as important entities has usually been attributed to functional requisites of policy-orientated problem solving, much of the relevant research is framed in optimistic terms: Networks constitute adaptive institutional responses to the 'wicked-problem' (Rittel and Webber 1973) aspects of the contemporary policy world and to the governance challenges of today (e.g., see Chisholm 1989; Powell, Koput, and Smith-Doerr 1996; Kickert, Klijn and Koppenjan 1997; Börzel 1998; Mandell 2001; O'Toole and Hanf 2002). A few European scholars in particular have voiced at least partial exception to this point (see Scharpf 1997), but the dominant trend has been to encourage an acceptance, even an embrace, of networked forms of governance (for detailed documentation, see the literature analysis in Raab and Milward 2003).[1] Policy problems, after all, often add pressure for multi-actor

1 Raab and Milward (2003) provide a very useful coverage of the positive treatment usually given the networks theme in the research literature, but we are not convinced the empirical units at the heart of their own coverage are all themselves networks.

collaborative responses. Coproduction, a common collaborative policy instrument, can indeed result in performance improvements. Some of the most systematic research available on networks and networking for public management demonstrates that in policy fields like public education and law enforcement, networks and networking are positively related to an array of policy outcomes (Meier and O'Toole 2001, 2003; O'Toole and Meier 2003, 2004b; Nicholson-Crotty and O'Toole 2004; O'Toole, Meier, and Nicholson-Crotty 2005). There are reasons to treat the governance theme seriously, and managers who ignore the possible effectiveness gains from working the network could be missing an important contributor to performance.

Fool's gold?

There would seem to be gold in them-thar networks. Nevertheless, despite the bulk of the literature, and despite the rather persuasive evidence generated on the relationships between networks and public programme performance, there are good reasons to temper the general point with some scepticism, at least on some particulars.

Three general reasons can be offered as to why the impact of public management in complicatedly networked settings might be lessened under some circumstances: (1) issues of managerial quality, and the associated matters of complexity and the costs of complex decision making; (2) ineffective or suboptimal agreement among parties, thus constituting a 'harmony trap'; and (3) goal conflict and the realities of politics.

On the first point, networks represent distinctive managerial vehicles, and offer challenges for a single organization and its traditional mode of management. Managerial quality, shown to be positively related to programme outcomes during execution, now embraces managers' ability to create, sustain, and nourish networks (Meier and O'Toole 2002). Still, the importance of management quality depends in part on the complexity of the network setting; some evidence indicates that as network complexity increases, the impact of quality management declines (O'Toole and Meier 2003). Cognitive demands are likely to be especially severe for managers facing the responsibility of generating policy results in networked contexts. Certainly the impact of institutional settings on the decision-making quality of individuals has been a key point of organization theory at least since the work of Simon (1997). Using game theory, Scharpf (1997) has illustrated how decision makers might play the wrong game or make the wrong move in complex and sometimes shifting settings of multiactor interdependence.

On the second point, we can suggest the notion of an 'iron net' as the analogue to the venerable concept of the 'iron triangle' in the analysis of public policy and public management. An 'iron net' is a close-knit set of relationships formed among a particular set of network nodes via consistent, long-running interaction or networking. Such stable interaction patterns carry advantages, but established relationships can make it difficult for nodes representing new or less well-known interests to access the net. In addition, the harmonious relationships among network nodes can bias (or trap) decision making by failing to present alternatives for consideration and by weakening legitimate accountability checks. As Bardach and Lesser (1996) point out, the traditional forms of accountability may not be sufficient in networked settings.

On the third point, adding nodes to a network obviously complicates the value-maximization problem faced by any public programme and any manager. This pattern can be expected in particular when networks deal with 'wicked problems' and when networks include some actors who are there for reasons of generating political support rather than adding capacity to deliver results during the management of programmes. More actors likely mean more goals, and often a wider or potentially more conflictual set of goals across the interdependent actors. Individual organizations themselves attend to multiple goals. When the nodes in a network are populated by many organizations, the full set of goals is likely to be long, and the conflicts among some of them significant.

This third point is the primary focus of the chapter. We do imply that networks are settings experiencing overt and visible clashes on a regular basis. A public manager's efforts to generate programme support across the nodes, however, might well run into complications as pressures to tilt results in one direction or another have to be considered. This theme is largely absent from the literature on public management and networks where networks are often conceived in terms of self-organizing sets of actors who have common interests in effective performance (see e.g., Ostrom 1990 on the management of common-pool resources). In contrast, the theme has received longstanding attention from researchers in political science and public administration in terms of the phenomenon of 'cooptation' of administrative action by parts of a program's political environment (Selznick 1949). In a precursor study, O'Toole and Meier (2004a) explored the cooptation hypothesis with regard to public management and networks and reported on evidence that managerial networking produces the most sizable gains in programme performance for those goals most important to powerful elements in the networked environment. Networking by managers, in short, tends to help the most powerful. This chapter concentrates on the research question related to the theme of goal conflict and politics: even if, overall, network activity by public managers has a positive result on delivering policy results, does managerial networking with *different* nodes have different impacts on performance? In short, we are panning for gold. By moving to each of several sets of dyads, we intend to ground the overall network pattern in the causal realities of more discrete links.

Public management: a formal treatment

Theoretical ideas about public management and how it shapes action and results are not in short supply, but until recently, little systematic effort has been made to model the impact of public management on public programme performance. We start with a formal model of such relationships – a model constructed from an analysis of the mass of theoretical and empirical (mostly case-study) material on public management and performance, and using some of the prominent notions of how management might matter in complex, or networked, institutional settings (see O'Toole 2000). The model, in turn, has been modified as the result of extensive empirical analysis. The model can be outlined briefly, and its application to the present study sketched.

Our general model of public management and performance is:

$$O_t = \beta_1(S + M_1)O_{t-1} + \beta_2(X_t/S)(M_3/M_4) + \varepsilon_t \qquad [1]$$

where:

O is some measure of outcome,
S is a measure of stability,
M denotes management, which can be divided into three parts
    M_1 management's contribution to organizational stability through additions
        to hierarchy/structure as well as regular operations,
    M_3 management's efforts to exploit the environment,
    M_4 management's effort to buffer environmental shocks,
X is a vector of environmental forces,
ε is an error term,
the other subscripts denote time periods, and
β_1 and β_2 are estimable parameters.

The two terms related to managing the environment can be combined where $M_2 = M_3/M_4$. Thus M_2 incorporates all efforts to manage externally in the environment, in contrast to managing the organization, M_1:

$$O_t = \beta_1(S + M_1)O_{t-1} + \beta_2(X_t/S)(M_2) + \varepsilon_t \qquad [2]$$

This M_2, which we define as managerial networking, can be disaggregated into a set of components reflecting managerial interactions with the other actors in the network of interdependence. The disaggregation of M_2 will be a focus of this chapter.

The complexities of the overall model make estimation in a single study difficult. Our strategy for testing, therefore, has been to undertake systematic exploration of limited parts of the model, seriatim. We have shown non-linear impacts of managerial networking overall on performance (Meier and O'Toole 2001;

2003), expanded tests of this relationship across multiple performance measures (O'Toole and Meier 2004b), analysed the separate contributions that structure and behaviour can make to performance (O'Toole and Meier 2004b), and begun to extend the work to other policy fields (Nicholson-Crotty and O'Toole 2004). In this chapter, to provide a better view of managing in the network, we simplify the model for the key research question here by dropping the autoregressive term, and the non-linear interactive relationship component, thus resulting in equation [3]:

$$O_t = \beta_1(M_2) + \beta_2(X_t) + \beta_3(M_1) + \varepsilon_t \qquad [3]$$

The goldfield: units of analysis

Public education is an important and appropriate setting for studying network-related public management questions. Our data are drawn from the 1000+ Texas school districts. School districts in the United States are generally independent[2] local governments with their own taxing powers. All districts in the sample are organized in this way. The sample of districts is highly diverse; they range from monoracial to multiracial, great affluence to considerable poverty, rural to suburban to urban, and tiny to very large.

Public education has become an increasingly complex policy challenge; and although production takes place almost entirely within the school district as organization, a wide array of stakeholders claim some interest in, or jurisdiction over, parts of the educational function. School district managers, accordingly, find themselves operating in networks of interdependent actors surrounding the core district organization. Interacting with this array constitutes one of the responsibilities of school district top managers, the superintendents.

District superintendents in Texas were sent a mail questionnaire on management styles, goals, and time allocations (return rate 55 per cent with 523 useable responses).[3] For the present investigation, we pool three recent years of data (2000–2002) on performance and control variables to produce a total of 1,532 cases for analysis. All non-survey data were from the Texas Education Agency.

---

2 Independent means that a school district is not subordinate to another unit such as a city. Independent districts have their own elected board, possess the ability to tax and set budgets, and acquire bonding authority by vote of the residents.

3 Districts responding to the survey, conducted during 2000, were no different from non-respondents in enrollment, enrollment growth, students' race, ethnicity and poverty, or test scores. There were slight differences in a few other factors. Respondents had 0.48 more students per class, paid their teachers $200 more per year, but had annual operating budgets of about $100 per student less.

Measures

We divide management functions for the purpose of this paper into M_2, managing in the network, and M_1, all other forms of management. Our measures will be discussed in terms of the model: networking (M_2), management (M_1), the vector of environmental forces (X), and programme outcomes (O) or performance. These items are covered in order.

Networking

The networking measure focuses on the frequency and extent of interaction by top managers with several nodes in the school districts' environment. Because school districts operate within a network of other organizations and actors who influence their students, resources, programmes, goals, and reputation, the extent to which a superintendent manages in the school district's interdependent network should be related to school district performance (Meier and O'Toole 2001; 2003).[4]

To measure managing in the network or the managerial networking activity of school superintendents, we selected five sets of actors from the organization's environment: the school board, local business leaders, other school superintendents, state legislators, and the Texas Education Agency.[5] In our mail survey, we asked each superintendent how often s/he interacted with each actor, on a six-point scale ranging from daily to never. Superintendents with a networking management approach, that is those who focus on managing outward, should interact more frequently with all five actors than should superintendents with an approach focused on internal management. A composite network management-style scale was created via factor analysis. All five items loaded positively on the first factor, producing an eigenvalue of 2.07; no other factors were significant.[6] Factor scores from this analysis were then used as a measure

4 In other work we have disaggregated the networking activity in terms of interactions upward, downward, and outward (O'Toole, Meier, and Nicholson-Crotty 2005). In the present study, the measure is fully disaggregated by node.
5 In recent work, we have tested to see whether asking about additional nodes with which these top managers might interact would provide a better measure of managing outward (see Moore 1995). We have asked about interactions with three other actors along with those included here. The five-node networking measure correlates very highly (.97) with the eight-node measure and thus seems an appropriate measure for M_2. See Meier and O'Toole (2005).
6 The network management factor correlates at –.27 with time spent managing the district (in contrast to time spent in contacts outside the organization). In some work we use a four-node network measure and exclude the school board (O'Toole, Meier, and Nicholson-Crotty 2005) because the school board can be considered external to the organization and part of the network. At the same time links with the board are principal-agent relationships and could be seen as part of hierarchically oriented management. The two measures of network management (five-nodes v four-nodes) correlate at .97 with each other, but school board interactions correlate only at .40 with the four-node factor. Because this chapter disaggregates the network into individual nodes, whether school boards are part of the network or a principal-agent relationship is not relevant.

of managerial networking, with higher scores indicating a greater networking orientation. Because we are interested in distinguishing gold from pyrite, we will also use individual network nodes in the analysis and examine separate dyadic interactions as well.

Other management variables

We incorporate two additional aspects of management in this study, as developed in earlier analysis (Meier and O'Toole 2002, O'Toole and Meier 2003). The first is managerial quality, a notoriously difficult concept to measure. In earlier work, we validated a measure based on the residual from a model explaining salaries of district superintendents. The rationale is that in the competitive salary-setting process such as that utilized in Texas school districts, managerial quality should be positively rewarded in salaries. After removing as many 'non-quality' factors as possible from the superintendent's salary, we use the remaining residual as a measure that should be correlated with managerial quality. Although this measure is not perfect, a systematic validation for this variable produced encouraging results (see Meier and O'Toole 2002).

The second aspect is personnel management – to be more precise, personnel stability. We include two aspects of school districts' personnel stability in this study: the longevity of top managers in their organizations and the extent to which the teaching corps in a school district remains in place from one year to the next. The reasons to expect more stable personnel patterns to boost performance, *ceteris paribus*, are explained in earlier work (O'Toole and Meier 2003). *Managerial stability* is measured by the number of years a superintendent has been employed by the district in any capacity. *Teacher stability* is the proportion of the teaching staff in a district that does not change from one year to the next. While not totally under the control of school district leaders, these variables are susceptible to influence by the individuals who make decisions about how such organizations are run, and thus tap aspects of personnel management.

Control variables

Any assessment of public programme performance must control for both task difficulty and programme resources. For school districts, neither of these types of elements is completely under the control of the districts, and therefore they can be considered key parts of the vector of environmentally influenced ('X') forces represented in the model. Fortunately, a well-developed literature on educational production functions (Hanushek 1996; Hedges and Greenwald 1996) can be used for guidance. Eight variables, all commonly used in education analyses, are included in our investigation – three measures of task difficulty and five measures of resources.

Schools and school districts clearly vary in how difficult it is to educate their students. Some districts have homogeneous student populations from upper middle-class backgrounds. Such students often do well in school regardless of what the school does (Burtless 1996). Other districts with many poor students and a highly diverse student body will find it more difficult to attain high levels of performance because the schools must make up for a less supportive home environment and deal with more complex and more varied learning problems (Jencks and Phillips 1998). Our three measures of task difficulty are the percentages of students who are black, Latino, and poor. The last-mentioned variable is measured by the percentage who are eligible for free or reduced-price school lunch. All three measures should be negatively related to performance.

While the linkage between resources and performance in schools has been controversial (see Hanushek 1996; Hedges and Greenwald 1996), a growing literature of well-designed, longitudinal studies confirms that like other organizations, schools with more resources generally fare better (Wenglinsky 1997). Five measures of resources are included. The average teacher salary, percentage of funds from state government and class size are directly tied to monetary resources. Average years of teaching experience and the percentage of teachers who are not certified are related to the human resources of the school district. Class size, non-certified teachers, and state aid (because it is correlated with poverty and other need factors) should be negatively related to student performance; teacher experience and teacher salaries should be positively related to performance.

Performance measures

Finally, we introduce measures for O, or performance (outcomes), for the school districts in our analysis. Acknowledging that all programmes have multiple goals, this study incorporates ten different performance indicators in an effort to determine how the different network nodes affect a variety of organizational processes.

Although each performance indicator is salient to some portion of the educational environment, the most salient by far is the overall student pass rate on the Texas Assessment of Academic Skills (TAAS).[7] The TAAS is a standardized, criterion-based test that all students in grades 3 to 8 and 11 must take. TAAS scores are used to rank districts and this performance measure is without question the most visible indicator used to assess the quality of schools and school districts. Our measure is the percentage of students in a district who pass all (reading, writing, and maths) sections of the TAAS.

---

7 The TAAS was replaced by a new examination in 2003.

Four other TAAS measures are also useful as performance indicators. The state accountability system assesses performance of subgroups of students, and districts must perform well on all these indicators to attain various state rankings. TAAS scores for Anglo, black, Latino and low-income students are included as measures of performance.[8]

Many parents and policy makers are also concerned with the performance of school districts regarding college-bound students. Three measures of college-bound student performance are used – average ACT score, average SAT score, and the percentage of students who score above 1,110 on the SAT (or its ACT equivalent, termed the 'college percentage' by the TEA). The ACT and SAT are standardized tests that are administered nationwide, primarily to students intending to enroll in higher education. Texas is one of a few states where both the ACT and the SAT are taken by sufficient numbers to provide reliable indicators of both. There is generally no correlation between these scores and the number of students taking the tests if the proportion tested is more than 30 per cent of the total eligible to take the test (see Smith 2003); Texas scores only weakly correlated with the percentage of students taking the exams.[9]

The final two measures of performance might be termed bottom-end indicators – attendance rates and dropout rates. High attendance rates are valued for two reasons. Students are unlikely to learn if they are not in class and state aid is allocated to the school district based on average daily attendance. Attendance, as a result, is a good indicator of low-end performance by these organizations; the measure is simply the average percentage of students who are not absent. Dropout rates, while conceded to contain a great deal of error, are frequently also used to evaluate the performance of school districts. The official state measure of dropouts is the four-year total percentage of students who leave school from eighth grade onward.

Nuggets: the findings

Table 9.1 displays the results for the overall TAAS pass-rate. The adjusted R-square is .42, indicating a reasonable amount of variance explained. All variables except *Teacher experience* are significant in the expected direction ($p < .05$). The other management-related variables developed from earlier studies (*Managerial quality*, *Teacher stability*, and *Managerial stability*) produce consistent results in this study. The quality of superintendent management boosts

---

8 Low-income students are defined as those who are eligible for free or reduced price school lunches under that federal programme. The various pass rates do not correlate as highly as one might imagine. The intercorrelations between low income, black, and Latino pass rates are all in the neighbourhood of .6, thus suggesting the overlap is only a bit more than one-third.

9 During 2000–2002 the relationship between the percentage of students taking the tests and the test scores in Texas is positive, but this explains only two to four per cent of the variance depending on the test.

Table 9.1 The impact of managerial networking on organizational performance

Dependent variable = Overall Student TAAS Pass Rate

Independent variables	Slope	t	P<|t|
Managerial networking	0.4269	2.76	0.006
Managerial quality	0.6202	3.80	0.000
Teacher's stability	0.1327	5.92	0.000
Managerial stability	0.0411	2.43	0.015
Control variables			
Teacher's salaries (000s)	0.5488	5.54	0.000
Class size	−0.6114	−4.56	0.000
Teacher experience	−0.0610	−0.68	0.494
Non-certified teachers (%)	−0.1122	−3.60	0.000
Per cent state aid	−0.7628	−2.54	0.011
Per cent black students	−0.1801	−10.78	0.000
Per cent latino students	−0.0714	−6.90	0.000
Per cent low income	−0.1236	−8.85	0.000
Students			
Dummy_Iyear_2001	1.7458	4.66	0.000
Dummy_Iyear_2002	4.4622	11.72	0.000
cons	85.7092	24.85	0.000
R-squared	0.43		
Adjusted R-squared	0.42		
F	80.87		
Number of cases	1532		

performance, as does managerial stability. Higher teacher stability is positively related to the TAAS pass rate, as expected. Of particular interest is the impact of managerial networking. Because the network measure is a standardized score, it has an effective range of −3 to +3, the maximum effect size for this variable is about 2.5 points on districts' overall pass rate. This figure may seem modest, but it can be seen as substantial, given that we examine only one level of networking – by top managers. In addition, the measure represents the net effect of overall networking – the influence of interactions with different external actors may sometimes cancel each other out. As we disaggregate the analysis of networking, the effect of networking with particular nodes that are relevant and instrumental to educational goals may be found to be higher. For the most salient performance indicator – overall TAAS pass rates – managerial networking thus contributes to positive results. This finding fits with the expectations developed from the research tradition of Selznick (1949) and others.

How does networking effort play out across the range of performance measures? Tables 9.2 and 9.3 show the regression coefficients for the managerial networking variable in nine different multiple regressions that use each of the outcome indicators as dependent variables. The controls, including the

Table 9.2 Impact of network activity on *disadvantaged* students indicators
Independent variable = Five-node networking factor score

Performance measures	Network slope	t	R-squared	N
Latino pass rate	0.0533	0.20	0.17	1426
Black pass rate	0.2816	0.64	0.15	951
Low income pass rate	**0.4325***	2.12	0.28	1523
8–12 grade dropouts	−0.1271	−1.12	0.19	1447
Class attendance	−0.0044	−0.23	0.20	1532

All equations control for managerial quality, teacher's stability, managerial stability, teacher's salaries, class size, teacher experience, non-certified teachers, percentage of state aid, percentage of black students, percentage of Latino students, percentage of low income students, and year dummies.

* $p < .05$ two tailed test

Table 9.3 Impact of network activity on *advantaged* students indicators
Independent variable = Five-node networking factor score

Performance measures	Network Slope	t	R-squared	N
Anglo pass rate	**0.4833***	3.23	0.24	1517
Average ACT scores	**0.1044***	2.99	0.40	1317
Average SAT scores	**4.2472***	2.15	0.28	1083
College bound Students (%)	**0.5498***	2.08	0.29	1398

All equations control for managerial quality, teacher's stability, managerial stability, teacher's salaries, class size, teacher experience, non-certified teachers, percentage of state aid, percentage of black students, percentage of Latino students, percentage of low income students, and year dummies.

* $p < .05$ two tailed test

other measures of management, are identical to those sketched earlier for all equations. The other management variables (*Managerial quality, Teacher stability*, and *Managerial stability*) continue to contribute in the expected directions, but the detailed findings on these are omitted from the tables in the interest of concentrating on the impacts of networking. (Overall, of the twenty-seven relevant coefficients – three management variables for each of the nine estimations – eighteen show statistically significant impacts in the desired direction, and none have impacts in the opposite direction.) These results reinforce the notion that networking can have positive performance impacts. Networking by superintendents is associated with statistically significant and desired organizational results in six of the full set of ten cases (including performance for the all-pass rate for TAAS). Of particular interest is the pattern observable when the performance indicators are organized into two groups: those tapping performance among advantaged students and those focused on disadvantaged students.

Table 9.2 summarizes the results for the five indicators targeting performance for the relatively disadvantaged portions of the educational constituency. The effect of networking is rather muted. For four of these five indicators (Latino pass rate, Black pass rate, dropouts and class attendance), managerial networking does not influence performance. The only disadvantaged-students indicator that receives a statistically significant benefit from managerial networking is the pass rate for low-income students.

However, in Table 9.3 a striking pattern emerges for the four indicators targeting the relatively advantaged parts of the educational constituency.[10] Managerial networking has a significant positive impact on all advantaged student indicators (Anglo pass rate, ACT scores, SAT scores, and per cent above 1,110). This pattern is what one would expect, given that all these indicators are of considerable interest to advantaged constituencies toward whom superintendents may channel their efforts.

Overall, the results from Tables 9.2 and 9.3 are clear: Managerial networking contributes considerably more to advantaged-students' performance but little to outputs linked to disadvantaged students. These results support Selznick's argument and confirm our suspicion: Managerial networking is more instrumental in assisting issues that concern influential parts of an interdependent constituency than those related to the less influential. The effects of managerial networking, therefore, are not evenly distributed.

Further insight can be gained by disaggregating the overall networking composite factor into its five components and examining the impacts of each. To separate, in effect, the bull from the bullion, we ran fifty additional regressions each including a single network node as an independent variable (and each including both the other management variables and the same set of controls), and reported the results in Table 9.4.

A glance at Table 9.4 clearly indicates that interactions with different network nodes affect performance in different ways. Some contacts are associated with significant improvements in performance: twenty-two of the fifty relationships are positively and significantly related to desired organizational outcomes. A substantial number of individual interaction dyads are unrelated to organizational performance: twenty-six of the fifty relationships fit this pattern. Two other relationships are negatively correlated with performance. While the general positives far outweigh the negatives, interacting with nodes is a lot like prospecting for gold. Sometimes one finds riches, sometimes one finds nothing and sometimes the mine collapses in on the prospector.[11]

---

10 The overall TAAS pass rate can also be considered as a part of this cluster of performance measures, since it is a salient measure generally for local communities.

11 An examination of these relationships for Texas school district data for 1995–99 produces similar and in some respects even more pronounced, results. These are not reported here – for a summary of parts of the earlier pattern (see O'Toole and Meier 2004a).

Table 9.4 All that glitters: The influences of *individual* network activity on all organizational performance measures

Disadvantaged students indicators

Performance measures	School board members	Local business leaders	Other superintendents	State legislators	Texas Education Agency
Latino pass rate	−0.1215	−0.1348	0.3391	0.0272	0.1517
Black pass rate	−0.467	0.1784	0.1112	**1.6270***	0.2392
Low income pass rate	−0.1904	0.0681	**0.7116***	**0.6945***	**0.5803***
8–12 grade dropouts	0.0877	0.0462	−0.1523	**−0.2983#**	**−0.2677#**
Class attendance	**−0.0731**	**−0.0478***	**0.0818***	−0.0012	**0.0548***

Advantaged students indicators

Anglo rate	−0.1483	**0.3034***	**0.6337***	**0.8925***	**0.3588#**
Average ACT scores	0.0252	**0.1147***	0.0402	**0.1457***	0.0725
Average SAT scores	−2.4132	**4.7436#**	**4.5256***	**7.6468***	0.6439
College bound students (%)	0.1288	**0.7595***	0.3111	**0.7749#**	−0.1504
Overall pass rate	−0.1879	0.2324	**0.6290***	**0.4380***	**0.4547***

All equations control for managerial quality, teacher's stability, managerial stability, teacher's salaries, class size, teacher experience, non-certified teachers, percentage of state aid, percentage of black students, percentage of Latino students, percentage of low income students, and year dummies.
* $p < .05$ two tailed test
\# $p < .10$ two tailed test

Examining the performance impacts of interactions with individual nodes provides some additional information. First, interactions with the school board never produce statistically significant positive results (see also O'Toole, Meier and Nicholson-Crotty 2005) and a significant negative relationship was found: for class attendance. Two prominent critics lay much of the blame for what they see as the poor quality of public education on school-board attempts to impose their preferences on school districts (Chubb and Moe 1990). While schools are generally open systems, school boards, as elected bodies, might be the focal point for efforts to limit administrative actions. Micromanagement, the logic asserts, results in lower performance.

Local business leaders provide a consistent set of impacts on the more elite aspects of education, those for college-bound students.[12] Positive relationships for Anglo test scores, SAT scores, ACT scores, and high college-board scores are offset by a negative relationship with class attendance. Such a pattern is consistent with business leaders pushing schools to provide better education for advantaged students.

12 This pattern is even clearer for the 1995–99 period (see O'Toole and Meier 2004a).

Contacts with fellow superintendents generally provide a consistently positive pattern. Managerial networking contributes to five out of ten performance indicators, two of these in the group of disadvantaged students' indicators and three for advantaged students. This set of results indicates that interactions with other superintendents influence both high- and low-end performance. Interviews with superintendents suggest that those with good contacts among other superintendents use that network as a source of new ideas on curriculum and practices.

Contact with legislators is part of the normal pattern of working the political environment in either searching for political support for school policies or seeking additional aid from the state. Networking with them has the most positive impacts (eight of them; the dropout sign should be negative). State legislators are also the only node related to a positive impact for African-American students, and the impact is sizable. Although we do not have information on the race of the state legislators in this data set, one might speculate that black legislators constitute a political force advocating that more attention be paid to the performance of black students.

Finally, the TEA has an accountability function, and superintendent interactions with the agency are associated with improved performance on the basic evaluation criteria – TAAS scores, attendance, and dropouts. Each of these factors is used in the TEA assessment that assigns grades to schools and school districts.

Overall, the pattern in Table 9.4 is clear and intriguing: Managerial networking with certain network nodes improves some of the results for disadvantaged students, while other interactions boost results for the advantaged students. The broader pattern of distributional impacts of networking takes on a more nuanced shape when the networking results are examined on a dyad-by-dyad basis. It is notable that the mine is more in danger of collapse when the prospecting centres around managerial interactions with school board members. This point might signal a larger issue in the board/superintendent school governance relationship than merely the managerial networking theme per se. On the other hand, the seams of gold evident in the horizontal networking among superintendents and state legislators bear more systematic attention, since some informal and horizontal networking relationships prove to be valuable for performance. Finally, interactions with local business elites show the clearest distributional impact, with those who are advantaged being helped and the disadvantaged possibly being hurt. The likelihood of uncovering riches depends on the lie of the land.

Conclusion

This study has examined the widely asserted view that networks and networking action are an unambiguously positive factor in organizational performance.

Using a large set of public organizations and controlling for other managerial impacts, we demonstrate that managerial networking with other actors is associated with improved performance for some, but only some, of the goals that organizations pursue. Examining the influence of individual nodes in the networked environment of Texas public schools, we have found an even more varied pattern. Some interactions are positively related to performance, some are unrelated to performance, and some are actually negatively linked to organizational performance.

A great deal of evidence has now accumulated to demonstrate that management matters for public services performance. In broad terms, this chapter provides further substantiation, along with some intriguing details. Several measures of management – managerial quality, along with personnel stability at two levels in public educational systems – contribute positively to services performance on multiple criteria. These, in turn, can be distinguished from managerial networking, which also performs as a good deal of the literature suggests – but not unambiguously so. Networking by managers involves no benign Midas touch. Interaction by top managers with the interdependent actors in the environment improves performance on metrics more important to the more powerful elements of the setting, not much for those who are weaker. Searching for the precious metal is not alchemy, nor a mere engineering task. The challenge exposes those involved to the fault lines and predictable seams of political life. Further, behind the notion of an abstract network node are the identities of particular kinds of interested actors. Networking by managers offers prospects of gain, wasted effort, or loss – the devil, as well as the payoff, lies in the details.

To the emerging line of research on networks and public services performance, then, this chapter contributes a cautionary note. Attention to the details of managerial interaction, actor identity, and the political lie of the land can help point prospectors toward discoveries of lasting value.

Acknowledgement

An earlier version of this chapter was presented at the 2003 Annual Meeting of the Association for Public Policy Analysis and Management, Washington, DC, 6–8 November.

This chapter is part of an ongoing research agenda on the role of public management in complex policy settings. We have benefited from the helpful comments of George Boyne, Stuart Bretschneider, Gene Brewer, Amy Kneedler Donahue, Sergio Fernandez, H. George Frederickson, Carolyn Heinrich, Patricia Ingraham, J. Edward Kellough, Laurence E. Lynn, Jr., H. Brinton Milward, Sean Nicholson-Crotty, David Peterson, Hal G. Rainey, Bob Stein, and Richard M. Walker on various aspects of this research programme. Needless to say, this chapter is the responsibility of the authors only.

REFERENCES

Agranoff, R. and McGuire, M. (2003) *Collaborative public management: New strategies for local governments*. Washington, DC: Georgetown University Press.

Bardach, E. and Lesser, C. (1996) 'Accountability in human services collaboratives – for what? and to whom?', *Journal of Public Administration Research and Theory*, **6**: 197–224.

Bogason, P. and Toonen, T. A. J. (eds.) (1998) Comparing networks', Symposium in *Public Administration*, **72**: 205–407.

Börzel, T. A. (1998) 'Organizing Babylon: On the different conceptions of policy networks', *Public Administration*, **76**: 253–274.

Burtless, G. (ed.) (1996) *Does money matter?* Washington, D.C.: Brookings Institution.

Chisholm, D. (1989) *Coordination without hierarchy*. Berkeley: University of California Press.

Chubb, J. and Moe, T. M. (1990) *Politics, markets, and America's schools*. Washington D.C.: The Brookings Institution.

Cline, K. D. (2000) 'Defining the implementation problem: Organizational management versus cooperation', *Journal of Public Administration Research and Theory*, **10**: 551–572.

Hall, T. E. and O'Toole, L. J., Jr. (2000) 'Structures for policy implementation: An analysis of national legislation, 1965–1966 and 1993–1994', *Administration and Society*, **31**: 667–686.

Hall, T. E. and O'Toole, L. J., Jr. (2004) 'Shaping formal networks through the regulatory process', *Administration and Society*, **36**: 186–207.

Hanushek, E. (1996) 'School Resources and Student Performance', in Gary Burtless (ed.) *Does money matter?* Washington D.C.: Brookings Institution. pp. 43–72.

Hedges, L. V. and Greenwald, R. (1996) 'Have times changed? The relation between school resources and student performance', in Gary Burtless (ed.) *Does money matter?* Washington D.C.: Brookings Institution. pp. 74–91.

Heinrich, C. J. and Lynn, L. E., Jr. (eds.) (2000) *Governance and performance: New perspectives*. Washington, D.C.: Georgetown University Press.

Held, D. (1996) *Democracy and the global order: From the modern state to cosmopolitan governance*. London: Polity Press.

Hjern, B. and Porter, D. O. (1982) 'Implementation structures: A new unit for administrative analysis', *Organization Studies*, **2**: 211–237.

Howse, R. and Nicolaidis, K. (eds.) (2002) *The federal vision: Legitimacy and levels of governance in the U.S. and the EU*. Oxford: Oxford University Press.

Jencks, C. and Phillips, M. (eds.) (1998) *The black-white test score gap*. Washington, D.C.: The Brookings Institution.

Kettl, D. F. (2000) 'The transformation of governance: Globalization, devolution, and the role of government', *Public Administration Review*, **60**: 488–497.

Kickert, W. J. M., Klijn, E. H. and Koppenjan, J. F. M. (eds.) (1997) *Managing complex networks: Strategies for the public sector*. London: Sage.

Kohler-Koch, B. and Eising, R. (eds.) (1999) *The transformation of governance in the European Union*. New York: Routledge.

Lynn, L. E., Jr., Heinrich, C. J. and Hill, C. J. (2001) *Improving governance: A new logic for empirical research*. Washington, DC: Georgetown University Press.

Mandell, M. P. (2001) *Getting results through collaboration: Networks and network structures for public policy and management*. Westport, CT: Quorum Press.

McGuire, M. (2002) 'Managing networks: Propositions on what managers do and why they do it', *Public Administration Review*, **62**: 599–609.

Meier, K. J. and O'Toole, L. J., Jr. (2001) 'Managerial strategies and behavior in networks: A model with evidence from U.S. public education', *Journal of Public Administration Research and Theory*, **11**: 271–293.

Meier, K. J. and O'Toole, L. J., Jr. (2002) 'Public management and organizational performance: The impact of managerial quality', *Journal of Policy Analysis and Management*, **21**: 629–643.

Meier, K. J. and O'Toole, L. J., Jr. (2003) 'Public management and educational performance: The impact of managerial networking', *Public Administration Review*, **63**: 689–699.

Meier, K. J. and O'Toole, L. J., Jr. (2005) 'Managing the network: Issues of measurement and research design', *Administration and Society*, **37** (5): 523–541.

Milward, H. B. and Provan, K. G. (2000) 'Governing the hollow state', *Journal of Public Administration Research and Theory*, **20**: 359–379.

Moore, M. H. (1995) *Creating public value: Strategic management in government*. Cambridge MA: Harvard University Press.

Nicholson-Crotty, S. and O'Toole, L. J., Jr. (2004) 'Testing a model of public management and organizational performance: The case of law enforcement agencies', *Journal of Public Administration Research and Theory*, **14**: 1–18.

O'Toole, L. J., Jr. (1997) 'Treating networks seriously: Practical and research-based agendas in public administration', *Public Administration Review*, **57**: 45–52.

O'Toole, L. J., Jr. (2000) 'Different public managements? Implications of structural context in hierarchies and networks' in J. Brudney, L. J. O'Toole, Jr. and H. G. Rainey (eds.) *Advancing public management: New developments in theory, methods and practice*. Washington, DC: Georgetown University Press, pp. 19–32.

O'Toole, L. J. and Hanf, K. I. (2002) 'American public administration and impacts of international governance', *Public Administration Review*, **62**: 158–169.

O'Toole, L. J., Jr. and Meier, K. J. (2003) '*Plus ça change*: Public management, personnel stability, and organizational performance', *Journal of Public Administration Research and Theory*, **13**: 43–64.

O'Toole, L. J., Jr. and Meier, K. J. (2004a) 'Desperately seeking Selznick: Cooptation and the dark side of public management in networks', *Public Administration Review*, **64**: 681–693.

O'Toole, L. J., Jr. and Meier, K. J. (2004b) 'Public management in intergovernmental networks: Matching structural networks and managerial networking', *Journal of Public Administration Research and Theory*, **14**: 469–494.

O'Toole, L. J., Jr. and Meier, K. J. (2005) 'Networking in the penumbra: Public management, cooptative links, and distributional consequences', Paper presented at colloquium of the European Group for Organizational Studies (EGOS), Berlin, Germany, June–July.

O'Toole, L. J., Jr. and Meier, K. J. and Nicholson-Crotty, S. (2005) 'Managing upward, downward, and outward: Networks, hierarchical relationships and performance', *Public Management Review*, **7**: 45–68.

Ostrom, E. (1990) *Governing the commons*. New York: Cambridge University Press.

Pierre, J. and Peters, G. B. (2000) *Governance, politics, and the state*. London: Macmillan.

Powell, W. W., Koput, K. W. and Smith-Doerr, L. (1996) 'Interorganizational collaboration and the locus of innovation: Networks of learning in biotechnology', *Administrative Science Quarterly*, **41**: 116–145.

Provan, K. G. and Milward, H. B. (1995) 'A preliminary theory of interorganizational effectiveness: A comparative study of four community mental health systems', *Administrative Science Quarterly*, **40**: 1–33.

Raab, J. and Milward, H. B. (2003) 'Dark networks as problems', *Journal of Public Administration Research and Theory*, **13**: 413–439.

Rhodes, R. A. W. (1997) *Understanding governance: Policy networks, reflexivity and accountability*. Buckingham, UK: Open University Press.

Rittel, H. W. J. and Webber, M. (1973) 'Dilemmas in a general theory of planning', *Policy Sciences*, **4**: 155–169.

Scharpf, F. W. (1997) *Games real actors play: Actor-centered institutionalism in policy research.* Boulder, CO: Westview Press.

Selznick, P. (1949) *TVA and the grass roots.* Berkeley: University of California Press.

Simon, H. A. (1997) *Administrative behavior.* 4th edn. New York: Free Press.

Smith, K. B. (2003) *The ideology of education.* Albany, NY: SUNY Press.

Wenglinsky, H. (1997) *How educational expenditures improve student performance and how they don't.* Princeton, NJ: Educational Testing Service.

10 Network evolution and performance under public contracting for mental health services

Keith G. Provan, H. Brinton Milward and Kimberley Roussin Isett

Introduction

Since the early 1990s, a major movement has been underway in the US and elsewhere (Jones and Kettl 2003) to 'reinvent' government (Osborne and Gaebler 1992), reducing its role from one of service provider, to service contractor. In the US, this movement has occurred at both the federal level, where states have assumed greater responsibility for services in such areas as welfare and health and human services, and the state level, where state government has increasingly turned to both the non-profit and private sectors to provide services that were previously considered to be in the public domain. This process of contracting out public services, referred to ominously as the 'hollow state' by Milward and Provan (1993), has both advantages and problems, as Smith and Lipsky (1993) point out. Despite some concerns, however, most notably in the costs of monitoring, state government contracting of services, especially in health and human services, has become widespread, becoming a key component of a worldwide movement that has been referred to as the New Public Management (Hood 1995; Kettl 1997).

In health care, one major area which has been contracted out in the US has been the provision of mental health services (Milward and Provan 1993). This trend actually started in the 1960s with the deinstitutionalization movement. Services to people with serious mental illness (SMI) had traditionally been provided in state-run mental hospitals, where patients were often kept for many years. With the advent of modern psychotropic medication, many SMI patients were able to gain considerable relief from their illness, enabling them to function reasonably well in a community-based setting, as long as sufficient support services were provided. These support services were to be paid for in part by federal programmes, like the Community Mental Health Centers Act of 1963, but also from funds saved by the state through major cutbacks in the costs of hospitalization.

By the 1980s and into the 1990s, however, it became apparent that government funding for mental health would not meet earlier expectations and hopes.

Direct federal spending for mental health shifted to more fungible block grants to the states and state dollars saved by deinstitutionalization were only partially channelled into community-based programmes. At the community level, some states, like Ohio, actually set up locally-run state government entities to distribute funding and even provide essential services to the SMI. In most other states, however, the state contracted with mostly non-profit local mental health agencies to provide core services needed by SMI clients.

One of the critical components of community-based mental health was, and continues to be, the integration of services across a network of health and related human service providers. Once SMI treatment became deinstitutionalized, a fundamental ideology emerged among service professionals that effective delivery of services could only occur if agencies worked collaboratively through an integrated network of care. This ideology was both fostered and facilitated through the Community Support Programme of the National Institute of Mental Health (Weiss, 1990). The effectiveness of services integration has been tested empirically in a small number of key studies (Lehman *et al.* 1994; Provan and Milward 1995; Bickman 1996). This work has provided only limited empirical support for the implied positive link between services integration and effective client outcomes. However, the fundamental belief in the need to integrate services through a network of organizations remains strong and generally has widespread support among researchers and practitioners, not only in mental health, but across a wide range of health and human services (Weiner and Alexander 1998; Provan *et al.* 2003).

The study presented here is an examination of the structure, performance, and evolution of a publicly-funded, non-profit network of agencies providing a community-based system of care for adults with serious mental illness. The newly-established system was funded by the state under a risk-based managed care contract to a local, non-profit behavioural health authority. In turn, this organization both funded (again, through risk-based contracts) and coordinated the network of local non-profit agencies, which provided the actual services to SMI clients. As in most mental health systems, provider agencies faced normative pressures to collaborate with one another and form an integrated network of services for their SMI clients. A strong network, in theory, would be good for clients and overall system performance. However, the agencies also had to operate within the new, risk-based managed care environment imposed by the state through its public funding mechanism. This setting promoted norms of efficiency, pressures to control costs, and competition for clients and funding – values that were not necessarily consistent with norms of collaboration. The little research that has been done on the topic suggests that the impact of managed care on services integration is negative, based on pressures to compete (Johnsen *et al.* 1998). Thus, the key question we examined in this research was whether or not the non-profit service providers that comprised the system could work together under these conditions to form an effective service delivery network and, if so, how such a system evolved.

There is an implicit assumption among practitioners and even those who study networks that increased network connectedness and collaboration will result in improved network-level performance (Huxham and Vangen 2005). While this view may be appealing, the empirical evidence to support the view is limited, due primarily to the lack of data on network evolution, difficulties in assessing network performance (Provan and Milward 2001), and difficulties in drawing an explicit causal link between network indicators and performance. While our work has its own shortcomings, especially regarding the last two concerns, we attempt to bring additional understanding to this complicated topic. To do this, we present findings from a longitudinal study of network evolution and performance focusing on the mental health delivery system in Pima County (Tucson area), Arizona.

Managed care and the Arizona model

Managed care has been an integral part of health care funding in the state of Arizona since the early 1980s, when it implemented the first Medicaid managed care programme in the US. Mental health funding was not part of the model until the early 1990s, however, and even then, risk was simply passed on to a local funding entity, called a Regional Behavioural Health Authority (RBHA). The problem with this model was that the RBHA, sometimes a provider itself, then had to pay for the full range of services needed by developing contracts with other local providers that were not at risk financially. These provider agencies typically continued to offer services based on the assumption that they would be reimbursed by the local funding entity. Not surprisingly, the outcome of this model, in both Phoenix and Tucson, the state's two urban metropolitan areas, was that SMI spending for the RBHAs in these cities rapidly exceeded the state's contract and both were closed down.

In Tucson/Pima County, a new model was developed to remedy this problem. In mid-1995, the state's mental health contract for Pima County and southern Arizona was won by a RBHA called the Community Partnership of Southern Arizona, or CPSA. Starting in October 1995, CPSA would commence operations under a new type of managed care arrangement. As with the earlier model, CPSA would be fully at-risk to the state. Unlike the earlier model, however, CPSA would contract directly with three large and one smaller provider agencies, whose contracts were fully at risk financially. These four At-Risk Providers (ARPs) would work closely with CPSA to ensure that performance would be maintained and costs controlled. If an ARP could not control its spending, then it would either have to make up the difference through revenue from other sources or go out of business. Thus, even though CPSA was at-risk, it passed on its risk to these four

ARPs, which were directly responsible for service provision and case management. While each of the ARPs had a somewhat different focus concerning how clients might best be served and what specific services it might provide, each was ultimately responsible for the breadth and depth of care for its clients (see Table 10.1). Thus, each ARP needed to work with other agencies in the system to provide a full range of services.

A key aspect of the new model was that all of the county's approximately 3,600 assigned SMI clients would be allocated randomly to the four ARPs. Thus, no one ARP would have to serve a client group that was significantly more impaired and thus, more costly, than any other ARP. This would be critical to the success of the system, avoiding problems of 'adverse selection' that can plague managed care plans. The ARPs were paid on a group capitation basis. That is, each ARP was allocated a yearly fixed-dollar amount based on the number of clients it was assigned. If more clients were added over the year, as typically happened, no additional funds would flow to the ARP, which would have to pay for services for these clients out of its existing funding. For the ARPs, this increased risk and pressure significantly.

When the new CPSA system was first set up, it was viewed by many in the provider community with considerable scepticism. Although three of the four ARPs had joined with CPSA in its successful bid, the idea of running a mental health system on principles of managed care, especially financial risk, was seen as potentially damaging both to clients and providers. A major concern was that the four ARPs would be pitted against each another. Capitation rates were not viewed as being high enough to cover unexpected client costs, there were not enough clients assigned to any single ARP to spread risk sufficiently and CPSA's monitoring activities were seen as threatening. Under these conditions, many felt that strong norms of competition would soon emerge among the ARPs, as each struggled to capture inadequate resources from the other. The expectation was that only one or two of the most efficient ARPs would survive and that client services would suffer.

In general, what was happening was that the state's method of funding mental health services was shaping the way in which these services were delivered, at both the organizational and client levels. Although the details were left up to the local RBHA and its providers, the macrostructure of the system was strongly influenced by the way in which the state government's funding mechanisms were structured and implemented.

This model of indirect government influence over local structures is consistent with institutional theory explanations, especially the work of Meyer *et al.* (1987) on school district complexity. These authors found that local school districts developed high levels of administrative complexity in response to federal funding, which was highly fragmented. While the federal agencies did not specifically require local complexity and thus no mandates were imposed, local districts developed their own structures as a way of coping with the various demands

Table 10.1 Characteristics of the four at-risk providers – 1996 and 1999

At-risk provider	Assigned SMI clients 1996	Actual number of SMI clients served		SMI funding*		Service focus***
		1996	1999	1996**	1999	
Carondelet	1,000	1,265	1,411	$4,193,969	$5,336,568	Hospital-centred crisis stabilization and intensive outpatient
CODAC	250	334	436	$466,460	$1,333,650	Outpatient mental health and substance abuse
COPE, Inc.	1,200	1,418	1,608	$5,032,764	$6,403,882	Psych-social rehabilitation
La Frontera Centre	1,150	1,459	1,595	$5,405,698	$6,137,545	Comprehensive community behavioral health
Totals	3,600	4,476	5,050	$15,098,891 ($4,194/client, 3,600 clients)	$19,211,645 ($3,804/client, 5,050 clients)	

* Funding based on case rate data.

** Fiscal year 1996 was only nine months long. Reported figures are extrapolated to twelve months.

*** The service focus of three of the ARPs remained more or less stable from 1996 to 1999. La Frontera Center retained its multi-service focus, but shifted resources out of vocational rehabilitation and into housing services.

and expectations of federal funders. Thus, it was the institutional environment to which local districts had to respond that shaped the way these districts were structured. In a similar vein, we argue here that the shape of the local mental health system will be affected by its broader institutional environment: specifically, by the funding mechanism adopted by the state.

The research study

The focus of the study reported here is on the impact of the managed care system on the network structure and performance of the four at-risk providers. As noted above, these four agencies comprised the core of the mental health service delivery system which was funded and monitored by CPSA. All four ARPs had been service providers in the previous system that went bankrupt. When the new system was first set up in 1995, each of these ARPs received their own specific allocation of clients and were then supposed to develop their own networks of sub-providers for such services as housing, hospitalization, rehabilitation, and social services. The assumption was that the agencies within each ARP network would work closely with each other to provide services to their particular set of clients. Cooperation across networks could occur, but this would probably be informal.

Research methods

The data for this study were collected at two points in time. The first wave of data collection took place in 1996, about six months after the new managed care system was first implemented. At that time, we only collected data on the links between the agencies that comprised the system. These agencies were identified using a reputational sampling procedure (Knoke and Kuklinski 1982). Specifically, key personnel were first contacted at CPSA and asked to list all agencies in the community that provided any type of regular service to SMI adults. This list was then reviewed and expanded by personnel at each of the four ARPs. After eliminating some agencies that turned out not to be involved with adult SMI clients, 45 remained, which became our research population. We actually collected data from 42 of these, for a 93.3 per cent response rate. Surveys were mailed to the executive director or the head of the SMI programme at each agency and followed up with repeated phone calls until a response was obtained.

   In late 1999, we once again collected data from the agencies that comprised the adult SMI provider system. We used our 1996 list as a starting point from which we added or deleted agencies based on their involvement with our target client group as determined by CPSA and the four ARPs. We surveyed 44 agencies from November 1999 to April 2000, collecting data from 40 of these for a response rate of 90.9 per cent. Of the 42 agencies surveyed in 1996, 39 (or 92.9 per cent), were identical to those surveyed in 1999/2000.

Our 1999/2000 data collection effort was much more extensive than in 1996. We not only collected data on interagency links, but also on such measures as relationship quality, attitudes toward services under the managed care system, and network governance. We also conducted in-depth interviews with nearly all our respondents. Finally, we obtained secondary data on the four ARPs and the system as a whole from CPSA. This included data on costs of services and ARP performance profiles based on their compliance with a series of thirteen quality management indicators. No data were available on actual indicators of client satisfaction, well-being, or quality of treatment.

Measures

Two categories of dependent variables were used in the study: ARP network structure and ARP performance. ARP network structure was assessed using a modified version of a measure developed by Provan and Milward (1995). Specifically, we collected data on the links agencies maintained with one another (including the four ARPs) by asking respondents to report their network ties with every agency on our list. Respondents had to report their relationships regarding each of three different types of links: formal contracts (i.e., funding relationships) and two types of client referrals, sent and received. In addition, in the 1999/2000 data collection effort, links based on shared information were also assessed. Finally, respondents were asked to indicate, for each linkage they maintained, the quality of that relationship on a one (poor) to four (excellent) scale. For all of the linkage data, respondents were asked to report the relationships they had 'over the past six months'. Thus, the 1996 data represents links back to the earliest months of the new system, while the data collected mostly in early 2000, represents links in place during the last part of 1999, approximately four years after the system started.

To maximize reliability of the data, links between individual agencies were only counted if they were confirmed (Marsden, 1990). Each confirmed link type – contracts, shared information, or referrals, was coded as a '1' and each unconfirmed link, or the confirmed absence of a link, was coded as a '0'. Network data were analysed using UCINET (Borgatti *et al.* 1999).

ARP performance data were obtained directly from CPSA records. As part of their monitoring activities, CPSA has, since its inception, been collecting data on the performance of its four principal providers in five areas: contracts, data reporting, quality management, utilization management and finance. We were concerned here only with the quality management data, since these related most closely to how effectively each ARP was serving its adult SMI clients. QM data were collected by CPSA for every year, 1996 to 1999, on each of thirteen dimensions of quality including: coordination of services with a primary care provider; conducting a comprehensive assessment of each client's condition and needs; maintaining and updating client treatment plans; appropriate and timely referrals; speed of intake and the like. These are not direct measures of effectiveness, such as client satisfaction or quality of life, but they do reflect the extent to which each ARP pays attention to various process indicators that are related to client quality. One hundred points were assigned for each of 11 dimensions while two dimensions were assigned 200 points each, for a total of 1,500 points. Final scores used a 0 to 100 scale, determined by the points earned by the ARP as a percentage of the total possible 1,500 points.

Findings

Network data

Table 10.1 reports some of the basic characteristics of the four at-risk providers, or ARPs, in both 1996 and 1999. These include data on clients, funding, and service focus.

Table 10.2 shows the basic network data for the four ARPs in both 1996 and 1999. Three statistics are presented: the actual number of agencies linked to each ARP, the density of each ARP relative to the full network and the ARP's within-network density. ARP density simply reflects the number of agencies linked to each ARP expressed as a percentage of the total possible number of links, which was 41 in 1996 (n − 1) and 43 in 1999 (n − 1). Within-network density reflects the density of the network of providers actually linked to a particular ARP. For instance, if an ARP had only five contractual links, but all five of these other SMI service providers were themselves linked to one another, then the density score would be 1.0. Within-network density was calculated by dividing the actual number of links maintained by the agencies in the ARP's network by the total possible number of such links.

The findings from Table 10.2 indicate several things. First, all four ARPs increased their links to other providers in the system from 1996 to 1999, for both contracts and referrals. Thus, despite the pressures of managed care, the four ARPs managed to build their relationship base over the four-year period since implementation of the new system. Each ARP became more central within the network as a whole. The overall increase in formal, contractual ties was modest, ranging from 2.8% for La Frontera (see Table 10.2 showing an increase in ARP density of .317 to .326) to over 43% for both Carondelet and CODAC. For referrals, however, which are typically informal, the increase in ARP density was more substantial ranging from 63.6% for COPE to 170.5% for CODAC.

Second, the within-network density scores mostly declined or stayed about the same, with sizable density increases only for COPE's contract network (+27.3%).

Table 10.2 Comparative statistics for the four At-Risk Provider (ARP) Networks – 1996 and 1999

ARP network measures	Contracts		Referrals		Combined		Shared information
	1996	1999	1996	1999	1996	1999	1999
Carondelet							
Number of agencies linked to the ARP	8	12	9	21	16	23	13
ARP connectedness	.195	.279	.220	.488	.390	.535	.302
Within-network density	.417	.308	.444	.279	.276	.295	.725
CODAC							
Number of agencies linked to the ARP	6	9	6	17	11	19	29
ARP connectedness	.146	.209	.146	.395	.268	.442	.674
Within-network density	.619	.489	.333	.359	.409	.371	.448
COPE							
Number of agencies linked to the ARP	9	13	14	24	21	27	27
ARP connectedness	.220	.302	.341	.558	.512	.628	.628
Within-network density	.311	.396	.267	.268	.242	.265	.479
La Frontera Centre							
Number of agencies linked to the ARP	13	14	17	30	23	32	32
ARP connectedness	.317	.326	.415	.698	.561	.744	.774
Within-network density	.308	.343	.261	.226	.226	.232	.383
Full Network	.049	.062	.086	.133	.125	.160	.257

* Full network sizes: n = 42 agencies in 1996 and n = 44 agencies in 1999 (CPSA not included).

Table 10.3 Mean multiplexity scores for the four At-Risk Provider (ARP) Networks – 1996 and 1999.

At-Risk Provider	ARP network multiplexity		ARP to APR multiplexity	
	1996	1999	1996	1999
Carondelet	1.313	2.000	1.000	2.333
CODAC	1.091	1.579	1.000	2.000
COPE	1.333	2.185	1.000	2.667
La Frontera Center	1.522	1.906	1.667	3.000

At first glance, these findings may seem inconsistent with the general pattern of increased integration across the ARP networks. However, density scores are very sensitive to increases in network size (Scott, 1995), and all of the ARP networks grew in size from 1996 to 1999, especially the referral networks. Thus, despite the fact that each ARP maintained more links in 1999 than in 1996 for both contracts and referrals, this increase in the number of other provider agencies in each ARP's network meant that it was now more difficult (and less likely) for each of these other providers to maintain ties to one another. It is actually an indication of the strength of some of the ARP networks (most notably, COPE) that within-network density increased or was maintained despite sometimes substantial increases in the number of other providers that became part of the ARP network.

Another point of comparison for the ARPs is their multiplexity which is an indicator of the strength of a particular agency-to-agency link. Relationships that are multiplex have two or more types of links (e.g., contracts and referrals sent). If one of these links is broken, then the relationship is still maintained since at least one other link remains viable. In this case, the maximum multiplexity score is three, which would mean that an ARP maintains ties to every agency in its network through all three types of confirmed links: contracts, referrals sent and referrals received (shared information links were excluded). Table 10.3 reports these multiplexity results.

The results in Table 10.3 indicate that ARP multiplexity with the other provider agencies in their network increased from 1996 to 1999 for all four ARPs. This increase was especially impressive since it occurred at the same time as the number of other agencies to which each ARP was linked also increased. Thus, both the breadth and depth of ARP-network relationships grew over the period studied. For two of the ARPs, Carondelet and COPE, multiplexity scores in 1999 between these ARPs and their network agencies were 2.0 or greater. In 1996, the highest multiplexity score was 1.522.

The ARPs were also strongly linked to each other in 1999, although this was not the case in 1996. At that time, all four ARPs had mean multiplexity scores

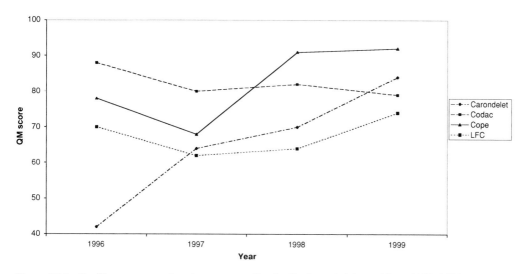

Figure 10.1 Quality management performance profiles for the four at-risk providers, 1996–1999

with one another of only 1.0 to 1.5, and two of the ARPs, COPE and CODAC, were not linked to one another at all (not shown in the table). In contrast, by 1999, multiplexity among the ARPs had increased substantially. Not only were all four ARPs linked to one another (not shown), but their multiplexity scores ranged from a low of 2.0 for CODAC to 3.0 for La Frontera Centre. In other words, La Frontera was linked to the other three ARPs through all three types of links: contracts, referrals sent and referrals received. These findings indicate that by 1999, the four ARPs were not only working closely with other non-ARP agencies in their networks, but also with one another.

Performance data

Figure 10.1 reports the overall scores from the quality management performance profiles for each ARP. In the first year of the system's operation, QM scores (on a 0 to 100 scale) showed considerable variance across ARPs, ranging from 42 for Carondelet to 88 for CODAC, with COPE at 78 and La Frontera at 70. This large gap narrowed over the years and the relative rankings have also changed. In 1999, COPE was the top ARP (92) followed by Carondelet (84), CODAC (79), and La Frontera (74). Most striking was the relative increase in performance of Carondelet and COPE and the relatively stagnant performance of the other two ARPs. For Carondelet, the biggest performance gain came between 1996 and 1997. While some performance problems no doubt were in evidence for this ARP, it was the only one of the four to not have participated in the original bid submitted by CPSA. Thus, its knowledge of the new system and its reporting methods lagged well behind the other three ARPs, who were part of CPSA from the beginning. Overall, the mean quality of services, based on QM scores, improved from 69.5 in 1996 to 82.3 in 1999, suggesting positive client-centred benefits from the managed care system.

These overall scores must be interpreted with caution, however, as they were collected by CPSA and not by an independent entity. It is, of course, in the best interests of CPSA to demonstrate that all their providers have done a better job serving clients since it (CPSA) took over the system. Nonetheless, the data are useful in noting a change in the overall system regarding the time and attention paid to clients and client services (as reflected by the higher mean score), as well as a shift in the relative differences in performance across the four ARPs, from substantial variance to only modest variance.

Although no data were collected directly from clients on system performance, our 1999/2000 survey data offer additional evidence that clients were not being treated poorly. No measures were available to assess the separate performance of each of the ARPs, other than the QM data reported above. However, we asked a question of all respondents requesting that they evaluate the impact of managed care under the CPSA system on their agency's adult SMI services. Respondents were asked to indicate their responses on a five point Likert-type scale, ranging from 1 ('at-risk system has had a significant *negative* impact') to 5 ('at-risk system has had a significant *positive* impact'). A response of 3 indicated that 'the impact has been pretty much neutral'. Respondents were asked to apply these ratings to each of six aspects of client services and operations (mean response in parentheses): number of SMI services offered (2.6); number of SMI clients served (2.81); quality of SMI services (3.03); controlling cost of SMI services (3.09); coordinating SMI care with other agencies (2.94); and stabilizing the system of SMI care (3.14). The mean for all six items is 2.94, which indicates a mostly neutral overall view of how the system of care for SMI clients has evolved under managed care. These same respondents generally approved of the job CPSA was doing regarding 'the overall management and governance of the adult SMI delivery system' since becoming the RBHA in late 1995, with a mean score of 3.63 (scale ranged from 1 = 'system management is much worse than before' to 5 = 'system management is much better than before'). Overall, even with no clinical performance measures, it seems reasonable to conclude that service delivery, as judged by those who were most involved in the network, did not suffer appreciably under the new system of funding.

Discussion

Although this study is unusual in that it is a longitudinal examination of the evolution of an organizational network, it is essentially a comparative case study, limiting the extent to which formal theory testing is possible. Nonetheless, theory helped inform the research and some important conclusions can be drawn that can extend what is known about both theory and practice.

Most notably, the study offered a unique look at how a community-based health network adapted to the introduction of risk-based public contracting. In their discussion of coercive isomorphism, DiMaggio and Powell (1983) argued that coercion by the state need not be direct for its impact to be felt and responded to. For instance, organizations may alter their structures and processes to adapt to the implicit and anticipated demands and expectations of funders and regulators (Meyer *et al.* 1987). What we found in our study was that a major change in the way provider agencies were funded led to local-level adaptation mechanisms and structures that could provide client services while accommodating financial risk. What the nature of that structural response would be was not at all certain when the system was first established. Since risk-based managed-care models emphasize cost control and even competition, it was not unreasonable to expect that the system of service delivery would be competitive and consistent with findings by Johnsen *et al.* (1998), network integration would decline. This assumption was reinforced by the structure of the new system, which was built around four providers, all of which were at-risk financially, all of which were assigned clients randomly and all of which were competing for resources from a single regional behavioural health authority.

What we found, however, was that instead of competing, the ARPs developed denser, more multiplex ties with one another and with the network as a whole. In addition, rather than becoming less effective in treating clients due to pressures on costs regarding service delivery, the four ARPs improved their performance based on CPSA-generated QM data, and showed no noticeable degradation of services based on survey data.

Why did this happen? Although we have no hard data to report, our observations lead us to offer three possible explanations, all of which are closely related: professional norms, system stability and non-profit context. Professional norms can be a powerful force in influencing adoption of similar organizational structures. Despite a mandate by the state to adopt and implement risk-based managed care, there were few direct efforts by the state to impose a specific structure on the local system. Thus, adaptation became a local issue. While administrative pressure to compete was very real, professional pressure to cooperate was also strong. In health care in general and in mental health in particular, these normative pressures can be significant, especially those related to services integration as a way of delivering services effectively and efficiently (Weiss 1990; Alter and Hage 1993). These norms were no doubt in place when the managed-care system was first implemented, but the threat of competition and the disruption caused by implementation of an entirely new system initially kept collaboration and cooperation at modest levels, especially across ARP networks.

In an earlier comparative study of mental health networks, Provan and Milward (1995) found that a critical factor for explaining system effectiveness was stability. While funding was important to ensure that essential services were actually offered, a system that was frequently changed and disrupted, typically by a change in the state's funding mechanism or by a major change in the local funding entity, was unlikely to be effective. The system we studied in Pima County had a long history of frequent and major changes in the system. For instance, the previous RBHA, which provided both case management and the allocation of state funding, lasted only two years before experiencing major financial problems that culminated in the loss of the state contract. In this environment, providers viewed the new managed-care system run by CPSA as an experiment that would probably either quickly fail or produce even more instability, forcing the ARPs to fight with each other for scarce resources. However, once the system was firmly established and it became apparent that CPSA was trying to work closely with the ARPs to ensure they would survive, norms of cooperation among agency professionals seem likely to have become an important force in shaping the system.

The third factor that may have contributed to the increase in integration was the non-profit context. Even though managed care is based on a number of sound principles of health care, such as preventive care, utilization management and cost control, most of the publicity surrounding the concept over the past decade has been negative. A major reason for this is that so many managed-care systems are run by for-profit entities that put pressure on providers to control costs while using savings for enhanced profits and salaries. Managed care can be effective, however, especially if non-profit (Himmelstein *et al.* 1999).

As a non-profit entity, CPSA was subject to the non-distribution constraint (Hansmann 1980) and thus, had no incentive to use system-wide cost savings to enhance its own well-being at the expense of its providers. While CPSA made major efforts to keep costs down, it did not do this in a way that alienated the ARPs and other providers, in part because it also tried to maintain or enhance the quality of services. In part, the focus of CPSA on system-wide outcomes, rather than on its own well-being, appeared to be the result of the norms of cooperation that were held not only by the providers, but also the management of CPSA, which was headed by the former executive director of one of the ARPs. But it also seems likely that norms of professional cooperation would be less likely in a for-profit system where the efforts of the ARPs to manage care and costs might well be undermined by a management entity interested mostly in its own financial survival.

As noted above, all three possible explanations – professional norms, system stability, and non-profit context, were closely tied to the system of contracting used. In the new public management literature on privatization (Savas 2000), competitive contracting is viewed as a driver of efficiency in the provision of public services. We found that competitive contracting, which was how the system was initially set up, was not at all welcomed by key providers. Competitive contracting was seen as being inconsistent with professional norms and had the potential of being a major source of instability, ultimately resulting in detrimental effects on service outcomes.

But we also found that the local risk-sharing aspect of the contract proved not to have the detrimental effects initially envisioned. The incentives created by risk-sharing by the key local providers led to a substantial increase in collaboration among the ARPs over the period covered in this study, mostly because CPSA and the ARPs were all in the same boat – if the system failed, they all failed. Thus, even though the contract won by CPSA from the state was competitive, the local contracting mechanism between CPSA and the four ARPs was not competitive, but relational. Relational contracting holds that building trusting relationships for hard-to-specify services is more effective than competitive contracting (Sclar 2000). In 'thin markets' with only a limited number of buyers and sellers, relational contracting can be a more effective method of holding sellers accountable for their output (Macaulay 1963; Smith and Smyth 1996). Stability, which is much more likely under relational contracting, increases the cost of defection and lengthens the shadow of the future (Axelrod 1984). In a mental health system, it takes time and effort to develop network-wide management systems to track the flow of clients and funding. If competition causes the contract to be won by new bidders with some frequency, there will be little incentive to invest in infrastructure, since the payoff is likely to be low. Of course, every management strategy has its Achilles' heal. If not closely watched, relational contracting can degenerate into collusion between the buyer and the seller at the expense of the taxpayer.

Conclusion

Our research has demonstrated that a community-based system of health and human services can adapt rather well to a state-imposed managed-care mechanism, even when that system is fragmented into a small number of potentially competitive providers. In fact, it may be that the presence of several key providers, with equal risk and mostly equal client loads, acts as a stimulus to do well, in much the same way that Wiewel and Hunter (1985) found community development organizations to benefit from the existence of other, similar, organizations in their community for attracting scarce resources, including legitimacy.

This study adds to the literature on the New Public Management (Osborne and Gaebler 1992; Hood 1995), which has been criticized for being long on generalities and ideology but short on empirical evidence (Pollitt 2000; Jones and Kettl 2003). Our findings offer empirical evidence that local non-profit entities like CPSA that are established to receive public contracts, distribute public funds to service providers and monitor the provision of these services, need not assume the rigidity and insensitivity of government bureaucracies, even when acting as an agent of the state. Such organizations can establish and build inter-organizational governance structures; specifically, networks, that satisfy the requirements of the state while ensuring that the local needs of both clients and their provider organizations are addressed. Although our study does not offer a direct test of the relationship between the evolution of network structure and network-level outcomes measured at the client level, it does demonstrate the impact of public funding mechanisms on network performance, especially measured in terms of sustainability and continued service to clients.

Our research has also demonstrated that some assumptions of the New Public Management, like the efficiency of competitive contracting, does not necessarily hold, especially when focusing on health and human service agencies. Any gains from increasing the efficiency of the system through competitive contracting must be balanced against the losses in collaboration that are likely to occur in changing to a new system (Provan and Milward 1995). By relaxing the part of contracting that calls for competition (but not monitoring, evaluation and joint training) we believe that overall system performance can be enhanced. Relational contracting, even when risk-based, is likely to present fewer problems than competitive contracting in a health and human services context, while being highly supportive of professional norms of collaboration.

The implication of our research for practice is that the imposition of risk-based (but not competitive) contracting models by states, as is the case with managed care, need not result in degradation of services at the local level, despite efforts to control spending. While the initial shift to risk-based contracts may be disruptive and create considerable uncertainty, once relative stability can be attained, key organizational players can then work to build the system's infrastructure and maintain performance.

Acknowledgement

This project was funded by a grant from the Nonprofit Sector Research Fund of the Aspen Institute (No. 99-NSRF-19). Portions of this chapter were published previously in *Nonprofit and Voluntary Sector Quarterly*, 2004, Vol. 33(3): 489–514.

REFERENCES

Alter, C. and Hage, J. (1993) *Organizations working together*. Newbury Park, CA: Sage.

Axelrod, R. M. (1984) *The evolution of cooperation*. New York: Basic Books.

Bickman, L. (1996) 'Implications of a children's mental health managed care demonstration evaluation', *Journal of Mental Health Administration*, **23**: 107–117.

Borgatti, S., Everett, M. and Freeman, L. (1999) *UCINET V Version 1.0*. Natick, MA: Analytic Technologies.

DiMaggio, P. J. and Powell, W. W. (1983) 'The iron cage revisited: Institutional isomorphism and collective rationality in organizational fields', *American Journal of Sociology*, **48**: 147–160.

Hansmann, H. B. (1980) 'The role of nonprofit enterprise', *Yale Law Journal*. **89**: 835–901.

Himmelstein, D. U., Woolhandler, S., Hellander, I. and Wolfe, S. M. (1999) 'Quality of care in investor-owned vs not-for-profit HMOs', *Journal of the American Medical Association*, **282**: 159–163.

Hood, C. (1995) 'The new public management in the 1980s: Variations on a theme', *Accounting, Organizations and Society*, **20**: 93–109.

Huxham, C. and Vangen, S. (2005) *Managing to collaborate*. London: Routledge.

Johnsen, M. C., Morrissey, J. P., Landow, W. J., Starrett, B. E., Calloway, M. O. and Ullman, M. (1998) 'The impact of managed care on service systems for persons who are homeless and mentally ill' in J. P. Morrissey (ed.) *Research in community mental health*, Vol. 10 pp. 115–137. Greenwich, CT: JAI Press.

Jones, L. R. and Kettl, D. F. (2003) 'Assessing public management reform in an international context', *International Public Management Review*, **4**: 1–18.

Kettl, D. F. (1997) 'The global revolution in public management: Driving themes, missing links', *Journal of Policy Analysis and Management*, **16**: 446–462.

Knoke, D. and Kuklinski, J. H. (1982) *Network analysis*. Newbury Park, CA: Sage.

Lehman, A. F., Postrado, L. T., Roth, D., McNary, S. W. and Goldman, H. H. (1994) 'Continuity of care and client outcomes in the Robert Wood Johnson Foundation program on chronic mental illness', *Milbank Memorial Quarterly*, **72**: 105–122.

Macaulay, S. (1963) 'Non-contractual relations in business: a preliminary study', *American Sociological Review*, **28**: 55–67.

Marsden, P. (1990) 'Network data and measurement' in W. R. Scott (ed.), *Annual Review of Sociology*, **16**: 435–463. Palo Alto, CA: Annual Reviews.

Meyer, J., Scott, W. R. and Strang, D. (1987) 'Centralization, fragmentation, and school district complexity', *Administrative Science Quarterly*, **32**: 186–201.

Milward, H. B. and Provan, K. (1993) 'The hollow state: Private provision of public services' in H. Ingram and S. R. Smith (eds.) *Public policy for democracy*. Washington, D.C.: Brookings, pp. 222–237.

Osborne, D. and Gaebler, T. (1992) *Reinventing government: How the entrepreneurial spirit is transforming the public sector*. Reading, MA: Addison-Wesley.

Pollitt, C. (2000) 'Is the emperor in his underwear?', *Public Management*, **2**: 181–199.

Provan, K. G., Nakama, L., Veazie, M. A., Teufel-Shone, N. I. and Huddleston, C. (2003) 'Building community capacity around chronic disease services through a collaborative interorganizational network', *Health Education and Behavior*, **30**: 646–662.

Provan, K. G. and Milward, H. B. (1995) 'A preliminary theory of interorganizational network effectiveness: A comparative study of four community mental health systems', *Administrative Science Quarterly*, **40**: 1–33.

Provan, K. G. and Milward, H. B. (2001) 'Do networks really work? A framework for evaluating public-sector organizational networks', *Public Administration Review*, **61**: 414–423.

Savas, E. S. (2000) *Privatization and public-private partnerships*. New York: Seven Bridges Press.

Sclar, E. D. (2000) *You don't always get what you pay for: The economics of privatization*. Ithaca, NY: Cornell University Press.

Scott, W. R. (1995) *Institutions and organizations*. Thousand Oaks, CA: Sage.

Smith, S. R. and Lipsky, M. (1993) *Nonprofits for hire: The welfare state in the age of contracting*. Cambridge, MA: Harvard University Press.

Smith, S. R. and Smyth, J. (1996) 'Contracting for services in a decentralized system', *Journal of Public Administration Research and Theory*, **6**: 277–296.

Weiner, B. J. and Alexander, J. A. (1998) 'The challenges of governing public-private community health partnerships', *Health Care Management Review*, **23**(2): 39–55.

Weiss, J. A. (1990) 'Ideas and inducements in mental health policy', *Journal of Policy Analysis and Management*, **9**: 178–200.

Wiewel, W. and Hunter, A. (1985) 'The interorganizational network as a resource: A comparative study on organizational genesis', *Administrative Science Quarterly*, **30**: 482–496.

11 The design and management of performance-based contracts for public welfare services

Youseok Choi and Carolyn J. Heinrich

Introduction

In the United States, the Wisconsin Works (W-2) programme is widely regarded as a pioneer in public welfare reform (Mead 2004). Beginning in 1997, Wisconsin made major changes in the administrative structures for the delivery of welfare services, ending the county government monopoly on public assistance administration and inviting private sector agencies to compete for contracts to manage local level programmes. Performance-based contracting was also introduced to motivate and monitor the performance of W-2 agencies by setting performance standards (and target levels) in advance and making payment and performance bonuses contingent on the achievement of performance goals.

Wisconsin is just one of many states that has increased contracting for public welfare services in the Temporary Assistance for Needy Families (TANF) programme. The US Government Accounting Office (GAO 2002) reported extensive contracting out for TANF services delivery in every state except one, with most funds (88 per cent) in state-level contracts (and close to three-fourths of these contracts with non-profit providers). The percentage of total TANF funds in contracts between states and for-profit providers ranged from 0–100 per cent in 2001; in addition, the majority of state funds were in traditional cost-reimbursement contracts (about 60 per cent); only about one-fifth of contracts included incentives to improve performance.

Designing performance-based contracts that align the interests of public and private providers with policy goals and effectively enforcing contract provisions are challenging tasks. This chapter describes the development of performance-based contracting in the W-2 programme and the state's efforts to improve contract design over time. We trace changes in the contract terms, particularly the evolution of performance standards, and discuss how the state government and W-2 service providers addressed problems associated with incomplete and imperfectly enforceable contracts.

We employ the case study method – an intensive study of performance-based contracting for public welfare programmes in a single state – relying on temporal variation and empirical analyses of subunits' (contractor) performance to draw out insights for public welfare programme administration and more general implications for performance-based contracting. Several state-level case studies on the administration of TANF programmes have documented major administrative changes, including the devolution of responsibility for welfare/job service provision to lower level governments and subsequent coordination problems among various administrative bodies (Norris and Thompson 1995; Liebschutz 2000; Weissert 2000; Sanger 2003; Van Slyke 2003). However, except for Van Slyke's study, these studies lack an in-depth analysis of the contracts governing relationships among the involved parties.

We begin with a brief theoretical discussion that frames our analysis of government contracting decisions. Applying this theoretical frame, we then analyse contract design and administration in W-2 over four contract periods, focusing on management issues and problems in the transition from government administration to a performance-based contracting regime with competing public and private providers. We conclude with recommendations for public sector contracting and suggestions for future research.

Theoretical framework

Formal models of government contracting decisions and processes suggest that the decision about whether to contract out service provision should not be made without consideration of how the contracting process will work given the nature of the service and other relevant factors (political and economic). Both theory and empirical research also suggest that contracting for *complex* public services – in which it is difficult to fully specify job tasks and performance expectations, that is, a *complete* contract – presents greater risks, management challenges and costs to implementation.

In their study of public sector contracting, Brown and Potoski (2003) consider two service-specific characteristics, *asset specificity* and *service measurability*, drawn from Williamson's (1981) transactions costs framework for analysing alternative contracting structures. They note that services with a greater degree of asset specificity require more specialized investments to produce them, thus barriers to entry and the risks of monopolization in service delivery are likely to be greater. The challenges (and costs) of writing an effective performance-based contract are also greater when the outcomes or value added of these services are difficult to observe or evaluate (i.e., a lower level of service measurability). In these circumstances, contract negotiations become critical, as the contracting parties determine the terms or mechanisms (e.g., performance incentives or sanctions) that will allow them to address the problems associated with contract incompleteness.

Thus, the government has to determine how the uncertainty and risk inherent in incomplete contracts – e.g., the potential for unforeseeable increases in the costs of service provision or unforeseeable difficulties in fulfilling contract obligations or objectives – will be shared between the government and private providers. McAfee and McMillan (1989) argue from a strictly economic perspective that the government is in a favourable position to assume a greater share of the risk associated with unknown or unforeseen contingencies and to assume more control over how these non-contracted contingencies are handled, as it is typically involved in many different activities and the risks (and costs) associated with any one activity are distributed across all taxpayers.[1] And in bearing more of the risk, the government should also pay less (or a lower risk premium) for services delivered by the private provider. They also acknowledge, however, that government contracting does not occur in a political vacuum, and that failed projects, cost overruns and unintended consequences take a political toll, even if unfairly attributed to government decision making that was appropriate at the outset. Thus, these political influences may compel government officials to be more risk averse than is socially (and economically) efficient.

In addition, the effective design and management of contracts is also critically dependent on internal government capacity (DeHoog 1984; Donahue 1989; Kettl 1993). Although there are clearly some capabilities required for effective contract management that are also pertinent to in-house service provision (e.g., financial management, planning and performance analysis), other tasks such as negotiating contract terms and monitoring provider activities are likely to require new levels of expertise or types of management tools and structures (Kettl 1993; Romzek and Johnston 2002). In their study of state contracting for social services in Kansas, Romzek and Johnston found that the contracting process required exceptional capabilities and experience in advance planning, contract design, negotiation and implementation on the part of the state that were not always present at the outset of the contracting relationship. Furthermore, the levels of capacity and resources required for effective contract management are also likely to be influenced by some of the factors associated with contract completeness, that is, the ability to anticipate contingencies (political and economic), measure value (outcomes) and to separate providers' efforts from outside (environmental) influences or risks.

Recognizing the importance of these factors, we use the heuristic framework (or logic of governance reduced form model) set forth by Lynn *et al.* (2000)[2] to

---

1 An exception to this presumption might occur in the case of a small government unit (e.g., a municipality) contracting with a larger firm.
2 The logic of governance reduced form model – represented by the function, $O = f(E, C, T, S, M)$ – consists of the following components: O = outputs/outcomes (individual-level and/or organizational outputs/outcomes); E = environmental factors; C = client characteristics; T = treatments

more broadly conceptualize the contracting decision (and resulting organizational outcomes, O), as a function of not only service-specific characteristics (or the treatment, T), but also environmental factors (E – e.g., political and market structures, economic conditions, external authorities, etc.), organizational structures (S – centralization of control, administrative rules/incentives, contractual arrangements, etc.), and management (M – e.g., leadership, monitoring, control and accountability mechanisms). In the next section, we consider the general implications of theory for contract design and management and then follow with our analysis of contracting in the W-2 programme and the role and influence of the above factors. This case study elucidates the progression of W-2 to an increasingly complex performance-based contracting system – from unrestricted bonuses to restricted rewards, process-orientated to outcome-based performance measures and unweighted to weighted performance standards – followed by a major retrenchment, brought about in part by environmental and management/structural constraints that impeded the effectiveness of these contract features.

Implications of theory for contract design and management

One option for reducing uncertainty or handling unforeseen environmental contingencies is to incorporate a mechanism for automatically adjusting expectations for contract outcomes or performance at particular times or under specific circumstances over the course of the contract. For example, in the Job Training Partnership Act (JTPA) programme, performance standards in contracts between states and local service delivery areas that were tied to total contract payments were adjusted annually by a mathematical formula to account for local characteristics (including client characteristics) that might change over time and influence programme outcomes. In fact, the use of performance standards and incentives in contracts between the government and private providers has become increasingly popular, in part because of the flexibility offered for balancing risks with rewards for improved performance.

However, in public welfare programmes, there are often multiple programme objectives (sometimes politically ascribed) and no single, verifiable measure of contractor performance that adequately characterizes the value of the services provided. In these cases, a performance measure may not generate appropriate incentives for service providers, nor will it always provide an accurate signal to the government of the total value produced by the provider. Baker (1992) shows in a formal model that if the variances of the performance measure and total value produced are highly (or perfectly) correlated, an optimal contract

(primary work/core processes/technology); S = structures, and M = managerial roles and actions. See also Heinrich and Lynn (2000) for examples of applications of this framework in research on government performance.

can be written.[3] Empirical studies have since shown that this may be difficult (and costly) to achieve in practice, with some finding weak and even negative correlations between performance measures and programme value or impacts (Burghardt and Schochet 2001; Heckman *et al.* 2002).

The problems associated with weak relationships between performance measures and service value are magnified when the effort or actions of the contractor (or agent, as discussed in principal-agent theory) are not fully observable by the government (i.e., principal), and/or the interests and goals of the principal and agent diverge (Dixit 2002). Any efficiency gains potentially achieved through a competitive market with a wider range of provider alternatives may be counterbalanced by inefficiencies generated by employees engaging in 'gaming' activities that increase measured performance but not service value. In addition, if monetary rewards for performance are included in a poorly designed (or inadequately managed) incentive contract, further distortions in the efficient allocation of resources may be introduced.

Other challenges in designing performance-based contracts include setting benchmark levels for the standards and assigning appropriate weights to standards when multiple performance measures are used to evaluate contractor performance. Courty and Marschke (2004) developed an economic model of the performance-standard setting process, noting the tradeoffs in terms of the costs associated with determining more accurate benchmarks (e.g., accounting for the effects of factors outside the control of managers) and the returns associated with assessing the value of services more accurately. Better distinguishing agents' contributions to performance by establishing more accurate measures should benefit the principal (i.e., government), who will pay a lower risk premium to the agent and will more efficiently allocate resources based on measured performance.

Courty and Marschke underscore the point, however, that identifying factors that are within versus those outside the control of programme managers or employees (e.g., separating agents' efforts from external influences or risks) becomes more complex in the case where multiple contract objectives and performance measures are established. Holmstrom and Milgrom (1987) model the allocation of an agent's effort among multiple activities and consider the weights that should be assigned to different measures of performance across the activities. They show that if one activity is subject to more exogenous variance than another, then the incentive scheme should reward the latter (i.e., which is less subject to factors outside the agent's control) more highly. At the same time, it is not uncommon for political priorities and management and monitoring constraints to have some bearing on the relative emphasis placed on performance

---

3 Baker makes this same point in defining a 'simple metric' for the 'goodness' of a performance measure: 'when the marginal product of the agent's actions on the performance measure is highly correlated with the marginal product of these actions on the principal's objective, then the performance measure is a good one and the resulting contract will be efficient' (Baker, 1992: 612).

goals. As the W-2 case study shows, this, in turn, can have important implications for client outcomes and programme performance.

Wisconsin works case study

Background: The new public welfare administration

In its decision to award W-2 contracts on a competitive basis, the state of Wisconsin allowed any public or private agency to bid to manage the programme and at the same time, advanced performance-based contracting for both public and private providers. Prior to W-2, counties administering AFDC and public/private agencies managing JOBS programmes had been paid on a cost-reimbursement basis where, regardless of performance, agencies were reimbursed in full for welfare benefit payments and job training and administration activities (Dodenhoff 1998). Another important change in programme administration was the merger of welfare (income support) administration and employment assistance services into a single programme (W-2), evidently to reduce the coordination problems that had hampered service delivery in the separately administered AFDC and JOBS programmes (Sandfort 1999).

Before the first W-2 contracts were awarded, the Wisconsin legislature intervened and imposed a 'right of first selection' rule. Counties could achieve the right to operate the W-2 programme without having to compete with other public or private agencies, as long as they met specific criteria indicating that their performance under AFDC had been satisfactory.[4] Thus, the programme began with strictly limited competition – of the seventy-two Wisconsin counties, sixty-seven earned the right of first selection. Private agencies were contracted to run the W-2 programme in nine counties, including Milwaukee, where at the time nearly three-quarters of all W-2 recipients were enrolled.[5] These services included: determining eligibility for W-2; placing participants into one of the four programme tiers (unsubsidized employment, trial jobs, community service jobs, or transition activities) and providing particular services within each tier.

The state also built into the contracts a provision for biannual renegotiation that, in theory, should help to reduce the risks associated with the incomplete nature of the contracts. The state can change contract awards and reallocate

4 All county welfare agencies were subject to a pre-W-2 trial period (1 September 1995 to 30 August 1996). The state government set caseload reduction and job-placement criteria for counties to meet. If the counties met those standards, they would earn the 'right of first selection' in W-2 (Dodenhoff, 1998).

5 The state divided Milwaukee county into six regions to facilitate service accessibility (Wisconsin Legislative Audit Bureau, 1999). Among the five agencies that received contracts – United Migrant Opportunity Services Inc. (UMOS), Maximus, Opportunities Industrialization Center of Greater Milwaukee (OIC), YW Works and Employment Solutions Inc. (ESI) – ESI received contracts for two of the regions.

funding, modify performance expectations, or make other adjustments in the face of changing economic conditions, legislative priorities or budget constraints.[6] However, the downside is that a two-year contract period allows little time for the recovery of start-up costs for new providers and might discourage service provider investments in qualities that are not immediately realized. To some extent, the W-2 'right of first selection' rule could silence this concern by contributing to stability in government-provider contracting relationships. Yet the tradeoffs among these features are important to recognize: both the right of first selection and two-year contract periods might discourage the entry of new providers and limit the potential benefits of competition in contracting; at the same time, limited competition might promote greater stability and reduce uncertainty for the contracted providers.

Evolution of W-2 contracts

We now examine changes in the W-2 contracts over four contract periods – primarily changes in performance standards, incentives and bonuses and monitoring provisions – and consider how they influence and distribute risk between the state and its contractors. To the extent that data are available, we also analyse the performance of W-2 contractors, and more generally, the state's capacity to manage the system and improve programme results over time.

Phase 1 (9/1997–12/1999): High-powered incentives for caseload reduction

The 1997–1999 contract period opened the first opportunity for W-2 agencies to make large profits in administering public welfare programmes. Although the contracts required W-2 agencies to assume financial responsibility for any programme costs exceeding the contract budget, they were not tied to minimum spending levels. By allowing contractors to keep some portion of their unspent funds, the state, in effect, paid a 'risk premium' in the form of profits earned by W-2 agencies, encouraging them to bid for the opportunity to operate the new programme and compensating them for taking the risks of unpredictable costs or cost overruns. Ostensibly, these profits should also reward agencies that improve programme management or efficiency and support their development of innovative ways to serve W-2 participants.

Three levels of performance achievement were established to determine incentive payments: base performance level; first bonus level and second bonus level. Table 11.1 shows that in the first contract period, agencies achieving the first bonus level could keep up to 7 per cent of unspent funds as unrestricted

---

6 However, the ex-post renegotiation might contribute to a moral hazard problem. If W-2 agencies and the state anticipate the possibility of renegotiation at the time of the first contract signing, they may not exert their best efforts to generate the desired outcomes in the first round.

Table 11.1 Components of performance reward and payment system

		1997–1999	2000–2001	2002–2003	2004–2005
Base contract Performance	Right of first selection (RFS)	Earned when meeting specified performance level			
	Community reinvestment fund (CR)	45% of remaining surplus	3% of contract amount	Replaced by emergency fund	Replaced by emergency fund
Level I Bonus	Bonus I	Up to 7% of unspent budget and 10% of remaining surplus (when unspent fund exceeds 7% of budget)	2% of contract amount (unrestricted)	Amount is not specified (unrestricted)	Bonus eliminated
Level II Bonus	Bonus II		2% of contract amount (unrestricted)	Amount is not specified (unrestricted)	Bonus eliminated

Source: Wisconsin Legislative Audit Bureau (2001), DWD (2003a), DWD (2003b)

profits. If the unspent funds exceeded 7 per cent of the contract budget, the remaining funds after the initial distribution of profits were divided between the state and the agency, with an additional 10 per cent given to the agency as unrestricted profit. Among the remaining 90 per cent of funds, 45 per cent was allocated to the agency for community reinvestment funds for services to needy people. The other 45 per cent was retained by the state (Wisconsin Legislative Audit Bureau 1999:12). These rules for the distribution of unspent W-2 contract funds were known to agencies at the beginning of the contract and provided a clear indication of the potential or maximum amount of bonuses and community reinvestment funds that they could earn. The prospect of large bonuses in return for meeting contract performance goals thus served as a high-powered incentive for W-2 agencies.

It is also important to recognize, however, that in the first contract period, the criteria or standards by which providers were judged were primarily process-orientated measures. These administrative measures included: the ratio of staff to clients; percentage of cases meeting full-activity requirements; percentage of clients with an employability plan; client participation in a high school equivalency degree programme, and the development of contractual arrangements with faith-based organizations. The single outcome-orientated measure was the percentage of W-2 cases that returned to a W-2 grant after being placed in a job (Kaplan 2000). Consistent with the pre-PRWORA emphasis on (and political goal of) reducing welfare caseloads, the overall administrative focus was on processing clients quickly and getting them into jobs (Mead 2004).

With funding fixed for the first contract period based on caseloads existing in August 1996, no minimum spending levels and little emphasis on outcomes in the first period, it should not come as a surprise that contract under-spending was significant. The initial budget allocation was based on an estimated 41,402 cash benefit cases; however, the actual caseload at the onset of W-2 in September 1997 was 23,182 – only 56 per cent of the projection. Statewide expenditure during the first year was only 60 per cent of the contract budget amount and the gap between projected and actual caseloads became greater by August 1998 (Wisconsin Legislative Audit Bureau 1999: 25). As a result, most W-2 agencies readily earned the right of first selection for the 2000–2001 contract – a total of sixty-two of the seventy-five agencies administering W-2 and all five of Milwaukee County's private agencies that handled the bulk of the W-2 caseload. During the first contract period, these five Milwaukee agencies' profits totalled $26.2 million, with an average profit rate of 8.5 per cent.

Concerns were subsequently raised about whether these large agency profits were appropriate (Wisconsin Legislative Audit Bureau 1999). While the state regarded the surplus as evidence of the W-2 programme's success in reducing costs, critics, including community welfare advocates and American Federation of State, County and Municipal Employees (AFSCME), argued that the contract terms would encourage W-2 agencies to provide fewer services to needy people and would transfer taxpayer dollars to agencies in the form of surpluses or profits (Huston 1998). Changes in the second round of W-2 contracts responded to these issues.

Phase 2 (1/2000–12/2001): Increased monitoring, restricted profits

The new provisions of the second round of contracting were aimed at increasing contract performance requirements and monitoring. These contract revisions came under the pressure of public opinion to improve accountability in the face of concerns about excessive agency profits. A key change under this new contract was the determination of performance achievements by outcomes-based standards rather than administrative actions orientated toward reducing caseloads. The 2000–2001 W-2 contract included five measures of participant outcomes: employment rate; average wage rate; two-job retention measures; employer health insurance benefits and two programme process measures (see Appendix 1). W-2 agencies had to achieve the base performance level for all seven measures in order to earn the right of first selection for the next contract period and to be eligible for a performance bonus. The base level expected outcomes are also shown in Appendix 1.

In addition, the second-round contracts reduced the level of profits agencies could earn to a total of 7 per cent of the contract amount (see again Table 11.1). Upon achieving the base level of performance, agencies could retain 3 per cent of the contract amount as a restricted-use bonus (e.g., for community reinvestment uses). By achieving a higher level of performance across all standards (the first bonus level), agencies could earn an *unrestricted* 2 per cent bonus; another 2 per cent of unrestricted funds were allowed upon attaining the highest (second bonus) level. The Milwaukee agencies' profits in the 2000–2001 contract period totaled $8.9 million, with a profit rate of 3.5 per cent. This compared to $26.2 million and an 8.5 per cent profit rate in the 1997–1999 contract period. In effect, at the same time that performance requirements were becoming more stringent, opportunities to earn profits were becoming more limited.[7]

It is also important to consider, however, the level of the performance standards set for the providers and how challenging they were to attain. If it is relatively undemanding for agencies to achieve these standards and the risk of failure is minimal, the state should not be expected to pay a high risk premium in the form of large bonuses to agencies who meet the standards. In fact, a majority of the seventy-two agencies achieved the highest level of performance across all standards in the 2000–2001 contract period. Only eight smaller counties failed to achieve the base performance level across these standards. The W-2 agencies' average performance on the entered employment rate was about three percentage points above the national average and their performance on the earnings gain measure was double the national average (see www.acf.hhs.gov//programs/ofa/). Thus, the reduction in available incentive payments might not only have helped to placate public concerns about excessive profit allowances, but might also have signaled a move by the government toward a more efficient contracting arrangement (i.e., offering smaller bonus awards in light of the low apparent risks).

The increased monitoring and scrutiny of contracting agencies in 2000–2001 uncovered a series of management problems, primarily from inappropriate use of funds in the first round W-2 contracts. A state government review confirmed that some W-2 funds intended to support those in need of public assistance in Milwaukee County were being used for other purposes, for example, to expand these agencies' business in other states.

Why did these problems occur early in the operation of W-2? Evidence suggests that the state's monitoring of agencies' financial management in the first period was lacking. The state had contracted with the Milwaukee Private Industry Council (PIC) to audit W-2 agencies' financial performance, but local officials indicated that the state did not allocate adequate resources for monitoring.[8] A Wisconsin Legislative Audit Bureau report (2001) criticized both the state and PIC for failing to properly monitor the programme and concluded that confusion over who was responsible for providing financial and programme oversight of W-2 probably contributed to the abuse. Hefetz and Warner (2004) found that high levels of monitoring were key to the success of government contracting

---

7 The performance bonuses earned by W-2 agencies during the 2000–2001 contract period were further reduced by the 2002–2003 Biennial Budget Act (DWD, 2002a). The act cut about $2.0 million of statewide performance bonuses – from $14,826,200 to $12,820,800.

8 According to PIC, the focus was changed by the state to remove any financial oversight. The council only checked to see whether W-2 agency spending stayed within the overall contract budget limit (Schultze 2000).

out, although they acknowledged that it does not come cheaply. The studies they cited estimated that the costs of monitoring average close to 20 per cent of total contract costs.

Phase 3: (1/2002–12/2003): Refining the W-2 contracts

Changes made in the W-2 contracting process during the third period again reflected the state's interest in improving contract management and fine-tuning contract provisions to increase efficiency. Significant changes were made to the W-2 performance standards during this period to address the early contracting problems. The state classified the major performance standards into four categories: 1) priority outcomes for participants; 2) high quality and effective case management services; 3) customer satisfaction; and 4) agency accountability (DWD 2001). A total of six new criteria were simultaneously introduced (see Appendix 1).[9] For example, in response to the improper billing problems, 'financial management' and 'contract compliance' standards were added.[10] A 'customer satisfaction' standard and new administrative standards for case assessments and processing were also adopted to encourage W-2 agencies to focus on meeting participants' needs.[11]

Importantly, coupled with these changes, different weights were applied to the four categories of performance standards in determining bonus payments and the right of first selection. Previously, no weights had been assigned to the performance standards. These weights also differed according to the two levels of bonuses used in the contracts (i.e., bonuses with and without restrictions on their use) (DWD, 2001). For the level one performance bonus, 'the priority outcomes' performance standards were accorded a weight of sixty-five per cent, and the other 35 per cent was based on standards measuring the 'delivery of high quality and effective case management services'. The weights on performance standards for level two bonuses were slightly different from those of level one, including a small allotment for customer satisfaction.[12] All performance measures were calculated based on data for the twenty-four month contract period and provisions were also made to adjust for risks associated with local labour market conditions (DWD 2001). Performance benchmarks

---

9 In addition, eight standards were introduced for 'information only' (e.g., average wage rate at placement) and were not linked to performance payments (DWD, 2001).

10 In order to prevent improper billing problems, a penalty for unallowable expenses was introduced (DWD, 2001). This made a W-2 agency automatically liable to DWD for a penalty equal to 50 per cent of the amount of unallowable expenses.

11 The new administrative standards, 'assessment for appropriate W-2 placement and extension' and 'timely and complete processing of 24- and 60-month extension requests', were also a response to problems with inappropriate client sanctions (DWD, 2001).

12 Sixty per cent for the priority outcomes for participant's performance standards, 30 per cent for the delivery of high quality and effective case management services performance standards and 10 per cent for the 'delivery of services that meet customer expectations' performance standard (DWD 2001).

(or targets) were adjusted when high unemployment rates were recorded over a period of at least three months.

In general, these changes are consistent with provisions that, in theory, should improve the contracting relationships between the state and W-2 agencies. For example, categorizing performance standards and assigning weights to them that signal the government's programme priorities should generate clearer and more cogent incentives for service providers. In addition, the adjustments for local economic conditions should lower agencies' risk of poor performance due to factors that are outside the control of programme managers. And to the extent that the new performance measures are more strongly correlated with the impact or value of the W-2 services being contracted out, programme outcomes for W-2 participants should be improved through managers' focus on achieving these standards.

However, as the state worked to develop a more accountable W-2 contracting system and to improve programme quality, the legislature imposed substantial constraints. These problems were driven in part by a disparity between the biennial budget fiscal years (e.g., 1 July 2001 to 30 June 2003 for the 2001–2003 Biennial Budget) and the W-2 contract period (1 January 2002 to 31 December 2003 for 2002–2003 W-2 contract). In effect, the budget for the last six months of the W-2 contract became subject to the outcome of the next round of biennial budget act negotiations, to the extent that the state could be forced to rewrite the W-2 contract for the final months of the contract period, changing the contract terms retroactively.

The contract changes driven by the Biennial Budget Act in the 2002–2003 contract period thus had important implications for the agencies' financial incentives, for example, performance bonuses or funds available for community reinvestment. The 2001–2003 Biennial Budget Act reduced the final amount of performance bonus and community reinvestment funds available by about $2.0 million in performance bonuses (DWD 2002a) and $1.99 million in community reinvestment funds (DWD 2003a). Furthermore, the bonuses earned during the 2002–2003 contract period would not be paid until about one year after the end of the contract. These changes have contributed to considerable uncertainty not only about the level of performance bonuses that will be paid, but also *if* they will be paid, particularly in times of tight budgets and weak economic conditions. In theory, one would expect that the prospect of late-period contract revisions and the breach in the link between agencies' performance and the amount of performance bonus they can earn could have a negative impact on agencies' motivation to achieve performance goals.

Performance results of two contract periods: 2000–2001 and 2002–2003

There are important differences in how performance was evaluated between the 2000–2001 and 2002–2003 periods; thus, in comparing results across the

Table 11.2 W-2 agency performance in 2000–2001 and 2002–2003 contract periods

	2000–2001	2002–2003
Number of agencies meeting all base level standards	63 (89%)	15 (22%)
Number of agencies failing to meet 1 base level standard	4 (6%)	21 (31%)
Number of agencies failing to meet 2 base level standards	3 (4%)	17 (25%)
Number of agencies failing to meet 3 or more base level standards	1 (1%)	14 (21%)
Total Number of Agencies	71	67*

*Performance data are not available for Waushara County, as the provider contract ended early in 31 July 2002
Source: DWD (2002), DWD (2004)

two periods, we consider how measurement and management changes in the system may have affected these performance outcomes. Table 11.2 shows that there were, in fact, significant differences in the performance outcomes of W-2 agencies between these two contract periods. The number of agencies that met base performance levels for all of the standards declined dramatically in the 2002–2003 contract period, down from sixty-three (89 per cent) to just fifteen (22 per cent) of the agencies. Table 11.2 also shows the number of performance standards that agencies failed to meet. While only 5 per cent of the agencies failed to meet more than one standard in the 2000–2001 period, this proportion climbed to nearly half of the W-2 agencies in the 2002–2003 contract period.

However, the much smaller number of agencies meeting all base level performance standards does not necessarily imply that agencies' performance during 2002–2003 was considerably poorer than in the 2000–2001 period. Table 11.3 shows the base, first bonus and second bonus performance achievements for each of the performance standards in the two contract periods. Among these, the target performance levels were the same across contract periods for the first five (of seven) 'priority outcomes for participants' standards shown in Table 11.3. Although it appears that the W-2 agencies' 2002–2003 performance fell short of 2000–2001 achievements on these five standards (entered employment, job retention – 30 and 180 days, full and appropriate engagement, and basic education activities), the differences are small and statistically negligible.

For the other two priority outcome standards – educational activities attainment and wage rate or earnings gain – the measures and their use in the performance-based contracts, in addition to agencies' performance on them, differed between the 2000–2001 and 2002–2003 periods. In the 2000–2001 contract, the educational attainment performance measure was optional and only three of seventy-one agencies met the base performance level. This same measure was required in the 2002–2003 contract and 88 per cent of W-2 agencies met the minimum (base) performance level, with 76 per cent of these achieving a bonus level. Alternatively, while all agencies met the base performance targets for wage increases in the 2000–2001 period, less than half met the earnings gains

Table 11.3 W-2 agency performance by standard (2000–2001 vs 2002–2003 contracts)

Performance standards and target levels	2000–2001		2002–2003	
	Number of agencies achieved	%	Number of agencies achieved	%
Entered employment				
Base Performance Level (35%)	70	**99%**	64	**94%**
1st Bonus Level (40%)	70	99%	57	84%
2nd Bonus Level (45%)	61	86%	51	75%
Job retention: 30 days				
Base Performance Level (75%)	71	**100%**	65	**96%**
1st Bonus Level (80%)	65	92%	55	81%
2nd Bonus Level (85%)	46	65%	43	63%
Job retention: 180 days				
Base Performance Level (50%)	70	**99%**	64	**94%**
1st Bonus Level (55%)	69	97%	57	84%
2nd Bonus Level (60%)	59	83%	42	62%
Full and appropriate engagement				
Base Performance Level (80%)	68	**96%**	63	**93%**
1st Bonus Level (85%)	66	93%	62	91%
2nd Bonus Level (90%)	59	83%	55	81%
Basic education activities				
Base Performance Level (80%)	64	**90%**	60	**88%**
1st Bonus Level (85%)	58	82%	54	79%
2nd Bonus Level (90%)	46	65%	44	65%
Educational activities attainment				
Base Performance Level (*Optional* in 2000–2001 = 50%) (2002–2003 = 35%)	3	4%	59	88%
1st and 2nd Bonus Level in 2002–2003 (40%)	N/A		51	76%
Average wage rate (2000–2001)/Earnings gain (2002–2003)				
Base performance level (Wage rate:100% of base wage) (Earnings gain: 50%) *Changed to optional, information only*)	71	100%	28	42%
1st Bonus Level (wage = 102.5%)	71	100%	N/A	
2nd Bonus Level (wage = 105.5%)	69	97%	N/A	
New performance standards for 2002–2003 contract				
Assessment for appropriate W-2 placement and extension				
Base Performance Level (80%) (1st Bonus = 85%, 2nd Bonus = 90%)	N/A		24	36%
Timely and complete processing of 24- and 60-month extension requests				
Base Performance Level (form submission = 80%, data entry = 95%)	N/A		12	18%
W-2 agency staff training				
Base Performance Level (90%) (1st Bonus = 85%, 2nd Bonus = 90%)	N/A		63	94%
Financial management				
Timely audit and no significant audit findings (Met/Not Met)	N/A		67	100%
Contract compliance				
Met/Not Met	N/A		67	100%
Customer satisfaction survey				
Base Performance Level (average score 6.5)	N/A		64	94%

Source: DWD (2002), DWD (2004)

base performance levels in 2002–2003. Although the W-2 agencies began their 2002–2003 contracts with the earnings gain standard as a required performance measure, the state changed it to an 'information-only' standard midway through the contract period. In an administrative memo proposing this change, a case was made that there were 'too many complexities and difficulties in getting accurate data', leading to 'questionable' performance data entries (DWD 2002b).

Continuing down Table 11.3, it is evident that W-2 agencies' performance on the new 'high quality and effective case management' standards was considerably poorer. In fact, the higher failure rates on these standards account for a large part of the decline in the number of agencies meeting base performance levels in the 2002–2003 contract period. Just over one-third of the agencies met base performance standards for 'assessment for appropriate W-2 placement and extension' and less than one-fifth met the minimum standard for 'timely and complete processing of 24- and 60-month extension request'. Recall that these standards were accorded less weight than the priority outcome standards (35 per cent compared to 65 per cent) in the determination of performance bonuses. In addition, the same November 2002 memo on proposed performance standard modifications claimed that the assessment standard was complex, confusing and poorly implemented and should be disregarded for the first half of 2002 (DWD 2002b). Although this administrative memo suggests it was the measure – not agency performance – that was poor, subsequent state audits and scrutiny of W-2 case management activities in Milwaukee have shown casework activities in W-2 to be deficient.

At the same time, 100 per cent of W-2 agencies met the requirements for 'financial management' (timely audits with no significant findings) and 'contract compliance' (with Department Policies and Procedures) – standards that were essential to earn the right of first selection for the 2004–2005 contract period. Considering the W-2 agencies' performance across all measures shown in Table 11.3 and the relative emphasis placed on each in the performance calculations under the two contracts, it appears that the agencies performed best or consistently highly on the measures that were accorded the greatest weight in the contracts (and were of the highest political priority). On the performance standards that were established as (or changed to) optional, the agencies' performance was comparatively poor. This pattern is consistent with the findings of other studies of contractors' responses to performance incentives, which show that they will emphasize achieving standards that are given the most weight in contract renewal and funding decisions (Heinrich 1999; Heinrich and Lynn 2000; Courty and Marschke 2004).

Phase 2004–2005: Another step back from performance-based contracting?

The Biennial Budget for 2004–2005 does not include any performance bonus funding, although the W-2 contracts specify criteria under which bonuses may be earned if performance bonus funding becomes available. The primary reward for agencies achieving performance targets in the 2004–2005 contract period is the right of first selection. The performance standards have been similarly scaled back: the priority outcome 'earnings gain' and 'job retention' performance measures are now used only for bonus allocations, if performance bonus funding becomes available (see Appendix 1). In effect, the financial incentives – the main administrative tool for steering W-2 agencies – have dried up in this period and the state's administrative focus has reverted back to securing basic W-2 benefits and job placement services for clients.

The state has also had to contend with additional W-2 contract failures and financial losses, among them, the largest Milwaukee area contractor, OIC. The Governor of Wisconsin recently called for the break up of the large Milwaukee contracts and suggested that the funds should instead be distributed to many agencies that would deliver specific services (Schultze, 2005). The state will also have to determine, however, how it will rekindle and promote competition among public and private agencies to provide W-2 services, regardless of the size of contract awards. Public and private contractors have recently expressed concerns that their current contract allocations are insufficient to meet their caseload obligations, and new providers are not coming forward to bid for the contracts of failed providers. As Sanger (2003: 18) remarked in her study of privatization and welfare reform: 'contracting may be the mantra, but it is competition that drives reforms in service delivery'.

Conclusion

Many of the problems that challenged the state and its contractors seemed to be inherent in the 'incomplete' nature of the contracting arrangements, that is, the inability to fully specify in advance all relevant contingencies and the courses of action that should follow their occurrence. The unexpectedly rapid welfare caseload decline, changing economic circumstances, legislative mandates, shifting political priorities and improper financial activities are just a few examples of unforeseen developments that affected programme administration and performance.

As a result, each of the contract periods was characterized by a significant degree of uncertainty. For example, in addition to the planned contract renegotiations every two years, the state was forced to renegotiate contract terms at the behest of the legislature following Biennial Budget Act decisions. It was only in the first contract period that contractors were informed in advance of the amount of performance bonuses that they could earn. In addition, the contract performance standards changed from period to period, in part to improve incentives for achieving service quality and to better convey the priorities of the state. As the state made an effort to improve contract terms, however, it was constrained both politically (e.g., public disapproval of private contractor profits) and economically (e.g., tight budgets that hindered a timely response to rising caseloads). These types of political and economic factors that impinge on efforts to negotiate an optimal contract (e.g., to establish a fair and efficient risk premium) will always be present in public sector programmes.

At the same time, there is increasing evidence that deficiencies in programme administration and contract management are in part to blame for the failures and setbacks in W-2. The state has publicly acknowledged that monitoring of W-2 service providers and contract compliance was inadequate. For example, one of the firms hired by the state to conduct audits of W-2 contractors was also found to be providing auditing and accounting services to the largest (and now failed) W-2 agency (OIC). Similar problems have been reported in other states, including New York, which Sanger (2003: 39) described as 'notoriously poor' at monitoring, with backlogs in accounting and inadequate assessments of contractor expenditures and performance. She argues that contracting should not be viewed as an opportunity to 'offload' administrative functions and that significant resources are required to achieve, but will not guarantee, contract compliance.

More generally, this study suggests that prescriptions to improve public sector contracting are likely to be inadequate if based solely on economic theories of contracting that centre on contract completeness and efficiency. In the W-2 programme, the state steadily progressed toward what in theory should have been a more efficient and complete contract design, but these efforts were frustrated in part by a lack of internal management capacity and the political pressures/backlash that followed. The fact that, on average, governments 'contract back in' four services for every six services they contract out is likewise indicative of the costs and difficulties associated with public sector contract design and management (Hefetz and Warner 2004). We urge other researchers to similarly use a broader framework to account for such factors in their investigations of public sector contracting.

It is also important to acknowledge that we have given greater attention to the contract management activities of the state than to those of the contracted agencies. Further exploration of agencies' goals, strategies and perceptions of the contracting relationship would enhance our understanding of the contracting system and how it could be improved. For example, future research could pursue questions about how performance incentives influence the behavior of individual actors (e.g., agency administrators or case managers), or how their effects vary across public and private agencies with different organizational characteristics or management practices. In addition, one could take advantage of the diverse administrative arrangements of welfare services across states to expand this type of research beyond the Wisconsin case and to further explore and disentangle the relationships between state and local administrative structures and programme performance. And to the extent that data are available, larger empirical studies of contracting out/contracting back in, like that of Hefetz and Warner (2004), could make a very important contribution to this literature, although in-depth comparative case studies could also produce rich insights about contracting relationships.

REFERENCES

Baker, G. P. (1992) 'Incentive contracts and performance measurement', *Journal of Political Economy*, **100**: 598–614.

Brown, T. L. and Potoski, M. (2003) 'Managing contract performance: A transaction costs approach', *Journal of Policy Analysis and Management*, **22**: 275–297.

Burghardt, J. and Schochet, P. (2001) *National Job Corps study: Impacts by center characteristics*. Princeton, N.J.: Mathematical Policy Research.

Courty, P. and Marschke, G. (2004) 'An empirical investigation of gaming responses to performance incentives', *Journal of Labor Economics*, **22**: 23–56.

DeHoog, R. (1984) *Contracting out for human services: Economic, political, and organizational perspectives*. Albany: State University of New York Press.

DeParle, J. (2004) *American Dream: Three women, ten kids, and a nation's drive to end welfare*. New York: Viking Books.

Dixit, A. (2002) 'Incentives and organizations in the public sector: An interpretative review', *Journal of Human Resources* **37**: 696–727.

Dodenhoff, D. (1998) *Privatizing welfare in Wisconsin: Ending administrative entitlements – W-2 untold story*. Report 11(1), Madison: Wisconsin Policy Research Institute.

Donahue, J. D. (1989) *The privatization decision: Public ends, private means*. New York: Basic Books.

Heckman, J., Heinrich, C. and Smith, J. (2002) 'The performance of performance standards', *Journal of Human Resources*, **38**: 778–811.

Heinrich, C. J. (1999) Do government bureaucrats make effective use of performance management information?', *Journal of Public Administration Research and Theory*, **9**: 363–393.

Heinrich, C. and Lynn, L. E. Jr. (2000) 'Governance and performance: The influence of program structure and management on Job Training Partnership Act (JTPA) program outcomes' in Heinrich, C. J. and Lynn, L. E. Jr. (eds.) *Governance and performance: New perspectives*, Washington, D.C.: Georgetown University Press pp. 75–123.

Hefetz, A. and Warner, M. (2004) 'Privatization and its reverse: Explaining the dynamics of the government contracting process', *Journal of Public Administration Research and Theory* **14**: 171–190.

Holmstrom, B. and Milgrom, P. (1987) 'Aggregation and linearity in the provision of intertemporal incentives', *Econometrica* **55**: 303–328.

Huston, M. (1998) 'Private W-2 agencies to share in profits', *Milwaukee Journal Sentinel*, 13 October.

Kaplan, T. (2000) 'Wisconsin's W-2 program: Welfare as we might come to know it?' in Weissert, C. S. (ed.) *Learning from the leaders: Welfare reform and policy in five midwestern states*. Albany: Rockefeller Institute Press pp. 77–118.

Kettl, D. F. (1993) *Sharing power: public governance and private markets.* Washington, D.C.: The Brookings Institution.

Liebschutz, S. (2000) *Managing welfare reform in five states: The challenge of devolution.* Albany: The Rockefeller Institute Press.

Lynn, L. E., Jr., Heinrich, C. and Hill, C. (2000) 'Studying governance and public management: Why? How?' in Heinrich, C. J. and Lynn, L. E. Jr. (eds.) *Governance and performance: New perspectives,* Washington, D.C.: Georgetown University Press pp. 2–34.

McAfee, R. P. and J. McMillan. (1989). *Incentives in government contracting.* Toronto: University of Toronto Press.

Mead, L. M. (2004) *Government matters: Welfare reform in Wisconsin.* Princeton: Princeton University Press.

Norris, Donald F. and Thompson, Lyke (eds.) (1995) *The politics of welfare reform.* Thousand Oaks: Sage.

Romzek, B. and Johnston, J. (2002) 'Effective contract implementation and management: A preliminary model', *Journal of Public Administration Research and Theory,* **12**: 423–453.

Sandfort, J. (1999) 'The structural impediments to human service collaboration: examining welfare reform as the front lines', *Social Service Review,* **73**: 314–339.

Sanger, M. B. (2003) *The welfare marketplace: Privatization and welfare reform.* Washington, D.C.: The Brookings Institution.

State of Wisconsin (Department of Workforce Development (DWD)). (2001) *Notice of changes in W-2 contract documents as a result of the 2002–2003 Biennial Budget (2001 Wis. Act 16).* Memorandum. ADM 01–20, 31 October.

State of Wisconsin (Department of Workforce Development (DWD)). (2002a) *Performance bonuses for the 2000–2001 Wisconsin Works (W-2) and related programs implementation contract.* Memorandum. ADM 02–14, 1 July.

State of Wisconsin (Department of Workforce Development (DWD)). (2002b) *DWS recommendation to DWD Secretary: Proposed modifications to the W-2 performance standards.* 21 November.

State of Wisconsin (Department of Workforce Development (DWD)). (2003a) *Community reinvestment funds – Revised amounts based on 2003–2005 Biennial Budget Enactment.* Memorandum. ADM 03–19, 16 September.

State of Wisconsin (Department of Workforce Development (DWD)). (2003b) *Updated allocations for 2004–05 W-2 and related programs contract.* Memorandum. ADM 03–23, 5 November.

State of Wisconsin (Department of Workforce Development (DWD)). (2004) *Wisconsin Works (W-2) 2002–03 final performance standards results.* Retrieved from www.dwd.state.wi.us/dws/W2/pdf/PS2002-03.pdf. 3 December.

Schultze, S. (2000) 'Regulators accused of being easy on W-2 agencies', *Milwaukee Journal Sentinel,* 31 August.

Schultze, S. (2005) 'Doyle proposes breaking up W-2 contracts', *Milwaukee Journal Sentinel,* 9 February.

Van Slyke, D. (2003) 'The mythology of privatization in contracting for social services', *Public Administration Review,* **63**: 296–315.

Weissert, C. (ed.), (2000) 'Learning from Midwestern Leaders' in Weissert, C. S. (ed.) *Learning from leaders: Welfare reform politics and policies in five midwestern states.* Albany: The Rockefeller Institute Press.

Williamson, O. (1981) 'The economics of organization', *American Journal of Sociology,* **87**: 548–557.

Wisconsin Legislative Audit Bureau (1999) *A review: Wisconsin Works (W-2) expenditures.* Madison: Legislative Audit Bureau.

Wisconsin Legislative Audit Bureau (2001) *An evaluation: Wisconsin Works (W-2) program: Department of Workforce Development.* Madison: Legislative Audit Bureau.

U.S. General Accounting Office (2002) *Welfare reform: Interim report on potential ways to strengthen federal oversight of state and local contracting.* GAO-02-245. Washington D.C.: US General Accounting Office.

Appendix 1. Performance standards: Changes in target levels

Performance standards and Levels		2000–2001	2002–2003	2004–2005
Primary outcomes for participants	Entered employment			
	Base performance level (RFS)	35% of participants	35%	35% of participants
	1st Bonus Level	40%	35%	35% (only if bonus is available)
	2nd Bonus Level	45%	40%	
	Average wage rate (2000–2001) / Earning gain (2002–2003, changed to information only)			
	Base Performance Level (RFS)	Equal to or greater than base wage rate (in 1998)	50% with any monthly earning gain	
	1st Bonus Level	Base wage rate + 2.5%	50% with any monthly earning gain of $50	19.3% (only if bonus is available)
	2nd Bonus Level	Base wage rate + 5%	50% with any monthly earning gain of $100	
	Job retention: 30 days			
	Base Performance Level (RFS)	75% of participants employed–30 days	75%	
	1st Bonus Level	80%	80%	32% (only if bonus is available)
	2nd Bonus Level	85%	85%	
	Job retention: 180 days			
	Base Performance Level (RFS)	50% of participants employed–180 days	50%	
	1st Bonus Level	55%	55%	
	2nd Bonus Level	60%	60%	
	Full and appropriate engagement			
	Base Performance Level (RFS)	80% of participants engaged (min. hours)	80%	
	1st Bonus Level	85%	85%	
	2nd Bonus Level	90%	90%	

Goal	Measure	Level			
	Employer health insurance benefits	Base Performance Level (RFS)	30% of employed participants	Not primary outcome: Changed to optional standard: available with the first 180 days of employment	
		1st Bonus Level	35%		
		2nd Bonus Level	40%		
	Basic education activities	Base Performance Level (RFS)	80% of participants attending basic ed.	80%	66% of participants attending basic ed.
		1st Bonus Level	85%	85%	
		2nd Bonus Level	90%	90%	
	Education activities attainment	Base Performance Level (RFS)		35% of participants completing education activities	45%
		1st Bonus Level		40%	
		2nd Bonus Level		40%	
High quality and effective case management services	Literacy and numeracy gains	Base Performance Level (RFS)			45%
	W-2 agency staff training requirements	Base Performance Level (RFS)		90% of staff	
		1st Bonus Level		95%	
		2nd Bonus Level		100%	
	Assessment for appropriate W-2 placement and extension	Base Performance Level (RFS)		80%	
		1st Bonus Level		85%	
		2nd Bonus Level		90%	
	Timely and complete processing of 24- and 60-month extension requests	Base Performance Level (RFS)		85% of requests meeting timeliness policies/95% of extention info is to be entered into CARES on time	80% 95%

(cont.)

Appendix 1. (cont.)

	Performance standards and Levels	2000–2001	2002–2003	2004–2005
Services meeting customer expectations	Customer satisfaction	Base Performance Level (RFS)	10 point scale on 10 items 6.5 avg score on each item	10 point scale on 4 items Q1:7.4, Q2:7.0 Q3:7.3, Q4:7.4
	1st Bonus Level		Proportionately allocated to the agencies having 10 highest cum scores	10 point scale on 4 items Q1:7.8, Q2:7.4 Q3:7.9, Q4:7.9 Q4–7.9 (only if bonus is available)
	2nd Bonus Level			
Agency accountability	Financial management	Base Performance Level (RFS)	Must submit timely audits and no significant audit findings	
	Contract compliance	Base Performance Level (RFS)	Must meet	UI employment: 48.1% UI job retention: 30.8% UI earnings gain: 17.5%
	Acceptable level of performance	Base Performance Level (RFS)		UI employment: 49.8% UI job retention: 32% UI earnings gain: 19.3%
	Bonus Level			
Information Only	• Average placement wage rate • Addressing barriers • Work supports (EITC, CC, MA, FS, CS) • Recidivism rates	• 18 and 19 year-olds in school • Moving out of poverty indicator • Expanded caseload: Serving broader population of working poor • Financial and Employment Planner (FEP) to caseload ratio		

Source: Wisconsin Legislative Audit Bureau (2001), DWD (2003a), DWD (2003b)

12 Outsourcing government information technology services: An Australian case study

Graeme A. Hodge and Anne C. Rouse

INTRODUCTION

Over the past two decades governments all around the world have been contracting out services as a key part of public sector reforms. Their objectives initially focused on simple cost-savings, but with experience, broadened to include
access to better services and an enhanced capacity for managers to focus on the
'core business' of their organizations.

Empirical evidence on the effectiveness of contracting-out services such as
refuse collection and cleaning in local government has been widely evaluated, but there is a scarcity of analysis with others. Notwithstanding this, it has
almost become an article of faith that outsourcing government services saves
resources and improves service quality. But what does the empirical evidence
tell us about the outsourcing of major government information technology (IT)
services?

This chapter looks firstly at the policy promises made when outsourcing IT
services, and reviews the range of global evidence to date on the effectiveness of
this technique in the context of the broader outsourcing debate. It then looks in
detail at the outcomes of an $AUD1.5 billion outsourcing exercise undertaken
by the Australian Federal Government. The empirical analysis of the exercise is
contrasted with the political promises made and reasons why savings projections of 15 per cent were not achieved are explored. Finally, the chapter discusses
a series of general lessons on the outsourcing of IT in the context of third-way
governments increasingly intent on adopting private means for providing public
sector services and infrastructure.

The rhetoric and reality of outsourcing government services

Over the past decade, we have begun to differentiate between the rhetoric of
policy reforms on the one hand, and the reality of empirical evidence on the
other. Policy promises made through the global era of government 're-invention,'

can now be contrasted against a growing body of evidence which suggests that although policy reforms such as contracting-out government services have delivered something, they have also often fallen far short of initial expectations.

Contracting-out government services has been part of a broader movement towards the privatization of public sector activities. And in line with the efficiency ideal, the promise of '20% savings' has become mythologized in the public sector reform hymn book.

Comprehensive analyses of the available global empirical measurements have suggested a more complex and rich story. Hodge's analysis suggests (2000: 233) an average saving of around 6 per cent[1] for contracting public sector services overall – a figure markedly lower than the 20 per cent often quoted by proponents of outsourcing. However Hodge did find evidence for savings (i.e., between 19 and 30 per cent) in the specific areas of garbage collection, cleaning and maintenance services, thus supporting the notion that large cost savings can be made through this reform in these instances. For many other services, particularly those more difficult to define and measure, little or no savings were found. In these instances, average cost savings estimates varied between an 8 per cent saving and a 24 per cent increase.

Importantly, from a research perspective, Hodge found cost savings measured for different services were statistically different (i.e., heterogeneous). This was in strong contrast to the savings claims made by proponents who continue to prescribe large-scale contracting-out of government services as some sort of cure-all medicine for public sector ills.[2]

On the matter of service quality, the sparse empirical global evidence indicated that on average, service quality was unaffected by contracting (Hodge 2000: 156). Sometimes it was better, sometimes not. The implication of this was that the claims of both sides of the contracting-out debate were extreme. Service quality was not, as a rule, generally improved, as claimed by one side, or generally reduced, as claimed by the other.

Another critical finding from the meta-review was that *contracting* either in-house or outside the organization both led to cost savings. Thus, service specification and competition appeared to drive efficiencies, rather than the sector doing the work. A significant flow-on effect also seemed to operate, in that agencies not contracting services, but in areas adjacent to those doing so, also showed cost reductions of around two-thirds of that for areas contracting out. Perhaps

1 This meta-analysis of the global empirical evidence found an average cost savings figure for all services (with each service type equally weighted) of around 6 per cent. The analysis acknowledged, however, that most cost savings evidence for contracting out was from studies of local government garbage collection, cleaning and maintenance services and that these service types had yielded larger costs savings than other services such as health or corporate services. When an average was calculated simply across all empirical measurements undertaken, a higher average cost savings figure of around 12 per cent was found in the meta-analysis.

2 Domberger was quoted in a press interview as finding strong heterogeneity – with IT outsourcing on average costing around 8 per cent more than in-house services. These observations, attributed to ineffective management, have never been acknowledged in the formal literature.

cost savings could effectively be achieved without comprehensively contracting out all services, as a little bit of contracting reform appears to go a long way.

This meta-review of international evidence also showed that some unintended social impacts occurred with contracting reforms. Women and minority groups unfortunately bore much of the brunt of efficiencies, increased potential existed for businesses to exert undue influence over political decisions and less transparency often occurred due to arrangements now being deemed 'commercial-in-confidence'.[3] All of these were seen as increasing risks to government and to citizens.[4]

Overall, then, whilst recognizing the shortfalls in the evidential base,[5] the meta-analytic evidence on the effectiveness of contracting-out services in government (from some 20,131 'before and after' measurements) suggests that modest positive outcomes are possible, on average, from contracting out policy initiatives in the field. These outcomes include cost savings of probably around one-third of government's expectations (at 6 per cent); cost savings that are very different for different services (with strong savings in some areas but none in others); and the finding that contracting in-house also leads to similar cost savings to contracting externally. At best, there is only limited evidence that outsourcing complex business services leads to savings. With marked differences in policy effectiveness under different circumstances, it is clear that one size does not fit all in outsourcing policy.

But where does this leave the outsourcing of information technology (IT) in government? It is to this matter that we now turn. Policy objectives were initially heavily focused simply on cost-savings. Later objectives emphasized value for money, better services, the capacity for managers to focus their time on the 'core business' of their organizations, greater innovation, the acquisition of the best skills for the firm's needs and broad economic growth through industry development.

One central philosophy underpinning the outsourcing of both traditional services and IT has been the notion that all functions not central to a business are potentially outsourceable. Osborne and Gaebler's 1990s popular theme of '*steering not rowing*', borrowed from Savas (1987), encompassed this thrust for

---

3 We note that some of Australia's 'high cost-saving' contracting-out exercises have been reversed in recent years, with Australian courts determining that businesses had illegally used outsourcing for transmission of business in order to avoid paying employees at award conditions. In these instances, contracting companies have been forced to pay award entitlements due to the staff and this has negated many of the cost-savings.

4 A fundamental, but often overlooked, point here was the recurring finding that the strongest statistical observation found in studies was simply between the amount of work done and the cost of that work.

5 Hodge (2000: 125) also discussed the lack of any reliable measurements to form the basis of estimates for the various transaction costs involved in contracting government services. Compared to traditional methods, contracting is likely to require the development of detailed specifications, a public tender, and the fair assessment and awarding of competitive contracts either in-house or externally.

government (Osborne and Gaebler 1993). For the private sector, McKinsey had previously suggested that better performing companies usually 'stick to the knitting' (Peters and Waterman 1982).[6] Nowadays, organizations are encouraged to focus on 'core business'.[7]

Reflecting on this, we ought to comment that the 'make or buy' decision for business managers has been around for decades, but appears to have taken on a consulting mystique of its own more recently, particularly in technical areas such as IT. Here, the technical complexity of the tasks is high, the professional language of solutions is unique and the rate of change in developments is extreme. On top of these characteristics, there is also a layer of marketing practice in which organizational reform techniques regularly evolve to become big business for consulting companies and for advisors to companies eager to learn of the latest methods of improving efficiency. The recent trend in the IT sector towards Business Process Outsourcing (BPO) is an example of this.[8]

To the degree that IT service can be regarded as simply 'another government service', outsourcing IT services also promises smaller government at reduced costs. Across the board reforms to government over the past two decades seem to have regarded IT in this way. But what do we know of the effectiveness of IT outsourcing reforms? Focusing on the most prominent objective, that of cost savings, what does the international evidence on IT outsourcing say? Whilst no comprehensive meta-analyses of evidence exist, a number of useful analyses provide clues to begin piecing together the jigsaw.

Outsourcing IT services: The empirical performance

IT services are complex, and in contrast to most of the services studied by Hodge (2000) and Domberger *et al.* (1986; 1987), are generally difficult to specify and evaluate. Furthermore, there are often several, sometimes conflicting, goals sought when IT services are outsourced. The criterion most commonly

---

6 Whilst both of these publications have been discredited from the perspective of rigorous research, there is also no doubt that they have strongly influenced the thinking of political leaders and organizational managers. One example of this is the fact that each of the newly arriving Ministers of Victoria's reformist and privatizing state government was told by the newly-elected Premier, Jeff Kennett, to read Osborne and Gaebler in order to understand the path ahead (Hunt 2001).
7 We might well ask what is 'core business', and who says? Mulgan (1998) suggests that for governments, the questions of what is 'core' or 'non-core' might utilize any one of three separate definitions depending on personal philosophy. Mulgan's three definitions of 'core' have adopted institutional, objective-based and non-contractable bases. In his words, these meanings have varied from being empty tautology at one end, to highly-loaded statements supporting the private external provision of services as a priority at the other.
8 Irrespective of concerns around what might be deemed 'core' and 'non-core' business, BPO certainly appears to be a reform of current relevancy and with a bright future. Lam (2002) reports that 93 per cent of companies outsourced some IT and BPO functions, and that 68.3 per cent of companies already engaged in BPO. Likewise, Dunne (2002), Pollard (2002) and Lam (2002) report high annual growth rates and potentially large market sizes for services.

reported in the IT outsourcing arena is the degree to which cost-savings expectations have been met. But establishing how widespread cost savings are in reality, proves difficult. The most widely cited research into cost-savings outcomes comes from the work of Lacity, Hirschheim, Willcocks and Feeny (Lacity and Hirschheim 1993, 1995; Lacity *et al.* 1997; Willcocks *et al.* 1997; and Willcocks and Lacity 1998). This body of work reports a series of IT sourcing case studies that began with those reported in Lacity and Hirschheim (1993). Not all involved outsourcing, and there is some confusion about the findings, which are nevertheless widely quoted in the trade literature. For example, in Lacity *et al.* (1997: 281) the authors report that cost savings expectations were met or exceeded in some thirty-five cases, or 66 per cent of the time. A later analysis on essentially the same cases in Willcocks *et al.* (1997) argued that out of 41 cases of IT outsourcing, twenty-three (56 per cent) achieved cost savings, five (12 per cent) achieved mixed results and thirteen (31 per cent) did not report savings. The authors also reported that in eight further cases, savings could not be determined. In yet another report on the same data, Lacity and Willcocks (1998) reported cost-savings expectations were achieved in 71 per cent of cases.[9] This 71 per cent 'success rate' also included organizations that did not outsource IT, but instead contracted with their internal providers in competition with market bids. The variability of reported success rates for the same set of cases illustrates the dependence of success on which cases are counted by researchers and how these are categorized.[10]

Modest cost savings estimates have also been reported in other international research into information technology outsourcing. Willcocks (1998) looked at 116 companies in the US and Britain that pursued large-scale, single-vendor outsourcing contracts. He reported that 53 per cent were not making savings overall and that unsurprisingly, 37 per cent regarded outsourcing as a failure whilst 27 per cent experienced mixed results. Most organizations were reported to have underestimated the cost of outsourcing and the number of people and capabilities needed to oversee the project.

Several other studies suggest either modest savings or cost increases from IT outsourcing. Aubert *et al.* (1999), in a longitudinal study of seventy Canadian organizations, found that 49 per cent of respondents reported IT costs had increased. Domberger, in a trade report of 7,500 outsourcing contracts (CTC Consultants 1999) reported that while savings for certain simple services like cleaning, garbage collection and hospital services were in the realm of

---

9 Since most of these cases had begun in the mid- to late eighties, it might be assumed that by 1998 those that did not know whether they achieved savings did not reap them.

10 Importantly, the cases aggregated by Lacity, Willcocks and colleagues were essentially opportunistic, and in no way statistically representative of the experiences that organizations in the field might encounter (Rouse and Corbitt 2003b), so their reported success rates cannot reasonably be extrapolated, a point made by Lacity and Willcocks (1998). There is also a systematic bias in the academic literature against negative cases, because respondents are rarely willing to discuss failed policies in public.

30 per cent, costs for IT services had increased, on average, by 8 per cent. Hodge (2000), also found that whilst simple services such as cleaning, maintenance and garbage collection had yielded real cost savings, corporate services, such as IT, on average showed an increase of 5 per cent.

In the case of Australasian IT outsourcing, Cullen *et al.* (2001) reported on a survey of 235 public and private organizations in a vendor publication. They found that organizations were spending around 30 per cent of their IT budgets on outsourcing, and reported that 'the majority of organizations largely achieved their primary objectives with outsourcing'. This claim has subsequently been disputed by other researchers, as it ignored failures to obtain secondary expectations (largely cost savings) that had led many respondents to report low levels of satisfaction (Rouse 2002).

Cullen *et al.* (2001) noted that although a majority of respondents expected to achieve some cost savings, the main reason given for outsourcing IT at this time was to gain access to better skills and expertise. This contrasted research in United States and the United Kingdom which showed the top two ranked reasons for outsourcing to be cost reduction and improved service quality objectives.

The Cullen *et al.* (2001) findings were the latest from a series of earlier survey reports from management consulting companies. PA Consulting (1997) reported an average cost reduction for IT outsourcing in Australia at just 2 per cent. Deloitte and Touche (1997), looking at both private and public organizations, were even more circumspect, noting for their recent survey as well as earlier surveys that 'then, as now, significant savings are rarely realized' for IT outsourcing.

Rouse and Corbitt (2003b) in their careful re-evaluation of the survey data used by Cullen *et al.* found that whilst some of the widely promised benefits of outsourcing were observed (access to skilled staff, positive vendor service and improved business flexibility), other strategic benefits were not (such as cost savings, concentration on core business, economies of scale and technology benefits). They summarized their findings by saying that once value for money was included as an aspect of satisfaction, 'only around a third (36 per cent) of respondents reported satisfaction with their outsourcing arrangements'. They also noted that cost savings had been reported by only a minority of organizations, and that cost increases had occurred in more than 20 per cent.

In summary, while government outsourcing of IT services does lead to a reduced headcount, the academic evidence supporting the policy promises of reduced costs or improved service from the outsourcing of IT services is limited. Furthermore, the extant evidence tends, if anything, to bring into doubt the likely achievement of such policy promises.

How might we view this evidence? Overall, we could make several observations. The first is a surprise regarding the sparsity of the empirical evidence compared to the size of the financial transactions being undertaken. The new face of IT outsourcing, BPO, for instance, is reputed to have a current annual growth rate of from 4 per cent up to 10 per cent, with estimates for the size of global BPO markets at between \$AUD129 billion to US\$234 billion (Dunne 2002, Pollard 2002 and Lam 2002). Given the magnitudes of market transactions and the size of financial commitments evidently being made to IT outsourcing by firms around the globe, the evidence on cost and quality gains is thin indeed.[11] Second, at a minimum,[12] what we may be observing is that the risks taken in IT outsourcing are more prevalent and more tricky to manage than previously acknowledged. At best, the real gains appear to have been modest on average.[13] Third, adopting the language of the economists, the transaction costs associated with organizational changes inherent in IT outsourcing are also probably higher than initially estimated. Fourth, as Rouse and Corbitt (2003b) hint, it may well be that outcomes are more complex than commonly assumed and that as a consequence, trade-offs are being made as we outsource. In some areas we gain and in others we do not. Perhaps there is even a need to better manage the optimism of policy proponents and managers leading these change projects.[14] Last, and perhaps critical to our current analysis, there has been little distinction to date between the logic and performance of IT outsourcing in the context of private business firms and the challenges of outsourcing government IT functions. The base assumption thus far has been that it works equally well in both environments.

In the midst of many of these findings being published, the Australian government was already planning to embark on a bold experiment in IT outsourcing. We now turn to this case study.

An Australian case study

This section reports a study conducted by Rouse (2002) of the Australian federal government's foray into large-scale IT outsourcing between 1997 and 2001. Rouse's research is based on a detailed investigation of published secondary sources, including the Australian Auditor-General's review of the first four

---

11 This is also the case for the more recent BPO trend, notwithstanding the glowing industry case studies of BPO such as Norman (2002) and Clark (2002) advertising cost savings of around 10 to 40 per cent.

12 What may be occurring here is advertising from suppliers and the pursuit of business transactions rather than the delivery of cost savings and better performance. This comment may also be directed against the entire 'consultocracy' (Correy 1999) that is central to today's business world.

13 Cost comparisons 'before and after' IT outsourcing are treacherously difficult and uncertain. It may be that significant new investments are made after the event (Dunne 2002) but more generally, assessments of IT outsourcing effectiveness involve a range of imprecise projections concerning service bundles over the life of the contract, in-house costs of suppliers, changes to business requirements and volumes, complex contractual terminology and evolving technologies.

14 These sobering sentiments are also supported by industry reports such as those suggesting 'Gartner sees the chances of strategic sourcing deals succeeding at about 50/50' (Gartner 2002), and those suggesting that for outsourcing, the anecdotal success rate is around 30%.

outsourcing exercises; ANAO (2000). This was supplemented by anonymous interviews with twenty highly-placed informants from public sector agencies and IT vendors involved in the IT outsourcing arrangements.[15]

The national policy context for IT outsourcing

In Australia it was the public sector, not the private sector that spearheaded IT outsourcing. The public sector accounts for around one-half of the country's large IT sites and historically, the federal government has been the largest purchaser of IT products and services (Rouse 2002).

During the 1990s, Australian state and federal governments were largely controlled by liberal coalitions, whose strong philosophy was to both privatize government businesses and outsource services. In Victoria, New South Wales, Western Australia, and South Australia, liberal coalition governments had introduced competitive market testing for large proportions of local government and were exploring the outsourcing of large proportions of government business under a purchaser-provider model (Walker and Walker 2000). Under this philosophy, governments moved away from delivering public services to specifying of services, which were then delivered by private sector agencies under contract. In Osborne and Gaebler's (1993) parlance, governments steered and left the rowing to others.

With IT accounting for a large proportion of government expense, the delivery of IT services was an early target for outsourcing. The policy directions taken were bold – in 1994 the liberal Victorian state government announced that it was to outsource up to 70 per cent of its IT services and the South Australian state government announced it would outsource all its IT services both to save money and enhance state industry development.

The Australian federal government case

In 1997, the Australian federal government announced that by 1999 it intended to outsource the delivery of IT infrastructure for most federal agencies, including mainframe, server, desktop services and in some cases telecommunications. The Whole of Government IT Infrastructure Outsourcing Initiative, commonly referred to as 'WOGITIOI', amounted to some 50 per cent of the federal IT budget (SFPARC 1997). The initiative was promoted as saving 'up to $AUD 1billion' through the use of external vendors and the consolidation of requirements across government agencies which would be clustered to form cross-agency contracts. The WOGITIOI initiative was a symbolic move by the liberal coalition government to ensure that the market sector 'rowed' in the future, with the

---

15 Some of Rouse's findings were earlier reported in Rouse and Corbitt (2003a).

Table 12.1 Federal government 'Whole of Government IT Infrastructure Outsourcing Initiative' IT outsourcing arrangements

Agency	Value $AUD	Won by	Date
'Cluster 3' – two large and four small agencies[*]	$160m	CSC	March 98
Department of Employment, Training and Youth Affairs[*]	$300m	Cancelled due to lack of bidders	June 98
Australian Tax Office (ATO)[*]	$490m	IBM/GSA	June 99
'Group 5' – five small agencies[*]	$90m	Advantra	July 99
Department of Health, Health Insurance Commission, and Medibank Private[**]	$351m	IBM/GSA	Jan–July 2000
'Group 8' – seven small agencies[**]	$130m	Ipex ITG	June 2000

[*] Reviewed by the federal Auditor-General. [**] Not audited, and not reviewed in Rouse's (2002) study
Sources: Davis (1998: 54); Humphry (2000: 45).

government 'steering' IT service provision. This controversial decision became the subject of examination by an ongoing Senate Inquiry (SFPARC 1997). In 1999, the Auditor General independently decided to review the outcomes of the first four contracts under this WOGITIOI initiative (ANAO 2000). These four contracts were valued at about $AUD1.04 billion dollars and are the subject of this analysis.[16] They are detailed in Table 12.1, which also notes two later, and thus unaudited, WOGITIOI arrangements. By 2001, the WOGITIOI had been disbanded.

The WOGITIOI context and timing

The WOGITIOI initiative had been the subject of considerable attention and some criticism from the start. This came particularly from unions, opposition parties, and the opposition-dominated *Senate Finance and Public Administration References Committee Outsourcing Inquiry*, which first met in 1997. A range of concerns were expressed, including privacy provisions, effects on departmental business initiatives, industry development and staffing implications.[17] Cost savings projections were also subject to scrutiny and challenge (e.g., Darcy

16 Earlier major IT outsourcing initiatives had amounted to some $AUD295 million and by 1997 included a Department of Veteran's Affairs contract ($AUD65m to IBM/GSA), a Department of Finance and Administration contract (IBM/GSA) for $AUD30m and an Australian Customs Services contract ($AUD200m to EDS). The contracts let under the WOGITIOI Policy, however, represented a quantum leap, amounting to around $AUD1.521billion.
17 Based on a review of newspaper reports, as well as the findings of the first Senate Inquiry into IT outsourcing (SFPARC 1997).

1996:[18] *Canberra Times* 1997a, 1997b; Background Briefing 1997). However, these concerns were largely presented in the context of political debate and as such were somewhat remote from the day-to-day issues affecting decision makers involved in IT sourcing.

This changed when the Auditor-General[19] released his report on the first four federal government WOGITIOI contracts; ANAO (2000). This extensive 243-page review examined the goals, tender evaluations, implementation and outcomes arrangements and was damning in its criticism of the IT outsourcing initiative.

The report had enormous impact in public sector circles and this according to vendor informants, was also felt in the private sector. Unlike earlier Senate inquiries, the strong community perception was that the Auditor-General's findings were independent and highly credible. For the first time, the public could examine how the promised 'savings' being reported by vendors, consultants and governments were being calculated; (Mitchell 2000).

The negative elements of the Auditor-General's report were highly publicized and vocal public and media criticism forced the government to act quickly to avoid further political damage. It established another review of the initiative headed by Richard Humphry, Chairman of the Australian Stock Exchange.[20] This in turn generated negative public reaction and the *Review of the Whole of Government Information Technology Outsourcing Initiative* (the 'Humphry Report') released in January 2001, led to the public abandonment of key aspects of the strategy.

When the government announced that it would accept the recommendations of the Humphry Review (Humphry 2000) and allow individual departments to decide whether and how to outsource their IT services, the WOGITIOI decision was, in effect, abandoned. The final policy evaluation curtain then came down on this experiment with the subsequent release of the *Report of the Senate Finance and Public Administration References Inquiry* in 2001.

So, to what degree were the policy promises made in this case actually achieved? And what do we make of this case study in the context of the broader contracting-out policy debates?

Policy promises made

As Australia embraced outsourcing of government IT through the 1990s, the policy arguments put forward had been twofold. First, outsourcing would save taxpayer funds through cost savings while improving business service

---

18 'IT Cuts Won't Save' was, for instance, the lead headline in *Computer Week* magazine (Darcy 1996).
19 The Auditor-General reports directly to Parliament, not to the government, and has many statutory protections to ensure independence.
20 Richard Humphry was also a former member of the 1997 IT and Telecommunications Advisory Committee that had initially recommended the outsourcing strategy.

operations and second, outsourcing would lead to the development and enhancement of an effective IT industry (Industry Commission 1996).[21]

In terms of quantum, the federal government sought savings of 20 per cent or more. This figure was based on a submission made by IBM 'assuming a net benefit of 20%' to an industry-centred expert panel (the IT Review Group), commissioned by the Department of Finance in 1995 (ITRG 1995). The Minister for Finance and Administration later used this estimate to support claims that 'across budget funded agencies, potential savings in the order of $AUD1 billion are realizable, over the term of multiple, seven year contracts'. Moreover, the Minister was confident, further stating that 'the savings to the budget are robust and they are conservative'[22].

While some inside government initially suggested that savings of around 28 per cent were possible, a more conservative cost-savings target figure of 15 per cent was adopted by government for a strategy that encompassed outsourcing and the consolidation and standardization of data centres and infrastructure services (ANAO 2000: 11, 195; Costello 1997).

Groups of departments ('clusters') were created that supposedly shared similar IT needs in response to vendor arguments that doing so would deliver economies of scale (Humphry 2000) and to analyses such as Lacity *et al.* (1996) of strategies most likely to lead to cost savings: that is, consolidating data centres or standardizing other services. The federal government was thus following the 'best practice' advice of Lacity *et al.* (1996: 17) to 'empower [management] to overcome the resistance of users' by encouraging users to 'manage demand by consolidating data centers into one site or by standardizing software'.

An important part of the government's strategy was the *selective* outsourcing of infrastructure services including mainframe and midrange operations, operations of distributed servers and desktops and in some cases, data networks, which at that time accounted for 'about half of the Commonwealth's total IT expenditure of approximately $AUD2 billion' (SFPARC 1997: Chapter 2, final paragraph). Government decision-makers saw this as being consistent with Lacity *et al.*'s (1996) 'best practice' recommendations that selective outsourcing (less than 80 per cent of IT expenditure), and outsourcing of commodity-like services, would be most likely to achieve significant savings. The contracts were

---

21 South Australia's reported success in achieving industry development goals (described in Lacity and Willcocks 2001) would have been an important influencing factor on other states and on the Federal government. According to informants, however, the industry development goal was secondary to the cost savings goal and this is supported by the reduction in attention paid to it in later WOGITIOI contracts (ANAO 2000).

22 Minister for Finance and Administration, in an address to the Information Technology Outsourcing Seminar, Freehill, Hollingdale and Page, 29 July 1998. The basis of this claim was inconsistent with the Minister's earlier statement that 'IT outsourcing was expected to save the Commonwealth some $AUD1 billion *over seven years*' (emphasis added); Mr John Fahey, Questions without Notice, House of Representatives, Hansard, 28 May 1997, p. 4265.

kept short,[23] ranging from three to five years, following best practice recommendations at the time (e.g. Lacity *et al.* 1996).

Building on a belief that there were considerable inefficiencies in the delivery of IT services and the reassurance that cost savings would be made, decision makers within the government required agencies to accept budget reductions up front.[24]

Policy performance

The IT outsourcing initiative of the Australian federal government was subject to intense scrutiny through public inquiries. After several inquiries and assessments, three central findings emerged.

The large cost-savings promised for the initiative (around one billion dollars) were not delivered

The Auditor-General (ANAO 2000) found that cost blow outs had nullified expected savings. As Rouse and Corbitt (2003a: 82) put it: 'Most of these cost blow outs were related to the costs of specialist international consultants, including "Big 5" accounting firms, outsourcing advisors, and the outsourcing legal specialists, Shaw Pitman . . .'. The Auditor-General also found that only one of the four contracts examined was likely to deliver any savings[25] and that actual savings were less than half of those projected.' In fact, the Auditor-General reported that actual savings for this contract amounted to around 12 per cent rather than the 28 per cent initially projected (Rouse 2002). Given that this contract was a minor part of the value of the whole WOGITIOI initiative, the overall cost savings for the group of agencies probably amounted to something closer to a few per cent – far smaller than the initial policy promise.[26]

---

23 The shorter contracts covered fast changing technology e.g., networks. The longer contracts covered mainframe services (ANAO 2000). Nonetheless, while 'short contracts' were described in Lacity *et al.* (1996) as less than four years, informants suggested vendors could not accept such short contracts for many services, as they did not allow time for the vendor to recoup the significant cost of winning the contract.

24 They saw this strategy as consistent with practices suggested by Lacity and Hirschheim (1995) who demonstrated that organizations, whether in-sourcing, or outsourcing, can save considerably on their IT budgets by instituting unpopular reforms, like consolidating data centres, and restricting the rate of technology change by sticking with equipment that is one to two generations behind. The strategy of mandating budget savings up–front was also consistent with competitive tendering contracting reforms introduced in Victoria a few years earlier.

25 Rouse and Corbitt (2003a: 83) further noted that despite relying on world-class consulting advice, the cost and savings projections were flawed, because decision makers had failed to take into account additional cash streams associated with equipment that would have been available at the end of the contract if the services were not outsourced. They had also underestimated the costs of leasing risks absorbed by the agencies.

26 It is important to note that in calculating cost savings significant outlays spent on the Office of the Asset Sales and IT Outsourcing organization were not included. These costs were viewed as a separate sunk overhead and not as an additional cost to these four contracts.

The 'failure' to achieve cost reductions occurred despite being a textbook case of outsourcing using 'Best Practice'

Decision makers in this case study went to considerable trouble to follow 'industry best practice' and recommended procedures spending $AUD25million on specialist consultant advice. This was in addition to advice from the IT Review group (ITRG), the IT&T Policy Advisory Committee, panels of industry specialists and the Australian Industries Commission which all supported the notion that if the process was carefully managed, the government could succeed in achieving the target 15 per cent savings (and possibly more). Considerable time went into planning and implementing the initiative. Indeed, Rouse and Corbitt (2003a) argue that the government essentially followed nine of Seddon's 'ten commandments' for best practice (Seddon 2001).[27] The adoption of such best practices was in marked contrast to many of the prior observations of IT outsourcing, where organizations had naïvely failed to know their own market costs and signed long-term contracts with a single vendor for a large proportion of their IT budget.

Even well-managed IT outsourcing is a risky business

The third finding reinforced the view that IT outsourcing as a privatization policy activity was far more risky than is commonly acknowledged. In the WOGITIOI initiative the business cases were complex and associated projections assumed idealistic best case outcomes, despite the fact that academic research was available warning of the risks. Being generous, the adoption of such assumptions in the business cases led, according to the Auditor-General, to incorrect predictions of the likely outcomes. Put simply, cost savings were predicted which in fact would not occur. This raises issues of stewardship versus policy advocacy at the centre of government and the degree to which this conflict can cloud policy judgements – no matter the financial size of the policy stakes. With IT, the risks of outsourcing appear to have been discounted amidst policy promotion.

A further aspect of policy effectiveness is the question of trade-offs possible during outsourcing where multiple goals are initially established. In the case of the WOGITIOI initiative, the Australian Tax Office reported substantial technology improvements, but not cost savings. Humphry (2000) reported that industry development goals conflicted with federal agency operational goals. Likewise, the review of South Australia's outsourcing arrangements by Lacity and Willcocks

---

27 Seddon's ten commandments were based largely on earlier work by Lacity and Hirschheim (1993; 1995). The commandments followed in the WOGITIOI initiative included 'selective outsourcing (of 50 per cent of the IT budget), targeting of "non-core" services, short (three–five-year) contracts, detailed contracts prepared under the advice of international specialists, retaining highly skilled staff to manage the arrangement, involving both line and IT management in decision making, conducting extensive analyses of vendor offerings and implementing detailed post-contract management and monitoring structures' (Rouse and Corbitt 2003a, 84). The single practice not followed was the option of allowing internal service groups to bid against external vendors. This option was judged as expensive, and would have been an ideologically risky one to allow as well.

(2001) reported the achievement of substantial industry development, but slim evidence of cost savings.

How generalizable is the WOGITIOI experience?

One central problem with case study research is that a case might be unusual and generally not applicable to the wider world. To the statistician, case study analysis lacks a control group, or counterfactual. In reality, however, this WOGITIOI study had been carried out as part of a larger body of research. This enables us to review wider corroborative quantitative data and assess the degree to which these WOGITIOI study results may have been typical of broader experience in the business sector.

Using Australian data gathered by Seddon *et al.* (2000) at the time the WOGITIOI case was being studied, Rouse (2002) statistically tested whether there were differences in outsourcing outcomes between public and private sector organizations. Her research looked at twenty-seven outcome measures across 240 organizations and is reported in Table 12.2. This shows that for the large majority of outsourcing outcomes, no statistical difference existed in perceived levels of performance. The table is sorted by frequency of reporting with those outcomes towards the bottom of the table being reported more rarely by respondents.

Importantly, Rouse found there were no statistically significant differences for the *key* success measures: technical benefits, strategic benefits, vendor service, cost savings, business flexibility, economies of scale and access to skilled personnel. Nor were there statistical differences in overall satisfaction and perceptions of value – government respondents reported the same relatively poor success outcomes as those in non-government organizations.

There were also no statistically significant differences for these success measures between those organizations, like the WOGITIOI, engaged in 'selective' outsourcing and those engaged in 'total' outsourcing.[28]

When she subjected the survey data to additional statistical analysis, Rouse (2002) found that a major cause of the relatively poor satisfaction (the 36 per cent 'success rate' reported in Rouse and Corbitt 2003b) was the low level of cost savings resulting from IT outsourcing. Only a minority (42 per cent) reported any savings at all from outsourcing IT, and only a handful (7 per cent) reported substantial savings. As noted above, there were no differences between public and private sector respondents for this outcome. Other causes of dissatisfaction reported by Rouse (2002) included failure to obtain expected strategic benefits,

---

28 Indeed, contrary to trade claims, those engaged in 'total' outsourcing reported more positive outcomes, although the difference was not statistically significant. This finding was also duplicated by Lee, Shaila and Yong-Mi (2004) in their study of IT outsourcing in 311 Korean organizations.

Table 12.2 Statistically significant differences between public sector and private sector outsourcers

Outcome	Public sector	Private sector
Overall satisfaction and perceived value of outsourcing	–	–
Vendor service/performance	–	–
Increased technical benefits/avoidance of obsolescence	–	–
Access to skilled personnel	–	–
Economies of scale or HR (scope economies)	–	–
Strategic benefits	–	–
Access to services that could not be provided internally	Less likely to report	More likely to report
Access to better/more skills and expertise	–	–
Better use of in-house personnel	Less likely	More likely
Better match of supply and demand	–	–
Greater concentration on core business	–	–
Better service through outsourcing	–	–
Access to better/more technology	–	–
Improved flexibility for the business	–	–
Enhanced management control	–	–
Shift from capital to operating expense	–	–
Reduced staff numbers	–	–
More flexible work practices	–	–
Changed users' accountabilities	–	–
Rationalized assets	More likely Less likely	Less likely
Reduced costs	–	–
Greater control of costs	–	–
Penalties for non-performance	More likely	Less likely
Outsourcing provided a temporary solution	–	–
Improved cash flow	–	–
Compliance with a corporate/government mandate to outsource	More likely	Less likely
Increased industry/or economic development	More likely	Less likely

* Statistically significant differences in mean ranks based on Mann-Whitney U test using alpha = .05.

A dash signifies there was no statistical difference between the groups.

particularly control over costs and not being able to concentrate on core business as a result of outsourcing IT.

So, while the majority of organizations (both government and private sector) reported improved vendor service and access to skilled staff as a result of outsourcing, these benefits were counteracted by the failure to save on costs and to obtain expected strategic benefits.

Thus, the contemporary Seddon *et al.* survey, acting as 'control' for the WOGITIOI case, reveals that the experiences reported for the case were by no means unusual. In fact, in achieving savings of 12 per cent, the first of the WOGITIOI contracts achieved a relatively rare success. Furthermore, the contemporary survey reveals the 'hit rate' of one arrangement in three succeeding is quite typical of other contemporary Australian organizations.

Discussion

The findings of the WOGITIOI outsourcing case show that despite the modest success reported for outsourcing simple government services, the determinants of successful IT outsourcing (both public and private sector) are still elusive. What we do know from both this case study and the empirical research to date is that when services are complex, like IT, outsourcing success appears relatively uncommon. This occurs even when governments spend substantially on advice, and implement 'best practice' management strategies.

The outsourcing effectiveness assessments conducted for this initiative were interesting from several public policy perspectives. First, the continuing degree to which both governments and the outsourcing industry overestimate results is evident. It may be that this is done in order to ensure implementation of a privatization policy initiative (in the former case) or to gain a slice of the coming transactions (in the latter case).

With the WOGITIOI initiative, there appeared to be considerable confidence that the policy would deliver substantial cost savings and this was bolstered by the large allocation of resources to planning the changes. If government IT facilities and operations were inefficiently managed, such a promise would have been easy to achieve. But the reality was far more complex. The Auditor General's finding that substantial savings were being achieved in only one of four contracts implies that, rather than achieving the initial political promise of 'up to a billion dollars (in savings)', real savings were in fact probably closer to $AUD27 million. Of course this broken political promise could be played either way during policy debates. Opposition parties could point out the folly of having little or no cost savings for all the reform effort. On the other hand, advocating governments could also claim that the IT work had been successfully moved to the sector most able to undertake the work in the long term with little operational interruption.

Second, we might muse whether, at the end of the day, the achievement of cost savings were really ever at the heart of the policy initiative. Governments are certainly being urged to become a *smart buyer* (Kettl, 1993), a more *intelligent buyer* (Hodge, 2002) and a more *informed buyer* (Yates, 2000) when purchasing contract services and the IT business literature is replete with rhetoric such as *smart-sourcing, right-sourcing*[29] and *strategic sourcing*. But *evidence-based* policy development is rarer than belief-based policies. In reality, policy advocacy is as much about power and persuasion as it is about finance. In this light, there is considerable room for doubt on the primacy of financial objectives in IT outsourcing. When one author quizzed a federal Minister on the commercial sense of outsourcing federal IT, the Minister replied that government should simply not be in the business of IT and the task was to get government out of there. On this basis, our assumption that relative cost-efficiency is a key driver of policy decisions to outsource IT services may be misplaced. Rather than tackling this policy arena through accounting eyes, perhaps the whole outsourcing policy field ought to be reframed through a political lens and the inevitable pressures for smaller government in terms of personnel numbers (Guttman 2003). Through this lens, higher IT costs after outsourcing may become a less important side-effect of policy directions, rather than a policy performance measure in its own right. Notwithstanding these comments, all commentators and parties agreed that the transition to outsourcing had been much more difficult than expected (Rouse 2002).

Third, comparing our earlier brief review of some of the global IT outsourc-ing evidence with the findings of the WOGITIOI case study, we could reflect on the large initial planning efforts put into this IT outsourcing case. The degree to which these efforts were truly independent, however, is questionable. Put simply, the existence of a large IT outsourcing industry worth hundreds of bil-lions of dollars would make it difficult to come to any other conclusion than to recommend that outsourcing be undertaken, albeit with costly advisors in tow. In the same way that share advisors throughout the 1990s profited well from their own recommendations to deal in shares no matter which way share prices turned, so do current IT industry advisors. A renewed search may be needed for independent analysts with fewer conflicts of interest. This is particularly the case when we recall that the risks in IT outsourcing are clearly more prevalent and more difficult to manage than were previously acknowledged. Real gains are at best, modest, and transaction costs are high.

Fourth, governments have probably failed to learn enough from the perfor-mance evaluations of IT outsourcing in the private sector, let alone contem-plating any further logics that might be relevant in comparing IT performance in the two sectors. There has been a simple assumption that the business of

29 See Lacity, Willcocks and Feeny (1997).

government is little different to the business of a private enterprise and insufficient attention has been paid to understanding either the uniqueness or complexity of some government services or the public sector environment.[30] The lack of such detailed analyses is important in the context of the observation by Willcocks (2001) that 'one common finding in both private and public sectors, across especially the large deals, is that they are pervaded by voodoo economics'.

There is also a worrying lack of appreciation among policy makers that IT outsourcing, like other management strategies, tends to follow a 'hype cycle'. It is initially talked up and then eventually seen in a more sober light. In the heyday of the early 1990s, when the press regularly announced the benefits IT outsourcing was going to bring, expectations for the strategy were high. This was reflected in the stock market's reaction to IT outsourcing announcements, which as Loh and Venkatraman (1992) showed, led to abnormal increases in stock prices. With the benefit of hindsight it is clear these stock market reactions were based on projected, not realized, benefits. Thirteen years later, Gewald and Gellrich (2005) have demonstrated that IT outsourcing announcements are now more likely to produce a decrease in stock prices, reflecting more informed market perceptions that the strategy has substantial risks (Gewald and Gellrich 2005).

The warning signs here are clear. Governments need to keep a steady head during decision making and act with skill and care if they are to provide strong stewardship of public funds. Above all, they ought to act without outsourcing their brains!

Conclusion

The global evidence on IT outsourcing suggests that the policy promises of this reform are often not met. The performance criteria potentially relevant to the evaluation of government outsourcing efforts are broad and may include cost savings, value for money, service improvement, management time and skill levels in addition to improved firm innovation and industry development. Recognizing that the number of effectiveness studies published is thin, IT outsourcing appears to lead at best to only modest improvements in public and private organizations. Looking specifically at the experience of the Australian government's $AUD1.5 billion outsourcing initiative, it is concluded that the key initial policy promise of cost savings to citizens amounting to one billion dollars was

---

30 For instance, few private firms are required to conduct a national election under strict legislative rules and little serious analysis has been undertaken at the policy level on the degree to which government services may or may not be handled in an identical manner to those of private firms.

not achieved. Interestingly, this failure to meet well-advertised policy promises was not because reforms were poorly managed. Indeed, considerable effort and resources were mounted to ensure that best practices were consistently applied throughout the reform process.

IT outsourcing appears therefore to be more complex and more risky than hitherto acknowledged. The implication of this is that third-way governments, who are increasingly intent on adopting private means for providing public sector services and infrastructure, will in future need to take a more careful and independent eye to their own outsourcing policies. The pressures for both better government as well as smaller government will further increase this need.

REFERENCES

Aubert, B., Patry, M. and Rivard, S. (1999) 'L'impartation des services informatique au Canada: Une comparaison 1993–1997 in Poitevin', Michel (ed.) *Impartition: Fondements et analyses*. Montreal, Canada: University of Laval Press; pp. 202–220.

Australian National Audit Office (2000) *'Implementation of "Whole-of-Government Information Technology and Infrastructure Consolidation and Outsourcing Initiative"'*, Audit Report No. 9, Canberra.

Background Briefing (1997) 'Bonanza: Outsourcing information' Technology Transcript of Radio National Broadcast Background Briefing 13 July. www.abc.net.au/Talks/bbing/stories/S10588.Htr Accessed August 1998.

Canberra Times (1997a) 'Outsourcing needs tight contracts', *Canberra Times*, 4 May.

Canberra Times (1997b) 'Still opposition to outsourcing', *Canberra Times*, 28 July.

Clark, G. 2002. *'Using business process outsourcing to transform the finance function – a case study in the retail sector'*. Presentation to the Business Process Outsourcing Australia Conference, Sydney, 3–5 December 2002.

Correy, S. (1979) 'The consultocracy', Radio National Background Briefing, 20 June 1999. Transcript available from: www.abe.net.ac/ru/background briefing/stories/1499/31095.htm.

Costello, P. (1997) Budget Speech 1997–1998. www.treasury.gov.au/[publications/CommonwealthBudget/1997-1998/budgetsp.asp. Accessed September 2000.

CTC Consultants (1999) *Government outsourcing: What has been learnt?* Sydney, Australia: CTC Consultants.

Cullen, S., Willcocks, L. and Seddon, P. (2001) *Information technology outsourcing practices in Australia*, Melbourne: Deloitte Touche Tohmatsu.

Deloitte and Touche Consulting Group (1997) *Information technology outsourcing survey: A comprehensive analysis of IT outsourcing in Australia* Version 3.1, November, Melbourne, Deloitte and Touche Consulting Group.

Darcy, B. (1996) 'IT cuts won't save', *Computer Week: Australia's Newspaper of Corporate Computing*, Network Edition, 24 July: 1

Davis, I. (1998) 'IT shifts from costs to better service'. *Australian Financial Review*. 11 October: 60.

Domberger, S., Meadowcroft, S. A. and Thompson, D. J. (1986) 'Competitive tendering and efficiency: The case of refuse collection', *Fiscal Studies*, **7**(4): 69–87.

Domberger, S., Meadowcroft, S. A. and Thompson, D. J. (1987) 'The impact of competitive tendering on the costs of hospital domestic services', *Fiscal Studies*, **8**(4): 39–54.

Dunne, J. (2002) '*Developing an understanding of the market landscape and maturity for BPO*'. Presentation to the Business Process Outsourcing Australia Conference, Sydney, 3–5 December 2002.

Gartner (2002) 'Gartner Insight' cited in TPI: '50% of outsourcing deals will fail in next 12 months because of poor management,' M2 *Presswire*, Coventry, 30 August 2002.

Gewald, H. and Gellrich, T. (2005) '*The impact of perceived risk on the capital market's reaction on outsourcing announcements*', Proceedings of 9th Pacific Asia Conference on Information Systems (PACIS), Bangkok, Thailand. July 7–10.

Guttman, D. (2003) *Contracting, an American way of governance: Post 9/11 constitutional choices*, Johns Hopkins University, National Academy of Public Administration Symposium, October 2003.

Hodge, G. A. (2000) *Privatization: An international review of performance*, Westview Press: Colorado.

Hodge, G. A. (2002) '*Business process outsourcing: Improving services, reducing costs and the intelligent buyer*'. Paper presented at the Business Process Outsourcing Australia Conference, Sydney, 3–5 December 2002.

Humphry, R. (2000) *Review of the 'Whole of Government Information Technology Outsourcing Initiative'*. Ausinfo: Canberra.

Hunt, A. (2001) *Personal communication with the author*, Bangkok.

Industry Commission (Australian) (1996) *Competitive tendering and contracting by public sector agencies: Report No 48*. Melbourne: AGPS.

ITRG (Information Technology Review Group) (1995) *Clients first: The challenge for government of information technology. Report of the minister for finance's information technology review group*. Canberra: Commonwealth of Australia.

Kettle, D. (1993) *Sharing power: Public governance and private markets*. Washington, D.C.: The Brookings Institution:

Lacity, M. C. and Hirschheim, R. (1993) *Information systems outsourcing: Myths, metaphors and realities*. Chichester, UK: Wiley.

Lacity, M. C. and Hirschheim, R. (1995) *Beyond the information systems outsourcing bandwagon: The insourcing response*. New York: Wiley and Sons.

Lacity, M. C. and Willcocks, L. P. (1998) 'An empirical investigation of information technology sourcing practices: Lessons from experience', *MIS Quarterly*, **33**: 363–408.

Lacity, M. C. and Willcocks, L. P. (2001) *Global information technology outsourcing: In search of business advantage*. Chichester, UK: Wiley and Sons.

Lacity, M. C., Willcocks, L. and Feeny, D. F. (1996) 'The value of selective IT outsourcing', *Sloan Management Review*, **37**: 3, 13–25.

Lam, A. K. (2002) '*Developing relationship management principles to ensure BPO success*'. Presentation to the Business Process Outsourcing Australia Conference, Sydney, 3–5 Dec 2002.

Lee, J.-N., Shaila, M. and Yong-Mi, K. (2004) 'IT outsourcing strategies: Universalistic, contingency, and configurational explanations of success', *Information Systems Research*, **14**(2): 110–131.

Loh, L. and Venkatraman, N. (1992) '*Stock market reaction to IT outsourcing: An event study*', Sloan School of Management, Massachusetts Institute of Technology Working Paper.

Mulgan, R. (1998) 'Identifying the "core" public service', *Canberra Bulletin of Public Administration*, **87**: February: 1–7.

Mitchell, S. (2000) 'Audit report slams federal outsourcing', *Australian IT (The Australian)*, 9 December: 31.

Norman, R. (2002) '*Using a document management solution to allow you to focus on your main business expertise*'. Presentation to the Business Process Outsourcing Australia Conference, Sydney, 3–5 December, 2002.

Osborne, D. and Gaebler, T. (1993) *Reinventing government: How the entrepreneurial spirit is transforming the public sector,* Reading, MA: Addison-Wesley.

PA Consulting Group (1997) *Strategic sourcing survey 1998: Australia in the international context,* Melbourne: PA Consulting Group.

Peters, T. and Waterman, R. H. (1982) *In search of excellence: Lessons from America's best-run companies,* New York: Harper and Row.

Pollard, S. (2002) *'BPO: In the trenches'.* Presentation to the Business Process Outsourcing Australia Conference, Sydney, 3–5 Dec 2002.

Rouse, A. C. (2002) *Information technology outsourcing revisited: Success factors and risks.* Unpublished PhD Thesis: University of Melbourne.

Rouse, A. C. and Corbitt, B. (2003a) 'The Australian government's abandoned infrastructure outsourcing program: What can be learned?', *Australian Journal of Information Systems,* **10**(2): 81–90.

Rouse, A. C. and Corbitt, B. (2003b) *'Revisiting IT outsourcing risks: Analysis of a survey of Australia's Top 1,000 organizations',* Proceedings of the 14th Australasian Conference on Information Systems, 26–28 November 2003, Perth, Australia.

Savas, E. S. (1987) *Privatisation: The key to better government,* Chatham, NJ: Chatham House Publishers.

Seddon, P. (2001) 'The Australian federal government's clustered-agency IT outsourcing experiment', *Communications of the Association for Information Systems,* **5**(13), 1–33.

Seddon, P., Cullen, S., Willcocks, L. P., Rouse, A. C. and Reilly, C. (2000) *'Report on information technology outsourcing practices in Australia 2000'* (Version 1, October). Melbourne, Australia: Department of Information Systems, University of Melbourne.

SFPARC (Senate Finance and Public Administration References Committee, (1997) *Contracting out of government services. First report: Information technology.* Canberra: Commonwealth of Australia.

Walker, B. and Walker, B. C. (2000) *Privatization: sell off or sell out? The Australian experience,* Sydney: ABC Books.

Willcocks, L. (1998) Personal communication, following 'Warning: Outsourcing can blow your budget', *Australian Financial Review,* 3 November, p. 27.

Willcocks, L. (2001) *'Submission to the Senate Standing Committee on Finance and Public Administration into the 'Whole of Government Information Technology Outsourcing Initiative',* Canberra: Commonwealth of Australia.

Willcocks, L. and Lacity, M. C. (1998) *Strategic sourcing of information systems: Perspectives and practices.* Chichester: John Wiley and Sons.

Willcocks, L., Lacity, M. and Fitzgerald, G. (1997) 'IT outsourcing in Europe and the USA: Assessment issues' in Willcocks, L., Feeny, D., and Islei, G. (eds.) *Managing IT as a strategic resource.* New York: McGraw Hill.

Yates, A. (2000) Government as an informed buyer. Recognising technical expertise as a crucial factor in the success of engineering contracts. Institute of Engineers, Australia. Available from: www.lea.org.an/policy/res/downloads/publications/Government as an informed Buyer.pdf.

13 International comparisons of output and productivity in public service provision: A review

Mary O'Mahony and Philip Stevens

Introduction

This chapter reviews the theoretical and empirical issues involved in undertaking international comparisons of output and productivity (outputs per inputs used) in the provision of public services. The primary focus of the chapter is on performance in aggregate sectors such as health and education, although many of the arguments carry through to more detailed comparisons such as the treatment of specific diseases or types of education. A host of measures of performance are available in the existing literature, from indexes of activity rates to surveys of consumer satisfaction, but there has been little effort to evaluate their relative merits. The purpose of the chapter is both to review existing measures and argue for a unifying framework to ensure that the measures are comprehensive in coverage and place the appropriate weights on various aspects of provision. This framework puts consumer preferences centre stage and draws from the methods employed to measure performance in the private sector.

The chapter begins with a review of existing measures used to evaluate international comparisons of performance, first considering measures for the private sector and then considering available indicators for public services. This highlights the confused picture that emerges for public services in contrast to the useful insights that arise for the private sector. The chapter considers alternative approaches that can be employed for public services and argues in favour of including information on final outcomes. It sketches the steps taken by the authors to employ this framework to compare productivity in the US and UK education sectors, and illustrates how the method could be employed in practice. The chapter concludes with observations on extensions of the method and the data requirements to take forward this approach.

International comparisons of outputs and productivity

Performance measures for market sectors

International comparisons of productivity levels and growth rates in both the aggregate and the private market economy have informed both research and policy for many years. Such comparisons, undertaken independently by researchers and international organizations, yield a set of stylized facts which are useful in explaining comparative performance and benchmarking policy initiatives.[1]

Productivity growth is defined as the growth in goods or services produced minus the growth in inputs. Productivity growth is probably the most important long-term indicator of performance in any sector since it measures the extent to which changes in input use and organizational procedures translate to increases in living standards of citizens. Measures employed in the literature include labour productivity, output per hour worked and total factor productivity (or TFP, the output per unit of multiple inputs). Labour productivity growth is the most commonly reported measure as it is the simplest to calculate. Relative productivity levels compare countries at a point in time and are useful both as benchmarks and as indicative of what might be expected in terms of productivity growth. A well known result is that countries far behind the productivity leader have greater potential for productivity growth because they can imitate production methods and technological advances and hence catch up with the leader.

Total economy labour productivity is shown in Figure 13.1, which combines both levels and growth rates in real gross domestic product (GDP) per hour worked for a number of industrial nations from 1950 to 2002. The US was the productivity leader throughout most of the post-war period, although France and the former West Germany caught up with the US in the 1990s. Two striking features of the graph are Japan's position throughout and the failure of the UK to follow France and Germany in catching up with the US. In the 1980s much of the economics literature was devoted to the perceived threat from Japan, with the implied policy recommendation that the US and other countries should seek to emulate Japanese production methods. However, this argument confused productivity levels and growth rates. While it was true that growth was much higher in Japan in the 1970s and 1980s, this was largely catch-up to levels in other countries. Once this was recognized and Japan ran into constraints following the end of catch-up growth, it ceased to be the country to follow. Examination of productivity by sector subsequently showed that Japan's higher growth up to the 1990s was largely confined to a few industries within manufacturing.

The figures showing the poor relative position of the UK and its failure to catch up with the US were an important background to subsequent research.

---

1 Recent publications on international comparisons of productivity growth rates and levels include e.g., O'Mahony and DeBoer (2002), O'Mahony and Van Ark (2003) and OECD (2003a).

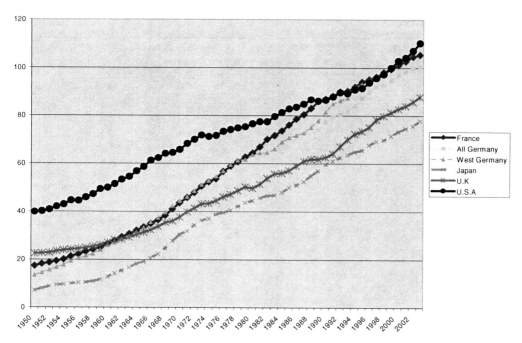

Figure 13.1 GDP per hour worked: US 1996 = 100

Results based on industry and firm data then pointed to skill deficiencies as one of the most likely explanatory factors, although many researchers also highlight problems with UK management, regulation and the propensity to innovate. From this discussion we can see that measuring aggregate performance can be useful in both dispelling myths and a spur to research to explain differences in performance across countries.

There are some measurement issues surrounding the estimates shown in Figure 13.1, but many of the problems are practical or data-based rather than conceptual. Nevertheless the broad conclusions on international comparative productivity in market sectors have proved to be robust to many revisions and changes in methodology.[2]

Existing measures for the public sector

It would be useful also to have a set of stylized facts that could inform policy on the effectiveness of public service provision. Suppose we were to ask what is the US productivity position in health care provision relative to other industrial countries or how does the UK perform in education? Are reliable and robust estimates available with which to answer these questions? A review of the

2 Examples of international comparisons that are broadly consistent with those in Figure 13.1 are Broadberry (1998) and Maddison (2001).

Table 13.1 Life expectancy in the EU and US

	Male life expectancy at birth		Female life expectancy at birth		Life expectancy at 65 years, male and female	
	1990	2000	1990	2000	1990	2000
Belgium	72.8	74.2[a]	79.6	80.8[a]	16.9	17.6[a]
Denmark	72.3	74.1[b]	78.0	78.9[b]	16.2	16.8[b]
Germany	72.1	75.2	78.6	81.3	16.4	18.1
Greece	74.8	75. 8[b]	79.6	81.0[b]	17.1	18.0[b]
Spain	73.4	76.0	80.6	83.0	17.5	19.0
France	73.4	75.2[b]	81.8	82.8[b]	18.7	19.2[b]
Ireland	72.1	74.0	77.7	79.3	15.2	16.5
Italy	73.8	76.8	80.5	83.0	17.3	19.0
Luxembourg	72.2	75.0	78.7	81.9	16.5	18.5
Netherlands	73.9	75.7	80.4	80.8	17.1	17.6
Austria	72.5	75.6	79.1	81.5	16.8	18.4
Portugal	70.5	72.6	77.5	79.7	15.7	16.7
Finland	71.0	74.3	79.1	81.3	16.2	17.9
Sweden	74.9	77.5	80.7	82.3	17.5	18.7
United Kingdom	73.1	75.7	78.7	80.5	16.4	17.7
EU-15	*73.1*	*75.6*	*79.8*	*81.7*	*17.1*	*18.4*
US	*71.8*	*74.1*	*78.8*	*79.5*	*17.2*	*18.0*
Cyprus	–	75.6	–	80.2	–	17.3
Czech Republic	67.6	71.8	75.5	78.6	13.8	15.8
Estonia	64.7	65.4	75.0	76.3	14.5	15.3
Hungary	65.2	67.6	73.9	76.3	14.0	15.2
Lithuania	66.5	66.8	76.4	77.6	15.7	16.3
Latvia	64.2	64.9	74.6	76.1	14.5	15.3
Malta	73.8	76.0	78.4	80.3	15.7	17.0
Poland	66.6	69.8	75.6	78.1	14.6	15.9
Slovenia	70.0	72.3	78.0	80.1	15.8	17.0
Slovak Republic	66.8	69.3	75.8	77.6	14.4	15.2

[a] indicates 1997 data, [b] indicates 1999 data.
Source: OECD Health Data 2003; WHO European Health for All Database 2004; Health, United States, 2003, National Center for Health Statistics.

literature on performance measures in health and education found that exist-ing internationally comparable measures were sparse and those that do exist frequently lead to inconsistent conclusions. A few examples from both sectors illustrate the problems.

In this brief discussion of the health sector we focus attention on the relative position of the United States. The majority of international evidence for the health sector is collected by the World Health Organization (WHO) and the OECD. Life expectancy is a commonly used measure of the health status of a population. Table 13.1 shows measures of life expectancy for the US and EU

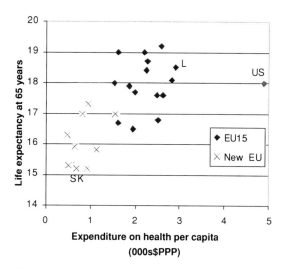

Figure 13.2 Life expectancy and expenditure on health

member states, dividing the latter into the original fifteen states and the recent new members. Male life expectancy in 2000 in the EU ranged from 74 years in Ireland to 77.5 years in Sweden whereas female life expectancy varied from 79 years in Denmark to 83 years in France. In the US, male life expectancy was 74 years, while female life expectancy was 79.5 years. Hence on this indicator, the US is at the bottom end of the country distribution, in stark contrast to its highest position in terms of expenditure on health care per capita. Life expectancy rose in both the US and EU between 1990 and 2000, continuing trends observed for the entire post-war period (Cutler and Richardson 1997). The relative position of the US compares more favourably to other countries when the indicator employed is life expectancy at age 65 years; its value is close to the EU average in both 1990 and 2000. The difference in the relative position of the US when examining total population or population aged 65 years or over can be partly explained by the considerably higher neonatal mortality rates in the US (Baily and Garber 1997). The latter in turn is likely to be related to the lack of universal insurance coverage in the US, in particular among poorer sections of the population and immigrants. Again, this is an indicator that has been increasing in all countries between 1990 and 2000 but the US has lost some ground on EU countries over this decade. Thus while only four of the original EU-15 member states had higher life expectancy at age 65 in 1990, by 2000 eight of these countries surpassed the US.

Figure 13.2 shows life expectancy for the elderly population relative to per capita expenditure on health. At first glance, and excluding the US, the chart suggests a positive and significant correlation between health expenditure and longevity. However, this is an artifact of the differences in overall wealth

Table 13.2 Mortality rates for malignant neoplasms and diseases of the circulatory system per 100 000 population[a]

	Malignant neoplasms	Diseases of the circulatory system
Belgium[b]	271.9	385.7
Denmark[c]	286.4	401.2
Germany	256.8	494.7
Greece	222.2	493.7
Spain[c]	227.7	341.7
France	245.4	281.3
Ireland	201.4	357.3
Italy	263.3	427.1
Luxembourg[d]	225.6	329.0
Netherlands	241.2	313.6
Austria[d]	231.2	494.6
Portugal[d]	210.2	401.5
Finland[d]	197.7	413.4
Sweden	238.3	503.0
United Kingdom	256.3	420.7
EU-15	248.4	406.3
US	201.6	350.0
Czech Republic[d]	277.8	566.5
Estonia[d]	245.6	728.6
Hungary[d]	332.0	687.0
Lithuania[d]	209.0	566.3
Latvia[d]	234.7	752.9
Malta	187.9	391.0
Poland[d]	218.8	453.9
Slovenia	241.6	388.0
Slovak Republic[d]	219.8	534.8

[a] data refers to 1999 unless stated otherwise [b] indicates 1996 data [c] indicates 1998 data [d] indicates 2000 data.
Source: WHO mortality database. Mortality rates calculated as number of registered deaths divided by population. WHO advise caution with regard to the level of coverage of the data – in the EU and US however, the estimated level of coverage is normally close to 100%.

between the old and new EU countries and is not significant when attention is confined to the original fifteen EU member states or when the US is included.

An alternative to using life expectancy is to consider the rates of fatality from major illnesses. Table 13.2 shows death rates per 100,000 population for two major disease categories, malignant neoplasms (cancer) and diseases of the circulatory system (various types of heart disease). In both cases death rates

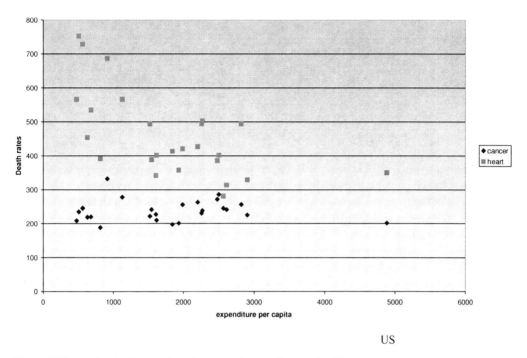

US

Figure 13.3 Death rates from major diseases and expenditure on health

are lower in the US than for the entire EU-15 population, with some EU countries, notably Belgium, Denmark and the UK showing very high death rates. More EU countries perform better or on a par with the US in terms of circulatory diseases, namely France, Spain, the Netherlands and Luxembourg, with again some very high rates among EU countries. When these death rates are plotted against expenditure per capita (Figure 13.3) we see a significant negative relationship between death rates and health expenditures for heart disease, regardless of whether the US is included or not.[3] Nevertheless the US is again an outlier. There is no obvious relationship between death rates from cancer and expenditures but in this case arguably a more appropriate measure would also take account of morbidity since many treatments merely represent palliative care rather than curing this disease.

This brief examination of aggregate data gives conflicting results on US relative performance. There is no doubt that the US spends far more per capita on health than other industrialized countries, but it is unclear to date if this is worthwhile.

3 Note endogeneity considerations imply care should be taken in interpreting this finding as a causal relationship between rising expenditures and declining death rates, at least in the short term. The causation could run the other way with high expenditures targeted at problem areas such as heart disease.

Table 13.3 Results from PISA

Country	Combined reading literacy Mean	Rank (OECD)	Mathematical literacy Mean	Rank (OECD)	Scientific literacy Mean	Rank (OECD)
OECD Countries						
Canada	534.31	2	533	6	529.36	5
Finland	546.47	1	536.16	4	537.74	3
France	504.74	14	517.15	10	500.49	12
Germany	483.99	21	489.8	19	487.11	20
Hungary	479.97	22	488.04	20	496.08	15
Italy	487.47	20	457.35	23	477.6	23
Japan	522.23	8	556.61	1	550.4	2
Korea	524.75	6	546.84	2	552.12	1
United Kingdom	**523.44**	**7**	**529.2**	**8**	**532.02**	**4**
United States	504.42	15	493.15	18	499.46	14
OECD total	498.83		497.52		502.18	
OECD average	500		500		500	

Source: Home Knowledge and Skills for Life – First Results from PISA 2000, Appendix B1, Tables 2.3a, 3.1, and 3.3.

The above discussion suggests that the answers depend on how the services are measured. In addition, the link between outcomes and medical treatment inputs is not clear cut, because many factors outside the health care system affect outcomes (a point which we explore in more detail, below). Considerable progress has been made in examining healthcare performance and its link to technology diffusion at the micro-disease-based level (see e.g., OECD 2003c; McClellan and Kessler 2003). These micro studies may at the end of the day be the best method of gaining an aggregate perspective of international performance in the health sector. But these studies are costly in research time and effort and so it will be some years before a sufficiently large number of diseases are studied to provide a comprehensive picture. In the meantime, since there is little by way of aggregate health sector estimates available to date, it is worth pursuing alternative methods.

Turning to education, there have been a number of league tables produced showing test score results across a selection of countries. The most recent is the OECD Programme for International Student Assessment (PISA), which was a survey of fifteen-year-olds in some thirty mainly OECD countries conducted in 2000. PISA 2000 sampled more than a quarter of a million fifteen-year-olds and covered three domains: reading literacy, mathematical literacy and scientific literacy. Table 13.3 presents the results from the PISA study, showing the

Table 13.4 Trends in maths achievement (TIMMS)

	1995 Average scale score	1999 Average scale score	Difference in average achievement between 1995 and 1999
Netherlands	529 (6.1)	540 (7.1)	11 (9.5)
Canada	521 (2.2)	531 (2.5)	10 (3.2)
United States	492 (4.7)	502 (4.0)	9 (6.2)
Korea, Rep. of	581 (2.0)	587 (2.0)	6 (2.8)
Hungary	527 (3.2)	532 (3.7)	5 (4.9)
International avg.	**519 (0.9)**	**521 (0.9)**	**2 (1.3)**
England	498 (3.0)	496 (4.1)	−1 (5.2)
Japan	581 (1.6)	579 (1.7)	−2 (2.2)
Italy	491 (3.4)	485 (4.8)	−6 (6.0)

Source: TIMMS 1999, International Mathematics Report (standard errors in parenthesis)

OECD average and results for selected countries. Interestingly the UK ranks in the top ten in all three tests, a result that surprised many researchers on UK education.

The UK's relatively good performance in PISA was not consistent with a previous similar study, the Third International Mathematics and Science Study (TIMSS) in 1995 and its follow up in 1999 (TIMMS-R). The maths results, shown again for selected countries in Table 13.4, put England well below average. This offers a more useful comparison over time than that between TIMSS 1999 and OECD-PISA 2000 due to the consistency of definitions. PISA created quite a stir when its results suggested a very different 'league table' to that suggested by the earlier TIMSS study (and the earlier studies conducted by the Institute of Economic Affairs). This was taken in many quarters to mean that, for example, the UK had experienced an enormous leap in the quality of its education provision. However, this jump in quality must have happened in one year since the difference between the TIMSS-R figures for 1999 and those of PISA for 2000 dwarfed the changes between TIMSS-R and the earlier TIMMS figures for 1995 (Prais 2003). Doubts have been expressed about the methodology and implementation of the PISA survey. There is some question mark over both the response rate of schools in the UK and of pupils within schools and this may have affected the UK's relative position (Prais 2003). Also the questions asked were very different in PISA relative to earlier studies, with PISA relying more on interpreting tables and graphs rather than solving equations. It is likely, therefore, that the results of these studies may pick up variations in teaching methods rather than in the true outcomes themselves. The divergent results in PISA and TIMMS have cast doubt on the reliability of these types of studies as indicators of international performance.

Although the existing measures based on aggregate indicators on health and education can give conflicting results, this does not stop commentators in the media and the academic community from expounding views on the merits of different forms of organizational structure, in particular the need for greater competition and deregulation. This is despite the fact that, at least in health care, the most readily available evidence suggests poor relative performance in the highly competitive and deregulated US system. Likewise, we frequently read about the poor productivity of UK public services, but there is little by way of international comparative evidence to support this. Since the UK spends far less than other countries on its public services we should expect worse outcomes. The main question is, given these low expenditures, are UK consumers getting value for money? In addition to this, we would like to predict what could be achieved by increasing expenditures on public services. A more comprehensive framework is required to examine these issues.

Measuring productivity in public services: A conceptual framework

Measurement in the private sector

In order to develop a measurement framework, it is worthwhile considering the methods used in the private sector that underlie Figure 13.1. Since transactions are recorded in the market place, the value of production in current prices can be calculated. Sales of any one product or service are equal to the quantity sold multiplied by their price. Therefore, estimating the volume of goods and services requires price indices, showing changes across time and differences in price levels across countries. Price indices in turn are constructed by weighting prices in two periods (countries) by base year quantities and summing across all items produced, equivalent to a weighted average of price changes with weights equal to each item's share in total sales. Prices are adjusted to remove any change due to differences in the product or service specification through time or across country that is, to account for quality. For example, the nominal prices paid for computers are adjusted to reflect the changing effectiveness of the machines through time in terms of their capacity to tackle specific tasks. National statistical agencies collect thousands of prices to calculate real growth in output. Calculating relative productivity levels in the private sector requires pricing matched bundles of goods and services, but again there is an internationally coordinated research programme designed to gather such prices. Some problems remain, relating to the reliability, coverage and comparability of the bundle of goods and services priced and to a greater need to adjust for quality change.

Aggregate measures need to be as comprehensive as possible, capturing the main services produced. In the market sector, output measures in the national accounts represent national statisticians' best attempt to provide comprehensive measures. Hence the discussion in much of this section relates to national accounting methods, with a brief discussion in the conclusion on going beyond national accounting conventions.

In the past, the national accounts of most countries measured non-market outputs by the inputs used. By definition, this method implies both that productivity growth is zero and that there are no differences in productivity levels across countries (although in practice, methods of calculating capital input varied so that slight differences emerged). Recently dissatisfaction with this approach has led national statistical offices to review their methods and attempts to get away from the dependence on inputs to measure outputs.

Measurement in the public sector: outcomes as alternatives to prices

In the private market economy, prices represent consumers' willingness to pay for goods and services. In the non-market sector the lack of prices means that alternative methods need to be employed to calculate output and productivity. The measurement approach advocated in this chapter essentially argues that the information incorporated in these alternatives should be the same as would be the case if prices were available. Quantity measures, such as numbers of operations or numbers of pupils educated, are frequently readily available for public services and so could be employed as an output measure. However this will only yield a measure unadjusted for quality and, given that quantities will be measured in different units, there is no natural aggregation method. It is therefore necessary to consider consumers' willingness to pay in terms of the characteristics of the product or service being consumed. Direct measures of these characteristics could be used as alternatives to prices, since they embody all the information contained in the price.

For the purposes of this chapter we distinguish:

Quantity or volume indices

These can be defined as *activities*, procedures or processes carried out within the public sector (e.g. number of operations in the health sector, hours of classroom lessons in education) or *outputs*, the translation of activities into services that can be consumed (e.g. finished treatment episodes or numbers of students educated to a particular level). In practice it is often difficult to distinguish activities and outputs. The UK Office for National Statistics currently employs activities in health sector measurement (Pritchard 2002). Volume output measures for education, based on number of pupils at various educational attainment levels are also commonly used (e.g., Pritchard 2002; Fraumeni *et al.* 2004; Kleima and Konijn 2003; Zhao and Jones 2003). In fact quantity indices have often been employed in the private sector where reliable data are unavailable, for example the use of passenger kilometres travelled in the transport sector.

Outcome indices

These can be defined as measures of well-being of persons consuming public services. In health this might be increases in life expectancy or in quality-adjusted life years (QALYs), which combine morbidity and mortality into a single measure. In education, easily measurable outcomes might be increases in pupils' earning power or increases in their probability of finding paid employment.[4]

Much of the recent literature on public service measurement has suggested that data on final outcomes, such as increased life expectancy or lifetime earnings from education, can be used as a measure of the benefit to consumers (see the discussion in Berndt *et al.* 2000; Triplett 2001). It is important to point out that it *is the marginal contribution* of the public service to outcomes that requires measuring since many factors apart from the services delivered affect outcomes. The use of outcomes, if measured to a reasonable degree of accuracy, can capture the characteristics of the service valued by consumers that are embodied in prices in the market sector. It also obviates the need to incorporate adjustments for quality of the service produced.

The measurement framework advocated in this chapter is to combine information on volumes with outcomes to evaluate public sector performance. This is the procedure adopted by the authors in comparing the UK and US education sectors (O'Mahony and Stevens 2005) and in evaluating the performance of the UK health sector through time (Dawson *et al.* 2004). Thus in many respects public and private services can be treated in a similar manner, since they essentially use the same information. Conceptually, the only difference is that the information is embedded in market prices in the private sector whereas direct measures of the marginal contribution of services to outcomes are required in the public sector.

Information based on outcomes can also be useful in measurement even when services are sold in a market. In particular, papers on the US health sector consider measurement issues in the face of asymmetric information whereby information is often in the hands of professionals whose preferences may diverge from those of the final consumer. Triplett considers the analogy between a private service, car repair and health, 'human repair' (Triplett 2001). He argues that in private services we are willing to assume that the more expensive ones must be better if the consumer chooses them. In health care the consumer has an inadequate basis for making this judgement, that is for making informed choices among both providers and types of interventions. In health care it is not correct to assume that because someone undertakes or approves a medical procedure it meets the consumer's willingness to pay test. Therefore Triplett concludes

---

4 Market-based outcome measures ignore both private benefits from educational services that go beyond the impact on market earnings such as education enhancing an individual's ability to enjoy leisure time and any external social benefits of education such as impacts on reducing crime rates etc. Both are likely to be important but nevertheless difficult to measure.

that we need data that show that more resource intensive medical procedures 'work'.

Measurement in practice

While in theory the framework discussed above, combining quantity and outcome information to mirror methods employed for the market economy, is useful in measuring the services produced by the public sector, a number of practical considerations arise when applying the method. Obviously, as with all applications, robust estimation requires good data (see the conclusion for further discussion of this issue). In addition, methodological issues include aggregation across diverse services, attribution and quality adjustments. This section considers these three issues in turn.

A typical study of performance in public service provision would start with data available at a detailed level, for example treatments for particular diseases or education at some level. An aggregate measure would then combine these indicators and compare them with the inputs used to provide the services. In the private sector, prices are generally employed when aggregating across quantities. These are the most appropriate weights because prices measure the marginal valuation to consumers. Problems arise when there is a divergence between prices and costs, for example due to the exercise of market power by producers. In that case, cost weights are used, but implicit in this is the assumption that the marginal products of resources employed are equalized. In simple terms, this means that budgets are allocated to areas of provision in a way that the benefit to the consumer is maximized.

Cost weights are also commonly used to aggregate across diverse public services. This is frequently justified on the grounds that costs are the only measurable weighting scheme available rather than the argument that budgets are optimally allocated. In public services, there are fewer grounds to believe that the latter in fact takes place as there may be a divergence between the goals of politicians/providers and consumers which is not readily observable because of information asymmetries. An alternative aggregation procedure is to translate each quantity indicator into its impact on a common outcome measure. This can be the impact of medical treatments on life expectancy or quality-adjusted life years (QALYs) in health care, quality of life in social services or earnings potential in education. Shares of the outcomes attributed to each quantity in total outcomes can then be employed as weights. Outcome weights can get around some of the problems associated with cost weights but are often much more difficult to measure. Also the more complicated measures such as QALYs may themselves be based on arbitrary weights in earlier stages of their calculations, for example weights on morbidity measures such as the extent of disability, pain suffered etc. Note that if the sole purpose is to aggregate across outputs within the one sector, then all that is required is that the aggregator is measured in a common unit and this need not be a monetary valuation. Thus in health care we do not require estimates of the value of a life saved; numbers of lives saved is a valid alternative. Against this, not all outcomes from each sector can be readily translated into a single aggregator, for example reductions in waiting lists or ensuring a high standard of cleanliness. Similarly, should aggregation across disparate services such as health and education be required, there is no escaping from monetary valuation.

The use of outcomes means we have to confront the issue of attribution, for example the extent to which changes in outcomes are due to public services or other outside influences. This issue has recently been discussed in the context of measuring health sector output (Triplett 2001). Medical interventions should add to the stock of health, but health is produced by many factors other than activities of the medical sector, for example diet, lifestyle, environmental factors and genetic endowments. Triplett represents this in a general form as:

Health = H (medical, diet, lifestyle, environment, genetic etc.)

The contribution of medical intervention needs to be measured by its incremental contribution:

effectiveness of the health sector = the change in health divided by the change in medical intervention, holding other influences constant.

Hence it is not worthwhile merely to explore whether there is a positive correlation between a society's level of health and medical expenditures. Rather the task is to compute the marginal value of a medical intervention on health, holding the other influences constant.

A number of methods exist to allow researchers to take account of the attribution problem. For example, the researcher could employ a method of standardization in order to remove extraneous influences. This is common in measuring population health, where standardization produces a measure of population health from which the effects of population structure (e.g. age and gender strata) have been removed so that one can make comparisons of mortality across periods or areas without the confounding effects of demographic structure. Regression analysis is also commonly employed whereby a set of control variables are included in an equation relating outcomes to public service provision; an example of this approach is discussed below.

If continuous outcome data on both characteristic dimensions and changes through time were available, weighting quantities by time varying outcomes attributable to the service would be sufficient to adjust for quality change. In practice data are only available at discrete observation points so that additional quality adjustments are necessary; an example of such a procedure is given below. It may also be the case that there are insufficient data to weight quantities but information exists on some important outcomes, such as changes in mortality rates, that can be attributed to the public service provided. In that case a proxy measure could be employed combining cost weights with quality adjustment factors providing the latter are based on estimates of the importance of these outcomes to consumers.

The approach advocated above should be distinguished from a direct outcome measurement method. The aggregate indicators of life expectancy and death rates from major diseases, presented above are one such example of direct measurement. The problem with these measures is that they address neither aggregation nor attribution. Direct outcome measures can however be useful if they are narrowly defined so that aggregation/attribution is not an issue. A large number of such studies are available in the literature, mostly for the US. For example, Cutler *et al.* have considered heart attacks where the outcome measure was the increase in life expectancy (Cutler *et al.* 1998). The studies on balance indicate a substantial rise in the productivity of healthcare (Cutler and McClellan 2001, see also Cutler and Berndt 2001 and references therein). However little has been achieved to date in including morbidity in addition to mortality, and chronic diseases such as many forms of cancer are underrepresented.

The potential to undertake international comparisons: An example for the education sector

For the education sector Jorgenson and Fraumeni present measures of the output of the US education sector where education was treated as an investment in human capital (Jorgenson and Fraumeni 1992). Hence the way the market values these skills can be employed as an outcome measure. The authors calculate a real output series by weighting pupil enrolments by lifetime earnings weights for each level of educational attainment. The research outlined in this section uses a similar framework. Note, if education levels are positively correlated with leisure or other non-income goods, the shares of higher skill groups might be underestimates. There are a number of additional problems with this approach, chief of which is the extent to which increased income of individuals is due to education versus inherent ability. Many economists think of schooling as involving the production of human capital in individuals, but an alternative perspective is that of screening or signalling (e.g., Spence 1973; Wolpin 1977; Weiss 1995). The extreme case of the screening model suggests that individuals begin schooling with differing abilities and that schooling merely allows employers to identify those with more ability. To the individuals themselves it does not matter what the source of earnings enhancement is – be it production by schools or screening – they will be equally induced to make schooling investments based on the comparison of returns and costs. It has been pointed out (Hanushek 2002) that the two may yield quite different incentives to governments to invest, because signalling may lead to different social and private returns to schooling. Dealing with this is difficult but available evidence suggests the impact may be less than first thought (Ashenfelter *et al.* 1999).

This section briefly discusses the steps taken in applying the above methods to compare the productivity of the UK and US education sectors; further details are available elsewhere (O'Mahony and Stevens 2005). Volume measures of the number of pupils/students educated are readily available in industrial countries. There have been some attempts to classify these for common groups. For example the International Standard Classification of Education (ISCED) is a system for classifying statistics on education in a way which is comparable internationally, dividing into categories such as primary, secondary and tertiary and divisions therein. These data could potentially be used to compare outputs across countries, weighting each type of education by its share of total cost. However there are many difficulties in matching qualifications to these groups, since in European countries vocational qualifications are common and there is no equivalent of the US high school graduation. Forcing qualifications into common groups may obscure important differences within countries. Therefore each country's education system is used to define the number of levels of education that capture its main feature. These groups are discussed further below.

The analysis uses data from both the UK Labour Force Survey (LFS) and the US Current Population Survey (CPS) to estimate the impact of education on earnings. The estimates are derived from a human capital earnings function which expresses the log of earnings as a function of years of schooling, a second or more-order polynomial of experience and other control variables. A variant of the basic estimates also took account of the effect of education on economic activity, that is the probability that the individual is employed, unemployed or inactive. The results are then applied to the volume data on school and higher education (HE) enrolments to derive an aggregate outcome weighted volume measure for education. Measures of quality change are then discussed with the main options being changes in test score results or age cohort impacts on earnings. The resulting output index is compared to labour input growth to derive an aggregate measure of labour productivity.

The education/qualification groups for which estimates were derived are shown in Tables 13.5 and 13.6 below. Note we do not attempt to match the categories in the two countries, in fact experience in working with these data suggests that it is not possible to match since there is no obvious UK equivalent of the US high school graduation. Instead the combination of enrolments and earnings yield a measure that can be compared across the two countries.

With time-varying weights, this approach is capable of adjusting for compositional or between-group changes in the quality of education output, by

Table 13.5 UK qualifications

Qualification level
No qualifications
Secondary education up to GCSE
Secondary education up to A-Level
Further education qualification
Higher education – Undergraduate, Masters
Higher education – Doctorates

Table 13.6 US qualifications

Qualification level
Less than 11th grade
11th grade
12th grade, but no diploma
12th grade, High School Diploma, GED[1]
Some college but no degree
Associate degree
Undergraduate degree
Postgraduate or professional degree

1. GED (General Education Development) qualifications are generally regarded as less valuable than high school diplomas but these two cannot be separated in the data employed in this chapter.

giving higher weight to 'higher quality' types of education and by incorporating differential growth in earnings. The fact that the quantity data are only observed at discrete intervals, however, means that this method misses within-group quality change. O'Mahony and Stevens also consider how to incorporate within-group quality change, or changes in the effectiveness of pupils through time (O'Mahony and Stevens 2005). This captures the idea that a pupil today may have been taught very different skills from those educated say ten years ago. An obvious candidate to take account of changing effectiveness of students is to use test score results but the authors suggest that it is difficult to use data on test scores without being able to translate them to a common metric, otherwise the results are sensitive to which test score measure is used. Also it may be that changes in the proportion of students reaching some score level may be merely capturing grade inflation. The impact of test scores on earnings is a possible candidate to employ in a quality adjustment (see Hanushek (2004) for evidence of a link between test scores and earnings for the US.

An alternative is to consider age cohort effects, that is comparing the earnings of persons with highest qualification at say A-level or university with persons receiving these qualifications some years earlier, adjusting for the impact of experience in the intervening years. This involves the assumption that any increased earnings of younger cohorts relative to older ones with the same qualification are due to improvements in the education system. Alternative explanations might be that younger workers are more flexible and more adept at using new technology. Hence earnings of younger relative to older cohorts might change in periods of rapid technological change such as is occurring at present with the wave of information technology innovations. A cohort quality adjustment might then be biased upwards.

The results of this exercise suggest about equal productivity levels in the UK and US education sectors by 2000, but significant differences in growth performance since 1979 with the UK in general outperforming the US. Thus in this sector the UK converged on the US in contrast to its failure to do so for the aggregate economy as shown above. Much of this is due to greater expansion of higher education in the UK than the US where the high growth occurred at a much earlier period, plus greater than average growth in the earnings of graduates.

Conclusion

This chapter has argued that measuring output and productivity in public services can be addressed within a framework which mirrors that employed for market sectors. This puts the benefits to the consumer centre stage while using available information on quantities and outcomes to measure these benefits. A common argument found in the existing literature is that measurement in this area is too difficult, since public services are fundamentally different from other services. Our approach suggests that such a negative view is unwarranted. Services, whether produced by the private or public sector, serve consumers and so consumer preferences should dictate how these services are evaluated. Thus measurement should begin by considering the characteristics valued by consumers, attempting to quantify the relative magnitudes of these and relate them to outcomes. It is easy to exaggerate the measurement issues in public services; all measurement is complex.

At the same time we acknowledge that the data requirements to derive robust and hence defendable estimates are daunting. Nevertheless data are increasingly becoming available that can produce better estimates, for example patient record data for health services and data that track pupils from education through work. In addition there is a rapidly growing literature valuing outcomes such as lives saved and QALYs. Lack of perfect data should not constrain researchers – attempting to measure, however imperfectly, will allow knowledge to accumulate on data requirements.

Finally the discussion above could be seen as constrained by taking a national accounts perspective. However there is no *a priori* reason to confine attention to this approach and so it could be extended in other directions. We might want to incorporate external benefits or spillovers, for example the impact of ensuring a healthy population on workforce productivity as an output of the health sector. The difference between social and private returns might well be of interest to policy makers but would not be incorporated in national accounts. Estimation of spillovers is frequently undertaken for private services by extending standard production models to include proxy variables in an econometric analysis. Such an approach could also be applied to public services once reasonable measures of private benefits were available.

Acknowledgement

The authors would like to acknowledge the support of the ESRC/EPSRC Advanced Institute of Management Research under grant number RES-331-25-0009 for this research. Initial research on this topic benefited from funding from the UK Treasury 'Evidence Based Policy Fund' with contributions from the Office for National Statistics, the Department for Education and Skills and the Department of Health. Thanks also to Lucy Stokes for research assistance.

REFERENCES

Ashenfelter, O., Harmon, C. and Oosterbeek, H. (1999) 'A review of the schooling/earnings relationship, with tests for publication bias', *Labour Economics*, **6**: 453–470.

Baily, M. and Garber, A. (1997) 'Health care productivity', *Brookings Papers on Economic Activity: Microeconomics*, 1997: 143–202.

Berndt, E. R., Cutler, D. M., Frank, R. G., Griliches, Z., Newhouse, J. P. and Triplett, J. E. (2000) 'Medical care prices and output' in Culyer, A. J. and Newhouse, J. P. (eds.) *Handbook of health economics*, Vol 1. Elsevier Science B.V., pp. 119–175.

Broadberry, S. N. (1998) 'How did the United States and Germany overtake Britain? A sectoral analysis of comparative productivity levels, 1870–1990', *Journal of Economic History*, **58**: 375–407.

Cutler, D. M. and Richardson, E. (1997) 'Measuring the health of the US population', *Brookings Papers on Economic Activity: Microeconomics* 1997: 217–271.

Cutler, D. M., McClellan, M., Newhouse, J. P. and Remler, D. (1998) 'Are medical prices declining? Evidence from heart attack treatments', *Quarterly Journal of Economics*, **113**: 991–1024.

Cutler, D. M. and McClellan, M. (2001) 'Productivity change in health care', *American Economic Review*, **91**: 281–286.

Cutler, David M. and Berndt, Ernst R. (eds.) (2001) *Medical care output and productivity.* Chicago: Chicago University Press.

Dawson, D., Gravelle, H., Kind, P., O'Mahony, M., Street, A. and Weale, M. (2004) 'Developing new approaches to measuring NHS outputs and productivity, first interim report', *CHE Technical Paper Series* No. 31, Centre for Health Economics: University of York.

Fraumeni, B. M. (2000) 'The output of the education sector as determined by education's effect on lifetime income'. Paper presented at 'Workshop on measuring the output of the education sector', Brookings Program on Output and Productivity Measurement in the Service Sector.

Fraumeni, B. M., Reinsdorf, M. B. and Robinson, B. P. (2004) *Real output measures for the education function of government, a first look at primary and secondary education.* Washington DC: US Bureau of Economic Analysis.

Hanushek, E. (2002) 'Publicly provided education' in Auerbach, A. J. and Feldstein, M. (eds.) *Handbook of public economics.* Amsterdam: North Holland, pp. 2047–2143.

Hanushek, E. (2004) 'Some simple analytics of school quality', *National Bureau of Economic Research, Working Paper No. 10229,* Cambridge, MA: NBER.

Jorgenson, D. W. and Fraumeni, B. M. (1992) 'The output of the education sector' in Griliches, Z. (ed.) *Output measurement in the services sector.* Chicago: University of Chicago Press.

Konijn, P. and Kleima, F. (2003) 'Volume measurement of education' in *Netherlands Official Statistics 2000–3.* Amsterdam: Statistics Netherlands, pp. 11–19.

McClellan, M. B. and Kessler, D. P. (eds.) (2003) *Technological change in health care. A global analysis of heart attack.* University of Michigan Press.

Maddison, A. (2001) *The world economy: A millennial perspective,* Paris: Organisation for Economic Co-operation and Development.

National Center for Health Statistics (2003) *Health, United States, 2003.* Hyattsville, Maryland: Department of Health and Human Services, Center for Disease Control and Prevention.

Organisation for Economic Co-operation and Development (2002) *Measuring up: improving health system performance in OECD countries.* Paris: Organisation for Economic Co-operation and Development.

Organisation for Economic Co-operation and Development (2003a) *The sources of economic growth in OECD countries.* Paris: Organisation for Economic Co-operation and Development.

Organisation for Economic Co-operation and Development (2003b) *OECD Health Data 2003.* Paris: Organisation for Economic Co-operation and Development.

Organisation for Economic Co-operation and Development (2003c) *A disease-based comparison of health systems. What is best and at what cost?* Paris: Organisation for Economic Co-operation and Development.

O'Mahony, M. and deBoer, W. (2002) 'Britain's relative productivity performance: Has anything changed?', *National Institute Economic Review,* **179**: 38–43.

O'Mahony, M. and Stevens, P. (2005) *International comparisons of performance in public services: outcome based measures for education.* Mimeo. London: NIESR.

O'Mahony, M. and Van Ark, B. (2003) *EU productivity and competitiveness: an industry perspective. Can Europe resume the catching-up process?* Luxembourg: Enterprise Publications, European Commission.

Prais, S. J. (2003) 'Cautions on OECD's recent educational survey (PISA)', *Oxford Review of Education* **29**: 139–163.

Pritchard, A. (2002) 'Measuring productivity change in the provision of public services', *Economic Trends* **582**: 20–32.

Spence, A. M. (1973) 'Job market signaling', *Quarterly Journal of Economics,* **87**: 355–374.

Triplett, J. E. (2001) 'What's different about health? Human repair and car repair in national accounts and national health accounts' in Cutler, D. M. and Berndt, E. R. (eds.), *Medical care output and productivity*. Chicago: Chicago University Press, pp. 15–95.

Weiss, A. (1995) 'Human capital vs signaling explanations of wages', *Journal of Economic Perspectives* **9**: 133–154.

Wolpin, K. I. (1977) 'Education and screening', *American Economic Review* **67**: 949–958.

World Health Organization (2003) WHO mortality database.

World Health Organization (2004) European Health for All database. WHO Regional Office for Europe.

Zhao, S. and Jones, M. (2003) 'The output of the government education sector – experimental estimates and issues', *Australian Bureau of Statistics Working Paper*.

14 Public management and government performance: an international review

Melissa Forbes, Carolyn J. Hill and Laurence E. Lynn Jr.

Introduction

Performance is seemingly an obsession with governments around the world. As Frederickson and Smith (2003: 208) point out, '[a]ccountability for conducting the public's business is increasingly about performance rather than discharging a specific policy goal within the confines of the law.'

Evidence for 'this general advocacy of a performance orientation' (Pollitt and Bouckaert 2004: 126) is found, for example, in the European Commission's commitment to 'more efficient, performance-orientated working methods' (EC 2000: 8), in the British government's widespread use of performance targets (James 2001) and in US President George W. Bush's 'management agenda' in particular, in the Office of Management and Budget (OMB) Program Assessment Rating Tool (PART), instituted in 2002. This tool represents the most recent effort by the US federal government to increase the emphasis on performance in government programmes and agencies, although the 1993 Government Performance and Results Act remains in effect. It was implemented by the Bush Administration as an explicit accountability strategy:

> The PART was developed to assess and improve program performance so that the Federal government can achieve better results. A PART review helps identify a program's strengths and weaknesses to inform funding and management decisions aimed at making the program more effective. The PART therefore looks at all factors that affect and reflect program performance including program purpose and design; performance measurement, evaluations, and strategic planning; program management; and program results. Because the PART includes a consistent series of analytical questions, it allows programs to show improvements over time, and allows comparisons between similar programs.
>
> (US OMB, 2005)

With so much attention being paid to performance by policy makers, the public management literature's neglect of relationships between management and performance came under mounting criticism. Peters and Savoie (1998) indicted the literature for being overly descriptive in regard to performance and only comparing measures of performance between countries. Additionally, Pollitt (2000) noted that very little effort has been devoted to rigorous empirical verification of claimed results or to the identification of causal relationships underlying them. Boyne *et al.* (2003: 2) asserted that ' . . . the academic community has not taken seriously the need to evaluate public management reforms.' Fortunately, public management scholars have begun to devote greater effort to determining how best to measure and achieve improved performance. Of particular note is the work of Pollitt (2000); Pollitt and Bouckaert (2004); Boyne (2003); Boyne *et al.* (2003); Hill and Lynn (2005) and Forbes and Lynn (2005) all of which synthesize research findings from individual studies in various countries in an effort to identify general relationships between public management and governmental performance.

This chapter synthesizes the findings of analyses by Hill and Lynn (2005) and Forbes and Lynn (2005) (hereafter referred to as HL and FL) of what public management scholars are studying, how they are modelling causal relationships between management and performance and, selectively and collectively, what they are finding. For the purposes of this chapter, we define government performance as *the character and consequences of service provision by public agencies.* The logic of governance framework utilized in this chapter (and explained below) considers performance measured in terms of: government/public sector outputs; markets, firms, or private sector outcomes; and outcomes for individuals, groups and societies.

Of special interest is the striking tendency in American and international empirical literatures toward hierarchical explanations of public service delivery and of the consequences of public policies and programmes, a finding at variance with the view of governance as increasingly networked and associational rather than traditionally hierarchical. Following discussion of the HL and FL research syntheses, we will review this finding and its implications for governance research and practice.

Evaluating research on public management and performance

A comparative, international view of public management and performance necessarily begins with a review of relevant empirical literature. A number of questions immediately arise. Should studies included in the review meet certain methodological standards? Should they be grouped by type of service such as human services or regulatory activities? Should they be restricted to certain types of functional activities such as implementation or contracting? How should 'public management' and 'performance' be defined? Clearly, no one right answer to each question exists. Rather, a research synthesis may differ with regard to focus, goals, organization, and other characteristic features (Cooper 1988).

In contrast to either literature reviews commonly seen in individual research papers, which appropriately focus on the specific substantive topics considered in the paper, or to more formal meta-analyses, which use statistical methods to summarize the findings of a number of individual studies (Glass 1976), our goal in HL and FL is to provide a synoptic view of the research on public sector governance from US and international (primarily European, English-language) sources. We describe the types of governance relationships that researchers are investigating across a wide range of disciplines, sub-disciplines and fields. Our goal is not to describe 'what works and how it works' but rather to describe '*how researchers understand* what works and how it works.' This fundamental step needs to be taken before considering 'what works' and is especially important in the context of international comparisons.

A number of options for pursuing this goal exist. One is to classify and describe research according to the methodology employed. Public governance has been analysed using experimental and non-experimental methods and, within the non-experimental category, both quantitative and qualitative methods. Within each of these categories are a number of specific approaches and analytical techniques. For example, included in the broad class of non-experimental quantitative methods are instrumental variable or time series models. Included in qualitative methods are observational or interviewing methods. Summarizing the methods across a number of studies can provide insight into the epistemology and comparability of research findings and, therefore, into one aspect of how researchers understand what works and why. Such a synthesis does not, however, report on the substance of the underlying research.

A second option, then, is to go straight to the subject matter by classifying and describing research that originates within a particular discipline, such as economics or public health. A third and related option is to classify and describe research that pertains to a particular substantive feature such as implementation or organization type (i.e., non-profit organizations). These options share the drawback that they unnecessarily restrict the breadth of comparison. For example, research on education occurs in departments of economics, education, human development, political science, public administration, public management, public policy, and sociology and appears in various disciplinary and field journals. Similarly, research findings in the context of one type of setting or organization may have parallels in other areas. While these options partly cover substantive issues, neither addresses the topic of how these issues can be understood across substantive fields.

Yet another option, which we have followed in the work reported below, is to select studies using a particular conceptual view of governance. Such a strategy would not be appropriate for a synthesis that sought, for example, to produce a statistical estimate of an overall effect size associated with a specific intervention. However, our strategy fits our goal of understanding *how* researchers conceptualize and understand what works and how it works, placing these questions in the wider conceptual construct of public governance.

A logic of governance

A common theme in the work of governance scholars is that the rule of law – including lawmaking, its adjudication, and its institutional expressions – is a useful starting point for analysing governance and interpreting relevant empirical research. Underlying this notion is recognition that governance involves means for achieving direction, control and coordination of individuals or organizational units on behalf of their common interests (Vickers 1983; Wamsley 1990; Lynn *et al.* 2001). From this starting point, it is possible to construct an analytic framework that provides conceptual order to the systematic empirical study of governance.

Public sector governance has been defined as 'regimes of laws, rules, judicial decisions, and administrative practices that constrain, prescribe, and enable the provision of publicly supported goods and services' through formal and informal relationships with agents in the public and private sectors (Lynn *et al.*, 2000a, 2000b, 2001: 7). Any governance regime is the outcome of a dynamic process that can be summarized in terms of a core logic.[1] This process links several aspects of collective action and may be expressed in the following set of hierarchical interactions that has been characterized by others as a 'chain of delegation' (Lupia and McCubbins 2000; Strøm 2000):

(a) between (a) citizen preferences and interests expressed politically and (b) public choice expressed in enacted legislation or executive policies;
(b) between (b) public choice and (c) formal structures and processes of public agencies;
(c) between (c) the structures of formal authority and (d) discretionary organization, management and administration;
(d) between (d) discretionary organization, management, and administration and (e) core technologies, primary work and service transactions overseen by public agencies;
(e) between (e) primary work and (f) consequences, outputs, or results;
(f) between (f) consequences, outputs, or results and (g) stakeholder assessments of agency or programme performance; and
(g) between (g) stakeholder assessments and (a) public interests and preferences.

This general approach is not new to the study of public governance. For example, Kiser and Ostrom (1982) distinguished among 'three worlds of action': constitutional choice, collective choice and operational choice. These refer, respectively, to decision making about rules that guide choice at the collective level,

---

1 For a fuller development of the ideas in this section, see Lynn *et al.* (2000a, 2000b, and 2001).

decision making about rules that guide choices at the operational level and decisions associated with frontline work or the day-to-day activities of 'street-level' administrative practice. Toonen (1998: 235) points out that '[t]he three worlds approach . . . opens up an understanding of public administration that goes very much beyond the organization. The three levels do not refer to different layers within a formal structure. Rather, they have to be understood as nested systems and subsystems of public policy, administrative behavior, or institutional macro structures.'

The approach is also not unique to the study of US public governance. Referring to parliamentary democracies as well as presidential democracies, Strøm (2000: 266; Lupia and McCubbins 2000) describes a 'chain of delegation' in 'contemporary democracies, from voters all the way to civil servants that ultimately implement public policy . . . in which those authorized to make political decisions conditionally designate others to make such decisions in their name and place.'

The logic of governance described above, and the one that we employ in our syntheses of US and international research, is consistent with, but more differentiated than, these other similar frames. In general, reference to a logic of governance encompassing interactions across different levels is useful in the design and in the synthesis of empirical research because it serves as a reminder of the endogeneity of complex governance processes and because it assists in integrating the findings of dispersed, but conceptually-related, literatures. Toonen (1998: 248) argued that Kiser and Ostrom's three-worlds 'framework clarifies, for example, that reform and change at one level of analysis presupposes certain conditions at other levels of analysis.' Stated differently, reference to a wider logic or framework makes explicit the types of factors that are 'presupposed' by the researcher, but that might in fact affect the relationships under study. Another advantageous feature of the three-worlds approach, in Toonen's (1998) view, is that it can accommodate 'more subtle and differentiated conceptualizations which allow us to go somewhat deeper into the actual operation of the system instead of simply scratching the surface' in comparative public administration research (237). The logic of governance just outlined provides even further leverage for assessing literature across space, time, method, and substance.

Syntheses of US and international governance research

HL and FL employed the logic of governance to map the terrain of US and international public governance research. The HL analysis focused on research concerning US public governance, drawing on over 800 articles published in over seventy academic journals covering the twelve-year period from 1990 to 2001 (inclusive). The FL analysis focused on research concerning international governance, drawing on over 190 articles from fifty-one academic journals published between 1990 and 2004 (inclusive). All the FL articles used non-US evidence; few of the authors were American and few of the studies were generated at US universities. All articles were published in English.

Articles were included in the FL and HL syntheses if they explicitly specified causal or reduced form relationships between variables from two or more not-necessarily adjacent levels of the logic of governance. Dependent variables were identified as being causally associated with independent variables at either higher or lower levels in the logic. Studies confined to a single level of governance were excluded from our reviews.

We used the analytic scheme summarized in Appendix 1 to code the dependent and independent variables whose causal relations were under investigation in each study.[2] Thus each study was characterized by its location within the logic of governance. The coded information was entered into a spreadsheet that included identifiers (author, date, journal), the governance relationships examined, the logic-of-governance codes, and the primary research method.[3] This information constituted our databases for the FL and HL studies.

Several caveats must be noted concerning these databases. First, individual studies meet the standards of quality established by the various journals, but these standards may vary across journals and over time. Second, our strategy for selecting publications introduces three possible kinds of bias: the tendency of academic journals to publish positive findings, our own bias in favour of articles that featured a verbally or formally transparent causal model and limitations on the journals and years of publication we included. Finally, the 'correct' way to characterize a study's variables and logic can be ambiguous: does 'coordination of care' refer to efforts by treatment personnel or the strategies of their supervisors and managers? To the extent possible, we coded these according to the stated or implied definitions employed in each study.

Our reviews characterized broad patterns of research strategies and findings relating to governance, allowing us to provide a synoptic view of governance research to draw out the implications for practice and research. Through canvassing public governance research across a wide range of disciplines and subfields and across US and international research, we can discover the types of governance relationships that researchers are examining. In HL and FL, we show the full distributions of studies across the logic of governance. In this chapter, we focus primarily on the results of our syntheses that pertain to public management and performance.

2 We generally did not code the control variables in each study. In a separate but related project, we are examining particular groups of studies in order to assess the uses and consequences of such controls for the validity of the studies' findings and for our ability to synthesize findings across studies.

3 The coding was done primarily by the authors, with occasional assistance by advanced graduate students. To ensure consistency, the coders conferred where there was any ambiguity and on subsequent discovery of any anomalies in coding.

Public management in a logic of governance

Within the multi-level logic of governance, the study of public management is concerned with managerial activity itself: the discretionary choices of actors in managerial roles, choices that are, of course, both enabled and constrained by formal authority. The need for management arises when legislation has explicitly delegated the authority to choose appropriate actions to executive agencies, when legislative mandates are ambiguous, necessitating decisions by managers as to how they should be interpreted and implemented and when fulfilling policy objectives requires managerial judgement in applying rules and standards in particular classes of cases. Because managerial discretion is virtually inevitable – few policy and service delivery domains can be completely governed by *a priori* rules – managerial choices are almost always a factor in government performance. But how much of a factor, under what circumstances, and compared to what?

To proceed, it will be helpful to define public management. Pollitt and Bouckaert (2004) imply that public management is concerned with adapting the structures and processes of public-sector organizations so as to ensure good organizational performance. A more elaborate version of this perspective is provided by Lynn (2003), who views public management as having three distinct but interrelated dimensions: the formal structures and processes of government, the practices and craftsmanship of individual public managers and the taken-for-granted beliefs and values that infuse public organizations and their managers, thereby transforming them into institutions. In the HL and FL studies, public management was regarded, in the first instance, as craft activity, that is, as comprising variables whose values are determined by the deliberate choices of public managers. We then surveyed the studies in our databases to see how public management activity was conceptualized and operationalized by investigators across a range of disciplines and domains.

From the 344 studies in the HL synthesis and eighty-eight studies in the FL synthesis that used public management as either a dependent or independent variable, three broad types of public management constructs were identified:

(1) *Administrative structures.* This category includes variables such as red tape, organizational and inter-organizational structures (such as partnership arrangements) and formalization of authority intended to constrain the behaviour of subordinate and other actors. While administrative structures are not, of course, wholly determined by managerial actors – many are defined in law or by overhead organizations (finance ministries, budget offices) – the discretionary actions of public managers either create or alter structures or infuse existing structures with distinction and meaning (e.g., by creating 'organizational effects' at national, state, or local office levels of administration).

Table 14.1 Public management in HL and FL syntheses

Subtype of management variable	Studies that use public management as a(n)			
	Independent variable		Dependent variable	
	Hill & Lynn	Forbes & Lynn	Hill & Lynn	Forbes & Lynn
Administrative structures	127 *(52%)*	22 *(29%)*	59 *(43%)*	12 *(25%)*
Managerial tools	52 *(22%)*	18 *(24%)*	33 *(24%)*	6 *(13%)*
Management values and strategies	104 *(43%)*	36 *(47%)*	52 *(38%)*	30 *(63%)*
Total	244	76	138	48

Sources: Hill and Lynn (2005), Table 4; Forbes and Lynn (forthcoming), Table 5.
Notes: Cells show the number of studies, then the *column percentages* for the studies in the HL and FL syntheses. For example, of the 76 studies in FL that examined a management-level independent variable, 36 of them, or 47 per cent, used a type of public management variable that could be classified as 'management values and strategies'. Column percentages do not sum to 100 per cent, because some studies used more than one subtype of management variable.

(2) *Managerial tools*. Within a given structural setting, managers may employ a number of different administrative instruments or mechanisms to design, implement, and evaluate policies and programmes. The use of performance incentives, coordination and networking techniques, and contracts are examples of managerial tools in this category.

(3) *Management values and strategies*. In contrast to structures and tools, managerial values and strategies reflect managerial choices with respect to goals, missions, priorities and adaptation to the institutional environment. Leadership, employee empowerment, inter-organizational cooperation (e.g., cooperative enforcement) and services integration, and the allocation of resources across programmes and activities are all included in this category.

As shown in the 'Total' row of Table 14.1, HL found that management variables were used almost twice as often as independent variables than as dependent variables (244 compared to 138). The ratio was slightly less, but still pronounced, for studies in the FL synthesis. Thus, both US and international studies tended towards using measures of public management to explain governance phenomena, rather than considering management as a phenomenon to be explained.

Other interesting patterns are evident in the table. First, the distribution among the three subtypes, across use as an independent and dependent variable, is quite similar for the US studies included in the HL synthesis: administrative structures are used most often, then values and strategies, and finally, tools. In US studies, administrative structures are even more heavily used as independent variables compared to their use as dependent variables (52 per cent compared to 43 per cent). In FL's international studies, we see a consistent – but different – pattern across independent and dependent management variables: values and strategies are used most often, then administrative structures, then tools. Moreover, values and strategies receive relatively more emphasis as dependent variables than as independent variables (63 per cent compared to 47 per cent).

To summarize, in terms of sheer numbers (without regard to study quality) we are amassing more information about how management affects other outcomes (usually further down the hierarchy, as will be discussed later in the chapter) than about how other levels of governance affect the administrative structures, tools, and values and strategies of managers. Moreover, US and international research diverge in their patterns of emphasis on administrative structures compared to values and strategies. But the two bodies of research share the characteristic that relatively little public management research attempts to understand what are the influences of, or what influences, managerial use of tools or instruments (quality control, planning), despite their importance in prescriptive literature.

Performance in a logic of governance

As noted earlier, government performance can be defined broadly as the character and consequences of service provision by public agencies. The definition of performance we employ is similar to, but distinct from, that used by other studies. For example, performance for Boyne (2003) means efficiency, responsiveness, or equity. Further subcategories, which align quite closely with particular e and f-level categorizations using a logic of governance framework, include quantity of outputs, quality of outputs, efficiency, equity, outcomes, value for money, and consumer satisfaction. Pollitt (2000) sets forth broader criteria for performance: savings, improved processes, improved efficiency, greater effectiveness and an increase in the overall capacity/flexibility/resilience of the administrative system as a whole.

Examined within a logic of governance, we define measures of performance at the service delivery, consequences/outcomes, and stakeholder assessment levels (see Appendix 1). At the level of primary work or service transactions (e-level), performance measures are primarily conceived as changes in accountability, efficiency, costs, or quality. Performance changes at the f-level largely measure broader changes in the final outputs/outcomes of a particular programme or changes in law.[4] Finally, stakeholder assessments of agency or programme performance (g-level) may themselves be considered measures of performance.

---

4 The distinction between e and f-levels can be somewhat subjective depending on how authors frame their research questions. Some variables coded as primary work measures of performance may be viewed as public sector outputs as well. However, in both analyses, the explanatory models are top-down in their orientation. Thus, the general findings of the study would not be affected by changing e-level to f-level classifications.

The distribution of performance variables examined in the HL and FL syntheses was quite similar: service-delivery and consequences (e-level and f-level) variables were by far the most common *dependent* variables overall, each used in about one-quarter to one-third of all studies examined. In contrast, these types of variables were infrequently used as *independent* variables.[5] As shown in Appendix A, f-level performance variables were classified as either outputs or outcomes, and within each of these categories, further subdivided into whether they measured results with respect to government/public sector, the private (market) sector, or individuals/society. The distribution of studies across these six subcategories was remarkably similar in the HL and FL syntheses, where the modal categories were individual/society outputs and outcomes. In contrast to the heavy use of e- and f-level dependent measures, stakeholder assessments of performance (g-level) were the least-frequently used dependent (and independent) variables in the HL synthesis and among the least-frequently used in the FL synthesis.

Overall, the body of relevant research on performance comprises primarily longitudinal studies, usually consisting of before-and-after or interrupted time series studies that attempt to associate results or improvements with the reforms that produced them, both with and without controlling for other factors that might have mediated reform results. At the level of primary work and service delivery (e-level), FL's review included studies that examined changes in the performance of entities like primary health centres in India (Varatharajan *et al.* 2004); technical efficiency of power generation in China (Lam and Shiu 2001); cost savings and effectiveness of a NPM merger in Welsh mental health care (Kitchener and Gask 2003); service efficiency, performance, and quality (Barnett and Newberry 2002); and changes in transportation service delivery efficiency (Pina and Torres 2001). HL's review included studies that examined e-level performance such as school district efficiency (Grosskopf *et al.* 2001); initiation, completion and pace of Superfund site clean up (Hird 1990); mental health service coverage (Grusky and Adams 1994); accessibility to disability benefits (Rosenheck *et al.* 1999); and expenditures on capital, water, sewers and highways (Nunn 1996).

Among studies that tested for performance changes at the output/outcome level (f-level), the primary focus of research included in both the HL and FL studies was on the individual/societal level rather than on outputs and outcomes for the public or private sectors. Examples of performance *outputs* at the individual/societal level in the studies examined by HL and FL include:

5 While many variables at the e-level are considered 'performance' variables, not all are. Such 'non-performance' variables at the e-level (subtypes e1 through e5 listed in Appendix A) are frequently employed as independent variables to model performance changes at the f-level. Twenty-nine per cent of HL studies and 17 per cent of FL studies use an e-level independent variable and an f-level dependent variable. For example, a study might test the effect of field worker/office discretion (e2) on the number of clients served (f11).

homicide rates; school test performance; school dropout rates; welfare payments and employment rates for welfare-to-work clients; households' expenditures on food; recidivism; use of bicycle helmets and citizen participation in local recycling programmes. Individual/societal *outcomes* included in the studies included: changes in workforce quality and productivity; development of active citizenship among young people; heightened public knowledge about health issues; earnings impacts for clients in local welfare-to-work programmes; exits from poverty and the life-saving effects of seat belts.

Among studies examining g-level dependent variables, most are concerned with stakeholder assessments of changes to government services and programmes. Examples include the privatization of services (Poister and Henry 1994, Becker *et al.* 2001), citizen opinions on drugs chosen by the legislature for higher reimbursement in Finland (Vuorenkoski *et al.* 2003) and the effects of client influence in programme decisions on their assessment of government programmes in the UK (Bache 2001).

What affects government performance?

The distributions of independent variables in studies that sought to explain dependent variables at the e, f or g-levels are shown in Table 14.2. We first examine the patterns for primary work variables (top panel). First, both HL and FL syntheses found very few studies that sought to explain primary work as a function of output/outcomes at the f-level, or of stakeholder assessments at the g-level: the explanations for primary work came from 'above' in the logic. Second, an emphasis on structural (c-level) and management (d-level) variables was evident as explanatory factors for primary work across both US and international studies. About half of the US and international studies used structural variables to explain primary work dependent variables.

A sharp divergence is evident, however, across the HL and FL results with respect to the role that management-level variables play in explaining primary work: 43 per cent of US studies used a d-level variable to explain primary work, while 63 per cent of international studies explored such a relationship. Studies in the US synthesis showed a greater tendency to explore multi-level relationships within the primary work level (almost 25 per cent, compared to only 8 per cent of international studies). With respect to explaining outputs or outcomes at the service delivery level, researchers of US governance tend to rely primarily on structure explanations, management, and service delivery activities in that order. International studies tend to investigate these same types of dependent variables primarily with management-level explanations and only secondarily with structural explanations.

The middle panel of Table 14.2 reports the distribution of independent variables for f-level dependent variables. In contrast to explanatory factors for

Table 14.2 Explanatory factors of performance in HL and FL syntheses

Level of dependent variable	Level of independent variable used to model the dependent variable							Total
	(a)	(b)	(c)	(d)	(e)	(f)	(g)	
(e) Primary work								
Hill & Lynn	40 (17%)	35 (15%)	125 (54%)	100 (43%)	56 (24%)	7 (3%)	2 (1%)	232
Forbes & Lynn	1 (2%)	7 (14%)	25 (49%)	32 (63%)	4 (8%)	0 (0%)	0 (0%)	51
(f) Outputs/outcomes								
Hill & Lynn	20 (7%)	76 (26%)	111 (37%)	91 (31%)	85 (29%)	7 (2%)	1 (<1%)	298
Forbes & Lynn	5 (6%)	15 (18%)	47 (56%)	15 (18%)	14 (17%)	1 (1%)	2 (2%)	84
(g) Stakeholder assessment								
Hill & Lynn	9 (39%)	0 (0%)	7 (30%)	3 (13%)	4 (17%)	7 (30%)	2 (9%)	23
Forbes & Lynn	1 (7%)	3 (21%)	6 (43%)	6 (43%)	4 (29%)	0 (0%)	0 (0%)	14

Sources: Hill & Lynn (2005), Table 1; Forbes and Lynn (2005), Table 1.
Notes: Cells show the number of studies, then the *row percentages* for the studies in the HL and FL syntheses. For example, of the 232 studies in HL that examined an e-level dependent variable, 100 of them, or 43 per cent, modelled that dependent variable using a d-level independent variable. Row percentages do not sum to 100 per cent, because some studies used more than one level of independent variable to model the dependent variable.

primary work just discussed, where divergence in approach between US and international governance research surfaced at the managerial level, here we see a marked difference in explanatory factors occurring at the structures level. Scanning across the HL row, f-level dependent variables were modeled using either c, d, or e-level variables in about one-third of the studies (37, 31 and 29 per cent, respectively). In contrast, the FL synthesis shows that structures are relied upon relatively more as explanatory factors, compared to management and primary work explanations (56, 18 and 17 per cent respectively). While not evident from the table, separate tabulations showed that over 60 per cent of the FL and HL studies employing d-level independent variables and f-level dependent variables focus on individual and societal level (rather than public or private sector) outputs or outcomes.[6]

As shown in the bottom panel of Table 14.2, significantly fewer studies in both the HL and FL databases use g-level stakeholder assessment dependent variables compared to e and f-level studies. Due to the very small number of studies in this category, it is difficult to draw firm conclusions about modelling tendencies or patterns.

Looking across e and f-level measures of performance, both HL and FL syntheses show that studies examining service delivery (e-level) or outputs/outcomes (f-level) often used explanatory variables at the structural level (c-level). These types of studies thus skip one or two levels of governance – management and service delivery – to explain performance changes. For example, Boex (2003) examined how central government budget transfers to local government in Tanzania (c-level) affected the redistributive effect of local government allocations (f-level). Such patterns of inquiry assume, in effect, that intervening managerial activity or implementation did not mediate how structures affect performance.

The tendency for researchers to use formal structures of authority as explanatory variables for changes in performance raises the question of whether public management researchers are neglecting potentially significant causal processes at intermediate levels of governance. To illustrate this potential problem, one might question whether the way in which budget transfers were handled administratively in the Boex (2003) study might also affect the redistributive effect of local government allocations. In another example, one of the studies included in the FL synthesis, Smith and Hardman (2000), treated the UK's National Literacy Strategy Programme's framework for teaching (c-level) as an explanatory variable for both teacher opinion about the programme (e-level) and school exam results (f-level). An obvious question, however, is whether teachers' attitudes toward the programme that resulted from the teaching framework imposed on them could also mediate the exam performance of their students.

---

6 An overwhelming majority (almost 85 per cent) of these studies employ quantitative methods to study the relationship between the (d) and (f) levels.

Table 14.3 How does public management influence performance?

| Level of dependent variable | Type of d-level independent variable | | |
	Administrative structures	Managerial tools	Management values and strategies
(e) *Primary work*			
Hill & Lynn	45	24	44
Forbes & Lynn	10	13	20
(f) *Outputs/outcomes*			
Hill & Lynn	43	20	39
Forbes & Lynn	6	3	9
Subtotal Hill & Lynn	88	44	83
Subtotal Forbes & Lynn	16	16	29
Total	104	60	112

Sources: Hill & Lynn (2005), Table 6; Forbes & Lynn (2005), Table 7.
Notes: Cells show the number of studies of that type in the HL and FL syntheses. For example, 45 studies in the HL synthesis used a d-level explanatory measure of administrative structures to explain an e-level variable.

In any social science inquiry, some explanatory variables will undeniably mediate the effects of other explanatory variables on performance, a point Boyne (2003: 389) emphasizes as well. The job of public management researchers is to tease out these often subtle, but potentially telling, complex causal relationships between public management variables and public sector performance. The logic of governance provides public management scholars with a framework to recognize (and either accept or reject) the role of mediating variables in their analyses.

Examining the types of relationships that researchers have explored between d-level independent variables and e or f-level dependent variables may illustrate possible missing pieces of the picture. Among international studies using d-level independent variables to explain variables at the e and f-levels, researchers seem particularly focused on the role management values and strategies play in determining performance (Table 14.3). Twenty-nine FL studies investigate the relationship between management values and strategies and e or f-level variables compared to sixteen studies each for administrative structures and managerial tools. A typical international study using managerial values or strategies to model performance changes is Valdivia's (2002) study of how management decisions regarding health infrastructure location has affected the utilization of outpatient health care services in Peru. In contrast, the number of d-level American studies employing managerial values and strategies and administrative structure explanatory variables to model e and f-level changes were almost the same (eighty-three and eighty-eight studies respectively). Only half as many HL studies used managerial tools to model e or f-level variables, such as Ehrenberg *et al.'s* (1991) study of how teacher leave policies were related to student academic performance.

The reality of complex causal processes and mediating variables raises a difficult methodological dilemma for public management scholars. Qualitative studies (for example, Bache 2001) may have access to more detailed, in-depth data that enable systematic consideration of the mediating effects of explanatory variables and how these might influence performance. (Interestingly, the FL synthesis of international studies included a larger number of qualitative articles in its database than the HL synthesis.) Testing for multi-causal processes affecting performance, however, poses difficulties for both quantitative and qualitative researchers. For the quantitative researcher, sufficiently large sample sizes may enable the use of an array of statistical controls, but data limitations may constrain the types of variables and levels of analysis that can be studied. For the qualitative researcher, rich detail may be available about many core and mediating factors, but sample size often precludes the ability to convincingly rule out confounding factors. Ultimately, the study of a phenomenon where endogeneity is as complex as public service performance will benefit from both quantitative and qualitative epistemologies.

Regardless of the methodology chosen by public management scholars, the logic of governance is a parsimonious and useful analytical tool for researchers to use when thinking about causal relationships related to performance. At the beginning of the research design process, it provides a systematic checklist for thinking about how explanatory variables operate in reality to affect service provision and outcomes. As the researcher proceeds, the logic of governance can also operate as a check on modelling causal relationships that neglect the mediating effect of variables which fall between explanatory variables and the dependent variable in the logic of governance. Finally, the logic of governance assists in the interpretation of findings, enabling investigators to speculate more precisely on how omitted variables might have influenced their findings, making explicit what is 'presupposed'.

Conclusion

As noted at the beginning of this chapter, a consensus exists among researchers that relatively little is known about determinants of performance. With almost 1,000 articles in our database of US and international governance research, we are still not able to say for certain what works, for whom and under what conditions. Yet as Cooper and Hedges (1994: 4) point out, when research results differ, one 'should not pretend that there is no problem or decide that just one study, perhaps the most recent one, produces the correct finding. If results that are expected to be similar show variability, the scientific instinct should be to account for the variability by further systematic work.' By describing how researchers of US and international public governance are trying to understand governance and performance, we can assess whether we, as a research community, are asking the right kinds of questions, where more detailed syntheses might be informative and where further research and replication of results is needed.

While the United States is not exactly an outlier among nations,[7] public governance is widely regarded as unique in the extent and influence on policy making and public management of its formal separation of powers and of its individualistic orientation. Yet the findings of the FL and HL analyses regarding how researchers understand what works and why both imply that the determinants of government performance are multifarious and are to be found at multiple hierarchical levels of governance that are interrelated in complex ways.

We also noted some key differences between approaches to the study of US and international governance research. International investigators exhibit somewhat different modelling strategies, tending, for example, to favour more linear managerialist hypotheses – changes in structure lead to changes in outcomes, for example – than US research, which is more concerned with inter-level complexities and the polycentric nature of governance. A possible justification for this difference is that US public management, heavily influenced by organized interests, the diffusion of power and legislative and judicial micro-management is, in fact, more constrained and polycentric than is the case in more unitary or statist regimes and should be expected to exhibit more complex patterns of outcome determination.

A particularly interesting substantive finding of both the FL and HL studies, as seen in Table 14.2 but exhibited for other levels of dependent variables as well, is the clear tendency toward hierarchical explanations of primary work and the consequences of government action. In the literature, hierarchy is the backbone of governance. This is not to say that hierarchical influences are necessarily decisive or even particularly effective. Evidence on the effectiveness of the chain of command is, at best, mixed. Nonetheless, our finding is notable because it is at considerable variance with the view of governance popular in both European and American literature as increasingly networked and associational. HL speculate that the widely-touted 'paradigmatic' shift away from hierarchical government toward horizontal governing (hence the increasing preference for 'governance' as an organizing concept) is less pervasive than is supposed and that it is usually tactical: polyarchic tools and administrative technologies are being employed, perhaps increasingly so, to facilitate public governance within constitutionally and financially hierarchical regimes. The work of Hall and O'Toole (2000, 2004) supports this view (at least at the federal level in the US). Their analysis of US laws and regulations spanning approximately thirty years found numerous instances of multi-actor relationships, but no marked

---

7 See, for example Lijphart (1999), Hofstede (2001) and Pollitt and Bouckaert (2004).

increase in networked relationships (at least as codified in laws and regulations) over this period.

As Frederickson and Smith (2003: 224) note: 'hierarchy is necessary for conjunction to exist' because the US political system remains hierarchical and jurisdictional. The 'chain of delegation' also characterizes parliamentary democracies (Strøm 2000). And, when it comes to answering multi-level 'why' questions, the evidence suggests that hierarchy preoccupies field researchers. The fact that relatively few studies in either database examined more complex patterns of causality incorporating the configurational, endogenous nature of governance may reflect the paucity of data, which constrains modelling efforts to postulating more straightforward, linear causality. It may well suggest something more revealing, however: conjectures by hundreds of investigators in specialized domains that the interesting questions of administration and management concern the effects of hierarchical interactions more than of horizontality. We cannot rule out that researchers are investigating these questions (instead of other questions) due to data constraints, but the consistency of research agendas across policy domains and intellectual subfields is suggestive of the kinds of questions and answers that are of interest to the audiences for empirical research throughout the worldwide public management community.

This issue warrants much further investigation, however. Achieving greater insights into the interactions between hierarchical authority and the interdependence of the many public and private-sector agents engaged in service delivery, as Provan and Milward and Isett do in chapter 10, would greatly enlighten our understanding of delegation and accountability, the efficacy of relying on polycentric arrangements to accomplish policy mandates, and the results of so-called 'post-bureaucratic' governance arrangements on public service performance and the satisfaction policy makers and citizens derive from it. While the data and conceptual demands of such research are often daunting, the complementarities and tensions between hierarchy and networks are a cutting edge issue for the public management field.

REFERENCES

Bache, I. (2001) 'Different seeds in the same plot? Competing models of capitalism and the incomplete contracts of partnership design', *Public Administration*, **79**: 337–359.

Barnett, P. and Newberry, S. (2002) 'Reshaping community mental health services in a restructured state: New Zealand 1984–97', *Public Management Review*, **4**: 187–208.

Becker, F. W., Dluhy, M. J. and Topinka, J. P. (2001) 'Choosing the rowers: Are private managers of public housing more successful than public managers?', *American Review of Public Administration*, **31**: 181–200.

Boex, J. (2003) 'The incidence of local government allocations in Tanzania', *Public Administration and Development*, **23**: 381–391.

Boyne, G. A. (2003) 'Sources of public service improvement: A critical review and research agenda', *Journal of Public Administration Research and Theory*, **13**: 367–394.

Boyne, G. A., Farrell, C., Law, J., Powell, M. and Walker, R. M. (2003) *Evaluating public management reforms: principles and practice*. Buckingham: Open University Press.

Cooper, H. M. (1988) 'Organizing knowledge synthesis: A taxonomy of literature reviews', *Knowledge in Society*, **1**: 104–126.

Cooper, H. and Hedges, L. V. (1994) 'Research synthesis as a scientific enterprise', in H. Cooper and L. V. Hedges (eds.) *The handbook of research synthesis*. New York: Russell Sage Foundation, pp. 1–14.

Commission on the European Communities (EC) (2000) *Reforming the Commission*. EU: Brussels.

Ehrenberg, R. G., Ehrenberg, R., Rees, D. L. and Ehrenberg, E. L. (1991) 'School district leave policies, teacher absenteeism, and student achievement,' *Journal of Human Resources*, **26**: 72–105.

Frederickson, H. G. and Smith, K. B. (2003) *The public administration theory primer*. Boulder, CO: Westview Press.

Forbes, M. and Lynn, L. E. Jr. (2005) 'How does public management affect government performance? Findings from international research', *Journal of Public Administration Research and Theory*, **15**: 559–584.

Glass, G. V. (1976) 'Primary, secondary, and meta-analysis', *Educational Researcher* **5**: 3–8.

Grosskopf, S., Hayes, K. J., Taylor, L. L. and Weber, W. L. (2001) 'On the determinants of school district efficiency: Competition and monitoring', *Journal of Urban Economics*, **49**: 453–478.

Grusky, O. and Adams, R. (1994) 'Organizational conflict and mental health service system effectiveness', *Administration and Policy in Mental Health*, **22**: 145–157.

Hall, T. E. and O'Toole, L. J. Jr. (2000) 'Structures for policy implementation: An analysis of national legislation, 1965–66 and 1993–1994', *Administration & Society*, **31**: 667–686.

Hall, T. E. and O'Toole, L. J. Jr. (2004) 'Shaping formal networks through the regulatory process', *Administration & Society*, **36**: 186–207.

Hill, C. J. and Lynn, L. E. Jr. (2005) 'Is hierarchical governance in decline? Evidence from empirical research', *Journal of Public Administration Research and Theory*, **15**: 173–195.

Hird, J. A. (1990) 'Superfund expenditures and cleanup priorities: Distributive politics or the public interest?' *Journal of Policy Analysis and Management*, **9**: 455–483.

Hofstede, G. (2001) *Culture's consequences: comparing values, behaviours, institutions, and organizations across nations*. Thousand Oaks, CA: Sage.

James, O. (2001) 'Business models and the transfer of businesslike central government agencies', *Governance: An International Journal of Policy and Administration*, **14**: 233–252.

Kiser, L. L. and Ostrom, E. (1982) 'The three worlds of action: a metatheoretical synthesis of institutional approaches' in Ostrom, E. (eds.) *Strategies of political inquiry*. Thousand Oaks, CA: Sage, pp. 179–222.

Kitchener, M. and Gask, L. (2003) 'NPM merger mania: lessons from an early case', *Public Management Review*, **5**: 20–44.

Lam, P-L. and Shiu, A. (2001) 'A data envelopment analysis of the efficiency of China's thermal power generation', *Utilities Policy*, **10**: 75–83.

Lijphart, A. (1999) *Patterns of democracy: Government forms and performance in thirty-six countries*. New Haven, CT: Yale University Press.

Lupia, A. and McCubbins, M. (2000) 'Representation or abdication? How citizens use institutions to help delegation succeed', *European Journal of Political Research*, **37**: 291–307.

Lynn, L. E., Jr. (2003) Public management, in Peters, B. G. and Pierre, J. (eds.), *Handbook of public administration*. Thousand Oaks, CA: Sage Publications, pp. 14–24.

Lynn, L. E. Jr., Heinrich, C. J. and Hill, C. J. (2000a) 'Studying governance and public management: Why? How?' in Heinrich, C. and Lynn, L. (eds.) *Governance and performance: New perspectives*. Washington, DC: Georgetown University Press, pp. 1–33.

Lynn, L. E. Jr., Heinrich, C. J. and Hill, C. J. (2000b) 'Studying governance and public management: Challenges and prospects', *Journal of Public Administration Research and Theory*, **10**: 233–261.

Lynn, L. E. Jr., Heinrich, C. J. and Hill, C. J. (2001) *Improving governance: A new logic for empirical research*. Washington, D.C.: Georgetown University Press.

Nunn, S. (1996) 'Urban infrastructure policies and capital spending in city manager and strong mayor cities', *American Review of Public Administration*, **26**: 93–113.

Office of Management and Budget. (2005) *Program assessment rating tool (PART)*. www.whitehouse.gov/omb/part/. (Accessed 25 March 2005.)

Peters, B. G. and Savoie, D. J. (eds.) (1998) *Taking stock: Assessing public sector reforms*. Montreal: McGill-Queens University Press.

Pina, V. and Torres, L. (2001) 'Analysis of the efficiency of local government services delivery: An application to urban public transport', *Transportation Research Part A*, **35**: 929–944.

Poister, T. H. and Henry, G. T. (1994) 'Citizen ratings of public and private service quality: A comparative perspective', *Public Administration Review*, **54**: 155–160.

Pollitt, C. (2000) 'Is the emperor in his underwear: An analysis of the impacts of public management reform', *Public Management Review*, **2**: 181–200.

Pollitt, C. and Bouckaert, G. (2004) *Public management reform: A comparative analysis*. 2nd edn. Oxford: Oxford University Press.

Rosenheck, R., Frisman, L. and Kasprow, W. (1999) 'Improving access to disability benefits among homeless persons with mental illness: An agency-specific approach to services integration', *American Journal of Public Health*, **89**: 524–528.

Smith, F. and Hardman, F. (2000) 'Evaluating the effectiveness of the national literacy strategy: Identifying indicators of success', *Educational Studies* **26**: 365–378.

Strøm, K. (2000) 'Delegation and accountability in parliamentary democracies', *European Journal of Political Research*, **37**: 261–289.

Toonen, T. A. J. (1998) 'Networks, management, and institutions: Public administration as "normal science"', *Public Administration*, **76**: 229–252.

Valdivia, M. (2002) 'Public health infrastructure and equity in the utilization of outpatient health care services in Peru', *Health Policy and Planning*, **17**: 12–19.

Varatharajan, D., Thankappan, R. and Jayapalan, S. (2004) 'Assessing the performance of primary health centers under decentralized government in Kerala, India', *Health Policy and Planning* **19**: 41–51.

Vickers, G. (1983) *The art of judgment: A study of policy making*. London: Harper & Row.

Vuorenkoski, L., Toiviainen, H. and Hemminki, E. (2003) 'Drug reimbursement in Finland – a case of explicit prioritizing in special categories', *Health Policy* **66**: 169–177.

Wamsley, G. L. (1990) 'Introduction' in Wamsley, G. L. and Wolf, J. F. (eds.) *Refounding public administration*. Newbury Park, CA: Sage Publications, pp. 19–29.

Appendix A A logic of governance identifies relationships between:

(a) citizen preferences and interests expressed politically, further disaggregated into:

(a1): primordial citizen preferences and interests;

(a2):   private firms, organizations, behavior, participation, etc.; and

(a3):   interest groups

and

(b) public sector decisions, activity and influence, which may be further disaggre-
     gated into:

(b1):   legislator preferences expressed in action or in enacted legislation;

(b2):   executive policies and, in a federal system, federal-level policies and
        influence; and

(b3):   court decisions;

between

(b) public sector influence, activity and choice

                                 and

(c) formally authorized structures and processes of public agencies at federal or
     state level, including regulatory authority, disaggregated into:

(c1):   hierarchy/structure

        (c11)   type of ownership

        (c12)   level/type of government

        (c13)   internal government entities

        (c14)   political atmosphere

(c2):   mandated behaviour

(c3):   policy design and elements

(c4):   fiscal situation

(c5):   other

between

(c) the structure of formal authority

                                 and

(d) the *de facto* or discretionary organization and management of the executive
     branch or of executive agencies, programs, and administrative activities, disag-
     gregated into:

(d1):   administrative structures;

(d2):   tools;

(d3):   values and strategies;

between

(d) discretionary organization, management and administration

                                 and

(e) primary work or service delivery activities of public agencies (the availability,
     type, quality, and cost of publicly-sponsored goods and services); which may be
     disaggregated into:

(e1):   programme design features

(e2):   field worker/office beliefs and values

(e3):   administrative processes and policies

(e4):   work/treatment/intervention

(e5):   client influence, behaviour, and/or preference

(e6):   use of resources and/or performance (i.e., efficiency, costs, quality, etc.)

between

(e) primary work activities/transactions

and

(f) consequences, outputs, outcomes, or results, which may be further disaggregated into:

    (f1):   outputs

        (f11):   government/public sector

        (f12):   market/firm/private sector

        (f13):   individual/society

    (f2):   outcomes

        (f21):   government/public sector

        (f22):   market/firm/private sector

        (f23):   individual/society

(g) performance assessments expressed politically

and

    (g1) public and private interests and preferences

15 What drives global e-government? An exploratory assessment of existing e-government performance measures

Eric W. Welch, M. Jae Moon and Wilson Wong

Introduction

Perceived to be a technological solution for a better, more efficient and more effective government, e-government has been presented and implemented in nations around the world as one of the most compelling advances for government since the mid-1990s (OECD 2003). Many governments, including those at both the national and sub-national levels, have begun various e-government initiatives to develop and advance their online functions by providing public information and services to citizens and businesses and by interacting with citizens to obtain policy inputs (Demchak *et al.* 1998; Demchak *et al.* 2000; Welch and Wong 2001; Wong and Welch 2004). E-government has often been hailed as a means of promoting more effective intra- and intergovernmental relations (Ho 2002; Moon 2002). However, efforts to measure e-government performance have tended to out-distance the conceptual and theoretical work necessary to justify the measures and explain the results.

So what is e-government performance? Recent work by Stowers (2004) proposes a multi-dimensional framework based on different levels of government performance: input measures, output measures, intermediate outcome measures and ultimate outcome measures. Input measures represent various resources used for e-government efforts to develop and maintain e-government applications. The input measures might be operationalized in terms of personnel and financial costs. Output measures reflect specific 'immediate actions' and visible indicators resulting from e-government initiatives such as the number of hits, completed downloads, number of e-mail requests and completed financial service/financial transactions. The intermediate outcomes are defined as the 'outcomes that are expected to lead to a desired end, but which are not ends in and of themselves' (Stowers 2004: 11). The measures include: information accuracy, timeliness, ease of use, user satisfaction, etc. Finally, ultimate outcome measures are designed to reflect the extent to which e-government actually achieves intended objectives such as cost-savings, time-savings and trust in government. Unfortunately, as will be shown in this chapter, the various methodologies currently used to assess performance do not typically adopt clear frameworks from which measures are derived. This is especially evident in the area of cross-national comparison of e-government performance – the subject of this chapter.

In the presence of active and large-scale pursuit of measures to assess global e-government, there is still a lack of consensus concerning which factors should be considered and how they should be weighted in developing e-government measures. More than that, despite ongoing use, scholars and policy-makers still do not know much about the validity and reliability of the global e-government measures. Research has not examined how the measures actually reflect 'e-government performance'. Furthermore, little is known about how the different global e-government performance measures are related or how differences in measures may affect the findings and conclusions reached in global e-government studies.

The objectives of this chapter are two-fold. First, it seeks to identify and explain the reasons for the differences that exist in current measures of e-government. For practitioners and academics alike, this sort of analysis will help explain, for example, why a United Nations e-government evaluation gave Finland very high marks while the Cyberspace Research Group had a more moderate assessment. What aspects and dimensions of e-government does each measure capture? Second, it seeks to examine the validity of the measures and to assess how measurement limitations may contribute to the variation in findings presented in e-government studies. The chapter should contribute guidance for developing a more comprehensive evaluation framework and better measures for the study of comparative global e-government.

The chapter first presents five prominent global e-government measures and explains their differences and similarities. It then identifies a set of country-level macro variables (political, economic, technological and social) that are typically used and models their effect on e-government development. Next, it reports a series of correlation and regression analyses to examine the relationships among and between the e-government measures and the selected explanatory variables of e-government. The chapter concludes with explanations of the findings and a discussion of the implications for e-government research.

Measuring global e-government

Responding to the increasing need for comparative e-government studies, scholars have developed various e-government performance indicators to compare the performance of countries in an objective way (Demchak *et al.* 1998; ASPA and UNDPEPA 2001; Kirkman 2002). To distinguish among different

Table 15.1 Typology of e-government measures and examples

Sophistication focus	Simple	Complex
Government website-focused	Web presence index	CyPRG openness measures WM e-government index
Societal enabling capacity integrated	NRI E-government score	BMEG E-government index

e-government performance measures, we present a typology that categorizes the different measures based on two dimensions: level of sophistication and focus of measurement (see Table 15.1). Measure sophistication ranges from simple (in which one or two indicators are used) to complex (in which multiple measures are employed). Focus of analysis distinguishes between measures that are primarily concerned with features and characteristics visible on the website from measures that also consider national enabling capacities that may foster e-government development.

When studying and comparing e-government performance among different countries using those measures, it is important to first understand what the measures represent and what data is used to create them. The following section surveys six recognized global e-government measures presented in various global e-government studies: Web Presence Index (WPI); E-government Index; Benchmarking of E-government (BMEG); Openness Measures: Transparency and Interactivity (CyPRG); E-Government Score, Network Readiness Index (NRI); and E-government Index, World Market (WM).

Web Presence Index

A global e-government project jointly conducted by the American Society for Public Administration (ASPA) and the United Nations Division for Public Economics and Public Administration (UNDPEPA 2001) developed a web presence measure that represents five different developmental stages of e-government: (1) emerging, (2) enhanced, (3) interactive, (4) transactional and (5) seamless. The emerging stage signals initial establishment of an official government online presence. In the enhanced stage, government sites become more numerous and information on the sites becomes more dynamic. The interactive stage is attained when users can download forms and communicate with government employees on the internet and when users can pay for services and conduct other similar operations online. A nation is categorized as transactional. The seamless stage represents a final stage of e-government when, for example e-services are integrated across administrative boundaries (ASPA and UNDPEPA 2001: 2).

This measure is developed based on the content and services available on government websites. Each stage is further divided into four sub-levels, using intervals of 0.25 to reflect detailed features and contents of selected government websites. A recent study by ASPA and UNDPEPA found that there are 32 emerging, 65 enhanced, 55 interactive, 17 transactional, and zero seamless countries (ASPA and UNDPEPA 2001). This measure is categorized as simple in terms of sophistication and focused only on government websites.

E-government index, benchmarking of e-government (BMEG)

Using three different indexes – the Web Presence Index described above, ICT infrastructure measures, and human capital measures – ASPA and UNDPEPA developed a global e-government index called 'Benchmarking of E-government (BMEG)'. BMEG is considered to be richer and more complex than the WPI because it also incorporates: (1) aspects of the country's e-government capacity; and (2) enabling factors such as national technological capacity and the capacity of society and citizens to take advantage of e-government. National ICT infrastructure capacity is measured using six proxy indicators: PCs per 100 people; internet hosts per 10,000 people; percentage of population online; telephone lines per 100 people; mobile phones per 100 people and TVs per 1,000 people. In order to 'capture a country's and its citizens' facility, opportunity and willingness to use online government', three variables – United Nation Human Development Index; Information Access Index and Urban as Percentage of Population – are used to form the human capital measures (ASPA and UNDPEPA 2001). The overall e-government index is calculated as a mean value of WPI, the combined ICT infrastructure measures, and the combined human capital measures, in which these three sets of measures are weighted equally.

Openness measures: Transparency and interactivity (CyPRG)

The openness measures are developed by the Cyberspace Policy Research Group (CyPRG) based in the University of Arizona (2004). CyPRG defines government website openness to be a function of transparency and interactivity. Transparency refers to 'the availability of information for navigating a large-scale social system' while interactivity represents 'a measure of the level of convenience or degree of immediate feedback.' Transparency is about the magnitude of online information available on official government websites, while interactivity is more about 'the convenience of the citizens and the speed of communication between the agency and its clients.' More strictly and clearly defined sub-dimensions are identified and used for calculating the scores for transparency and interactivity. Web-based transparency is measured based on five different elements including ownership; contact information; organizational/operational information; citizen consequences and freshness.[1]

---

1 Ownership tests to see how involved the agency is with the site. Contact information tests whether individuals or positions inside the organization can be reached by outsiders.

Interactivity is also measured using four different elements: ownership, reachability, organizational/operational information, and responses.[2] Openness is calculated as the sum of transparency and interactivity. Similar to the WPI, the openness measures focus mainly on the content and features of government websites though it includes somewhat sophisticated indicators that reflect the level of openness. Societal enabling factors and online public services are not a major focus of the openness measures.

e-government score, network readiness index

In conjunction with the Harvard University Center for International Development's Global Technology Project, Kirkman, Osorio and Sachs developed 'the network readiness index' (NRI) and have used it to rank seventy-five countries. The NRI is constructed with both institutional data and survey data and it represents the extent to which a government is prepared to take advantage of the critical role of information technology in economic development (Kirkman *et al.* 2002). The NRI is determined by two major components: network use and enabling factors, both of which comprise multiple sub-indexes. For example, 'network use' captures data on percentage of computers with internet connection; internet users per host; internet users per 100 people; cellular subscribers per 100 people and availability of public internet access.

'Enabling factors' include network access,[3] network policy,[4] networked society,[5] and networked economy,[6] which are all equally weighted. In addition,

Organizational/operational information tests for information about the organization's operation or its role in a wider issue network. Citizen consequences tests the extent to which the organization indicates what citizens are required to do to comply with laws or regulations, and helps them to do so. Freshness tests how up to date this information is by looking at how frequently key pages of the site are changed.

2 Interactivity tests for interactive or 'clickable' means to access information about citizen consequences. Ownership indicates whether the organization's addresses are hotlinked in the government websites for the convenient usage of citizens. Reachability tests whether the agency has provided clickable e-mail addresses. Organizational/operational information tests the extent to which the organization permits users to reach deeply inside the agency to a variety of staff. Responses test how smoothly users can find their way around the organization's structure or the wider issue area.

3 The sub-index of network access is formed by: information infrastructure micro-index (e.g., price and quality of internet connection, perceptions of broadband internet access, teledensity, telecommunication staff per 1,000 mainlines) and the micro-index of hardware, software and support (e.g., PCs per 100 inhabitants, availability of specialized IT services, software products fitting local needs). The two micro-indexes are equally weighted.

4 The sub-index of network policy is formed by: ICT policy micro-index (e.g., internet access cost, legal framework supporting IT businesses, ICTs as overall government priority) and the micro-index of business and economic environment (e.g., income per capita, rule of law, number of days to start a new firm, trust in public postal system). The two micro-indexes are equally weighted.

5 The sub-index of networked society is formed by: networked learning micro-index (e.g., investment in employees' development of IT skills, internet access in schools), ICT opportunity micro-index (e.g., brain drain of IT-skilled workforce), and social capital micro-index (e.g., illiteracy, political rights). The three micro-indexes are all equally weighted.

6 The networked economy index is formed by: e-commerce micro-index (e.g., commerce websites, competition in dotcom market, sophistication of online marketing), e-government micro-index

government characteristics and e-government policy form part of the enabling factors. To provide one example, the sub-index for networked economy includes four elements: availability of online government services; government effectiveness in promoting the use of ICTs; extent of government websites and business internet-based interactions with government. In general, NRI is an ambitious and complex measure that uses multiple indicators including website content and societal enabling factors.

e-government index, World Market

The World Market (WM) e-government index is developed jointly by World Markets Research Center and Brown University. West conducted a global e-government survey and ranked 196 countries based on twenty-eight e-government features in the areas of information availability, service delivery and public accessibility (West 2001, 2003a, 2003b; World Markets Research Center 2001). Some of the indicators include: type of site; name of nation; region of the world; office phone number; office address; online publication; online database; external links to non-governmental sites; audio clips; video clips; non-native languages or foreign language translation; commercial advertising; user payments or fees; subject index; handicap access; privacy policy; security features; presence of online services; number of different services; links to a government services portal; digital signatures; credit card payments; e-mail address; search capability; comment form or chat-room; broadcast of events; automatic e-mail updates and having an English version of the websites. The overall e-government ranking was determined as the average percentage of websites having the selected features in each country's government (executive offices, legislative offices, judicial offices, cabinet offices and major agencies of central government). Similar to the openness and WPI, this measure is developed based on an assessment of the features of government websites; it does not examine social enabling factors.

Using the typology identified earlier in this section, we categorize the different e-government measures along two dimensions: sophistication (simple or complex) and focus of analysis (government websites versus societal enabling capacity). As summarized in Table 15.1, the five different e-government measures can be classified into four different categories based on the two dimensions. While these five measures represent some of the primary measures being used to track e-government performance, it is not clear whether and how they concur. Nor is it clear that they measure the same qualities, dimensions and aspects of e-government. The coming sections will examine the correlations among different

(e.g., extent and availability of government e-services), and general infrastructure micro-index (e.g., TV penetration, quality of air transport).

measures of e-government to begin to explore the strengths and limitations of the selected measures and their impact on e-government research and policy.

Theoretical framework for an explanatory model

Recent studies have sought to evaluate e-government performance based on various measures by ranking municipal, state and national e-governments (Fountain 2001; Ho 2002; Moon 2002; Holzer and Kim 2003; Norris and Moon 2005). Despite growing interest in the development of e-government among practitioners and scholars, the current research has not made good progress in identifying clear and consistent factors that determine and affect the development of e-government. In other words, while scholars dependent variables have proliferated, explanatory variables and relationships have not been adequately investigated, though some studies have examined how government size and type as well as managerial innovativeness affect the development of e-government at the municipal level (Moon and Norris 2003). As part of our effort to assess the sensitivity of measures and variation in the findings from e-government studies, this section identifies some explanatory variables that might determine e-government performance at the national level.

Government decisions at the national level, like any major policy or administrative decision, are made through complicated internal political and bureaucratic processes; a government decision is also often an outcome of a compromise among multiple actors of interest (bureaucratic politics) or a decision mainly made by a political or administrative leader (methodological individualism). Similarly, when the nature of the decision goes beyond the government boundary and is related to the interests of many social actors or has extensive social and economic implications, the decision is often bounded by various political, social and economic conditions. For example, a country's public sector or economic reform might be determined by a political leader's policy preference, related social and economic actors' interests, or driven by citizens' interests and policy preferences.

Following this logic, a nation's e-government performance is most likely determined by both internal governmental factors and external societal factors; e-government is not only shaped by government's proactive innovation initiatives (including broad government reform efforts), but is also determined by political, economic and technological preparedness. Hence, two major forces affect the evolution of e-government in all nations: pulling factors and pushing factors. The pulling factors are the e-government driving forces that emerge within governments or politics through administrative reform initiatives, strong political or administrative leadership or political reform initiatives. As an example, the Clinton-Gore administration offered the blueprint of e-government as part of 'reinvention' reform in the early 1990s (Osborne and Gaebler 1992;

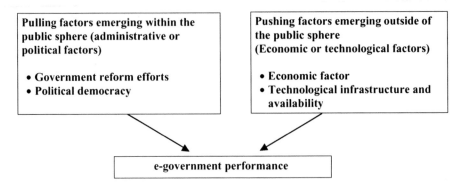

Figure 15.1 Factors affecting e-government performance

Kettl 1997). E-government pulling forces also include the political culture where citizenship and political participation values and expectations may set the standards for information provision and interaction between government and citizens.

Hence, the nature of e-government performance might be closely associated with the level of democracy in a society. In a less democratic society, where the power structure is more centralized and input to decision making is more closed, use of ICTs in ways that are especially suited for information disclosure, communication and transactions may be less favoured. As a result, core applications of e-government can conflict with core values of a governing regime under a less democratic political setting.

Pushing factors refer mainly to non-governmental or non-political forces that facilitate or promote e-government from the outside of the public sphere (politics or administration). They are societal forces (non-political and non-governmental) that promote and facilitate advances in e-government. For example, the prosperity of a nation's economy might facilitate government's interest and policy action on e-government. Additionally, the development, diffusion, and availability of information technology could spur e-government implementation.

Based on the model of pulling and pushing forces of e-government among nations, this chapter proposes an approach that includes four determinants of e-government: administrative, political, economic and technological factors (see Figure 15.1). We posit four exploratory propositions about how pushing and pulling forces are related to national e-government performance.

Proposition one: *Bureaucratic factor*: A more streamlined (efficient) government is more likely to advance national e-government performance than a big government.

Proposition two: *Political factor*: A more democratic country is more likely to advance e-government performance (particularly a higher level of interactivity and transparency).

Proposition three: *Economic factor.* A more economically prosperous country is more likely to advance e-government performance (particularly a higher stage of e-government).

Proposition four: *Technological factor.* A more technologically advanced country (a higher level of technological development and infrastructure) is more likely to advance e-government performance (particularly a higher stage of e-government).

Data and methods

The first part of the analysis examines the correlations among the major e-government performance measures described above. The second part explores the relationship between the e-government measures and seven well recognized macro-level explanatory variables, which we describe below and categorize as either pushing or pulling factors. Then correlation analysis examines the associations between the seven variables and the e-government performance measures. Finally, in the third part of the analysis, four of the seven variables – two pulling and two pushing – are regressed on each of four different e-government performance measures to test the hypotheses stated above.

Pulling factors

Democratic government

The Freedom House (2002) organization conducts an annual survey of selected experts who are considered to be knowledgeable about corruption, civil liberties and political rights in specific nations. A composite democratic government score is created from a combination of the political rights and civil liberties scores. *Political rights* measures whether elections of political leaders are free and fair, the fairness of electoral laws, self-determination by ethnic and minority groups and other political considerations. *Civil liberties* comprises media independence, freedom of assembly, religious expression and political organization, independence of the judiciary and other similar considerations (Lindley 2003). In this study, the combined 2002 *democratic government* score for 2002 operationalizes the political democracy pulling factor in the regression model. However, we present the separate *political rights* and *civil liberties* variables in the correlation analysis. The democracy score ranges on a scale from 1–7 – 'the most free' to 'the least free'.

Government expenditures

This is a proxy measure for the relative size of a government that is used by McArthur and Sachs (2001). It measures government expenditure as a percentage of GNP in 2000. Hence, it operationalizes the government reform pulling factor, with the assumption that a country with a larger public expenditure is less efficient, more interventionist and more cumbersome. This variable is included in both the correlation and regression analyses.

Public institutions

This is a composite measure that includes survey questions about contracts, laws and corruption, reported in the 2000 Executive Opinion Survey (McArthur and Sachs 2001). Respondents were asked for their perceptions about judiciary independence, protection by law of financial assets and wealth, neutrality of government in contracting, effects of organized crime on the costs of doing business and three separate questions about bribery practices. These variables generally reflect the level of corruption in government (Moon and Norris 2003).

Social capital

This measure, developed by Kirkman *et al.* at Harvard University's Center for International Development, also combines institutional and survey-based data (Kirkman *et al.* 2002). The institutional data include three education-related measures including percentage of no schooling in the population, average years of schooling in the population and the illiteracy rate. Survey data include responses about political rights, quality of schools and difference in quality of schooling for rich and poor children. This variable combines all six values at equal weight. In general, *social capital* measures educational capacity and social infrastructure.

Pushing factors

Macroeconomic stability

This measure, developed by McArthur and Sachs (2001), combines institutional and survey-based data into a single measure. Survey data originated from the Executive Opinion Survey and base institutional data came from the World Bank. Institutional data includes: the inflation rate in 2000; the lending to borrowing interest rate spread in 2000; the real exchange rate relative to the US in 2000; government surplus in 2000 and the national savings rate in 2000. Survey questions used include: perceived likelihood of a recession in the next year; and respondents' perceptions about the comparative ease or difficulty of obtaining credit in 2000 compared to the previous year (United Nations Development Program 2001). All seven measures are weighted equally.

Human Development Index – HDI (2001)

This is a composite index that considers multiple dimensions of a nation's society and economy. It combines United Nations Development Programme indexes for

Table 15.2 E-government correlations

	E-government Index (WM)	E-government Score (NRI)	E-government Index (BMEG)	Web Presence Index (WPI)	Transparency CyPRG 2000
E-government score (NRI)	0.60 74				
E-government index (BMEG)	0.64 132	0.80 71			
Web Presence Index (WPI)	0.65 132	0.71 71	0.92 132		
Transparency	0.30 142	0.30 74	0.47 119	0.45 119	
Interactivity	0.39 142	0.47 74	0.60 119	0.55 119	0.77 142

life expectancy, education and GDP. Because it incorporates health, education and economic indicators, this variable represents a broader measure of the well being of a nation.

Internet penetration

It is measured by the number of internet hosts per 10,000 and is a measure of the internet penetration in the nation. This data comes from the *Benchmarking of E-Government* study which identifies the ultimate source of the data to be the 2001 *International Telecommunications Union Report* (ITU 2001). Because this variable is a contributor to the BMEG e-government index, we expect to find a high correlation between the two measures. This measure operationalizes the pushing factor of technological infrastructure and its availability.

Analysis and findings

Relationship among e-government measures

Since the WPI captures the most basic elements of e-government – the developmental stage of official government websites – we expect that it has much in common with and a high correlation to, other e-government measures. For example, the WPI is folded into the BMEG e-government Index. This and the e-government Networked Index both contain common societal enabling elements. We also expect that the openness measures (interactivity and transparency) will be closely related with the WM e-government Index because of their emphases on various content-related aspects of government websites.

Table 15.2 summarizes the correlations among the different e-government measures. Placing these correlations into three categories of medium ($0.3 \leq r < 0.6$), high ($0.6 \leq r < 0.8$), and very high ($0.8 \leq r < 1.0$), the table results show very high correlations between BMEG and NRI and between WPI and BMEG. Findings also indicate medium correlations between transparency and all other measures. The other correlation coefficients fall into the 'high' category. Although results show strong positive correlations among all variables, substantial variation in the level of correlation raises obvious questions about which aspects of e-government each captures and why such variation exists – both topics of the next section.

Relationship between independent variables and e-government measures

Table 15.3 presents the rankings and values of correlations among the e-government measures and the explanatory variables in three tiers. In terms of rankings, the first tier (rows 1 and 2) shows that the Human Development Index (HDI) is the most consistently highly-correlated explanatory variable across all categories. Nations that are better able to satisfy basic education, economic and health-related needs may be more likely to be able to implement and utilize electronic government tools. In addition, public institutions rank either first or second highest for four of the six e-government measures; only in the case of transparency and interactivity is the variable ranked lower. In general, the last variable in each column shows that government expenditures are negatively associated with a majority of the e-government scores. We can interpret this to mean that relatively larger governments (in terms of expenditures as a percentage of GDP) are slower to implement e-government. This may be some evidence in support of our Proposition 1. Greater detail about the expenditure categories and levels is probably necessary before further insight is possible.

The middle tier (rows 3 to 7) presents a more complex set of findings. The explanatory variables of social capital, internet and macroeconomic stability rank higher for the e-government Index (WM) and e-government Score (NRI). However, public institutions, civil liberties and political rights variables are more highly ranked for transparency and interactivity. Therefore, the middle sections of these two sets of measures are nearly mirror images of each other; the CyPRG measures are to be more focused on the political variables and the e-government Index (WM) and e-government Score (NRI) appear to place more emphasis on the social, technical and economic aspects of e-government. The middle tier ranking of the correlates for the two benchmarkers of e-government variables (WPI and BMEG) fall between the two extremes: social capital ranks high, macroeconomic stability lower, with civil liberties and political rights falling in between (rows 3–5). Unexpectedly, there is little difference between the ranking for the two BMEG variables.

Examination of the correlation coefficients finds equally divergent results. For example, correlations between the political institutions and human development (HDI) variables on the one hand and the six e-government measures on the other range from approximately 0.22 to 0.85. The correlations between the explanatory variables and the e-government measures are higher and more

Table 15.3 Correlation analysis (* significant at the 5% level)

Correlation rank	E-government index (WM)	E-government score (NRI)	Web presence index (WPI)	E-government index (BMEG)	Transparency (CyPRG)	Interactivity (CyPRG)
1	Public institutions (0.61*)	Public institutions (0.85*)	HDI (0.80*)	Public institutions (0.76*)	HDI (0.40*)	HDI (0.54*)
2	HDI (0.59*)	HDI (0.76*)	Public institutions (0.60*)	Social capital (0.71*)	Civil liberties (0.37*)	Civil liberties (0.44*)
3	Internet (0.53*)	Macro-economic stability (0.70*)	Social capital (0.55*)	Civil liberties (0.57*)	Political rights (0.36*)	Public institutions (0.42*)
4	Social capital (0.52*)	Social capital (0.67*)	Civil liberties (0.54*)	Political rights (0.53*)	Internet (0.25*)	Macro-economic stability (0.42*)
5	Macro-economic stability. (0.51*)	Internet (0.60*)	Political rights (0.53*)	Macro-economic stability (0.53*)	Public institutions (0.22)	Political rights (0.40*)
6	Civil liberties (0.44*)	Civil liberties (0.56*)	Macro-economic stability (0.48*)	Government expenditure (−0.50*)	Macro-economic stability (0.15)	Internet (0.40*)
7	Political rights (0.43*)	Political rights (0.46*)	Government expenditure (−0.44*)		Social capital (0.13)	Social capital (0.39*)
8	Government expenditure (−0.17)	Government expenditure (−0.37*)	Internet (0.43*)		Government expenditure (−0.07)	Government expenditure (−0.22)

Notes: Two explanatory variables (HDI and Internet) are not included in the e-government index column because they are part of the calculation of 'E-government Index (BEMG)'.

Table 15.4 Difference of means based on the stages in *Web Presence Index*

Web Presence Stage	E-government index (WM)	E-government score (NRI)	E-government index (BMEG)	Transparency (CyPRG)	Interactivity (CyPRG)
1	25.00 (8.25)	3.98 (1.02)	**0.72 (0.17)**	9.58 (2.71)	3.39 (2.18)
2	**26.69 (6.39)**	2.95 (0.90)	**1.11 (0.32)**	10.16 (2.70)	3.30 (2.09)
3	**30.93 (4.87)**	3.18 (0.60)	1.67 (0.30)	11.37 (2.33)	4.17 (1.48)
4	37.04 (8.15)	4.33 (0.66)	2.28 (0.28)	13.28 (2.07)	6.54 (2.44)

Notes:1. Significant differences among successive stages are highlighted in bold typeface.
2. Standard deviations listed in parentheses.

similar among the 'stage' variables (WPI and e-government BMEG Index) than between the openness (CyPRG) variables. Overall correlations between the explanatory variables and the CyPRG measures are the lowest. Transparency has particularly low correlations. This indicates that the CyPRG openness measures may be capturing a fundamentally different type of variation of e-government quality than the other variables.

While transparency and interactivity do a reasonable job of capturing the political and HDI variation, they are not as sensitive to variation in many of the other explanatory variables. The CyPRG variables, compared to the e-government stage variables, appear to represent a different dimension of the qualities of e-government. Data density, information quality and the level of citizen-government interactivity through e-government do a relatively good job of capturing variation associated with political and civic freedoms. However, they do not cover economic or institutional factors well. It should be noted that the CyPRG measures were initially designed to capture variation in managerial control and, as a result, management-related explanatory variables may elicit higher correlations than the macro-level explanatory variables.

The final correlation analysis uses the stages designated by the BMEG WPI to separate the five other e-government measures. An ANOVA test was conducted to determine if the difference in means between the four stages (emerging stage; enhanced stage; interactive stage and transactional stage) is consistent across all e-government measures. Table 15.4 presents the results.

Findings continue to reflect inconsistency with little overall pattern. Differences between all stages were significant for the BMEG e-government index but this is not surprising as the Web Presence stage is incorporated in this measure. For the WM e-government index, difference of means tests are significant for all stages except between stages one and two. However, only the difference between stages three and four was significant for the NRI, transparency and interactivity measures. The most obvious implication of these findings is that all five e-government measures more consistently agree on advanced stages of e-government, but do a poorer job of consistently separating less advanced

Table 15.5 Regression analysis

	Model 1		Model 2	
	Openness (CyPRG)		E-government index (WM)	
	Estimate	Standard error	Estimate	Standard error
Intercept	8.37 ***	1.70	−1.10 *	0.65
Democracy score	0.20 **	0.09	0.04	0.04
Internet	0.001	0.001	0.001 ***	0.001
government expenditure score	−0.01	0.18	−0.02	0.07
Macro-economic score	0.34	0.40	0.41 ***	0.15
Adjusted R-squared	0.14		0.38	
N	69		69	
Model significance	***		***	

	Model 3		Model 4	
	E-Government score (NRI)		Web Presence index (WPI)	
	Estimate	Standard error	Estimate	Standard error
Intercept	−2.48 ***	0.47	2.06 ***	0.52
Democracy score	0.05 *	0.03	0.03	0.03
Internet	0.001 *	0.001	0.001	0.001
Government expenditure score	−0.23 ***	0.05	−0.21 ***	0.05
Macro-economic score	0.86 ***	0.11	0.48 ***	0.12
Adjusted R-squared	0.70		0.45	
N	69		69	
Model significance	***		***	

stages. Similarly, the table shows that a higher stage in one measure does not translate to a higher stage in another. Again, it appears that the measures represent different interpretations of performance and progress.

Regression analysis

Table 15.5 displays results from the regression analysis in which four different e-government measures are used as dependent variables in four identical regression equations. Independent variables in the equations represent the four macro-level explanatory variables identified in our four propositions: democracy, bureaucracy, technology and economy. These four independent variables are operationalized by the democracy score, government expenditure, internet and macroeconomic stability measures respectively. Other variables included in the correlation analysis such as the human development index and the social capital score were not used as explanatory variables due to high levels of collinearity. The models presented in Table 15.5 all conform to assumptions of normality; results from tolerance and variance inflation factor tests for multicollinearity were low.

In Model 1, only the democracy score is a significant indicator of CyPRG openness. Model 2 is primarily pull-orientated with technology and economic factors determining the e-government Index (WM). Findings for both of these models make sense as the focus of the CyPRG variable is openness, while the WM measure is more concerned with e-business and e-service dimensions.

Model 3 finds that all four variables are at least weakly associated with the NRI E-Government Score, while Model 4 shows that only government expenditure and macro-economic stability are significantly associated with the BMEG WPI. In both of these models government expenditures are negatively correlated meaning that relatively larger governments have lower e-government scores. While both of these e-government measures tend to recognize both pushing and pulling factors, the NRI score captures the greatest variety of explanatory dimensions. This finding may not be surprising because it is a complex index that incorporates a wide range of different dimensions.

Overall, findings show no consistent systematic support for our propositions. However, inconsistency simply reveals that the measures are capturing different dimensions of e-government. Hence, results show that e-government performance depends on how e-government is measured in the first place: different explanatory factors are associated with different dimensions of e-government. In light of these findings, we believe that one of the major obstacles to e-government research and developing e-government capacities is the validity problem in e-government measurement, which can be traced all the way back to the fundamental issues of inconsistency and limited scope in understanding e-government and the lack of a comprehensive theory of e-government guiding the construct design process.

Discussion and conclusion

This exploratory chapter finds significant variation in association among the different e-government measures and between those measures and the explanatory variables. Regression analyses clearly indicate that the various e-government measures do not capture the same phenomena. In sum, this study reveals substantial reliability and validity problems with the existing e-government measures. Which factors are relevant or irrelevant for the development and performance of e-government may be more related to the issue of how e-government is defined and measured rather than the real causal dynamics driven by the independent variables of e-government. Caution should be exercised in interpreting the findings of those studies in order to avoid over-generalizing the implications of the findings to dimensions and aspects that are not covered by the measures under question.

Ultimately, issues faced in the study of e-government and brought out in this chapter are broader than a measurement problem. At heart, the problems are definitional, theoretical, and empirical. The research and management literature defines the concept of e-government in many ways, often loosely, in an effort to fulfill the basic purpose of practical communication or general description. For research purposes, these definitions are too general and often inconsistent. According to the United Nations Division for Public Economics and Public Administration (UNDPEPA) and American Society for Public Administration (ASPA), 'e-government can include virtually all information and communication technology (ICT) platforms and applications in use by the public sector' (2001, p. 1). On its website, ASPA defines e-government as 'the pragmatic use of the most innovative information and communication technologies, like the internet, to deliver efficient and cost effective services, information and knowledge. It is an unequivocal commitment by decision makers to strengthening the partnership between the private citizen and the public sector' (Wong and Welch 2004: 292). The World Bank defines e-government as 'the use by government agencies of information technologies (such as Wide Area Networks, the Internet, and mobile computing) that have the ability to transform relations with citizens, businesses, and other aims of government . . . [for] better delivery of government services to citizens, improved interactions with business and industry, citizen empowerment . . .' (World Bank 2004). Brown University's Center for Public Policy defines e-government as 'public sector use of the Internet and other digital devices to deliver services and information' (World Markets Research Center 2001: 3). Clearly, the definitions are broad and lack consensus.

Furthermore, prior to studying the factors that affect e-government performance, it is useful to first develop a theory that suggests a valid and acceptable measure of e-government – in that way, empirical variation is explainable in terms of the theory. Under the present situation, the inconsistency in e-government measures can easily translate itself into inconsistency in the findings of an explanatory study of e-government. Stowers' (2004) work developing a framework for assessing e-government performance represents a strong effort toward identification of measurable, theoretically-derived constructs. Stowers' list of e-government performance measures, presented in the introduction of this chapter, indicates that there are many aspects and levels of measurements that must be considered to enable a reliable and valid assessment or comparison of national e-government performance. Other theoretical efforts include a more complex and sophisticated framework for assessing and measuring web content which incorporates detailed investigation inside the organization to learn about the pathways and procedures critical to placing information on the agency

Table 15.6 Scope and extent of measurements in e-government measures

E-government measures	Website content and features	Organizational factors	E-governance: openness, accountability and participation	External technological context	External economic context
Openness (CyPRG)	☐				
E-government index (WM)	■				
E-government score (NRI)				■	■
Web Presence index (WPI)	☐				
E-government index (BMEG)	☐			■	■

☐ Limited breadth
■ Comprehensive

website (Eschenfelder 2004). Welch and Fulla have also developed a theory and identified associated measures of cyber-interactivity between citizens and bureaucrats (2005).

Empirically, there are further limitations of the current e-government research paradigm. Generally, organizational factors and e-governance are neglected by all macro e-government measures we have examined. Organizational factors can be defined as those organizational features that are necessary or favourable for the development of e-government including a less bureaucratic structure which promotes innovation and the application of information technology to facilitate organizational change. In addition, comparisons are always more meaningful and more appropriate at more defined levels of analysis. Hence, comparison of e-government performance that focuses on an agency type or service may be more enlightening. Finally, many of the measures designed thus far capture the static nature of e-government performance, based mainly on web-content analysis. They do not seek to capture the dynamic effectiveness of e-government: Has the agency accomplished its e-government goals? Are citizens satisfied with the online interaction and information provision? Can agencies adequately use web applications to conduct critical procurement tasks? These and many other questions of performance suggest change over time that is relative to stakeholders and questions of governance.

Based on the above discussion and as shown in Table 15.6, e-government performance can include a broad spectrum of considerations including: website content and features; organizational factors, e-governance; external technological context and external economic context. Each of these different columns presents definitional, theoretical and empirical challenges that must be better addressed by researchers. While the current e-government performance measures used in previous global e-government research have merit, they are still incomplete and limited in scope and focus. A more complete conceptualization of e-government is needed before meaningful e-government measures can be develop, collected and interpreted.

REFERENCES

American Society for Public Administration (ASPA) and United Nations Division for Public Economics and Public Administration (UNDPEPA) (2001) *Benchmarking E-government: A Global Perspective*, Available at: www.unpan.org/e-government/Benchmarking%20E-gov%202001.pdf (accessed on 5 May 2004).

CyberSpace Policy Research Group (CyPRG), Available at: www.cyprg.arizona.edu (accessed on 10 May 2004).

Demchak, C., Friis, C. and LaPorte, T. (1998) 'Configuring public agencies in cyberspace: A conceptual investigation' in Snellen, T. M. and van de Donk, W. B. H. J. (eds.) *Public administration in an information age: A handbook*. Amsterdam: IOS Press.

Demchak, C., Friis, C. and LaPorte, T. (2000) 'Webbing governance: national differences in constructing the face of public organizations', in Garson, D. (ed.) *Handbook of public information systems*. New York: Marcel Dekker Publishers.

Eschenfelder, K. R. ((2004) 'How do government agencies review and approve text content for publication on their web sites? A framework to compare web content management practices', *Library and Information Science Research*, **26**: 463–481.

Fountain, J. (2001) *Building the virtual state: Information technology and institutional change*. Washington, D.C.: Brookings Institution Press.

Freedom House (2002) *Freedom in the world*. Available at: www.freedomhouse.org/research/index.htm (accessed on 20 May 2004).

Ho, A. T-K. (2002) 'Reinventing local governments and the e-government initiative', *Public Administration Review*, **62**: 434–444.

Holzer, M. and Kim, S-T. (2003) *Digital governance in municipalities worldwide*. US, New Jersey: The E-government Institute/The National Center for Public Productivity of the State University of New Jersey-Newark and The Global e-Policy e-Government Institute of Sungkyunkwan University. Available at: www.worldmarketsanalysis.com/e_gov_report.html (accessed on 4 October 2005).

International Telecommunications Union (ITU) (2001) *World telecommunications indicators*. Geneva, Switzerland: ITU.

Kettl, Donald (1997) 'The global revolution in public management: Driving themes, missing links', *Journal of Policy Analysis and Management*, **16**: 446–462.

Kirkman, G., Osorio, C. and Sachs, J. (2002) 'Networked readiness index: Measuring the preparedness of nations for the networked world', in Kirkman, G. (ed.) *The global information technology report 2001–2002: Readiness for the networked world*, New York: Oxford University Press, pp. 10–29.

Lindley, C. (2003) *World audit report*, available at: www.worldaudit.org/civillibs.htm (accessed on 5 May 2004).

McArthur, J. and Sachs, J. (2001) 'The growth competitiveness index: Measuring technological advancement and the stages of development', in Sachs, J., Porter, M. and Schwab, K. (eds.) *Global competitiveness report 2001–2002*, New York: Oxford University Press, pp. 28–51.

Moon, M. J. (2002) 'The evolution of e-government among municipalities: Rhetoric or reality?', *Public Administration Review*, **62**: 424–433.

Moon , M. J. and Norris, D. (2003) 'Linkage between managerial innovation and e-government.' Paper presented at Western Political Science Conference, April 2003, Denver, CO.

Norris, D. and Moon, M. J. (2005) 'Advances in electronic government at the grassroots: Hare or tortoise?', *Public Administration Review*, **65**: 64–75.

Organization for Economic Cooperation and Development (OECD) (2003) *OECD e-government studies: The e-government imperative*. Paris, France: OECD.

Osborne, D. and Gaebler, T. (1992) *Reinventing government*. Reading, MA: Addison-Wesley.

Stowers, G. (2004) *Measuring the performance of e-government*. Washington, D.C.: IBM Center for the Business of Government.

Welch, E. and Wong, W. (2001) 'Global information technology pressure and government accountability: The mediating effect of the domestic context on website openness', *Journal of Public Administration Theory and Research* **11**: 509–538.

Welch, E. and Fulla, S. (2005) 'Virtual interactivity between government and citizens: The Chicago Police Department's Citizen ICAM Application Demonstration Case', *Political Communication*, **22**: 215–236.

West, D. (2001) *Global e-government survey*. World Markets Research Centre. Available at: www.worldmarketsanalysis.com/e_gov_report.html (accessed on 15 May 2004).

West, D. (2003a) *The urban e-government, 2003*. Available at: www.insidepolitics.org/egovt03city.pdf (accessed on 15 May 2004).

West, D. (2003b) *State and federal e-government in the United States*. Available at: www.insidepolitics.org/egovt03us.pdf (accessed on 15 May 2004).

Wong, W. and Welch, E. (2004) 'Does e-government promote accountability? A comparative analysis of website openness and government accountability', *Governance*, **17**: 275–297.

World Bank (2004) *A definition of e-government*. Available at: www1.worldbank.org/publicsector/egov/definition.htm (accessed on 6 May 2004).

World Markets Research Center (2001) *Global e-government survey*. Available at: www.worldmarketsanalysis.com/e_gov_report.html (accessed on 15 May 2004).

16 Public management and organizational performance: An agenda for research

George A. Boyne, Kenneth J. Meier, Laurence J. O'Toole, Jr. and Richard M. Walker

Introduction

How can public services performance be improved? This question is central to both governmental reform efforts and the academic study of public management. If one leaves aside the possibility of pure dumb luck, effective policy and managerial prescriptions must be built upon a grounding of information – in particular, valid knowledge regarding the correlates of performance. This key step is necessary to both identify variables which can be adjusted to beneficial effect and provide input for policy makers' deliberations.

The work in this volume constitutes a systematic effort focused on three key questions entailed by such an objective. First, what are the appropriate ways to measure a public organization's performance? Second, what role does management play in enhancing – or, for that matter, inhibiting – performance? Third, how does the context of programmes and organizations, both political and organizational, create contingencies that enhance or suppress the various determinants of performance? The early parts of the book are organized around the first pair of these questions. The international comparisons sketched in the last part of the volume contribute directly to the third point, but most of the chapters also touch upon it.

Much credible work has been reported by the authors represented here and numerous insights regarding all three questions can be garnered from the foregoing contributions. Still, in this effort as with all dynamic research programmes, new questions arise as old ones are put to bed. Rather than recapitulating the findings of the various studies included, this chapter emphasizes where additional research is still needed. The chapters presented earlier highlight key puzzles as the research findings are unpacked and thus the challenges on the horizon deserve further attention here. The paths of the agenda as research moves forward are several: the need for greater theoretical development on the performance question; the benefits likely to accrue from enhancing research infrastructure in this field; the necessity of resolving methodological issues of causality, linearity and multiple goals; and the advantages of bringing structural factors into the performance mix. Each merits discussion in turn.

Theory

The development of a scholarly literature in any scientific specialty requires progress in both empirical research and the construction of theory – each should inform the other. What often passes for theory in public management, however, is discursive and speculative work without systematic empirical tests, or sometimes even empirical referents. The standard for theory construction is not met by descriptive coverage which fails to make tightly logical arguments which, in turn, generate hypotheses. Such work might be useful as preliminary forays that can offer some building blocks to theory, but – especially after a number of such sketches have been developed and little systematization or testing has followed – much of this cumulative product consists, in effect, of detritus littering the intellectual landscape. At its best, theory is marked by precision and by the generation of propositions that are at least, in part, not intuitively obvious. In this way the construction of theory both organizes earlier empirical findings into coherent and explanatory form and also points the way toward promising lines of future research. Theory need not be formally framed, despite some advantages of that genre, but it should be rigorously crafted – and with an eye to how it can be developed further and also translated into additional empirical studies. Note that some formal theory can definitely be shown to be wrong: Choi and Heinrich demonstrate in chapter 11 that well-developed economic theory based on notions of completeness and efficiency is of little value in predicting or explaining the performance of governmental contracting systems in practice, while in chapter 10, Provan, Milward and Isett document how misleading principal-agent theory can be in helping analysts understand the performance of contracting regimes in another policy specialty. A key virtue of explicit, precise, and particularly formal theory, however, is that it is possible to test it explicitly and it is often clear when it is wrong. Such steps constitute progress, and the study of public services performance will gain little traction without the development of theory with these features.

Good theory is also appropriately parsimonious, a characteristic that would be especially useful in the investigation of public management and its role in the provision of public services. The great mass of theoretical work in public management is richly descriptive or normative and often borrowed or adapted from contemporary theories of private management. In general, the theoretical work lacks precision and seeks, at a deeper level, to be so inclusive as to render most theories the equivalent of 'it all depends'. Essentially public management research, already with too many designated variables and implications regarding highly complex interactive and non-linear relationships, faces a trade-off. The field either needs to reduce the number of variables and focus on the complexity of the relationships or retain the universe of variables and limit the relationships to simpler – linear and additive – ones. While our preference is the former (O'Toole and Meier 1999), a choice that has demonstrated a track record of productive results, the best approach is ultimately an empirical question. Current analysis using standard statistical approaches, however, can generate false positives – that is, apparently significant relationships that are actually not – when too many variables are subjected to too many statistical tests. No theory of social phenomena can explain 100 per cent of the variance – a good theory consistently explains a large portion of the variance and recognizes that in the social world there are idiosyncratic events that should be recognized as such.

Good theory also builds on appropriate classifications of extant studies. The logic of governance effort (Lynn *et al.* 2001; also Chapter 14 of this volume) has generated a massive classification of managerial studies with a focus on identifying variables and levels of governance. Well-designed theory can use the information developed in the classificatory effort as a basis to expand upon and further specify the relationships, and functional form of the relationships, identified in this earlier effort.

One of the most promising areas to invest in developing theoretical work would probably be the topic of contingencies – that is, the features of the public services context that can influence the ways that variables like management can shape organizational performance. Context has been a major focus for the studies reported in this volume; investigations here have examined different types of organizations as well as similar organizations operating in different political and governance situations. Health performance has been studied – for instance in sub-national cancer networks in the UK, mental-health networks in the US Southwest, and a multilevel governance setting (see chapters 4, 5 and 10 in this volume). Performance questions have been explored in Welsh local authorities, US federal agencies, the Australian national government, the state of Wisconsin, school districts in Texas, as well as in explicitly cross-national form for education and e-government (chapters, 2, 3, 6, 9, 11, 12, 13 and 15 of this volume). The findings demonstrate that not only does organizational performance vary in difference contexts and locales, but that the relationships among variables can be expected to vary subject to contingencies. Here is where significant theoretical progress could be made. We need more precise predictions than that, for instance, New Public Management reforms will work in this country, but not in that country. We need to be able to specify the characteristics or contingencies that influence the size of the relationship between management or other factors and public services performance. Such a theory should have the precision to specify that, for example, a style of management involving networking with external actors will increase the positive relationship between resources and performance. Additional theoretical work should focus on the interaction *among* contingencies; for example, how does managerial experience interact with resources and human capital to affect performance? Is this relationship stronger or weaker in the long run than the short run?

The illustration of contingencies is only one of many that could be presented. Some theories have already suggested that management affects performance via a set of nonlinear interactions (see O'Toole and Meier 1999), and evidence in this volume indicates certain of the non-linearities that seem to be at work. Some, like the work on red tape and performance by Pandey and Moynihan in Chapter 8, not only explicates the importance of contingencies but also shows that conventional wisdom – in this case about the negative performance effects to be expected from red tape – can be in error. Further research could focus on how the mix of different management styles in an organization affects the translation of resources into outcomes, or how given organizational structures either facilitate or restrict the influence of various managerial strategies.

Building intellectual infrastructure

Beyond the development of clear and coherent theory, cumulative gains in knowledge on public services performance require an intellectual infrastructure that allows scholars to start from and build upon the work of others rather than beginning every study from scratch. We offer three proposals: two that can benefit both the individual studies involved and also the general research community – improving the systematic focus on measurement and generating variance on methodological approaches – and one which can generate benefits primarily for the broader community – investment in and storage of hybrid data sets.

Measurement

Empirical analysis of public services performance can be no better than the measurements used to assess it and estimate its correlates. Measurement is critical to both the research enterprise and the practice of public service. While measurement is often viewed as banal work to be avoided if possible, or at least de-emphasized in scholarly work, little progress can be expected without a focused effort on improving the reliability and validity of the measures that we use. On a subject as contentious and salient as public services performance, with so much potential for confusion, misunderstanding and politicization, measurement issues are crucial. The academic and public-sector literature on performance measurement has blossomed in recent years with the growth in interest in this subject (see Ingraham 2005), but further sustained attention to this topic is clearly required. In addition, the measurement of performance itself addresses only a portion of the measurement challenge. We can offer brief sketches of some of the work that still needs to be developed – on performance measurement and beyond.

Performance measurement

The chapters in this book have devoted a substantial effort to measuring programme performance in subjective and objective terms. It is clear, for instance, that there is no such thing as the perfect and unbiased measure of performance, as Andrews, Boyne, and Walker demonstrate in chapter 2. It is also apparent that particular caution needs to inform the use of some subjective measures, as Brewer indicates in chapter 3. Addicott and Ferlie in chapter 4 are correct in reminding analysts that diverse stakeholders can be expected to evaluate performance in markedly different terms (see also chapter 9 for the contribution by Meier, O'Toole, and Lu). Still, there is still much to be done in improving our understanding and use of performance measurement. Certainly in some public services specialties, like e-government performance, a great deal of work remains to be done in developing the basics of acceptable and appropriate measures – as chapter 15 by Welch, Moon and Wong clearly demonstrates. The same is true in numerous other public services.

Any empirical measure is composed of two parts – the true value of the concept being measured and some measurement error. While measurement researchers frequently assume that measurement error is randomly distributed and can thus be ignored for purposes of estimating relationships, such an assumption is ill-advised in studies of public organizational performance. Virtually all measures of public sector performance contain nonrandom measurement error or biases. The bias of subjective measures of performance – either in terms of tapping race (Andrews *et al.* 2005) or in reflecting the self-interest of managers (Brewer – chapter 3 of this volume) – has justifiably received some attention. Objective measures also have these biases: standardized tests do not measure the full extent of education (see Smith 2003); they emphasize some skills and ignore others. Such claims can be made for the criteria used to evaluate job placement programmes, hospital results and those of numerous other public programmes. To the extent that a performance indicator or set of indicators measures less than what is expected in terms of performance, measurement bias is a problem.

At this point it is important to understand the implications of various measurement biases for the systematic study of performance and management. For subjective measures, such implications are fairly straightforward. Objective measures can generate what are known as instrumentation effects, that is, the instrument used to measure performance interacts with the organizational processes to change the meaning of performance. One common instrumentation effect is goal displacement, as the organization seeks to produce numbers for the accountability system and downplays aspects of the job that are not measured by the accountability system (Blau 1956). Objective measures can also create governance system dysfunctions – sometimes particularly pernicious ones, in that many users of the measures may be deluded into thinking that such measures are free of bias and therefore to be trusted implicitly. Cheating is one such dysfunction that can take a variety of forms: spin control in interpreting numbers, organizational triage on the selection of cases that produce the most favorable set of numbers (Blau's famous case (1956) of an employment service agency's use of placement data to evaluate staff performance is one of a long line of well-documented instances), and perhaps even reporting false data (Bohte and Meier 2000). Not all of these dysfunctions are bureaucratic. Objective performance indicators can often create political pressure when electoral officials seek to intervene in the grade given to a programme.[1]

Scholars of public programmes also need to be more creative in their view of organizational performance. Boyne (2002) identifies sixteen dimensions of public organizational performance that can be clustered into five general groupings. His last general grouping is the least-studied democratic outcomes which includes probity, participation, accountability and cost per unit of democratic outcome (see e.g., Moynihan and Ingraham 2003). Measuring some of these is relatively easy (participation) with others likely to be more difficult (accountability). The difficulty of the task notwithstanding, a full understanding of governance, management and performance requires that greater attention be paid to the full range of performance indicators – perhaps all the more so since often the performance across the full range seems not to be highly correlated, as Addicott and Ferlie point out in chapter 4.

At the present time, most of the literature assumes that accountability systems and performance indicators are then incorporated into the governance process, that managers use them to manage and that policymakers use them to make future budgetary decisions. Certainly governmental jurisdictions in many settings have taken the 'performance' trend seriously and have committed themselves in principle to using performance data to make several kinds of key decisions, even if actual patterns of use tend to be more varied and complicated (Ingraham 2005). Performance indicators are in many ways simply a form of feedback, information that may or may not be useful to decision makers. While accountability systems create incentive to use the information that they generate, we need to know more about how they change the various incentives that employees have when implementing programmes. It is also important not to assume, as much of the literature does, that the control of performance is an entirely management-driven process. The contribution of Kenis in chapter 7 of this volume demonstrates that 'agent control' is not to be ignored; indeed, as

---

1 Political intervention to change performance numbers is probably even more likely when the performance indicator has a subjective element in it.

he hypothesizes, under some contingencies, performance control systems that are agent-driven can be expected to be more effective.

Management

Performance measurement is important, but it is far from the only issue. Aside from the actual design of public programmes, the most obviously important variable – and potential point of leverage – to affect performance is the management of such programmes. Compared to the extensive literature on public services performance and the progress made in measuring this performance, attempts to measure 'management' are still in their infancy. In part, the reluctance to invest time in measuring management might be the residual impact of disciplinary biases from economics (focusing on incentives and outcomes) and political science (concerned with environmental factors external to organizational units) that plague the study of public management. Before public management can become a true design science (see Simon 1996), one aimed at improving performance rather than merely explaining it, we first need to be able to measure the relevant aspects of management systematically in large and small studies – in reliable and valid ways. Management is likely to be one of the variables that is consistently manipulable.[2] Indeed, as Kenis indicates in chapter 7, systems of performance control are often present in public organizations, can be crafted in quite different fashions and deserve much more systematic attention from analysts. The managerial challenges inherent in such systems also require serious scrutiny. More generally, precise measurements of management in its various manifestations can both provide estimates of what difference it makes and also indicate how the various elements of what we call management interact with various contingencies.

Human resources management

Aside from the other multiple managerial functions that deserve attention as researchers work to improve on the measures necessary to explore the performance question systematically, at least one can be singled out for special emphasis. An extensive literature on human resources management contends that management practices can motivate employees, reduce turnover, and possibly affect overall performance (see Rainey 2003). A priority for the public services performance literature should be to integrate this well-developed work into our own studies. To do so will require the development of an efficient measure or set of measures of human resources management that can be used systematically

---

2 Referring to 'management' as a solitary variable is certainly an oversimplification. Management encompasses multiple functions, these can all be considered on both quality and quantity dimensions, and – according to some preliminary studies – the various aspects of management may not correlate empirically (see Meier *et al.* 2005).

across numerous organizations. Most current measures regarding human resources rely on large numbers of questions that are asked of both management and subordinates or are available for units aside from those that actually implement and deliver specific programmes. The Government Performance Project in the US, which sought to develop measures of management capacity in governmental units, including capacity to manage human resources, illustrates the highly labor-intensive aspects of such work (see Ingraham *et al.* 2003). To the extent that the human resources findings hold up in systematic analyses of organizational performance, the management of human resources provides another manipulable variable, or set of variables, of likely importance to the performance of public services.

Varied approaches

Virtually all the contributions in this volume are empirical. And while some useful qualitative studies are included in the collection, for instance the study of one large-scale contracting effort on the part of Australia (Hodge and Rouse in chapter 12) and the exploration of a small number of cancer networks in the United Kingdom (Addicott and Ferlie), most of the chapters contain large-n studies, thus distinguishing them from the overwhelming majority of public management studies. While there are clearly some advantages to these large-n empirical studies that range across multiple organizations, they are not the only way to study the management-performance linkage. A myriad of other approaches offer the potential to address different questions or to examine the same question, but in different ways. Indeed, the long-running debate about qualitative versus quantitative approaches often ignores certain valuable designs which are rarely considered. Experimental methods, for example, have been overlooked despite the strong preference for quasi-experimental designs. Whitford and Miller's (2002) work on the influence of incentives demonstrates the utility of the approach for public management. For those who feel that traditional experiments are difficult to generalize, one can embed experiments in the types of management surveys that are commonly used (see Chin *et al.* 2000 for an example in political organizations).

As the theoretical development of public management catches up with the empirical studies, computer simulations could be used in assessing different managerial tactics. Similarly, mathematical modelling, which has been used in the presentations of theory (O'Toole and Meier 1999; March and Simon 1958), could be used to tease out the implications of theoretical arguments or even to demonstrate the logical validity of a theory.

In short, then, the systematic study of public services performance will not advance much without significant improvement as well in the study of public management. And while the chapters in this book represent some of the best recent work at the nexus of performance and public management, the research approaches used to explore the subject can and should be expanded considerably.

Hybrid data sets

Progress in building a science of public management has been slowed by the lack of widely available data sets that permit a complete specification of the factors involved in determining organizational performance. Government data sources often provide a rich set of performance indicators but generally contain little or nothing that directly taps management or could be interpreted as a measure of management. Similarly, such data sets often take organizational or programme structure as a given and fail to document the obviously extensive structural variation among programmes. Archival or government data sets need to be merged with survey data sets that add management, structure and other variables into the mix. As some of the chapters in this volume show, even these combined data sets then need to be supplemented with interviews, site visits and qualitative methods of data gathering to provide explanations for the relationships found. If our purpose is to build theory in public management and organizational performance, only such hybrid data sets can provide the necessary triangulation to make convincing causal statements, and only by following such painstaking efforts can we be confident in the conclusions and recommendations that are offered to improve the performance of public services.

Given the data necessary for a solid intellectual infrastructure, archiving existing data sets is essential. Often archived data sets can be used to deal with management and performance questions not envisioned by the original researchers. Brehm and Gates' (1997) classic study of police departments using a principal-agent framework was conducted on a relatively dated data set that was not originally designed for this purpose. Archiving data sets and sharing intellectual property can also create a community among public management scholars that could facilitate interactions across theoretical orientations, methodological approaches, and substantive interests.

Methods

Public management, as an applied social science, borrows methods selectively from other social sciences. Because more traditional social sciences develop their methods for the specific problems that they consider important, these methods are not always optimal for the study of public management (see Gill and Meier 2000). Rather than repeating arguments about methodology published elsewhere (see Boyne *et al.* 2005), this section will focus on three items – causality, non-linearity, and the problems associated with multiple goals in a single programme, organization, or network.

Causality

Management theory is clearly based on the notion of cause, that is, a change in management activities will result in a subsequent improvement (one hopes) in organizational performance. Similarly, policy analysis focused on programme performance seeks variables that can be manipulated to improve performance. The traditional regression-based methods used in the study of management and programme performance, however, rarely deal with causality except perhaps to make assumptions that X causes Y. For those willing to make some additional assumptions, one common approach with cross-sectional data is to use two-stage or three-stage least squares. These techniques require the assumption that one can specify a set of exogenous variables that are determinants of X and a second set with at least one additional variable that are determinants of Y but not X. Those with access to data arrayed over time have the option of using the differences in time to apply versions of Granger causality analysis, a technique which tests whether a vector of X variables over a period of time adds additional explanation to Y over and above a lagged vector of the Y variable.

Causality becomes extremely important in design sciences because one purpose of the analysis is to change factors that will improve performance, rather than simply to explain performance. A change in an independent variable will consistently produce a subsequent change in a dependent variable only if a causal relationship exists. For scholars with only academic (that is to say, scientific but not primarily practical) concerns, the question of causality remains important. As an illustration, scholars working on multi-level governance models need to know if 'higher' levels of governance (those generally thought to reflect democratic institutions) affect 'lower' levels of governance or if the correlation between the two is the result of bottom-up processes – or both. Sorting out such relationships has significant implications for evaluations that seek to determine how democratic a process might be.

Non-linearities

A variety of theories precisely specify non-linear relationships or imply that such exist. The assumption of linearity, after all, is just that – an assumption based on the idea that simpler explanations are preferable to more complex ones. Systematic and critical assessments of linearity are important both in public management and the assessment of programme performance. For one thing, a great deal of case-study evidence accumulated over the years suggests that management, at a minimum, interacts with a variety of other contingencies to shape public programme results (see the coverage in O'Toole and Meier 1999). For another, an invalid assumption of linearity could result in inappropriate practical results. After all, a relationship that is subject to diminishing returns could produce an overly optimistic policy prescription if the diminishing returns are not incorporated into the analysis.

Three non-linearities appear to be particularly important. First, functional form is simply the question of whether or not the relationship between two variables is best summarized by a straight line or by a non-linear estimate. Such estimates can be done relatively simply via polynomial curve fitting or logistic or other variable transformations (Hamilton 1992). Second, variables might interact with each other and in the process produce relationships that are vastly different for some organizations than for others; chapter 8 in this volume illustrates just such a relationship with the impact of red tape contingent on an organization's culture. Although most interactions involve only two variables, there is no reason why three or more variables might not interact. Theories that specify multiple contingencies, in fact, call for exactly this type of specification. Third, the relationship between two variables might vary across organizations or for the same organization over time. Although such relationships can be handled by an interaction specification, for exploratory purposes, the use of substantively weighted analytical techniques (SWAT) is a more efficient way to identify such relationships.

The use of non-linear estimations in empirical work should also feed back into theoretical thinking. The common two-by-two table with different results in different cells is analogous to a statistical interaction. Theorists who frame their arguments in such terms are more likely to get the attention of empirical scholars.

Multiple goals

In chapter 5 of this volume Peter Smith proposes an innovative way to deal with programmes that have multiple indicators of performance. The problem addressed by Smith is endemic in modern programmes; few public programmes are created with a single goal. The politics of programme design is such that programmes might even be created with goals that are in conflict with each other. Smith's use of seemingly-unrelated regression, or SUR, techniques to deal with programme tradeoffs is the first step in addressing an equally important question: How do organizations deal with multiple goals?

Simon (1947) proposed a simple but elegant solution in his architecture of complexity. Programmes were simply disaggregated into smaller and smaller parts, the parts containing no more than one goal assigned to a single unit for a solution. The problems once solved or the programmes once designed were then assembled back together with the idea that the sum of the parts would produce an effective overall programme. 'Making a mesh of things', in Appleby's choice phrase (1949), then refers to the managerial challenge of aggregation and coordination. Unfortunately, we do not know that organizations actually operate in this fashion. Many programmes that rely on street-level bureaucrats (policing, welfare, mental health, education) do not appear to decompose programmes, but rather vest extensive discretion at the street level with no attempt to reconcile conflicting goals (see Maynard-Moody and Musheno 2003). Others operate parallel programmes but do not reconcile any resulting conflicts. Simon also suggested that in the face of the complex juggling required to achieve multiple goals, individual decision makers would likely attend sequentially to different objectives at different times. Testing this notion for many public programmes and organizations also requires extensive additional investigation, a task that researchers on public services performance have not yet begun to tackle.

Perhaps the most fruitful type of study to address the goals-tradeoff question is the analysis of large pooled time-series data sets that permit one to examine on an annual (or other time period) basis how changes in performance for programme A compare to changes in performance for programme B and how this ratio can be explained by other variables. The type of programme-elasticity analysis would essentially create new dependent variables from the year-to-year changes in the various programmes. While this type of analysis might not tell us what management intended to do with regard to goal conflicts, it would tell us how much the goals conflict in practice and what organizational or policy factors contribute to making the tradeoffs more or less severe. Such an analysis could also determine if it is possible to avoid the tradeoffs completely or even to design systems in which programme performance on one goal generates positive externalities for other goals.

Structure

Programme structure is the missing variable in the study of organizational performance. Although there is an extensive literature on public- versus private-sector delivery of services (Hodge 2000) and substantial literature on contracting, this aspect is only one among many dimensions of structure that might be related to performance. Provan and Milward (1995), for example, provide evidence that networks perform better when they take on some of the structural aspects of more traditional hierarchies. Many structural designs represent managerial choices that are thought to influence performance: centralization versus decentralization, coproduction, span of control, the mix of employee types, the number of field offices, and so forth.

One theoretically important structural dimension in need of systematic study is the distinction between hierarchies and networks. Of course the category 'networks' itself encompasses enormous structural variations, from two-organizational dyads to institutional arrangements encompassing dozens of interdependent organizations coproducing action on behalf of, for instance, a policy and set of clients (see Provan and Milward 1991). Aside from exploring how these variations themselves help to shape outcomes, we argue that a set of rather basic questions need to be addressed. One issue is suggested by the point that structural features of networks can be expected to shape results, and networking behaviour of managers also contribute to what happens (Meier and O'Toole 2003; see also Agranoff and McGuire 2003; Morgan *et al.* 1999; Rhodes 2002). How these structural and behavioural dimensions jointly operate, and interact, has barely begun to be explored (O'Toole and Meier 2004).

Further, although we know some things about the role of management in performance and the networking activities of managers, we have little information about management *of* networks (as opposed to management *in* networks – that is, management of hierarchical organizations that are in turn linked in networked arrays) and how it relates to performance (see Kickert *et al.* 1997). In theory, management of a network is far more complex than management in an organization – simply because it must reflect efforts to orchestrate the coordinated actions of various network partners (see Meier and O'Toole 2004), and how the actions of individual managers and their organizational units aggregate to the network level is unclear. In a sense, management at the network level represents a multilevel management challenge, with at least one level (the network) unlikely to be tightly coupled and operating with common perspectives and interests. This theoretical expectation is in turn supported in some of the chapters included in this volume, including chapters 4 and 10. Both suggest that the management challenges at the network level are likely to be considerable. The former analysis offers grounds for some optimism, in that some integrative forces like professional norms may help to shoulder some of the burden, but such possibilities are likely to be quite contingent on certain structural and other characteristics. This last point too indicates further reasons why we need serious investments in rigorous analyses of larger samples. The coverage earlier of non-linearities feeds directly into a number of the key questions worth probing on the subject of management in networks and performance-related results.

This is particularly so, given the large number of programmes structured as networks (Hall and O'Toole 2000, 2004). Accordingly, the study of networks, their management, and their performance should be a high priority. Addressing this agenda requires studying systematically networks that produce some type of measurable output and that are simple enough, structurally speaking, to allow investigators to be able to identify the intentions of various network actors. Small-n studies of this sort are valuable, as some of the chapters in this book demonstrate, but large-n explorations must also be undertaken (see Meier and O'Toole 2005).

Conclusion

This volume represents the best current work on public services performance and its effective management. As such, it suggests a high level of interest in the topic by able researchers on several continents, along with a rather large set of intriguing and provocative findings – these carrying myriad implications for both theory and practice. If it is not the case that the theme of public management and performance is itself an oxymoron – and it is not – it is also not true that measuring, explaining, and delivering strong performance in public services are straightforward or easy tasks.

In this chapter, we have concentrated almost totally on the agenda before us rather than the results reflected here, or for that matter in other studies completed thus far. We have argued that the serious development and implementation of such an agenda is a particularly critical task and the solid work contained in this book nonetheless amounts to but the initial steps in what should be an extensive and broadly-joined field of research.

Our brief for theoretical development is not especially novel, but it does call for a great deal from those specialists in public services performance and management who care about scholarly advance. As a subject of study, public management is a field rich in discursive partial arguments and thus-far-unvalidated ideas and assumptions. We need rigorous, parsimonious theoretical contributions, despite the sometimes-inconvenient richness and complexity of the world of public services. We need appropriate and sophisticated recognition of complications like contingencies, not just as excuses for theoretical weaknesses, but as building blocks of good and useful theory. And we also need ambitiously integrative analyses that map the full reach of the intellectual terrain and point toward the over- and underexamined theoretical and empirical linkages and themes.

Making significant improvements on the theoretical front will not be accomplished without simultaneous, and equally serious, development of what we call the intellectual infrastructure of the field. Building infrastructure in a research field has a good deal in common with building it in a city: the work is hard and unglamorous, the payoffs real and long term. Here we have emphasized a small set of the various kinds of intellectual bases upon which a flourishing field of performance and management can be constructed. Measurement has been a salient theme recently, particularly when the topic is performance. Here, as several contributions in this volume attest, things are neither straightforward nor simple. Beyond the measurement of performance, other knotty measurement challenges remain – particularly with regard to management in general and human resources management in particular.

Infrastructural developments are also called for in the nitty-gritty realms of methods used to explore the performance of public services, and we have tried to suggest the range of possible approaches, most of which are virtually ignored thus far by specialists in the field, that could be put to productive use. Doing so in most cases requires better and more creatively constructed data sets, also part of the necessary basis for research of the first rank.

We care about performance not primarily as an aesthetic or intellectual pastime but because the results of the delivery of public services have public value – or values. As a consequence, focusing on the improvement of public services requires addressing some questions of method from a perspective somewhat apart from social science as usual. Enhancing public services, and thus enhancing public values, involves designing improvements. As a design science, public management consequently needs to apply newly developed techniques to determine how to strengthen, rather than merely estimate, performance impacts. Similarly, some of these methodological improvements can gain leverage on the issue of contingencies and non-linearities that is clearly a key part of the puzzle. Other advanced methods can also bring practical improvements by allowing us to assess the prospects for and degree of goal tradeoff – or, alternatively, synergy – in complex public programmes.

Finally, as some of the contributions in this book emphasize, and as considerable other research has documented in systematic detail, the structural setting for the production and delivery of public services is a huge and barely explored terrain, at least so far as management and performance is concerned. Since much in the realm of public services now operates through networks, how to shape and manage performance in these more complex institutional arrays has become a highly salient question. The topic is likely to grow still more in visibility as governments resort to various forms of collaboration, contracting and partnership for a variety of reasons. Accordingly, those interested in the subject of performance must perforce become interested in management of and in networks.

In short, the agenda for the systematic exploration of public services performance is large, variegated, and – in relative terms – in its infancy. The questions are huge, the answers anything but simple, and the challenges for researchers both significant and stimulating. If this volume helps to catalyse serious attention to the topic, it will have been successful. Let the work commence.

REFERENCES

Agranoff, R. and McGuire, M. (2003) *Collaborative public management: New strategies for local governments*. Washington, D.C.: Georgetown University Press.

Andrews, R., Boyne, G. A., Meier, K. J., O'Toole, L. J. Jr. and Walker, R. M. (2005) 'Representative bureaucracy, organizational strategy, and public service performance: An empirical analysis of English local government', *Journal of Public Administration Research and Theory*, **15**: 489–504.

Appleby, P. H. (1949) *Big democracy*. New York: Knopf.

Blau, P. M. (1956) *Bureaucracy and modern society*. New York: Random House.

Bohte, J. and Meier, K. J. (2000) 'Goal displacement: Assessing the motivation for organizational cheating', *Public Administration Review*, **60**: 173–182.

Boyne, G. A. (2002) 'Concepts and indicators of local authority performance: An evaluation of the statutory framework in England and Wales', *Public Money and Management* **22**(2): 17–24.

Boyne, G. A., Meier, K. J., O'Toole, L. J. Jr. and Walker, R. M. (2005) 'Where Next? Research Directions on Performance in Public Organizations', *Journal of Public Administration Research and Theory*, **15**: 633–639.

Brehm, J. and Gates, S. (1997) *Working, shirking and sabotage: Bureaucratic response to a democratic public*. Ann Arbor: University Michigan Press.

Chin, M. L., Bond, J. R. and Geva, N. (2000) 'A foot in the door: An experimental study of PAC and constituency effects on access', *Journal of Politics*, **62**: 534–549.

Gill, J. and Meier, K. J. (2000) 'Public administration research and practice: A methodological manifesto', *Journal of Public Administration Research and Theory*, **10**: 157–200.

Hall, T. E. and O'Toole, L. J. Jr. (2000) 'Structures for policy implementation: An analysis of national legislation, 1965–1966 and 1993–1994', *Administration and Society*, **31**: 667–686.

Hall, T. E. and O'Toole, L. J. Jr. (2004) 'Shaping formal networks through the regulatory process', *Administration and Society*, **36**: 1–22.

Hamilton, L. C. (1992) *Regression with graphics*. Pacific Grove, CA: Brooks/Cole.

Hodge, G. A. (2000) *Privatization: An international review of performance*. Boulder, CO: Westview Press.

Ingraham, P. W. (2005) 'Performance: Promises to keep and miles to go', *Public Administration Review*, **65**: 390–395.

Ingraham, P. W., Joyce, P. G. and Donahue, A. K. (2003) *Government performance: Why management matters*. Baltimore, MD: Johns Hopkins University Press.

Kickert, W. J. M., Klijn, E-H. and Koppenjan, J. F. M. (eds.) (1997) *Managing complex networks*. London: Sage.

Lynn, L. E., Heinrich, C. J. and Hill, C. J. (2001) *Improving governance: A new logic for empirical research*. Washington: Georgetown University Press.

March, J. G. and Simon, H. A. (1958) *Organizations*. New York: John Wiley and Sons.

Maynard-Moody, S. and Musheno, M. (2003) *Cops, teachers, counselors*. Ann Arbor: University of Michigan Press.

Meier, K. J. and O'Toole, L. J. Jr. (2003) 'Public management and educational performance: The impact of managerial networking', *Public Administration Review* **63**: 689–699.

Meier, K. J. and O'Toole, L. J. Jr. (2004) 'Conceptual issues in modeling and measuring management and its impacts on performance' in Lynn, L. E. Jr. and Ingraham, P. W. (eds.) *Effective government: How organization and management affect performance*. Washington, D.C.: Georgetown University Press.

Meier, K. J. and O'Toole, L. J. Jr. (2005) 'Managerial Networking: Issues of Measurement and Research Design', *Administration and Society*, **37**, 5: 523–541.

Meier, K. J., O'Toole, L. J. Jr., Boyne, G. A. and Walker, R. M. (2005) 'Strategic management and the performance of public organizations: Testing venerable ideas against recent theories'. Paper presented at the annual meetings of the American Political Science Association, Washington, D.C., 4 September.

Morgan, K., Rees, G. and Garmise, S. (1999) 'Networking for local economic development' in G. Stoker, (ed.) *The new management of British local governance*. Basingstoke: Macmillan.

Moynihan, D. P. and Ingraham, P. W. (2003) 'Look for the silver lining: When performance based accountability systems work', *Journal of Public Administration Research and Theory*, **13**: 469–490.

O'Toole, L. J. Jr. and Meier, K. J. (1999) 'Modeling the impact of public management: implications of structural context', *Journal of Public Administration Research and Theory*, **9**: 505–526.

O'Toole, L. J. Jr. and Meier, K. J. (2004) 'Public management in intergovernmental networks: Matching structural and behavioral networks', *Journal of Public Administration Research and Theory*, **14**: 469–494.

Provan, K. G. and Milward, H. B. (1991) 'Institutional-level norms and organizational involvement in a service-implementation network', *Journal of Public Administration Research and Theory*, **1**: 391–418.

Provan, K. G. and Milward, H. B. (1995) 'A preliminary theory of interorganizational network effectiveness: A comparative study of four community mental health systems', *Administrative Science Quarterly*, **40**: 1–33.

Rainey, H. G. (2003) *Understanding and managing public organizations*. San Francisco: Jossey-Bass.

Rhodes, R. A. W. (2002) 'Putting people back into networks', *Australian Journal of Political Science*, **37**: 399–416.

Simon, H. A. (1947) *Administrative behavior*. New York: Free Press.

Simon, H. A. (1996) *The sciences of the artificial*. 3rd edn. Cambridge: MIT Press.

Smith, K. B. (2003) *The ideology of education*. Albany, NY: State University of New York Press.

Whitford, A. and Miller, G. (2002) 'Trust and incentives in principal-agent negotiations: The 'insurance/incentive trade-off', *Journal of Theoretical Politics*, **14**: 231–267.

Index

Lightning Source UK Ltd.
Milton Keynes UK
UKOW010234101012

200285UK00003B/12/P